BILL RAWLING

Surviving Trench Warfare
Technology and the Canadian Corps, 1914–1918

Second Edition

UNIVERSITY OF TORONTO PRESS
Toronto Buffalo London

© University of Toronto Press 2014
Toronto Buffalo London
www.utppublishing.com
Printed in the U.S.A.

First edition published in 1992 in cloth and paper.

ISBN 978-1-4426-4943-9 (cloth)
ISBN 978-1-4426-2678-2 (paper)

Printed on acid-free paper

Publication cataloguing information is available from Library and Archives Canada.

All photographs are from Library and Archives Canada: 'mudlarking' PA22705, training with a Colt PA4915, barbed wire entanglements C30360, personnel of the 55th Battery PA112412 (photo by J.G. Curry), members of the 109th Battalion PA61415, gun crew doing maintenance PA635, Lewis gun being demonstrated PA69844, a practice platoon attack PA4773, two soldiers with gas helmets PA001027, a heavy artillery piece PA2137, a German pillbox PA2329, armour-infantry tactics PA3257.

Cover illustrations: (front) two soldiers with gas helmets examining a Lee Enfield rifle, March 1917, W.I. Castle/Canada, Dept. of National Defence/ Library and Archives Canada/PA001027; (back) CEF Liberation of Mons, Belgium, *Toronto Telegram* Collection, York University Archives.

University of Toronto Press acknowledges the financial assistance to its publishing program of the Canada Council for the Arts and the Ontario Arts Council, an agency of the Government of Ontario.

Canada Council
for the Arts

Conseil des Arts
du Canada

ONTARIO ARTS COUNCIL
CONSEIL DES ARTS DE L'ONTARIO

an Ontario government agency
un organisme du gouvernement de l'Ontario

University of Toronto Press acknowledges the financial support of the Government of Canada through the Canada Book Fund for its publishing activities.

Surviving Trench Warfare
Technology and the Canadian Corps, 1914–1918

Second Edition

The horrors of the First World War were the product of a new and un-precedented type of industrial warfare. To survive and win demanded not just new technology but the techniques to use it effectively. In *Surviving Trench Warfare*, Bill Rawling takes a close look at how technology and tactics came together in the Canadian Corps.

Drawing on a wide range of sources, from interview transcripts to staff reports, Rawling makes clear that the decisive factor in the war was not the new technology itself but how the Canadians responded to it. The Canadian Corps devised a system based on specializing tasks within the infantry and artillery. Only through intensive training, close coordination, and communication could the Canadians overcome the deadly trinity of machine-guns, barbed wire, and artillery. *Surviving Trench Warfare* offers a whole new understanding of the First World War, replacing the image of a static trench war with one in which soldiers actively struggled for control over their weapons and their environment, and achieved it.

Released to coincide with the centenary of the First World War, this edition includes a new introduction reflecting on the book's origins.

BILL RAWLING is a historian with the Directorate of History, Department of National Defence.

Contents

Introduction to the Second Edition

This author is old enough to remember a 1960s documentary TV series, long before a History Channel was even conceived, entitled *The World at War*, narrated by Laurence Olivier. Part of one episode featured the failed raid on Dieppe of 19 August 1942, and as I was watching it with my grandparents they informed me that my uncle George had been killed there, the first time I was aware of war's impact on our family. I later found out that one of my middle names, George, commemorates my grandmother's brother, her only sibling, who joined the Royal Regiment of Canada in Toronto early in the conflict. If that was not enough to spark an interest in military history, my grandparents' home contained memorabilia from Vimy Ridge, a 1917 battle in which my great-grandfather, Charles Gillard, had participated as a member of the 75th Infantry Battalion. What particularly struck me were small sculptures fashioned from the chalk of that ridge, and since fortunately he was still alive (he died in 1983) he was able to explain how soldiers had dug out tunnels near the base of the ridge prior to the battle in order to provide shelter from shelling, and some of them made artefacts from the chalk they removed during excavations.

With interest piqued, and then deepened, I was one of the few teenagers to get history books for their birthday, and actually read them. While a student at the University of Ottawa in the late 70s and early 80s interests focused mainly on international affairs, with an eye to doing graduate work at the Norman Patterson School at Carleton University, but assigned a term paper for a course on the history of technology, taught by Don Davis, I chose a military topic, namely the use of various weapons in the capture of Vimy Ridge that my great-grandfather had described. Still, although I intended to focus on the history of viii / Introduction to the Second Edition

technology for my master's thesis, also done at the University of Ottawa (from 1982 to 1984), my original topic dealt with industrialization in Detroit and Windsor, notably the auto industry. I came across a story, however, which detailed how a graduate student going through the General Motors' archives had found the smoking gun proving that the corporation had indeed been seeking a monopoly in the 1930s, and that those archives were subsequently closed to all outside researchers. The story may well be apocryphal, but archival materials for my thesis were definitely not available, so I had to choose another topic – and time was running out.

Meanwhile, although my interest in history had taken a road other than military, I had joined what was then called the Militia in 1977, namely 3rd Field Engineer Squadron, and a professor at UofO, Robert Keyserlingk, suggested I combine my interest in the history of technology with my knowledge, limited as it might be, of military engineering and study the history of my own unit for my master's thesis. I therefore worked on the engineering units of the 1st Canadian Infantry Division in the Second World War, a thesis I defended in 1984. (That work formed the starting point for *Technicians of Battle*, published by the Canadian Institute of Strategic Studies in 2001.)

Having been accepted to study for a doctorate at the University of Toronto in 1984, I again needed to come up with a thesis subject and decided to avoid any detours, dead ends, or diversions by keeping to a military technology topic. Desmond Morton was already well known for his work in Canadian military history, so the department recommended I call him to help choose a fruitful area. Thinking back to my term paper on technology at Vimy Ridge, I thought it would be a simple matter to expand it to cover technology within the Canadian Corps for the duration of the conflict, and was somewhat taken aback by Morton's question: 'Are there any sources for that?' I said yes, although I was bluffing somewhat, having only vague recollections of war diaries and other materials held at the Public Archives of Canada, but with the intention of double checking when I next visited Ottawa, which was my home town.

It was then that I came across one of the classic finding aids of archival operations, which had been compiled by Barbara Wilson only a few years before. It listed all the units of the Canadian Expeditionary Force and their files, by title, so that I could easily pick out those, such as 'machine guns,' 'artillery,' and 'minor operations,' which would be of help in my dissertation, and was quickly able to put together a proposal that the department as quickly approved. Wilson was, however, only the first to help me maintain a proper course, the second being the above-mentioned Desmond Morton, who became my thesis advisor and, I must admit, my editor. Having failed my comprehensive exams in January 1986, I passed on my second attempt in April, but by then I was months behind schedule and Morton made it very clear he was not going to supervise a decade-long project.

Throwing myself in my research, and living within walking distance of the Public Archives, I came up with a 420-page manuscript that might be categorized as unadulterated gibberish or, more kindly, as a stream-of-consciousness approach to the topic, but which I thought would keep my advisor busy for some time while I focused on contract work that would actually pay my rent. Such was not to be, however, as Morton, within weeks, replied with a 22-page single-spaced editorial critique (if I remember correctly, he reduced chapter thirteen to a single sentence) which turned my six-inch brick into a dissertation, later published as *Surviving Trench Warfare*. Therefore, whatever works in this book is largely due to Desmond Morton.

And whatever works in the field of Canadian military history relating specifically to the First World War since the first edition of *Surviving Trench Warfare* appeared is due to scores of historians who have chosen to work on the subject. In the last twenty years or more *Canadian Military History*, published out of Sir Wilfrid Laurier University, has published so many articles in the area that they are difficult to count, including at least one that proved a corrective to some throw-away comments made in this author's work. Scholarly publications include books by Patrick Bouvier, Marcelle Cinq-Mars, Tim Cook, Sarah Glassford and Amy Shaw, J.L. Granatstein, Jack Hyatt and Nancy Geddes Poole, Teresa Iacobelli, Andrew Iarocci, Benjamin Isitt, Michel Litalien, Stéphane Thibault, Ian Miller, Mélanie Morin-Pelletier, Desmond Morton, James Pitsula, Ian Ross Robertson, Shane Shreiber, Amy Shaw, Timothy Winegard, Glenn Wright, and no doubt others this author needs to apologize to for not having listed them here. As for more popular accounts, they are so numerous this author can only recommend the reader consult Owen Cooke's comprehensive bibliography, *The Canadian Military Experience*, of which a fourth edition is currently in preparation. The same, fortunately, could be said for graduate work in universities, in the form of memoirs, theses, and dissertations, which easily number a hundred, and I can only suggest that the reader browse through the theses webpage of Library and Archives Canada to get an idea of what is available to researchers on microfiche or in electronic form.

As for this author, as a public servant since 1988 I have worked on the projects assigned to me, namely histories of the RCN and RCAF, but there were occasions when the First World War again caught my attention, notably with the publication of *Une façon de faire la guerre* in 2004. That conflict also figured as a chapter in each of *La mort pour ennemi* and *Technicians of Battle*, as well as a section in each of *Victor Brodeur: Officier de la marine canadienne*, and *Ottawa's Sappers: A History of 3rd Field Engineer Squadron*. Articles have included such topics as the use of machine guns in *Material History Review*, on communications in *Canadian Military History*, on the tactics of the last campaign of the war in *1918: Defining Victory*, and on preventive medicine in *La Première guerre mondiale et le Canada*. Throughout, I have attempted to link such studies to a common theme, which appears in the conclusion to this book, that military historians are not studying sheep led to slaughter but thinking human beings who sometimes had an impact on their own destiny. Another theme has also come to permeate this admittedly small body of work – that in a world where people are organized by Human Resources departments, a soldier is a resource not to be squandered.

Bill Rawling
Vanier, 2014

Surviving Trench Warfare
Technology and the Canadian Corps, 1914–1918

Second Edition

Introduction
Technology in the First World War

On 28 June 1914 an assassin's bullet shattered the peace of Europe and brought the nineteenth century to a close. The technology of the Industrial Revolution, which in the previous hundred years had enabled Europe to master the world, served to destroy that dominance as the old empires bled themselves white and two powers on the periphery rose to take their place. The seeds of post-Second World War nuclear confrontation were sown in 1914–18, when centuries of technological development culminated in an orgy of violence to which rifles, machine-guns, flame throwers, artillery pieces, tanks, submarines, poison gas, and aircraft all contributed. The First World War was an outstanding example of rapidly developing technology quickly brought to the battlefield. Aircraft, which in 1914 barely fit into the martial doctrine of any of the belligerent countries, by the end of the war not only were common in the skies over most battlefields but had created a new warrior caste. The tank, no more than a British Admiralty experiment in 1915, was an important part of Allied strategy and tactics at the end of the war and soon took over the cavalry's place and traditions. Only in two realms would the Second World War add to humanity's arsenal: electronics, especially communications and radar, engendered a whole new dimension in warfare; and nuclear fission made a Third World War suicidal if not unthinkable.

The years 1914–18 saw drastic transformations not only in the tools of war, but also in the tactics that governed their use. It was no longer enough to deploy one's troops and send them forward as in the wars of Napoleon or the Crimea; for new weapons and new versions of old weapons inflicted punishing casualties on massed soldiers. In a war where commanders-in-chief and political leaders in France and Britain insisted on recapturing ground lost to the Germans, it became necessary for officers and non-commissioned officers to find some way to ensure troops would get across intervening ground and invest the enemy's positions without suffering prohibitive casualties. Infantry battalions could not achieve their purpose if their soldiers lay dead or wounded in no man's land.

The First World War deeply marked those who experienced it, mainly because it was such a departure from the popular and mythical view of war as an opportunity for glory. The famous German author Erich Maria Remarque reflected on the role of technology in giving the Western Front its fearsome reputation: 'Bombardment, barrage, curtain-fire, mines, gas, tanks, machine-guns, hand-grenades – words, words, but they hold the horror of the world.'[1] Towards the end of the war a French soldier commented on the changes brought about by the industrialization of combat: 'Our men were not driven on ... by the chimera of glory – they died in obscurity and unknown – nor by the assurance given in times past by a strong arm and an intrepid heart – progress in armaments had overwhelmed the valour of old.'[2] Georges Blond commented on the inglorious tactics forced upon soldiers by the technology of war, 'Ramper est devenu un moyen de progression tout à fait normal pour les soldats de la guerre de Quatorze.'[3] Technology was so prevalent that some authors compared the war to one gigantic machine; Siegfried Sassoon, on returning from leave, remarked that he 'was in the machine again,'[4] and when the British Army replaced hats with helmets in 1916, Edmund Blunden saw the change as a symbol of what was happening around him: 'The dethronement of the soft cap clearly symbolized the change that was coming over the war, the induration from a personal crusade into a vast machine of violence';[5] while Sassoon described the war as 'undisguisedly mechanical and inhuman.'[6] Technology even supplanted disease, which in the Boer War had been responsible for 16,000 of 22,000 British deaths,[7] as the great killer during quiet periods; sniper and gunner ensured that even between battles, 'though nothing happened, men died.'[8]

Industrial warfare, like that of the American Civil War that preceded and the Second World War that followed, characterized operations and day-to-day life on the Western Front. But there is far more to technology than machines; one must also take into account the manner in which the machines were used and how they fit in with other forms of technology. Above all, one cannot neglect the role of the technician. As Tony Ashworth insisted,

The picture of combatants helpless before 'laws' working independently of their wills, causing misery and desperation, which is then passively endured, represents some part of the trench war experience; but if it is meant to describe either the whole or 'average' war experience, the image is misleading, and, perhaps, is less than just to trench fighters who were resourceful as well as brave ... For the fact is, soldiers strove with success for control over their environment and thereby radically changed the nature of their war experience.[9]

Technology was not enough; the troops themselves had to be involved in tactical change. The tank, lauded as a solution to the machine-gun and rifle, was vulnerable to shell fire, especially when the Germans sited artillery pieces to destroy oncoming tanks at close range; armoured vehicles needed accompanying infantry to keep them safe from such anti-tank guns. Furthermore, one can counter the machine-gunner or the rifleman by pouring bullets in his direction and forcing him to take shelter in his dugout, trench, or pillbox. Simultaneous fire and movement are not necessarily dependent on the combination of armour and the internal combustion engine; one can achieve the same results by splitting one's infantry units in two, with one group firing at the enemy to force him to keep under cover while another group moves towards him – more a matter of technique than of technology.

It has become common to view the First World War as a long series of bloody battles in which soldiers advanced towards their enemies in slow waves that shuddered and faltered as machine-guns cut them down, but such characterization ignores the war's many contrasts. On the Somme in 1916 the British moved less than eight miles in over four months, but at Amiens in 1918 they drove eleven miles in three days. Two years made a dramatic difference, and it was due only in small part to the Royal Navy's blockade, since the German Army of 1918 was still strong, even if the German economy was weakening. The difference between the slow, ponderous advance of 1916 and the quick, hard blow of 1918 was a change in attitude towards preparing soldiers for battle. In August 1914 Britain's War Office issued its instructions for infantry training, which emphasized the dominant role of the battalion and its commander in the assault.[10] Soon after the war, however, *Platoon Training* carried on its front cover the short message: 'The Platoon Commander came into his own in the Great War. On the vast battle-fronts in France and Belgium the leader of the small, self-contained fighting unit was proved to be the indispensable factor in victory.'[11]

Of interest here is the relationship between the soldiers of the Canadian Corps and the tools of war. Their experiences were similar to those of the British and American expeditionary forces, and the French and German armies, as they strove to find some way to break the deadlock of the Western Front. They were not entirely successful, but before passing judgment on their imperfections one must consider the technology of the day and the inherent conservatism of a social group like the British Army. Various tactical developments led to a different way of waging war, relying on fire and movement and the actions of small units. In their counter-offensive at Verdun the French made the platoon of some forty men their main unit of manoeuvre; in Operation Michael, the offensive of March 1918, the Germans relied on small groups of well-trained, well-motivated infantry to break through British defensive positions, creating a crisis equal to or worse than that of 1914; in the following August the British attacked at Amiens with tanks but also, more importantly, with platoons carrying their own fire-power and closely supported by artillery. In the end the combination of blockade, which weakened the German economy and struck a serious blow at morale; American manpower, which significantly strengthened French armies; and tactics, based on artillery support and small unit manoeuvre, defeated the German Empire.

The Canadians learned from their comrades and enemies on the Western Front, adopting and adapting lessons from the Somme, Verdun, and the March offensive to construct a tactical system which would allow them to cross no man's land, capture the enemy's defences, and hold them against counter-attack. The system involved fire and movement at two levels: the battalion, the soldier's home and family, made its way towards its objectives while artillery kept enemy soldiers in their protective dugouts; the platoons that made up the companies that made up the battalions then fought their own separate battles against trench systems and pillboxes and fought to hold on to the ground they gained. With rifle grenades as artillery, their own machine-guns, and tactics by which men supported one another with different weapons, Canadian infantrymen of 1918 fought their way from Amiens to Mons. Meanwhile, communications, by wireless, pigeon, observer aircraft, lamps, flags, and other means, were critical in ensuring that artillery batteries and infantry battalions indeed worked towards the same goal, and they underwent important developments in the course of the war.

The officers and men of the Canadian Corps were members of a relatively small formation – when compared with the huge armies of the British and French – and required less time to disseminate the lessons of the battlefield. As will be seen, the Canadians after April 1917, like the Anzacs as well as some British and French formations, moved from victory to victory, though always with heavy casualties. Amateur enthusiasm does not explain Canada's victories at Vimy, Hill 70, Amiens, and elsewhere, though Sam Hughes, minister of militia in the first years of the war, insisted that all he needed were men who could ride and shoot. Amateurs can sometimes be successful in war, but usually at prohibitive cost. The Canadians eventually became adept because they were well trained for their tasks.

The Canadian Corps at Vimy Ridge and after was able to break into German defences because it had learned from the battles of 1915 and 1916 that fire-power was as important as courage in taking enemy positions and that soldiers had to be technicians, not just rifle carriers. The commanders and staff officers of the Canadian Corps attempted, sometimes with success, to rationalize war, to plan for every contingency, and to give junior officers, non-commissioned officers, and simple soldiers the tools, the training, and the licence to solve the problems their higher command could not predict. Although in the opening stages of trench warfare courage could mean certain death, by 1918 technology and technique combined to give the brave a greater chance of survival.

Therefore, the Canadian Corps, like its British, French, and German counterparts on the Western Front, attempted to solve the problems of industrial warfare by adopting or devising a tactical system based on specializing tasks within the infantry and artillery and on the close integration of these specialists and their weapons through effective communications, the whole coordinated through detailed planning. Training was crucial, since only well-trained troops could survive in such a lethal environment. In industrial war, and perhaps any war, idealism soon waned; like their British, Australian, and New Zealand counterparts, the leaders, staff officers, and soldiers of the Canadian Corps found their patriotism burned out by the horror of the Western Front. 'What remained was a silent bonding together of men who knew there was no other way out but to see the thing through.'[12] The tactics that evolved from late 1916 to the summer of 1918 allowed the majority of those serving with the Canadian Corps to do just that.

1

The Learning Process Begins

In the nineteenth and early twentieth centuries Britain's empire allowed plenty of opportunity for its soldiers to practise their trade. Some of what they learned in these colonial wars was passed on to the Canadian Militia through the intermediary of Canada's small Permanent Force. Tactics and field operations received little or no attention in the last decades of the nineteenth century, however, and by 1900 only those who had experienced the 1885 North-West Rebellion had any idea of how to move and fight in battle.[1] Canadian inexperience was obvious when for the first time the dominion sent a contingent overseas, to fight in the Boer War. As Desmond Morton has shown, the 2nd (Special Service) Royal Canadian Regiment that landed in South Africa in December 1899 was a military unit in name only; many of its members were new to military life, and even those with militia experience were ignorant of drill, discipline, and military routine. The hastily selected officers knew little more, and even those who had come from the Permanent Force were not well trained.[2]

In other ways also the war in South Africa served as a prologue to the Canadian experience of 1915 and 1916. As a small colonial force with little experience in military affairs, the Canadian contingent served under British generals and followed their dictates and tactics. As representatives of a country where even imperialism was tinged with nationalism, the contingent was supplied with Canadian kit to carry out its small part in the war. The Oliver equipment, found only in Canadian units, was the collection of belts, pouches, and straps with which the soldier carried ammunition, rations, water, extra clothing, and other necessities. Colonel W.D. Otter, commanding the Canadian contingent, found much to be desired in 'the brown leather accoutrements'; in his report concerning the activities of the Canadians in South Africa he stated that 'personally, I am of the opinion that the main brace was not altogether satisfactory, it being inclined to rest too low from the shoulders and apt to gall, or pinch, under the arms.'[3] The water bottle was so small that it was useless, the bandolier stretched out of shape and allowed cartridges to fall out, and the kitbags accompanying the equipment were too small.[4] Soldiers had to avoid getting the equipment wet, for it cracked while drying.[5] The Canadian Contingent of 1914–15 would also have to put up with Oliver equipment, though it would thankfully see it replaced with British web kit before the Canadians went to France. The rifle was more satisfactory. Otter reported: 'In the matter of arms the battalion was as well equipped as any other in the Imperial service, and, I think, considering the rough usage and wear and tear which fell to the lot of both the Lee-Enfield rifle and bayonet, no fault can be found with either.'[6] As we shall see, the Canadian troops of 1915 and 1916 would be less fortunate.

While the Canadian Militia filed its reports, the British took a close look at the events of 1899 to 1901 to see if they could improve procedures, equipment, and tactics, because they had not done well in South Africa, requiring over two years and 22,000 fatalities to bring a small country to heel. The most important lesson the British learned in that war was the need to shoot fast and straight, since Boer musketry often brought attacks to a halt. Rifles, in the right hands, could be lethal up to 2,000 yards; at Spion Kop, Colenso, the Modder River, and Magersfontein the lesson was driven home as, time after time, the British advance withered in the face of accurate Boer musketry. Also, drill would have to take a back seat to field and battle craft; the Boers had fought from well-camouflaged positions and made effective use of South Africa's topography. Marching in battalion formation was useful only in getting troops to the battlefield; it was suicidal once the fighting started, and small units were easier to control and more effective in a type of war where mobility and accurate fire were far more important than mass. The British half-companies, further divided into sections of twenty-five men, made for unwieldly fire units; they were eventually replaced with platoons made up of ten-man sections, though the infantry's organization took longer to change than the British attitude towards musketry.[7]

Artillery tactics also had to change, as guns parked wheel to wheel proved far too vulnerable to Boer rifle fire. General Sir Redvers Buller gave a hint of what was possible when he crossed the Tugela River on

27 February 1900. The 'gunners could fully exploit Buller's revolutionary new tactic for co-ordinating artillery and infantry: to send, skimming over the heads of the creeping infantry, a creeping curtain of shell fire. Only a hundred yards ahead of them, the hillside foamed and thundered with rocks and earth and flying steel. While, on their side of the curtain, the sun still shone and the butterflies glittered on the rocks.'[8] South African knolls and mobile Boers stressed the need for quick-firing howitzers, which could lob shells over hills and other obstacles. To increase a gun's rate of fire it was necessary to control recoil, which forced an artillery piece to leap backwards and lose its alignment. Hydraulics, which tamped the barrel's rearward movement, combined with spring assemblies to push it back into position, provided the answer. Around 1862 the British had used hydraulic devices on coastal guns. Attached to the carriage was a piston rod which pulled a piston through a cylinder filled with a viscous mixture of water and glycerine. The liquid had to pass through a hole in the piston as it moved, acting as a brake. In 1897 the French introduced their famous 75-mm field gun, which worked on a similar principle. Its ammunition was 'fixed'; resembling an overgrown rifle cartridge it allowed for propellant and projectile to be loaded simultaneously and in a single motion. Loading was quick and the carriage remained stationary as the piston absorbed recoil, allowing the French 75 to sustain, easily, a rate of fire of six rounds per minute.[9] By 1906 the Royal Artillery had thirteen- and eighteen-pounder guns, each with a range of 6,000 yards and sights for indirect fire, as well as a 4.5-inch howitzer with a 7,000-yard range and a heavy sixty-pounder capable of firing a shell 9,500 yards. All four were quick firing and would remain with the British Army, and the Canadian Corps, until the end of the First World War and into the beginning of the Second.[10]

In 1904 and 1905 the Japanese, having developed a modern, well-equipped, and well-trained army and navy, clashed with Tsarist Russia as both empires expanded their domains into Manchuria. Machine-guns, heavy artillery, hand-grenades, and mortars contributed to the violence. The Japanese won, Tsar Nicholas II faced rebellion at home, and the western powers tried to derive lessons from the Manchurian battlefield. For the British, the lessons of the Boer War and Russo-Japanese War were summarized in a conference of general staff officers held in January 1910, but all was not clear. After the South African War, the War Office had concluded that fire-power was the decisive factor in armed conflict and that the sword and bayonet were anachronistic. Brigadier Launcelot Kiggell, a future chief of the general staff of the British Expeditionary Force, however, felt that such ideas were erroneous. The Japanese victory in Manchuria, won at such cost, had left the British with the impression that the bayonet was the dominant weapon in war; according to this line of thinking the Boer War had been an anomaly. The British, then, would enter the First World War with the best marksmen in the world but fervently believing that a vigorous assault could be pressed home against rifle and machine-gun fire.[11]

Canadians also tried to learn from their own and the British experience in the Boer War. In 1905 infantry training in Canada moved away from the drill square; though close-order drill remained, as it does today, it became a means of instilling in the soldier a sense of obedience and teamwork and was no longer intended to teach tactics. In fact, training tried to get away from the old formations, and the training guide for the infantry in 1905 stated that 'constant practice in a stereotyped formation inevitably leads to want of elasticity, accustoms all ranks to work by rule rather than by the exercise of their wits, and cramps both initiative and intelligence.'[12] Emphasis was on offensive action, what the French called *élan*, though this in itself could cause problems; for enthusiasm is rarely sufficient to deal with the enemy's weapons unless guided by tactics stressing simultaneous fire and movement.

British tactics called for British equipment, which the Canadians used whenever it was available. Rifles were a major stumbling block, since British manufacturers produced too few of them in time of peace and the British Army required the entire supply in time of war. An easy solution, or so it seemed, was for Canada to produce its own rifles.[13] Canadian infantry thus came to rely on a home-manufactured weapon (based on the Austrian Mannlicher), designed by Sir Charles Ross, a Scottish sportsman and entrepreneur. The rifle weighed nine pounds fourteen ounces, was 50.5 inches long, with a barrel length of 30.15 inches, while the British Lee-Enfield was six inches shorter, with a barrel length of only 25.2 inches. The Ross's muzzle velocity of 2,600 feet per second made it highly accurate at long range,[14] but it was abnormally long. A weapon's length was of little consequence when troops attacked over meadows and fields, but it would prove a serious encumbrance in the trenches.

A committee formed in June 1901, with Colonel W.D. Otter as its president, oversaw a series of a dozen tests in August. Machinists examined the Ross's breech action and declared themselves satisfied, and in the testing that followed the rifle seemed to do well. The straight-pull mechanism was considered 'a very important advantage over the Lee Enfield Action,' since it required only a single movement to clear a spent casing, while to operate a Lee-Enfield one first had to force the bolt a quarter-turn to the left before pulling it back. The committee was also impressed with the rifle's simplicity; a soldier could disassemble the weapon with an ordinary pocket knife and in less time than was required for the Lee-Enfield – evidence (supposedly) that the Canadian weapon was easier to maintain. The breech mechanism was stronger than that of the British rifle, allowing for increased velocities, and hence range and accuracy, if required. A week on the ranges in the hands of the Dominion Rifle Association brought forth no testimonials, but 'no adverse comments were known to have been made, and ... all seemed pleased with the action of the rifle.'[15] The Ross was also a pound lighter than the Lee-Enfield.

The British weapon, however, proved itself superior in one important respect, it could fire rapidly without jamming. 'The chief objection or difficulty which was found in connection with the tests to which the Ross rifle was subjected, was brought in the "endurance test." While in firing 1300 r[oun]ds out of each of the Rifles, the Lee Enfield stood the test quite satisfactorily. It was found after heating, the breech of the Ross Rifle closed with more or less difficulty, the action being very stiff with occasional jamming.'[16] Jamming was aggravated by the lack of leverage the breech mechanism allowed, making it more difficult to force a jammed casing out of the chamber, while that first quarter-turn to the left required with the Lee-Enfield was almost always sufficient to force a jammed casing loose. Sir Charles insisted, however, that the problem could be remedied. In its report the committee accepted the Ross, but with reservations: 'The Board do not profess to pronounce upon the question of a complete remedy of this objection, but having called attention to it, assume that due precaution and provision with reference thereto will be taken, in event of the Rifle being adopted.'[17] For the moment, the jamming problem was left in Sir Charles's lap, and the Ross Mark II would be manufactured with a breech having the same dimensions as the Lee-Enfield.

In 1906 Colonel W.D. Otter, the commander of the Western Ontario District, was directed to adapt the British Army's new, incremental training syllabus to the Permanent Force, which would thus start by teaching the individual the rudiments of his trade, then train men in sections, platoons, and, finally, companies. Five years later Camp Petawawa was the site of the first Permanent Force all-arms manoeuvres in Canada. Both moves were steps in the right direction if the goal was a small professional army, but Sam Hughes, Robert Borden's minister of militia, was not interested in professionals. He believed fervently that all Canada needed were citizen soldiers who could shoot and ride. Battalion commanders, who shared the minister's view, failed to train their subordinates; Lieutenant-Colonel N.M. Young, when interviewed in the 1960s, remembered: 'I had been qualified as a lieutenant in the militia, 35th Regiment, Simcoe Foresters, in 1912, and went to the comic opera camps in the red, ill-fitting uniforms.'[18] The director of artillery, Colonel E.W.B. Morrison, was a journalist friend of Hughes, though it should be said here that he had acquitted himself well in the Boer War and would do so again in 1914–18. In general, however, amateurism ruled the Militia, while the Permanent Force developed with little or no support from its minister, and equipment shortages added to the problem.[19] In the decade before the First World War Canada was at peace and expanding and could allocate few resources to its soldiers.

The arm that reflected technology most closely was the artillery. Here, also, enthusiasm was an important part of tactics as gunners, like everyone else, prepared for a war of movement. This sense of *élan* was most apparent when the artillery trained to pursue the enemy. 'Orders need not be waited for, risks may be freely incurred, and it should not be necessary to delay the pursuit until the immediate front is cleared of the enemy; isolated bodies will be accounted for by the troops which follow.'[20] As early as 1902, then, the concept of using troops to mop up behind the main assault was important to British tactics; it would reappear in the war to come. To emphasize the importance of initiative, the War Office, in one of its own manuals, warned that a training pamphlet was nothing more than a guide; while gun drills were to be followed to the letter to ensure gunners unfamiliar with one another could still maintain a steady rate of fire, any discussion of tactical questions was to be treated as suggestive only.[21]

Artillery's main role was to support the infantry's advance, but setting up such support could be complicated, even in the first decade of the century. Since the enemy's artillery was likely to fire upon assaulting troops, it was necessary to overcome it with one's own batteries. The gunners also had to shell the point or points selected for attack, and any areas from which the enemy could bring flanking fire to bear. From the gunner's standpoint, the battle could be carried out in three phases: first the enemy's guns would be beaten down; when the officer in charge had judged that this phase had been carried out, all available guns, except for a few retained to continue shelling enemy artillery, would then turn on defensive positions; finally, when the infantry began to advance, every gun available, regardless of enemy shell fire, would be used to support the assault by bombarding the enemy's main defensive works.[22]

The purpose of the shelling was not to destroy the enemy; for that required far more shells than the ammunition column could carry. Rather, it was up to the infantry to kill or capture the opponent's soldiers, while the artillery's goal was to limit their capacity to fight back while the infantry advanced. Thus,

At this period of the battle, the greatest result can be obtained, and the most effective support afforded to the attacking infantry, by the concentrated fire of guns and field howitzers. The former ties the defenders to their entrenchments ... distracts their attention from the advancing infantry, and tends to keep their heads down, while the shell fire from the field howitzers ... searches out the interior of the trenches, and the reverse slopes of the position, and checks the movement of reinforcements towards the threatened points.[23]

Artillery fire continued after the position had been won or lost. If the infantry was unable to capture it, the shelling would cover a retreat; if it was successful, the guns and howitzers could use concentrated fire to crush any enemy counter-attacks.[24] These basic goals remained the same until the end of the Great War.

In 1910 Sir John French, soon to be commander-in-chief of the British Expeditionary Force, inspected the Canadian artillery units then training at Petawawa and came away satisfied, though as a cavalry officer he may have judged the gunners more on their speed in coming into action than on their accuracy. He suggested that a third of the batteries were ready for war, another third would require a few weeks' training, and the remainder would be ready within a few months. Canadian artillery had thus learned and practised British tactics to the satisfaction of one of the empire's highest-ranking soldiers.[25] At the time, the gunners had, across Canada, 200 guns available for service, enough to support two infantry divisions, though they were sorely lacking in vehicles and horse-drawn transport.[26] From a British point of view, Canadian artillerymen would be ready in case of war, assuming the next war was similar to the one they had fought in South Africa.

Prior to 1914 the British envisaged using their army on the Continent as they had in the days of Napoleon, but they gave little thought to tactics, especially those of siege warfare. After the Russo-Japanese War engineers provided photographs of dugouts and defensive works, but the majority of high-ranking officers relied on the French for their tactical philosophy, and the French were not interested in dugouts. In 1908 British experiments showed that infantry firing on the move, with overhead machine-gun support, would hit men head and shoulders above a trench with 18 per cent of their rounds as they closed from 150 to fifty yards. Ironically, the British emphasized the offensive *because* of the increase in fire-power on the battlefield, but they did not take into account the possibility, evident in Manchuria, that any enemy would avoid exposing his head and shoulders to machine-gun and rifle fire.[27]

The moral approach to tactics, which emphasized morale and offensive spirit, was dominant in both artillery and infantry, but it did not go unchallenged. Some British officers, instructors at the musketry school at Hythe, proposed that modern fire-power made a breakthrough impossible, so one should aim at a deliberate advance, or what Tim Travers had called the 'bite-and-hold' approach. Certainly those who taught soldiers how to shoot had some idea of what their weapons could do; the musketry school insisted that, given a clear field of fire of 400 yards, the infantry could stop an attack, but its requests for Vickers machine-guns to make the defence even more effective went unheeded. The artillery had worse problems, since it did not have a centralized school until 1920. Though gunners had experienced the need for indirect fire in the Boer War, they never organized the necessary communications networks to make this effective. By 1912 British signal units were capable of setting up networks incorporating telegraph, telephone, and dispatch riders. Telephones were provided to the artillery, but since they were not connected to switchboards, no more than two telephones could be linked on a single line. Also, the instruments tended to break down.[28] In the 1913 manoeuvres the gunners acquired their targets by direct observation (not from the map), did no night shooting, carried out no calibration or adjustment for atmospheric conditions, and had almost nothing to do with the infantry, whom they were supposed to support. Finally, *Infantry Training*, the manual used to teach soldiers their trade, was amended in 1914, so that 'the decision is obtained by fire' became 'fire superiority makes the decision possible.' Thus, as Bidwell and Graham explain, 'The aim of the General Staff was to speed up movement towards the objective. The result was probably to indicate that the advocates of more fire-power were losing the battle against those, like Kiggell, who believed it was overrated.'[29]

In August 1914 Germany invaded Belgium and Great Britain declared war. The British Expeditionary Force (BEF) which began to make its way to France was certainly small, with six infantry and one cavalry divisions. Furthermore, they were divisions in name only; the formation introduced in 1907 had not yet developed into a team, though it went into battle with a full complement of infantry or cavalry, artillery, and ancillary troops.[30] Each infantry division comprised about 18,000 all ranks, 12,000 infantry, 4,000 gunners, and the balance was made up of divisional mounted troops, engineers, signallers, supply and transport sections, and members of field ambulance units. Each of a division's twelve battalions had two machine-guns, and divisional artillery comprised seventy-six guns: fifty-four eighteen-pounders, eighteen 4.5-inch howitzers, and four sixty-pounders. Starting in 1911, British and French staffs had worked out the details of getting the BEF to France and to the front;[31] and in the opening days of the war the British move went according to plan, and morale was high.

Canada was also at war. On 10 August an order-in-council authorized the formation of an expeditionary force, and on 18 August the government introduced the War Measures Act.[32] The minister of militia, Sam Hughes, abandoned plans for mobilization that staff officers had formulated in the previous months and decided on a massive levy: local contingents would be concentrated at Valcartier, just outside Quebec City, where they could organize and train. Infantry training concentrated on teaching the men of the Canadian contingent the use and maintenance of the Ross rifle. Like other military rifles of its day, it was a powerful weapon if fired accurately; at medium range – 300 yards – its bullet could penetrate nine inches of brickwork, eighteen inches of sandbags, or four and a half feet of earth.[33] Hughes told the troops at Valcartier that 'I want, first of all, men who can pink the enemy every time,'[34] so priority was on musketry, teaching soldiers to shoot straight, fast, and at long range.

Problems hampered training from the very beginning; though contractors built a huge rifle range, musketry had to compete with medical examinations, uniform-fitting, and all the other administrative details that go into forging an army from a mob of several thousand civilians. Sam Hughes had sent the Royal Canadian Regiment (RCR), Canada's Permanent Force infantry battalion, to Bermuda, thus creating an acute

shortage of competent instructors. As Vick Lewis recalled: 'I can remember they'd fall in in the morning and somebody would start giving
orders, playing at soldiers, somebody would have an argument, "You're
not doing it right" and I've seen one take off his coat and put it on and
say, "Well, if you know better than I do, come out here and do it" and
they would until we got some real old British sergeant-majors [sic] ...
We didn't actually soldier until 1915 when we were on Salisbury Plains.'[35]
Sending the RCR to Bermuda also created a lack of rifle instructors, only
nine men being available for such duty. They had to start on 25 August
by teaching seven battalions, about 7,000 men, how to shoot. Though
many had handled rifles in civilian life, this experience did not necessarily prepare them for battlefield musketry. Troops had to learn to
shoot at targets according to orders; otherwise, everyone might aim at
the same body of attacking soldiers, allowing others to get through.
Training consisted of firing fifty rounds at various targets, a program
many did not complete, and no one practised at ranges greater than 300
yards.[36] Despite the British emphasis on musketry, men who had to
rely on their rifles for their lives received little opportunity to practise
with their new weapons while in Canada.

The Ross rifle issued to the men at Valcartier, the Mark III, was far
different from the Mark I that had failed the rapid-fire test thirteen years
before, but soldiers found the newer versions still had their imperfections. The magazine, which stored and fed ammunition into the rifle,
held only five rounds and thus required much reloading. Even if it had
had a greater capacity the weapon could not have fired more quickly;
for the bolt, which the soldier pulled back and pushed forward to load
each round out of the magazine and into the rifle, grew hot enough
when firing rapidly to blister flesh.[37] Worse, the contingent reported a
blow-back, where the bolt burst out of the rifle into the firer's face,
though his injuries were minor.[38] Thankfully such incidents would be
exceedingly rare, but some troops were already beginning to lose confidence in the weapon they would have to use to stop German attacks.
The Ross, however, was not only for shooting. Throughout the conflict
the War Office stressed the importance of bayonet fighting, and men
were drilled in parrying, thrusting, slashing, and other movements.[39]
Even in the mobile war for which the Canadian contingent prepared,
planners expected the infantry to capture their objectives in hand-to-
hand combat. Here again, however, the Ross was a problem, because
the bayonet did not fit well onto the rifle and tended to fall off when
the weapon fired.[40]

If the problems of the Ross were worrisome, the history of another invention, the McAdam shovel, bordered on comedy. Ordered and issued by Sam Hughes, it was made of three-sixteenths-inch metal, supposedly thick enough to stop a bullet at 300 yards. The blade was 8.5 by 9.75 inches, or smaller than a page of foolscap, and in one upper quarter was a loophole 3.5 by two inches; the whole affair had a four-foot handle and weighed five pounds four ounces. Inspired by a pre-war Swiss invention, it was designed so the infantryman could use it either for digging or as a shield.[41] All in all, the McAdam may have been brilliant in conception, but it failed miserably in the field, serving, however, as comic relief for soldiers who had little else to laugh about.

In 1914 the machine-gun appeared in British training manuals. Though there were only about four Vickers machine-guns, and possibly a few of other types, at Valcartier, they were the nucleus of larger units to come, and how the War Office perceived them is of some interest here. According to British tactics, machine-guns were to be used in conjunction with artillery, and in fact they carried out an identical role. They were not deemed useful for defence, however, since one could not foresee the actions of the enemy and the machine-gun's arc of fire was limited.[42] That evaluation changed in late 1914, when trench warfare limited the enemy's avenues of approach and the machine-gun became an important defensive weapon; but when the Canadians mobilized at Valcartier, siege warfare was some months away and each battalion was allocated only two Colt machine-guns, or one for every 500 men.[43] Each British battalion went to France with two Vickers, while some German battalions had six machine-guns on strength.

Artillery units, still relying on horses for mobility, were also concentrated at Valcartier. The organization of an artillery battery included everything it would need to live and fight in the field. When Major Harry Crerar, an artillery officer from Hamilton (and commander of the First Canadian Army in the Second World War), prepared his battery for a parade on 31 September, it included six guns, eighteen ammunition wagons, four transport wagons, a water cart, six officers, 187 men and 183 horses.[44] Three such batteries were grouped together to form a brigade, which had its own ammunition column.[45] The gunners at Valcartier had little occasion to train; like the infantry they had to pass medical examinations and get inoculated, attested, and issued with clothing and equipment; unlike the infantry, they had no ranges on which to shoot, so they practised firing across the St Lawrence at a sheet pegged to the far bank.[46] In cleaning the guns, however, the artillerymen had plenty of opportunity to familiarize themselves with the mechanisms and devices that made them function. Their officers at least had time to think about the war's impact on their role and tactics, and one of them, Major A.G.L. McNaughton, a professor of chemistry from McGill (destined to command First Canadian Army before Crerar), gave a series of lectures in October, during the contingent's transatlantic crossing. He foresaw strong defensive positions based on trenches, machine-guns, and barbed wire, which could be breached only if artillery could clear a way for the attacking infantry.[47]

In early October the troops left Valcartier and embarked for England. Their training, which had barely begun while they were in Canada, continued in Bustard Camp, part of the major concentration complex on Salisbury Plain. Canadian inexperience was obvious, as Hughes's citizen-soldiers tried to mould themselves into a professional formation. Private Alex Sinclair of the 5th Battalion wrote in his diary on 9 February, 'There's an expectant stir in camp this morning, and there's more bustle, and sans doute, the usual confusion – the word "confusion" has become synonomous [sic] with "Canadian Contingent"; and just recently I have heard it referred to as the "Comedian Contingent." '[48]

Meanwhile, Canada raised its second contingent, though Sam Hughes did not send it to Valcartier for training. Four of the new battalions, soon to form the 4th Brigade, were from Ontario and went to the exhibition grounds in Toronto to prepare for war. There, the men drilled, fired their Ross rifles, practised bayonet fighting, and went on night manoeuvres through the northern part of Toronto, 'when it was good and dirty and mucky and wet and snowy and freezing.'[49] The artillery in Toronto followed the example set by its Valcartier brethren, firing at targets in Lake Ontario. In western Canada artillerymen trained at Winnipeg, like the Torontonians, with obsolete twelve-pounders, lacking recoil mechanisms, that were more useful for practising mounted manoeuvres than for shooting.[50]

At Bustard Camp the men also dealt with mud and sleet, and conditions were so severe that the Australians, expected to train on Salisbury Plain, diverted their contingent to Cairo. The Canadians had their hodgepodge of equipment replaced with British kit except, of course, for the Ross. Their Oliver equipment had to go because it could carry only fifty to eighty rounds of ammunition, and the British had learned that a soldier would have to start each battle with at least 150 rounds,[51] adding a little more than five pounds to an infantryman's load. Training continued as much as weather allowed, and in November route marches hardened the men. Lessons the British had learned in France were passed on to the recruits at Salisbury, and for ten minutes every day soldiers practised loading and rapid fire with dummy cartridges, since the British Expeditionary Force had brought many a German attack to a halt with rifles. About eight hours a week of musketry taught them to aim and fire their rifles, when they could wrest the ranges from British regiments.[52]

Companies of about 200 men each learned to attack enemy positions and spent nights out on manoeuvres, learning the techniques of silent patrolling. The changing nature of warfare was underlined when the men learned how to take cover from enemy aircraft, which could give away their positions to artillery.[53] In December the Canadian contingent, now the 1st Canadian Division, learned the intricacies of attacking woods or villages, artillery cooperation, occupying defensive positions, and, a necessity on the Western Front, how to dig hasty trenches. (Digging trenches and dugouts was important not only in static warfare but also to protect newly won positions after an assault, since German defensive tactics relied heavily on counter-attacks.) Troops trained in progressively larger and larger units, for five weeks as companies, two as battalions, and two as brigades.[54] On 11 December the entire division trained as a formation for the first time.[55]

In the meantime, the British had begun to learn the importance of the machine-gun in trench warfare. In January the Canadian contingent was advised that its allocation of personnel and equipment for machine-guns would double – to two machine-gun sections per battalion, each armed with two Colts. Machine-gunners were to be extensively trained for their tasks, learning drills, much as the artillery did, to ensure each man was at his post when the gun was placed into position, loaded, and fired. The men also learned to fill belts with bullets, some theory about how the mechanism worked, how to care for and clean the gun, different methods of fire – such as rapid or sniping – how to recognize targets, semaphore so they could communicate with the infantry they were supporting, tactics, how to dig in properly, how to judge distances, methods of determining range, how to select and occupy different gun positions, and how to use the gun to support an attack. Training in the last week of the three-week program included exercises with the entire battalion to practise supporting the infantry in the assault.[56] The machine-gun was a complex weapon which placed a heavy strain on the battalion's supply column – most of the fifteen men in the machine-gun section were detailed to carry ammunition. Machine-gunners were specialists, like gunners or sappers; the infantry of 1915 did not learn to handle automatic weapons.

At Salisbury the artillery trained as best it could in spite of bad weather and several changes in organization. It rained on eighty-nine of the 123 days the Canadians spent in England, often forcing commanders to cancel training. The first contingent had arrived with three brigades of artillery, each formed of a headquarters and three batteries of eighteen-pounders of six guns each and an ammunition column. The contingent also had a heavy battery of sixty-pounders and a division ammunition column. Normally each brigade would also contain a battery of 4.5-inch howitzers but these were not yet available. In November 1914, just as the front in France was stabilizing, this organization changed; the British had decided that six guns were too difficult to control in mobile warfare, so each battery was formed of four guns and each brigade now consisted of four batteries.[57] Even when rain and bureaucracy allowed, the artillery could not practise firing its guns, because many of the ranges were occupied by troops for lack of space anywhere else, and the ranges that were available had to be shared with the gunners of six British divisions. Daily training concentrated on equitation and driving, and it was not until the end of January 1915 that the guns were fired, fifty rounds per battery.[58] The gunners would have to wait until the move to France to gain any real experience with the tools of their trade.

While the Canadians trained, fighting on the Western Front quickly turned to deadlock; the first Canadian contingent would move to a continent dominated by siege warfare. German strategy, embodied in the Schlieffen Plan, called for a strong offensive against France while preparations were made to defend against Russia. Since a defensive posture on one front was an important element in their general plan, the Germans had already incorporated the machine-gun into their defensive tactics; so when the offensive against France failed, they had only to adopt the posture they had expected to use on the Eastern Front, deep in barbed wire and bristling with automatic weapons.[59] Thus the French, who bore the brunt of the fighting, saw their tactics change dramatically with the advent of trench warfare. In September 1914 tactical doctrine called upon the troops to advance to within 400 metres of the enemy, where they opened fire then advanced again in short bursts. After the front stabilized, however, a French officer wrote home: 'Je t'assure que cette guerre n'est plus une guerre honnête; c'est une guerre d'apache, une guerre à l'affût ... Oui, parle-moi [sic] de la guerre à la Napoléon, de la guerre en rase campagne ou l'on manœuvre, ou

Canadians 'mudlarking' on Salisbury Plain. Though these soldiers are smiling for the camera, they really had little to smile about. Only at Passchendaele would conditions be so wet again.

l'on change de place, comme au commencement. Mais maintenant c'est écœurant de voir cela. On se guette, comme on guette un lapin à l'affût. On se fait sauter, on se tue sans se voir. On se lance des bombes, des torpilles, on est à quarante mètres et on ne se voit pas. Nous sommes devenus des bandits.'[60]

In February 1915 the Canadian Expeditionary Force moved to France, where training continued. It was hardly a well-prepared formation, having had barely a few weeks to train as a division,[61] but trench warfare was new to the well-trained professional European armies as well.[62] Emphasis was on the local attack, involving limited objectives assaulted by battalion- or brigade-sized units. Before entering the trenches, Canadian troops repeatedly went over the procedures to be followed before, during, and after an assault, with the usual emphasis on bayonet fighting.[63] Tactics were simple; for by 1915 the British, like the Germans and French, had given up on some of their pre-war concepts of mobility. Heretofore, scouts had gone out in front of the assaulting infantry to find safe routes through no man's land and ensure the platoons behind them were moving towards their proper objectives. The scouts, however, tended to get caught in the wire, where the Germans soon slaughtered them with machine-gun and rifle fire. Understandably, platoons following the scouts had been slow to move; to solve this problem, the British did away with scouts except for major offensives. The detachments detailed for the assault were expected to leave their trenches at the same time and reach their objective without firing a shot. In practice platoons crossed no man's land in alternate rushes but did not attempt to support one another with fire. Then the artillery, which had been firing at the trenches, would be ordered to lengthen its range and isolate enemy positions from reinforcements. When the infantry had moved to within about fifty yards of the enemy trenches, commanders would give the signal to move forward as a body: 'On this signal the assault must be launched in one rush, this is essential if it is to succeed. The energy and courage of the troops will do the rest.'[64]

The War Office expected the artillery to play a major role in upcoming attacks, and the gunners trained accordingly. The battles of 1914 and the stalemate of 1915 had not changed the artillery's role, and its main task was still to bombard the enemy's positions during the assault and cut him off from his reserves.[65] To this Lieutenant-Colonel A.G.L. McNaughton, who kept in close touch with changing developments in the Royal Artillery, added the task of clearing no man's land of obstacles: 'You had to get some way over – to be able to smash your way through the barbed wire. And the only possible way to do it in the time available was by gunfire.'[66] Unlike the infantry, however, the artillery had some opportunity to train under realistic conditions, using the enemy's trenches as targets for practice shoots, but they could do this only if ammunition was available, and often it was not.[67]

Infantry training continued in the trenches. Between 17 February and

2 March each Canadian infantry brigade, accompanied by its supporting units, was attached for a week to a British division holding the line in order to learn the routines of trench warfare. The Canadians thus adopted British procedures which rotated units through the front trenches so only about 2,000 men of a division of 18,000 were actually in the front line at any given time.[68] Trench warfare followed a schedule that remained pretty much the same until 1918, each battalion usually spending four days in the front line, another four in support, and yet another four resting, 'a euphemistic term employed by the army to describe a strenuous program of training and work.'[69] While in reserve, battalions could carry out further training and general maintenance. The front line was a constant drain on those who guarded the parapets, even in quiet times. As George Bell, a one-time member of the 1st Battalion, explained, 'To the historian the phrase "a prolonged period of inactivity," means quiet; to the private it means cold, wet trenches, minor trench raids, counter attacks, all of which take their toll.'[70]

The front was characterized by long periods of tension and boredom sometimes punctuated by moments of excitement and terror. Though John Terraine could speak of the defensive power of artillery[71] and Tom Wintringham could insist on the stopping power of machine-guns,[72] the infantryman facing his enemies across no man's land was limited to two weapons with which to defend himself, the rifle and the bomb. The latter was a reinvention of an old weapon, as 'Once again one sees how the peculiar conditions of the Western Front forced men to delve back into history and rediscover weapons and techniques that had been developed hundreds of years before.'[73] The bombs in use at that time were hazardous, and bombers, like machine-gunners, were specialists. The first bombs were handmade in the trenches and reserve lines, and infantrymen called them 'Tommy Tickler's Artillery' because they were made with jam tins bearing that brand name. The tins were filled with explosive and metal fragments, such as nuts, bolts, and nails, and closed with a fuse showing at the top. One simply lit the fuse and tossed. Bomb-throwing was made perilous by the fact that atmospheric conditions and mishandling could shorten the length of time the fuse needed to burn, and some men were killed learning to use the devices. If the opposite occurred and the fuse took too long to burn, enemy soldiers could pick up the bomb and throw it back.[74]

Some infantrymen found ways to fight their enemies across no man's land with the rifle – as snipers. Sniping was a difficult business because, as instructors cold-bloodedly pointed out, the smallest of game animals presented more target area than a German face. In this vocation one of the preferred weapons was the Canadian-manufactured Ross rifle, which British snipers found as accurate as the American Springfield up to 600 yards. Its only disadvantage, deriving directly from the characteristics that made it a superior sniper weapon, was that it accepted only perfect ammunition or jammed.[75]

Another common feature of trench warfare awaiting the Canadians was the night patrol, where soldiers risked their lives to check on the enemy's defences, ensure that their own were up to standard, or simply establish a 'presence' in no man's land. Silence was all-important, so much so that ordinary fence stakes were eventually replaced with screw-type stakes so soldiers could put up barbed wire obstacles without making too much noise. Patrols were surrounded with ritual. As Denis Winter related, 'Pockets would be emptied, faces blackened with burnt cork and bayonets dulled with a covering sock. These were the preliminaries. Next, men would equip with knives and clubs; grenades were for emergencies only since noise in no-man's land spelled star shells and machine-guns.'[76] In accordance with orders from the commander-in-chief, Sir John French, Lieutenant-General Sir E.A.H. Alderson, the Canadian Division's British commander, instituted a policy of bold patrolling, persistent sniping, and quick attacks against enemy trenches being dug in no man's land to lower enemy morale and give him few opportunities to move to the offensive.

At the front the troops soon learned the dangers posed by enemy artillery. The Germans could shell Canadian defences without warning or fall into a routine whereby, for example, they fired at the troops before breakfast and after dinner. Casualties were common, and a typical infantry battalion reported a couple of men killed or wounded almost every day.[77] Lieutenant W.B. Foster described some of the shells the Germans used, each of which had been given a nickname by solders who were more interested in technology's effects than its jargon.

You ask what 'coal-box' is; well it is a howitzer shell, 5.9,, which explodes with a noise like thunder and throws up large volumes of thick black smoke. You can hear it coming quite plainly, and when it is just overhead the noise resembles an express train travelling at the rate of 65 to 70 miles an hour ... [while] Wooly Bears are high explosive shrapnel shells which explode in the air, throwing great clouds of dense white and yellow smoke; when the shrapnel comes over you the noise is terrific, and that is the time we hug the parapet pretty closely ... The Hun have a thing called an aerial torpedo which they delight in throwing at us; it is just a large 14-inch shell and full of explosive. You can hear a dull thud in the Hun lines and then you see this big shell rising into the air. It goes up to a tremendous height and at first it is very difficult to know just where it may land. It is a case of stand tight and judge its course as it comes down ... we have 'sausages' which are about 20 inches long and 4 inches in diameter. They go a great height too, and come down with a swishing noise; you can observe these quite clearly during their whole flight through the air.[78]

The Canadians, however, were not the only victims of indiscriminate shelling; they too had artillery support. Crerar reported the damage done by a particularly large artillery piece: 'The other day, I saw it shelling a German battery from my observation station, the explosion hurled things hundreds of feet in all directions.'[79] Artillery duels – somewhat misnamed – were common, though gunners shot not at each other but at the infantry opposite them. Every time Canadian gunners moved to a different position, however, they had to be careful to camouflage it properly before enemy aircraft spotted it; for not only could enemy observers call in their position to counter-battery sections, but already at this stage of the war planes carried bombs.[80]

Artilleryman faced other hazards at the front. Most of their targets were hidden; so battery commanders often went forward into the front trenches or sent subordinates to spot fire and send back corrections, each shift lasting forty-eight hours. Crerar related a conversation he had with one of his colleagues: 'They were shelled out of their dugout yesterday, very annoying. He also complained that one of his observing stations was a pet target for snipers – it's a ruined house and they take pot shots at him getting in out out.'[81] Many observers were killed or wounded while creeping forward into no man's land to get a better view. It was not long before the artillery began to train infantry officers to act as observers, and by March 1915 many infantry battalions called down their own fire. For the British, French, and their allies, it was crucial to be able to locate the German guns, which outnumbered and outranged them. Furthermore, ammunition supplies were a problem throughout 1915, as industry continued to gear itself up to the demands of a modern war, and accurate spotting made for a more economical expenditure of shells. One way to increase accuracy was to use aircraft to perform the spotting, and airplanes grew in importance as deadlock settled in; light cars both sides expected to use for reconnaissance could not penetrate into rear areas, and the same was true of cavalry. The only effective means for aircraft to call the fall of shot was through wireless, though this method brought with it disadvantages of its own. The transmitter was so bulky that there was no room for either an observer, who normally looked out for enemy aircraft, or a receiver; so the pilot could not receive new orders should gunners need to change targets. At least a simplified means of sending information existed through the clock code, which required the pilot to send only a two- or three-digit message to correct a battery's fire (see figure 1). In early 1915, however, there were too few training courses available for officers to learn the techniques of communicating with aircraft, and for the time being gunners or infantrymen performed the bulk of artillery observation.[82]

The Canadians' first experience of a set-piece battle was at Neuve Chapelle from 10 to 12 March 1915, though they were part of a diversion and so were not committed to the attack. Their artillery shelled German positions in front of the British for thirty-five minutes and, when the assault began, Canadian riflemen and machine-gunners fired in bursts, continuing to do so at fifteen-minute intervals throughout the day.[83] It was at Neuve Chapelle that the French term 'barrage,' meaning barrier, came into use for the first time, and it accurately described what the artillery was attempting to do – prevent the Germans from moving up reserves to reinforce their besieged front-line troops. It was also at Neuve Chapelle that British and Canadian gunners used the clock method of calling fall of shot for the first time, allowing gunners to zero in on their targets thousands of yards away with little loss of time. Added to Haig's insistence that each round be accurately observed, the technique was one of the first steps towards 'scientific gunnery.' The bombardment also lifted from objective to objective, the first time British artillery had attempted to protect the troops throughout the advance.[84] George Bell, a member of the 1st Battalion acting in a diversionary role on the left flank of the British assault, reported on how the barrage helped the infantry get forward: 'For about a half hour this merciless bombardment went on, the range was lifted and under protection of a creeping barrage, British infantry climbed out of trenches into No Man's Land. This was the first time this form of barrage had been used, and, in spite of instructions to time their pace with the lifting range of the big guns, advancing Tommies went too fast and ran into their own artillery fire.'[85] Taking casualties from one's own creeping barrage, gruesome as it may sound, would be considered a portent that infantry losses as a whole would be lower, since they would enter the German trenches before the

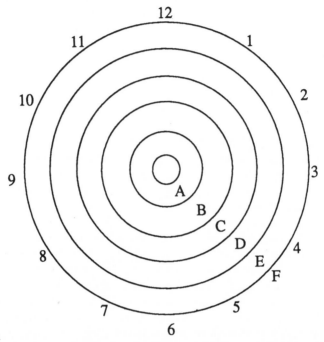

Figure 1

The Clock Code. The target is taken to be the centre of a clock with north at 12 o'clock, south at 6 o'clock, and concentric circles representing 10-, 25-, 50-, 100-, and then hundred-yard intervals, labelled Y, Z, then A through F (the two smaller circles have not been drawn here). Thus a miss of 200 yards to the right would be reported as C3, and 100 yards south-southwest would be reported as B7.

From DHist 83/98, *Co-operation of Aircraft with Artillery, December 1917*, 23–4

enemy could emerge from protective dugouts and take up defensive positions.

For the infantry Neuve Chapelle was more a time of frustration than innovation, because the Ross rifle demonstrated its deficiencies and often jammed. As Michael L'Abbé later remembered:

On our left the Scottish Rifles let loose and we took it up. What a din! But it was great to snuggle down and aim low at that trench in front, pumping the bolt as fast as one could ... In a few minutes my rifle started kicking like an old muzzle loader. I could hardly open the bolt. No use getting excited. 'Use some oil' I yelled at the others and did so myself ... I couldn't open the bolt. There was no dirt or mud in it. I took pride in my old gun. Kicking it open each time I fired became monotonous, and I grabbed a rifle that was lying unused in the trench. It was worse than mine ... On our left the Scottish Rifles were keeping up that deadly stream of fire, without any brakes in it, that denotes a regular battalion of the line. A steady rolling fire, like so many machine guns. And here we were with a few 'put-puts' a minute.

Hours later he tried to diagnose the problem: 'I began a systematic examination of my rifle, wondering why it should have failed when most needed. I had fired "rapid" before with this rifle. The bolt was working all right now. The rifle was cold, of course. Was it expansion? If so, why hadn't it happened on the ranges during the tests. Must be the ammunition. My faith still clung to the Ross Rifle.' The next day, on parade, officers blamed the jamming on faulty ammunition, just as L'Abbé had suspected: 'But why, Oh why, could the Scottish Rifles on the left keep up their fire without a break using the same make and brand of ammunition?'[86] He would have to wait upwards of a year for an answer; meanwhile many Canadian soldiers gave up on the Ross completely, and, since its shortcomings could not be repaired in the field, there was nothing left to do but to try to get Lee-Enfields, which used the same ammunition, from British casualties.[87]

By the spring of 1915 the infantryman in the trenches already had a wide variety of weapons at his disposal, including bombs and machine-guns, assuming men who had been trained to use them were available. He still had no effective means of dealing with enemy aircraft, however, except to hope that the Royal Flying Corps, itself still groping with effective ways to arm its planes, would come along to clear the enemy from the skies. Infantry battalions on the front line often complained that they were wide open to attack from bomb or machine-gun, or simply vulnerable to observation that could bring on severe shelling. One diarist wrote just before the battle of Ypres, 'Hostile aircraft in numbers hovering over our position. No friendly aircraft in sight – no friendly anti-aircraft guns. Enemy permitted to reconnoitre our position unmolested save for our own rifle and machine gun fire.'[88] Airplanes gathered the information they needed and a few days later the Germans launched their attack.

On 22 April the Germans, for the first time on the Western Front, used poison gas to create a breach in the lines; the battle, in fact, was essentially a testing ground for the new weapon, not a major offensive.[89] The 87th Territorial and 45th Algerian divisions of the French army, whose soldiers received full doses of the vapour, withdrew. As a weapon, gas was particularly advantageous when used against soldiers in defensive positions; for, heavier than air, the chlorine used at Ypres followed the ground's contours and sank into the trenches and shell holes soldiers used as protection against shrapnel and bullet, forcing them to abandon their defences. Those who stayed found it extremely difficult to fight with watery eyes, heaving stomachs, and burning lungs. It could thus be more effective than artillery, which had to be very accurate to do any damage to a defensive position, or rifle fire, which required the enemy to expose himself. The Canadians were not targets for gas attack on that first day of the Second Battle of Ypres, but some of them were witnesses to the German assault. The 10th Battalion's war diary reported the experiences of some of its officers: 'Maj. McLaren, Maj. Ormond and Capt. Glidden [the medical officer] riding between Elverdinge and Brielen hear bombardment from north east and see shells breaking also cloud of peculiar color (greyish, yellowish, greenish), darker near the ground and lighter in color near top.'[90] One Canadian officer, looking towards the French lines and seeing the greenish yellow mist, thought the infantry there were firing with a different kind of powder.[91] Such short reports announced the introduction of chemical warfare to the Western Front.

The breach in Allied lines was over four miles wide, and the Canadians, to the right of the gap, were called upon to help close it. That first night, the 10th and 16th battalions were ordered to recapture Kitchener's Wood, and their attacks are excellent examples of the tactics of the day; for the old professionals of the 1914 BEF were no more, and the citizen-soldiers of 1915 went into battle with only rudimentary tactical skills. The men formed up in a nearby field under cover of darkness and thus avoided German shelling. When the time came to attack, the 1,500 troops stood up in eight ranks at intervals of about thirty yards. The 10th Battalion's diary described in great detail the battle that unfolded. At about 10:30 in the evening, guides showed the troops to their positions, with A and C companies forming the first two lines and B and D companies forming the third and fourth lines. There was just enough light for these soldiers to see the woods they were to capture, 500–600 yards away. A house off to one side, suspected of harbouring machine-guns, they left alone, because officers determined it was not their job to take it. In years to come destroying such potential redoubts would become common practice. At 11:45 p.m. the attack began. At this point the two battalions were on their own, since they had no way to communicate with headquarters or supporting artillery, except through runners: 'The 16th Bn was reported all ready and the order to advance given, not a sound was audiable [sic] down the long waving lines but the soft pad of feet and the knock of bayonet scabbards against thighs. In C.17.a [a map reference] a hedge was unexpectedly encountered and the noise of breaking through brought on a hail of bullets, rifle and machine gun. Our two supporting field guns had ceased fire.'[92]

Artillery support having ceased, the Canadians had to rely on their rifles, bayonets, and bombs to carry out the assault, which took place just three minutes after setting out: 'There was a momentary pause at the hedge then those unhit burst forward at a fast run and struck the enemy trench, where brisk work with bayonet and butt cleared this trench, in less than a minute, the whole body pressing on into the wood where the enemy were making a fair resistance, the men were thoroughly aroused and pressed on clearing the wood.'[93] The 16th Battalion's experience was similar. Formed up in four lines behind the 10th, it advanced at about midnight: 'When about 300 yds. from enemy he opened rapid fire with rifles and machine guns. We then doubled and when flares went up lay down. When we made the charge the enemy fled.'[94] The actual assault, against hastily prepared positions, was a success, in spite of German rifle and machine-gun fire and the absence of Canadian artillery support. Casualties had been high, however, and holding the newly won line was to be more difficult than taking it had been. Informing brigade headquarters of the situation, so as to get reinforcements, was also a problem. On the whole, different levels of command knew little of what was happening to their subordinate formations and units.[95]

The Germans, as was common in 1915, organized their defences in depth, even if they had just recently captured the ground they were defending. The Canadians had managed to cave in the first line, but there were others from which German commanders could launch their men into counter-attacks. After their assault the 10th Battalion's survivors saw a redoubt only fifteen yards away: 'Lt. W.A. Lowry of the 10th Bn came up, he took 8 or 10 of the 34 O[ther] R[anks] and went into the wood, an effort was made to charge this position while the party in the wood opened rapid fire, this however was unsuccessful for as soon as the party made the attempt to charge they were cut down by machine gun fire or blown to pieces by bombs and grenades used by the enemy.'[96] The redoubt remained in German hands, as did other sections of the German defences.

At about 2:00 a.m. on 23 April the 10th Battalion reported that it was under fire from all directions except the southeast but was trying to consolidate its gains by digging new trenches and building up parapets. In addition, the two battalions, having become intermixed in the course of the fighting, sorted themselves out.[97] German fire from the second line of trenches was too intense, however, and the Canadians withdrew.[98] At 6:30 that morning, the 10th Battalion paraded. Five officers and 188 other ranks answered roll call; 816 other ranks had gone into the assault seven hours before. Casualties were not quite as high as the numbers might indicate, since many men were missing and would rejoin the battalion in the days to come. In all, the war diary estimated that nineteen officers and 460 other ranks were killed, wounded, or taken prisoner.[99] Tactics were perhaps costly, but the Canadians had learned no other way to conduct a night assault, and the cover of darkness had helped prevent the Germans from detecting the Canadian attack until the last moment.[100]

Counter-attacks continued. On the following day a company of the 2nd Battalion attempted to capture a strong point in Kitchener's Wood, but as they advanced, the ground mist lifted, revealing the 200 Canadians to German machine-gunners. Only fifteen men managed to crawl back to their trenches. The 1st and 4th battalions fared little better as they tried to retake Mauser Ridge, attacking at 5:25 in the morning without artillery support; German artillery, machine-gun, and rifle fire forced them to stop. Digging in 400 or 500 yards from the enemy's positions, the 4th Battalion came out of action at 9:00 that evening, having suffered 505 casualties. The 1st Battalion remained until the evening of 25 April, losing 402 men, almost all of them on the first day.[101] Enemy artillery shelled them as they formed up, machine-guns cut them down as they crossed no man's land, and rifle fire reduced their ranks as they approached the enemy's positions. They were less successful than their comrades of the 10th and 16th battalions had been the night before and did not even have the satisfaction of entering German trenches. The infantry required much more fire support than they themselves could supply, but artillery was unable to suppress machine-gunners and riflemen protected by trench works, and communications were too primitive to allow advancing infantry to call for help when it needed covering artillery fire.

On 24 April the Canadians felt the full force of a gas attack. The chlorine was released from cylinders just in front of the German lines or through portholes punched through the parapets. The breeze carried it towards the Canadians, who, without protection, could do little but withdraw; they evacuated the first line of trenches, the men moving back and lying on their stomachs, covering their mouths with wet cloths. The gas, however, which had come as a complete surprise to the Algerians, began to lose its novelty. Because the fumes made it difficult or impossible for German observers to call the fall of shot, at times their infantry advanced without artillery support, and the Canadians waited until they came upon their empty trenches and opened fire from ranges of less than 100 yards. German casualties were heavy.[102]

Gunners, who had become intimate with the workings of the eighteen-pounder, used the guns over open sights at ranges of 800 or 900 yards, firing shrapnel to stop German assaults. Then, they held back, waiting for the Germans to re-form before shelling them in their assembly areas.[103] Training before the war and on Salisbury Plain had prepared the gunners well for the crises they were asked to face; their positions changed several times a day, forcing them to move constantly, sometimes under German shell fire. One gas attack forced some of the Canadian units to evacuate the front trenches, but artillery, firing into no man's land, kept the Germans from taking the Canadian positions, which were reoccupied as soon as the vapours dissipated. In order for the Germans to hold the ground they had cleared with gas, they still had to use their infantry, which had not lost its vulnerability to shelling.[104] At Ypres the Canadian Division relied far more heavily on artillery than on machine-guns to defend its positions.

German artillery was also busy, and it managed to cut contact between front-line troops and brigade headquarters. Telephones were the most reliable means of communication as long as shelling did not cut the wires, and in the crisis situation at Ypres where headquarters, battalions, and batteries moved often, there was no time to bury it. Battalion commanders often knew little of what was happening, and the battlefield was a confused series of skirmishes, rushes, and withdrawals.[105] As the 7th Battalion reported: 'never succeeded in establishing communications. All wires broken,'[106] while the 5th Battalion experienced the same trouble: 'Very heavy Artillery bombardment of our position from 4 a.m. throughout the day. Great difficulty experienced in keeping telephonic communications open between Headquarters of Battn and fire trenches.'[107]

As for the gas, Canadian troops were capable of only limited precautions, and many suffered. A few were totally overcome and lost consciousness, and, for those who remained standing, breathing was difficult and it was hard to resist the temptation to tear away the damp rags and gulp air. Men in the trenches, where the gas collected, coughed, spat, cursed, grovelled, and tried to retch. The worst effects lasted about ten minutes, but later the men still felt weak and cold in their extremities.[108] One member of the 8th Battalion and two men of the 15th died, while the 1st Division as a whole lost 228 men injured by gas.[109] Casualties were thus not particularly high, but the symptoms the vapour induced made it very difficult for men to defend themselves effectively, and many of those killed or wounded by conventional arms no doubt fell because of their diminished fighting capacity.

Gas was far from the only weapon the Germans used in the battle, and traditional weapons also took their toll. After the gas came the shelling and machine-gun barrages, followed by the infantry with their rifles. When the 14th Battalion was forced back on its left, 1 Company of the 7th Battalion found itself under machine-gun fire from the flank. Enfilade fire was particularly deadly, since it was difficult to retaliate because only those on the extreme left flank could engage the machine-guns. After having beaten off three attacks that morning, the company was forced to withdraw; German machine-gunners had made the position untenable. The company suffered heavily from shell and bullet from 22 to 24 April; 308 men had entered the line, including stragglers and volunteers from other units, but by 12:00 noon on the 24th about fifty men were left fighting. When they were relieved on the 26th, a lieutenant and twenty-two men were all that could walk out of the trenches. On 23 April the 15th Battalion suffered 647 casualties while holding off German attacks, which were characterized by superior numbers of infantry supported by a preponderance of heavy artillery and automatic weapons.[110] Enemy machine-guns made it difficult to move, and the Germans used them to their advantage.[111]

The rifle was the Canadian infantryman's main weapon of defence. Firing as quickly as they could load, soldiers tried to stop the enemy from advancing or at least to delay his attack so they could withdraw in good order.[112] The Ross did not stand the test well, though some units described their experiences without mentioning any trouble with the rifle. R.C. Fetherstonhaugh devoted a chapter to Second Ypres in his history of the 13th Battalion without making any reference to the Ross, and the rifle did not figure in H.M. Urquhart's two chapters on the battle in his account of the 16th Battalion's experiences.[113] In his history of the 2nd Battalion, however, Colonel W.W. Murray wrote: 'It is a tragic commentary on these weapons that in a large number of cases the bolt-rings had ... been broken off when the men, in desperation, had striven to kick them open. The failure of their rifles to function properly was a disheartening feature of a disheartening situation.'[114] After the battle, however, Lieutenant-Colonel David Watson, commanding the 2nd Battalion, reported that 'Majority of opinion strongly in favour of Ross rifle,'[115] though his friendship with the minister of militia,[116] a strong supporter of the Ross, may have influenced his judgment. Lieutenant-Colonel F.O.W. Loomis, commanding the 13th Battalion, complained that 'after firing 15 to 30 rounds rapid fire, the rifles jam. To loosen the bolt it was necessary to use the boot heel or the handle of an entrenching tool.'[117] Evidence against the Canadian-manufactured weapon was slowly mounting.

The Canadians were withdrawn from the battle on 3 May. Losses had been heavy: of a maximum divisional strength of 18,000 that had started the battle on 22 April, 5,975 had become casualties, of whom over 1,000 were known to be dead;[118] so almost 6,000 men were lost in the Canadians' first major engagement of the war. The fighting of the first few days, as the Canadians counter-attacked to recapture lost ground, had been heavy, but the worst day for the division was 24 April, when it fought to defend its trenches against determined attacks supported by gas and shelling, suffering 3,058 casualties.[119] For those who subsequently insisted that defence was stronger than offence, Second Ypres should have provided food for thought; for sitting quietly in one's trenches could make one a target for attack. Second Ypres proved to be the worst battle the 1st Division would fight in the course of the war, half of its infantrymen becoming casualties.

The Canadians were not yet ready for the kind of war that had been thrust upon them, and the Ross rifle's defects made matters worse. The simple, linear tactics of 1915 were inappropriate against an enemy armed with magazine rifles and machine-guns. Artillery had proved itself in breaking up German attacks, and the Canadians would swear by the eighteen-pounder until after the war. The gunners' reliance on initiative, which had been bred into them since the turn of the century and before, stood them in good stead in defensive battles, but it was not sufficient to ensure that infantry advances could be pressed home without heavy casualties. The Canadians had to find some way to make their infantry weapons more effective, liaison between infantry and artillery more efficient, and the artillery's guns more accurate. They began the long road towards achieving these goals on their way to one of the bloodiest battles in history: the Somme.

2

The Road to the Somme

Second Ypres was a defensive battle, the Canadians trying to give up as little ground as possible in the face of German attacks. In the years that followed, the Canadian Corps would be mainly on the offensive, slowly developing the elements of fire and movement necessary to advance through German defences, though counting the dead and maimed of Ypres made it clear that the learning process would be brutal. The first phase of that harsh education began after Ypres and ended just as the Canadians moved to the Somme, in September 1916, to take part in one of the largest offensives of the conflict. At Festubert in May 1915, Givenchy in June of that year, St-Eloi in March and April 1916, and Mount Sorrel in the following June, the Canadians knew mostly failure, punctuated with a few successes. Through these assaults there developed a system of tactics more sophisticated than those that had led to disaster in the counter-attacks at Ypres, though not yet adequate to guarantee clear-cut victories. In the intervening periods of relative calm soldiers patrolled no man's land when in the trenches and trained for the next battle while in reserve. Eventually the corps developed some competence in the intricacies of trench warfare and the technology with which it was fought.

Some of that technology, however, was faulty. From March 1915 machine-gunners had complained that the Colt machine-gun, which they had been using since Valcartier, was not reliable in combat, but it was not until May that these complaints were investigated. The findings were striking. The 2nd Brigade had suffered a serious reverse at Keerselaere, on St Julien Ridge near Ypres, in part because the Colts failed. The 5th Battalion reported that, in one action, one of its four machine-guns became useless after firing only a few rounds, and its crew abandoned it in the subsequent withdrawal because the tripod was too heavy to carry in a quick retreat. It was simply not possible to keep the machine-gun clean enough in the trenches to ensure it would operate.[1] It was also a logistical nightmare; the list of suggested equipment for four guns was two pages long, with ninety-eight different items for a total of 348 pieces, including tools and spare parts, as opposed to 123 for the Vickers and ninety for the Lewis.[2]

Complaints centred mainly on the gun's extractor, which cleared the chamber in order to make way for the next live round. It had to repeat this action several hundred times a minute if the weapon was to work at full efficiency. When it broke, any defensive position relying on the gun's high rate of fire could face serious trouble – including annihilation – especially given problems with the Ross and shell shortages which limited artillery support. The 10th Battalion reported losing eleven of fifteen men from one gun crew when an extractor failed. Lieutenant-Colonel Victor Odlum, commanding the 7th Battalion, stated that the 'Machine Gun Officer who is believed to have been lost with his men, repeatedly condemned the guns.'[3] Lieutenant Edward Bellew, the missing officer in question, received the Victoria Cross for his actions at Second Ypres, where he was taken prisoner.[4] The 8th Battalion could not prepare an adequate report, for only eight men of its four crews survived.[5] Brigadier-General Arthur Currie of the 2nd Brigade insisted the unit's Colts be replaced with the British Service Maxim:[6] 'The reports received are almost unanimous in condemning the gun and I have reluctantly come to the conclusion that the weapon is from its complicated mechanism and cumbersome mounting unsuited for service conditions and is liable to fail at critical moments when machine gun fire is essential to save the situation.'[7] Years later, when asked whether the Vickers was superior to the Colt, John Lundie responded: 'There was no comparison ... [It would] jam in the dust and stopped firing just at the moment when it was needed most ... The Colt was a washout.'[8] There being too few Vickers to go around, however, the Colt was retained.

So was the Ross. After Second Ypres concerns about its suitability rose as high as Field Marshal Sir John French. In June he reported to the War Office that rumours of Canadians ridding themselves of their weapons – even though it was an offence to do so – in favour of Lee-Enfields had forced him to investigate the matter. He found that over 3,000 infantrymen of the 1st Division, or one in four, had made the change. A committee formed at General Headquarters in France was unanimous in condemning the Ross, which it said was reliable only

Training with a Colt machine-gun, the heaviest and hence least mobile automatic weapon issued to Canadian infantry in the First World War. Though it is difficult to see here, the gunner is sitting on a small seat attached to the third leg of the tripod.

when firing Canadian-manufactured ammunition, which was not available in any quantity on the Western Front. Because there were plans to use the Canadian Division in upcoming offensives, French admitted, 'I did not feel justified in sending this Division into battle with the Ross rifle.'[9] He hoped, however, that replacing the rifles with British weapons would prove a temporary measure: 'Owing to the difficulty at present experienced in turning out rifles in sufficient numbers for our requirements, I shall most heartily welcome an authoritative statement which will carry conviction to the men that their apprehensions are unfounded.'[10] He suggested that the Ross be rechambered to accept British ammunition.

Sam Hughes quickly authorized an inquiry, which found matters were worse than had been presented in French's report, for even some of the Canadian-manufactured ammunition jammed. An investigation soon revealed that ammunition marked DC 1915, made by the Dominion Cartridge Company, failed 15–20 per cent of the time, though it had no trouble chambering in the Lee-Enfield or the Ross Mark II. It seems the factory was using worn gauges that allowed defective ammunition to pass, but such defects were not the heart of the problem. As Colonel Greville Harston, chief inspector of arms and ammunition, pointed out, in wartime one could not expect mass-produced cartridges to be perfect. He suggested that the Ross Mark III, in the hands of the Canadian Corps, be fitted with Lee-Enfield chambers, as was the Ross Mark II. The Standing Small Arms Committee agreed. Greville had some Ross IIIs reamed out to expand the chamber, which seemed to do the trick; they all fired well, one managing thirty-five rounds in one minute without jamming. The first 500 rechambered rifles were delivered in Canada on 9 August,[11] destined for the 2nd, 3rd, and eventually 4th and 5th divisions, the 1st retaining the Lee-Enfield for the rest of the war.

After Ypres the Canadians had little time to muse over their mistakes and casualties before they participated in a series of difficult attacks near Festubert from 17 to 25 May, 1915. The British and French had long before agreed to conduct a joint offensive while the Germans were concentrated on the Eastern Front, and Second Ypres had not changed Allied plans to recapture French soil. The enemy's defences were strong and well organized; not only was each trench system protected by barbed wire and machine-guns, but within these defences were redoubts, each with its own trench system and barbed-wire obstacles and sited to allow any one of them to fire on enemy troops attacking its neighbours. The commander of the 5th Battalion referred to them as simply 'unbreakable,'[12] since attacking troops would have to take these islands within the German lines one by one. With no time to adopt the lessons of Second Ypres on a large scale, the Canadians had to rely on the know-how their soldiers and gunners had acquired in the previous months to capture this formidable position without heavy casualties. Like Ypres, Festubert was series of small battles, each beginning with the Canadians forming up for the attack and ending with the troops holding enemy ground or withdrawing to their own trenches.

The Canadians took steps to increase their chances of survival against German artillery and automatic weapons. While planning for the battle, brigade commanders allocated machine-guns to the assaulting battalions, not to take part in the battle proper but to be held ready to move forward and establish strong points in the new position should the infantry attack succeed.[13] At least one brigade commander, Brigadier-General Arthur Currie, asked for a trench mortar;[14] these primitive weapons were essentially a form of artillery, firing bombs at a very high angle over ridges and hills, where they could then plunge almost straight down into trenches. Though the Germans had incorporated them into their arsenals before the war, the British did not begin to redevelop mortars which, after all, were medieval siege pieces, until the end of 1914; the last time British soldiers had used them was in the Crimea. At first British Armies made their own from pipe or artillery cartridge casings, but in early 1915, a four-inch version manufactured at Woolwich Arsenal began to appear, which remained in service until 1916, firing eight-pound bombs about 900 yards.[15] As these mortars could be located in the trenches, they could be called upon to support the attack, potentially isolating German positions that were holding up the advance, but in order for the system to work, communications between the attacking infantry and the mortar operators had to be secure, and crews had to be well trained to hit their targets accurately and quickly. Relations were sometimes strained, as Lieutenant Bud O'Neil, an officer in a trench mortar battery, related: 'You see it was high angle fire, and the Infantry I can tell you hated us because they said they come in here and wherever the trench mortars are they draw fire.'[16]

The area's topography complicated the infantry's preparations. Ditches and old trenches criss-crossed the ground throughout no man's land, rendering any assault even more difficult, since the troops had to clamber in and out of these depressions. It was necessary to send bridging parties out at night to place ten-foot-long walkways over the ditches. In no man's land these patrols were within range of machine-gun fire, and the moonlight often aided the Germans in picking out their targets. As the 5th Battalion remarked about one of these patrols, 'This party naturally suffered heavy casualties.'[17]

While infantry officers planned their attacks, the artillery made its own preparations in accordance with tactical notions now at least fifteen years old, the idea being to pave the way for the infantry's assault before the troops entered no man's land. (In one attack, the infantry was drawn back before the artillery barrage began because its trenches were too close to those of the enemy.) The gunners bombarded the objective for several hours, at which time it was deemed that 'the assault will be made.'[18] These barrages were for the most part ineffective; for artillery had not yet found the means to increase its accuracy to the point where it could shell individual strong points and systematically destroy the enemy's defences, high explosive shells for the eighteen-pounders were too light to have any appreciable effect on defensive works, and shrapnel was only effective in killing riflemen exposed on a fire step. Furthermore, a shell shortage due to production difficulties in Great Britain seriously limited the amount of high explosive the heavier 4.5 and six-inch guns could deliver.[19] Since the barrage ceased before the infantry left the trenches, there was time for defenders to leave the security of their dugouts and other safe shelters and take their positions to fight off the Canadian assault. The Canadian barrage was an example of fire preceding movement but not accompanying it.

Once preparations, however incomplete, were deemed adequate, the infantry could be sent into battle on 19 May, after British artillery had bombarded German trenches from the 13th to the 17th and the British 7th Division had launched several attacks over the next two days. The Canadians, the 10th Battalion on the right, the 15th in the centre, and the 16 and 14th on the left, would press forward until 21 May. Casualties began to mount before the advance could even start; for German artillery fire was accurate enough to strike through the ranks of soldiers moving about in the open towards their assembly areas.[20] When the assault began, the troops adopted different formations than those taken at Ypres, which had allowed German artillery and machine-guns to concentrate on massed targets. Brigadier-General R.E.W. Turner, commanding the 3rd Brigade, specifically ordered that 'Attacks will be made in as open a formation as possible.'[21] When the 14th and 16th battalions went into the attack, each sent only two companies forward, keeping the other two to support the advance should the assaulting waves meet with difficulties or to take advantage of any breach the attackers might make in the enemy's defences.[22] The new formations were successful in keeping losses below the catastrophic levels experienced at Ypres; heavy shell fire in no man's land, potentially devastating, inflicted only sixty-seven casualties on the advancing 14th Battalion, as the unit deployed in four lines of skirmishers at fifty-yard intervals with five paces between each man.[23] In the attack, the Canadians had learned to deal with German artillery to some extent by diminishing its opportunities to do harm.

Open formations, however, could be defeated by a very unsophisticated technology – barbed wire. Artillery was short of ammunition and lacked a shell fuse sensitive enough to explode within the barrier, and the latter remained essentially untouched, forcing troops to pick their way through clinging, piercing metal as best they could. Caught on the wire, soldiers became targets for machine-gunners, who could not fail to miss men immobilized by the obstacle. On 19 May the 15th Battalion suffered heavy casualties and was unable to press home its assault because of wire and machine-gun; the 16th Battalion, however, found gaps in the barrier and managed to capture its objective.[24]

Bombers led the attack. Still using homemade bombs, these men made their way to within throwing range of the enemy and tried to clear the trenches with their grenades. At times whole companies bombed their way into and through the trenches, following the meandering ditches and attempting to force the Germans to withdraw. They were often successful.[25] Bombs were highly suited for this kind of warfare; while a rifle could be used only if there were no obstacles between the soldier and his enemy, and a bayonet required the attacker to close to within a couple of feet of his foe, a bomb could be thrown over parapets into trenches while the attackers took cover. Since defences followed a zig-zag pattern, bombs could be tossed into the next bay without the assaulting bombers' being exposed. In this manner whole trench systems were cleared of German defenders, though some of the bombers, such as M.C. McGowan, were doubtful of the tactic's effectiveness:

And at that time the bombers were supposed to lead the attack, that was for clearing the trenches on the attacking side. It was quite a setup which wasn't – I wouldn't think very practical or anything else. But nevertheless you just started out with bayonet men and so forth that led you and you were supposed to clear the trench by throwing these bombs ... I got hit with a German bomb clearing

Barbed-wire entanglements anchored with screw-type pickets. The difficulties of getting through such obstacles are obvious, and they were usually covered by machine-gun fire.

the trenches at that time. Which I was blown up with, I got 12 holes in the legs with it. But otherwise than that it was just a simple same thing you only kept on going. You only kept on going.[26]

Reaching one's objectives was only the first part of a successful operation; as Lieutenant J.S. Williams wrote: 'Everyone who has been out here is thoroughly acquainted with the fact that it is one of the easiest tasks in this war to *capture* a trench but to *hold* on to it is something totally different.'[27] Isolated outposts were thrown out to warn the attackers-turned-defenders of any counter-attack, and they were later joined to form a continuous trench line to replace the old German defences, damaged by artillery and facing the wrong way. It was while the infantry consolidated its positions that the gunners came into their own, surrounding the infantry with a ring of shrapnel which dissuaded the enemy from counter-attacking. Furthermore, the gunners had found their opponents' range and began to bombard their artillery positions, distracting them from lobbing shells on the as yet unprepared Canadian trenches. The enemy's repeated attempts to form up were broken up by shrapnel, allowing the Canadians time to dig in.[28] Artillery, almost useless against German machine-gunners and riflemen in defensive positions, was deadly effective against infantry counter-attacking in the open or German artillery set in positions that offered little or no protection. In 1915 the guns served best in a defensive role.

The action at Givenchy on 15 and 16 June followed a similar pattern, infantry capturing their objectives, if gaps could be found in the wire, and artillery helping to protect any gains made. It was time to take stock. The Canadians received much useful information from the British, who themselves sought ways to deal with the problems of trench warfare, and after Festubert they circulated reports of lessons learned, especially concerning artillery. Responsible for disseminating the lessons of the battlefield was the much-maligned staff officer. At corps level, these men were divided into general staff, concerned with training and operations, and a combined adjutant-quartermaster staff, which dealt with personnel and materiel. It is the former that concerns us here; in 1915 imperial officers filled key posts, and when the Canadian Contingent expanded to corps size in the fall, a third of its staff officers were British.[29] At the top of the staff pyramid was the brigadier-general, general staff, an imperial officer throughout the war, assisted by other staff officers who carried out the corp's planning and issued instructions to govern its training.[30] Each division also had its staff, again divided between the general staff branch and the adjutant and quartermaster branch; the GSO 1 was usually a colonel, with four other officers, lieutenant-colonels and majors, to assist him. Each brigade had a brigade major and two staff captains, while battalions had, aside from the commander and his second in command, an adjutant responsible for administration and a quartermaster who dealt with equipment, ammunition, and, most important from the soldiers' point of view, food. Attached to the battalion were a pay officer and medical officer.[31] The Canadian Corps was blessed with good staff officers, who either were British or had learned from them, and they ensured the lessons learned elsewhere on the Western Front became part of the training syllabus.

One of these lessons was that it was not enough to bombard the objective; one also had to pay attention to those areas on the enemy's flanks from which he could fire his weapons or launch counter-attacks. Furthermore, shelling should not stop as soon as the infantry left the trenches; rather, 'the salients, flanks, and areas in rear of the flanks, must be kept under *heavy fire for a considerable time after the assault is launched.*'[32] Infantry had suffered because artillery had not sufficiently shelled the enemy, but the infantry also had a role to play, for severe shelling 'is useless unless the infantry creep in during the bombardment as near the Artillery fire as possible, and assault the locality immediately the bombardment on that particular place ceases.'[33] If artillery cover was to be effective, it had to be continuous as long as infantrymen were above ground, and the latter had to ensure they used it to cover their movements.

Thus one of the most important lessons to come out of the fighting of mid-1915 was that artillery and infantry had to develop a closer relationship: 'It is impossible to take too many steps to ensure the closest and quickest cooperation between the two arms under all conceivable circumstances.'[34] The British 2nd Corps suggested that the two literally live together, with artillery officers in the infantry's dugouts. Every battery would have a telephone line to the infantry trenches, so the gunners could react quickly to enemy attacks or artillery bombardments; signalling with lamps, both day and night, should supplement the telephones, since wires were often shot out by artillery. The infantry was to make full use of the forward observation officers the artillery sent into the front lines; for these men were well trained to call down shells where they were needed.[35] In short, the best way to ensure cooperation between artillery and infantry was through effective and constant communication, either by telephone and lamp or by sharing the same shelter.

The role trench mortars could play – and their place in the military hierarchy – was far murkier. Paul Villiers reported that at Givenchy 'Trench mortars were being used for the first time, and a very hard time they had of it. They were handed over by [brigade] to [brigade], with the result that their crews got worked to death in a very short time for they never got any rest.'[36] That mortar crews were called upon until they were exhausted was a sign that they were thought useful for something, but what that 'thing' was no one had yet determined with any clarity.

Canadian troops and their leaders sought opportunities to experiment with the technology of war, and the laboratory for these experiments was the trench raid. Such minor operations were not invented by the Canadian Corps, and their origins are somewhat obscure; one of the first may well have been carried out by the 1st and 2nd battalions of the Gerwhal Rifles, an Indian unit, on the night of 9/10 November 1914. The Princess Patricia's Canadian Light Infantry raided on 28 February 1915, when the regiment was serving with a British brigade, and the 1st Worcester Regiment raided German trenches some time during that same month. Of interest is the fact that the 2nd Royal Welsh, which had developed close-combat skills useful for raiding, had been one of the units to instruct the Canadians in trench warfare when they arrived in France. By 1916 the Germans had become quite adept and used box barrages to cut off the target from any support; they called them 'winkle raids.' Whoever invented them, not everyone was happy with the idea, since raids disturbed the 'live and let live' system that sometimes arose between German and Allied units.[37] Siegfried Sassoon, the British war poet, wrote that 'The idea had been revived early this year, when some Canadian toughs had pulled off a fine effort, and since then such entertainments had become popular work with the Staff.'[38] Sassoon was also upset at the number of good soldiers killed on raids, since only the best from the battalion volunteered for such operations, and Edmond Blunden provided the most poetic condemnation of the trench raid: 'The word "raid" may be defined as the one in the whole vocabulary of the war which most instantly caused a sinking feeling in the stomach of ordinary mortals.'[39]

The war poets could well rage against what they saw as yet another insanity, but war is essentially an irrational enterprise, where it is impossible to take into account all the variables needed to calculate a successful solution to a tactical problem. For many of these variables are determined by an enemy, whose duty is to foil one's plans. If one was to develop techniques to survive and win in trench warfare, the final evaluation for such techniques would have to take place in the field. As one possible means of achieving local victory might lie in small-unit coordination, trench raids were an important step in developing effective tactics. One of the first involving members of the Canadian Corps was on the night of 16–17 November on the Douve River. The raid had several goals: to capture prisoners to identify the units opposite and gain other information through interrogation; to induce the enemy to send his reserves forward so they could be shelled; and, most difficult to achieve (or even measure), lower the enemy's morale. Aggressive patrolling prior to the attack forced the enemy to abandon his listening posts, so he would not be forewarned, while the ninety men who were to carry out the raid, all volunteers, rehearsed their tactics by day and night.[40]

A reproduction of the enemy's trenches was laid out in a nearby field through which the raiders practised bombing attacks, setting up blocks in the trenches to prevent the Germans from counter-attacking and withdrawing to their own lines. They built and tested bridging ladders to cross ditches in no man's land and rehearsed crossing barbed wire with mats. In the nights before the raid scouts took them over the ground they would cover on their way to the German trenches.[41] The men were trained to fill highly specialized roles, each of the two attacks comprising no less than seven parties. A small wire-cutting party would make gaps in the wire; bombing and blocking parties, loaded down with grenades, would assault the trench and seal it off, one on the left, the other on the right; in the centre a trench rifle party, complete with telephonist, would move into the trench, capture prisoners, and sketch the area; a bridge-covering party would protect the withdrawal while a listening party, again with telephonist, would warn of impending counter-attack; finally, a reserve party would be available to help if there was trouble.[42]

Artillery played a part in accordance with its general support role. On 16 November, the day of the raid, the guns opened fire at 9:00 in the morning, attempting to sever the wire that formed a barrier across no-man's land; it also bombarded the enemy front line and communication trenches to inflict casualties and hinder the movement of German reserves. A machine-gun emplacement that dominated the raiders' line of advance found itself the target of Canadian machine-guns and trench mortars, thus being bracketed by both direct and plunging fire. The bombardment was augmented by sniper fire, the battalion's rifle fire, and rifle-grenades.[43] The latter were a recent innovation, consisting of bombs attached to rods that could be inserted down the barrel of a rifle. To use the Hale Number 3, most common at this time, one inserted the rod down the rifle barrel, pulled the pin from the grenade, and fired it with a blank cartridge; a vane attached to the rear of the projectile armed it in flight, and it exploded on contact.[44]

After dark, preparations continued. Slow rifle fire on the flanks of the objective kept the Germans' heads down while scouts moved out into no man's land to place bridges over ditches and check the wire; machine-guns fired into rear areas, and the general bedlam both weapons created covered the scouts during their reconnaissance. Their task was difficult; since the wire in front of the raiding party on the left had remained uncut, they began to clear a gap through the obstacle with wire-cutters. The task took from 9:15 to 11:45 in the evening, the scouts working only when the moon was clouded; by the time they had finished, the lane came to within thirty feet of the German parapet. By 2:00 in the morning the Douve River, little more than a creek, was bridged and all was ready for the assault.[45]

The right party's attack was brief; for while crossing no man's land five men fell noisily into a water-filled ditch, giving themselves away to German defenders, who did not hesitate to open fire. Though they were silenced by a soldier dropping to his knees and vigorously throwing bombs into the trenches, the commander could find no way to enter the enemy's defences and ordered the raiders to withdraw. The night's work was over for them. The left party found a way into the trenches, fighting a brief skirmish, and at 2:34 a.m. the signaller set up his telephone and indicated to headquarters that all was well. Luck had been an important factor in the raid's success thus far; as the official report stated, 'Although the enemy's trench was very strong and was heavily manned (about 8 men per 10 yds. in the front line) and despite the bright night and other conditions favourable to them, the enemy absolutely failed to meet the attack.'[46] The element of surprise had served the Canadians well. Prisoners were sent back with the scouts, sketches were made of the trench system, and the raiding party withdrew, picking up its bridges along the way. Artillery, notified by phone that the Canadians were returning, moved its barrage, which had been cutting off the enemy's rear to prevent the Germans from moving reserves forward, into the front-line trenches to ensure the Germans did not fire on the retreating raiders. German artillery did not reply. Total casualties for the operation were one man slightly wounded and another killed accidentally when one of his comrades stumbled and his rifle went off.[47]

The Canadians derived four positive lessons from the raid: first, careful training and rehearsal over similar ground and preparations to meet every obvious contingency had prepared the men well for their task; second, artillery had proved most useful in cutting off the Germans from their reserves and supporting the infantry withdrawal; third, first-class scouting had averted disaster by discovering and removing wire left uncut by artillery; finally, the raiders had been well selected with a view to providing specialists who could work together.[48] These lessons influenced future raids, which became a common feature on the British portion of the front until the end of the war. They were also applied, eventually, to full-scale operations. The Germans also carried out raids, though their plans for the Western Front from 1915 to March 1918 called for them to concentrate on defending themselves until victory was assured against Russia, a reversal of the Schlieffen Plan; there was little incentive then, to patrol no man's land the way the Canadians did and risk suffering heavy casualties.[49]

When not engaged in trench raids or full-scale battles, the Canadians settled down to trench routine. Battalions rotated through the trenches as they had two months before, spending from four to six days at each of the defensive, support, and reserve positions, with casualties mounting slowly. Listening posts set up in no man's land were particularly dangerous; their only link with their comrades was a wire on which they were supposed to pull in case of danger; their only means of defence were the rifles and grenades they carried. It is not surprising that many listening posts simply disappeared.[50] In defensive positions, some men died when rifles discharged by accident; others shot themselves in the foot to get out of the cold, filthy trenches.[51] Competing for mastery were the snipers, who carried on a war of their own, crack shots on both sides of no-man's land attaching telescopic sights to their weapons, applying the art of camouflage, and spending their days firing at their enemies if the latter were careless enough to show themselves. There were some logistical problems with the Ross rifle, since the 'sniperscopes' designed for the Lee-Enfield would not fit properly,[52] but the problem was soon solved and sniping became an integral part of trench life – and death.

Other weapons were perhaps less personal; with the advent of the rifle-grenade, both German and Canadian infantry had the means to make each other's lives even more miserable. Trenches were often only fifty yards apart, well within the grenade's 100-yard range, and it took little time to set up a bombardment. All the infantryman had to do was load a blank cartridge into his rifle, insert the rod attached to the grenade into the barrel, pull the pin, and fire. While the gunners of both sides continued their intermittent duels, the infantry engaged in similar battles, smaller in scale but just as deadly. One officer in March 1916 fired 258 grenades at the enemy's front lines in a single night.[53] The 42nd Battalion's war diary described one of these grenade duels: 'Shortly before eight o'clock this morning, the enemy opened rifle grenade fire of twelve or fifteen rifle rounds on trenches 14-A and 15-A. The officer in charge of the latter asked O[fficer] C[ommanding] Mortar Battery to reply and 8 rounds were fired with apparent effect a breach being noticed in front line German trench.'[54] The rifle-grenade could be effective in trench warfare, but, like its hand-thrown cousin, it needed careful handling, because wind could make it drift to the left or right as much as 100 yards.[55] Given the trenches' zig-zag pattern, one had to be far forward to avoid hitting one's own positions.

Trench mortars, nestled somewhere between infantry and artillery in the hierarchy of destruction, were somewhat more accurate and had a much longer range than the rifle-grenades. In August 1915 the Stokes mortar entered British service; it was a simple weapon with a smooth-bore barrel resting on a steel baseplate, the muzzle supported on a bipod with a screw-elevating gear, and the bomb little more than a cylinder packed with explosives. To operate the mortar one removed a pin from the fuse and dropped the bomb down the muzzle; it slid down the barrel until a twelve-gauge cartridge fitted into the base of the round struck the firing pin at the bottom of the tube; a propelling charge sent it aloft. Clear of the muzzle, a safety lever flew off the bomb, a striker dropped and fired a cap which ignited a safety fuse, and the bomb then detonated a few seconds later.[56] Like the artillery's howitzer shells, bombs travelled with a very high trajectory and low velocity, making them subject to wind. Like machine-guns, mortars could be co-located with the infantry in the front lines, and they were often used as an adjunct to artillery in cutting barbed wire before raids, or in shelling enemy positions before an attack, or merely in harassing his troops.[57] Throughout the war their usefulness would be debated and discussed, and infantrymen were not happy having them in the trenches, since they invited retaliation. But they were never rejected, and before the Somme they served as a form of infantry artillery, capable of reacting quickly to enemy attacks thanks to their accessibility.

More ubiquitous than the sniping, the grenades, or the trench mortars was artillery, which throughout this period continued to harass infantrymen and gunners alike; so shell fire had come to be accepted as part of the normal routine in the trenches. War diary entries like 'Situation quiet. Usual artillery fire,'[58] or, 'Usual artillery practices both sides,'[59] or, 'Enemy delivered gas attack ... in early morning. Attack easily repulsed,'[60] were common. That is not to say that the infantry was ever happy with its lot.

One is ever conscious of the huge missiles going through the air in all directions, some hissing like huge snakes, some like a street car going over a large concrete bridge, some like the engine of a motor car starting up and some like a bee buzzing by. Then there is the constant Crump Crump Crump of the huge Hun shells bursting, and the Krupp Krupp Krupp of another kind, and the Bang Bang Bang and the Crack, Crack of others – Then there is the sound of our 18 pounders going off like two boards being clapped together in the distance and the howitzers that turn one around when they speak and worse still the huge 15. long barrelled guns that fairly lift everything and make the whole world shake ... Its not earthly and one cannot help but feel that he is in another world and very apt at any moment to be standing face to face with his maker.[61]

The artillery's role was to support the infantry, but communications between the two arms had not yet been perfected. When the shelling became too difficult to bear, front-line troops expected their gunners to relieve the pressure, but, though artillerymen were perfectly willing to help, they did not always know when infantrymen were in trouble. In the midst of one particularly tense rifle-grenade attack, the soldiers in the front line had problems getting artillery support: 'Owing to the congestion of telephone line there was some delay in getting artillery retaliation.'[62]

There were several attempts to mitigate the problem. First, it was made clear to infantry commanders that the heavier the gun, the more limited the ammunition supply; therefore they should not call for support against the enemy's artillery, which would require firing the larger guns, unless his shells were causing casualties or damaging trenches. Each infantry brigade had at its disposal three eighteen-pounder batteries and a battery of 4.5-inch howitzers; the former were in direct telephone communication with the portion of line for which they were responsible, while the latter, which had limited supplies of ammunition, could be raised either through the eighteen-pounder brigade or the infantry brigade. Also available for dire emergencies, such as a German assault, was a six-inch howitzer battery, which could be contacted through the eighteen-pounder brigade commander, who in turn would raise the officer commanding the six-inch howitzers. Furthermore, officers felt it was best if artillery commanders decided which guns would be most suitable to carry out a mission, though the infantry would have to supply the information required for the artillery to make its decision, such as the area being shelled, the type of shell used, the direction of the hostile battery, the intensity of the shelling, the approximate range, and the time of the barrage.[63] By maintaining more than one line of communication to the larger guns and leaving it up to the artillery to determine how best to deal with their opposite numbers, infantrymen and gunners alike hoped to increase protection for front-line troops.

To help defend the front line, the British Army adopted the SOS barrage; if the infantry should send up a prearranged emergency signal in the form of a rocket or flare, artillery would open fire on registered targets. For example, the eighteen-pounders would fire a shrapnel barrage for three minutes as close to friendly lines as was considered safe, then creep towards the enemy front trenches and remain there for about ten minutes. Heavy artillery, at the division commander's discretion, could either be superimposed on the eighteen-pounder barrage or used in a counter-battery role. After some initial problems, in which British units expended masses of ammunition on false alarms, the British decided to use the SOS only in case of imminent attack.[64] These techniques were important in two respects: first, the idea of marching the eighteen-pounders' shells up to the enemy trenches signalled the further use of the creeping barrage, which would be an important part of infantry assaults at the Somme and after; second, the SOS could also be used after an attack to protect the infantry during consolidation. The artillery, so useful at Ypres in this regard, would become even more valuable in future.

All of the weapons mentioned above – rifles, grenades, trench mortars, and artillery – were used above ground. Below, engineers fought another kind of war: mining. Revived by the Japanese in the siege of Port Arthur in 1904–5, by the end of 1915 mine warfare was considered by both sides on the Western Front an important part of what had become a huge siege campaign, much as it had been in the wars of the Renaissance. The Canadians gained a certain skill at underground operations, making full use of those in their ranks with mining experience. Engineers toiled by day and night, attempting to dig tunnels under no man's land and beneath the opponent's positions, which could then be destroyed with explosives. Tunnel systems could be almost as complicated as the trenches above, with protective galleries, each with a listening post, branching off from the main offensive tunnel.[65] Sappers used a variety of listening devices, the simplest consisting of two cans joined with a length of string; one was placed on the floor or wall of the tunnel while the other was held up against the ear, with the string pulled tight. In the early months of 1915 the geophone, a French-developed listening device similar to a stethoscope, appeared on the Western Front; it was far more sensitive than the homemade gadgets that had preceded it and after the war was used in mine rescue operations.[66] Having located enemy works, engineers could tunnel under his galleries and place explosives to destroy them.[67] This war of mine and counter mine was at times, as at St-Eloi, Mount Sorrel, or Messines, a critical factor in determining a battle's outcome.

High above the ground the Canadians faced a completely different problem – there the enemy was perfectly visible, but seemingly invulnerable. German aircraft had been in evidence since early in the war, but they were difficult to shoot down; for machine-guns and rifles firing against gravity at a quickly moving and very manoeuvrable target brought poor results. The British had too few anti-aircraft guns; so the front-line soldier had to rely on his own resources to destroy the airplanes that gave away his position to the enemy and sometimes bombed or strafed his trenches.[68] By the late summer of 1915 the British Army was issuing instructions on how to aim correctly at aircraft, by leading them, and on how to use available fire-power. Individual rifle fire was useless; whole companies firing volleys were preferable, mitigating problems of accuracy, like those of the musket 100 years before, through massed fire. Even machine-guns were told to fire not as individuals but in pairs. The Royal Flying Corps, meanwhile, was not actively seeking to shoot down the enemy in the early months of 1916, though from January to April its brigades fought 148 aerial combats and lost twenty-nine aircraft.[69]

Between battles or tours in the front line, battalions took time to train their men. The training was necessary in part because Sir Willoughby Gwatkin, Canada's chief of the general staff, was being left in the dark as to the special requirements for teaching the techniques of trench warfare; for Sam Hughes's ad hoc organization in Great Britain was not capable of digesting the lessons of the Western Front and imparting them to instructors in Canada.[70] Training in the British Isles was better, but it was still insufficient. Private Donald Fraser of the 31st Battalion noted that it was amateurish and impractical, consisting mainly of route marches, a little musketry, half an idea about bombs, and nothing at all about rifle-grenades; 'But in due time we learned from Fritz what bombs, rifle grenades, trench mortars and machine-guns really were.'[71] In 1915 and 1916 Major-General David Watson held on to the best troops for his 4th Division and, with Hughes's backing, sent inadequately trained soldiers to France. To make matters worse, Major-General Sam Steele and Brigadier-General J.C. MacDougall, commanding Bramshott and Shorncliffe camps, respectively, acted independently of one another and ignored Gwatkin's attempts to coordinate CEF training in Canada with what they were doing in England; each training camp followed a different syllabus. Hughes's policy of sending over entire battalions, which were then broken up in England, helped matters not all all; only non-commissioned and junior officers – and the troops themselves – were useful as replacements. The captains, majors, and lieutenant-colonels remained in England, employed in training positions that would have been better filled with veterans from the front.[72]

So the corps took care of its own, and after Second Ypres, it is not surprising that the Canadian Corps spent much time training in anti-gas techniques, on courses sometimes lasting three days. Soldiers were taught to look for signs of gas and warn their colleagues; they also learned how best to adjust their masks for maximum effect. Until 1916 the gunners and infantry had had little protection against poison fog: after Ypres they were issued with PH Helmets, which were nothing more than medicated bags that the men drew over their heads to ward off the gas, with eyepieces that fogged over as soon as they were put on.[73] To ensure the lesson was driven home, soldiers, after adjusting their masks, stood in a trench and were subjected to large doses of tear gas; if a mask did not fit properly, its wearer would soon know it.[74]

Musketry was still a high priority for training in the British Army, and if time was available, troops repeated the entire course of instruction for the rifle.[75] Refresher training was important in battalions whose casualties at the front had been replaced with inexperienced and sometimes badly trained reinforcements. Snipers received special training, though schools of sniper warfare did not form until the end of 1915, when they taught crack shots about telescopic sights, about camouflage until they could render themselves invisible at thirty yards, and interpretation of what they saw through their sights to provide information on enemy activities.[76] The rifle was not only the basic weapon of the infantryman but also a tool for specialists.

Next on the priority list for training was bombing instruction; for

Personnel of the 55th Battery, Canadian Field Artillery, undergoing training in Petawawa, Ontario, in 1916. They would have to be retrained once they arrived in Britain, since lessons from the Western Front were not yet part of the training system in Canada.

what in early 1915 had been a skill only for specialists became more generalized, as whole companies learned to use grenades, and new

Members of the 109th Battalion training in Leaside, Ontario, on 2 April 1915. Note the emphasis on providing as low a profile as possible. Such small-unit tactics were de rigueur in Canada before the First World War, when units were not large enough to do anything else.

bombing sections were formed often, rotating increasing numbers of soldiers through their ranks. Training was still hazardous, and there were still casualties; for though the fuses were timed for five seconds, damage to the bomb could seriously reduce this delay; in order to avoid unnecessary fatalities and injuries, the men first practised by throwing dummy grenades. Until the end of 1915 soldiers still learned to make their own bombs, but early in 1916 these were replaced with the Mills Number 5, manufactured in England. This device, the first of the modern grenades, had no external fuse to light; one pulled a pin and threw the grenade; a safety lever flew off in flight, allowing a plunger to strike a cap, igniting the internal fuse, which set off a detonator about five seconds later. Even after the pin was pulled, the grenade was still safe as long as the safety lever was held in place. Men learned to throw the grenades from inside a trench, or while kneeling or lying on their backs, and they were encouraged to adopt whatever throwing technique was most comfortable. There were still accidents in training as men unused to the new weapon released the safety lever *before* throwing, seriously cutting down their margin of safety. The men practised trench blocking and trench fighting, adopting tactics that allowed them to take cover while tossing their bombs.[77]

Training with machine-guns followed similar lines. Here also there was a gradual attempt to familiarize all ranks with what was still a specialist weapon, rather than concentrate on training only a small group of experts. These more general courses laster only a few days, however, and could do no more than teach men how to load and fire an automatic weapon should its crew become killed or wounded. The crews themselves spent two weeks behind the lines relearning how to assemble, disassemble, maintain, place in position, aim, and fire their guns. Vickers-gun drill was as follows: the number 1 moved with the tripod and placed it where he wanted the gun to fire from, then the number 2 placed the gun on the tripod, after which the number 1 locked it into place; the number 3 brought up 250 rounds of ammunition, the number 2 loaded the web, which contained the bullets, onto the weapon, and the number 1 cocked the machine-gun, which was then ready to fire.[78] In the course of 1915 and 1916 it became increasingly important to train crews as the number of machine-guns in each battalion increased; for as early as August 1915 the Second Army, of which the Canadian Corps was a part, suggested that four guns per battalion might not be sufficient for operations on the Western Front. By the end of the year a reorganization was in the offing; the Lewis gun had arrived in France, and Canadian battalion commanders suggested that it would be advantageous to assign four of these to each battalion and use the Colts to form a second machine-gun company for the brigade. They went so far as to hope that each battalion would receive eight machine-guns, allowing two per company. The Lewis gun had no water jacket, a reservoir that fit around the barrel to keep it cool, and thus could be fired not in long streams as the Vickers could, but only in bursts. Machine-gunners preferred it because it weighed less than thirty pounds, while the

Gun crew doing maintenance on a Vickers machine-gun. For firing, the number one would be squeezing the trigger, as he is here, while the number two sat to one side to ensure that the belt fed into the weapon properly.

Colt, complete with tripod, weighed more than seventy (one source says 101 pounds). In February 1916 the British decided to replace each battalion machine-gun section of four heavy machine-guns – Colts in the Canadian case – with two Lewis detachments of two guns each.[79] The Canadians would thus have an automatic weapon light enough to follow them in assaults and on raids.

At St-Eloi, the Canadians' next battle, bombs and machine-guns were of little use. The fighting began on 27 March, when the British detonated six large mines and launched an assault with their 3rd Division. The action was no more than retaliation, to avenge the German capture of

Lewis gun being demonstrated for recruits. It was usually fired from the prone position, the barrel supported on a light bipod. Later, slings would be developed so it could be fired from the hip during an attack. It was air cooled, so the tube-like jacket surrounding the barrel was much lighter than on water-cooled automatic weapons.

some British trenches at 'The Bluff' during the previous February.[80] Several days of fighting were inconclusive, and on 4 April the 6th Canadian Brigade arrived, heralding the 2nd Canadian Division's involvement in its first major battle. Attacks and counter-attacks, centred on the craters, continued until 16 April, but mining and shelling had broken the water table, and the mud was thick enough to prevent bombers from attacking German positions. Enemy artillery held sway over this portion of the front, cutting off one company for five days while other units withdrew to avoid annihilation.[81] Private Donald Fraser wrote: 'During these trying days the enemy was raining shells continually; the trenches were in a quagmire and unconnected; communications were entirely broken down; there was no such thing as a firing trench; the enemy gave us no peace to consolidate; neither could materials be brought up; our men, battered and weary had all their work cut out to shelter themselves from the devastation that was happening around.'[82] The situation was so confused that infantrymen could not even pinpoint their own positions, since the craters had so changed the local topography that maps became useless. Also, the fact that they were looking up a slope created problems of perspective. The Royal Flying Corps had been supplying British forces with intelligence through aerial photographs since February 1915, but bad weather prevented aircraft from taking off during the battles for the craters. On the 16th airplanes discovered that the Germans were in possession of the four largest craters at St-Eloi, and after two fruitless weeks, the Canadians were relieved. So was Lieutenant-General Sir E.A.H. Alderson, who turned over command of the corps to Lieutenant-General Sir Julian Byng.[83]

The British and Canadians learned much in the battles for the craters, especially about the murky world of communications, the 2nd Division allocating to the subject half of the 'Lessons Learned' section of its after-action report.[84] The division commander made it clear 'That information must be sent in early and often by subordinates.'[85] Most important, Canadians relearned that there was no such thing as perfect communications and that the battle would be won or lost by those on the ground; anyone above the rank of battalion commander could plan but not participate. The greatest lesson learned at St-Eloi was that technology was not sufficiently advanced to allow generals to retain control of their units once they had been sent into combat, and 'That all subordinates must be prepared to act on their own initiative. The one unforgivable sin when in difficulties is to do nothing and wait for orders.'[86] Brigade commanders should no doubt have gone forward to check on fighting conditions, especially the nature of the ground, but the best place for them to be when a battle started was in their own headquarters, where reports, albeit intermittent, could come in from different parts of the brigade's area of responsibility. With no truly portable wireless available, a commander outside his headquarters was in touch only with what was happening within sight and hearing. The platoon thus had to rely on its own resources and was slowly becoming the focus of Canadian tactics.

Unlike the frustrating battles of the craters, the rush on Mount Sorrel was a clear-cut victory for the Canadian Corps, though, like Second Ypres, it started as a defensive battle when the Germans attacked Canadian positions on 2 June 1916. It was an action typical of many medium-scale assaults that year; the enemy advanced after detonating several mines and pounding Canadian positions with artillery, tried-and-true methods of siege warfare, and the 8th Brigade bore the full brunt of the attack. Major-General M.S. Mercer, commanding the 3rd Division, was at the front when the Germans attacked and died in the shelling, while Brigadier-General V.A.S. Williams, commanding the 8th Brigade, was wounded and captured. The 4th Canadian Mounted Rifles lost almost 90 per cent of its troops, only seventy-six of 702 emerging from the battered trenches unscathed. The 1st Canadian Mounted Rifles was also hit hard. The Germans used flame-throwers, but they turned out to have little more than moral effect, since they were rudimentary devices composed of steel tubing attached to a base plate through which oil jets, ignited by automatic lighters, were propelled towards the target with compressed air. As the projectors were anchored to a fixed position, they had very limited range – about seventy yards – while the flame and smoke they generated made them easy targets; nor could they reach down into trenches to burn crouching infantry. German artillery, however, was effective, and even the Princes Patricia's Canadian Light Infantry, firing into the enemy's flank and rear as he poured through the gap, could not halt the advance. A counter-attack that evening failed to dislodge the Germans.[87]

Further counter-attacks were postponed. The Canadians had long before learned the importance of artillery support for an assault, and the gunners needed time for their observers to register the guns. The corps took several days to prepare and plan, waiting until the weather allowed airplanes to fly, an indication of the importance of aerial observation in artillery operations. By 13 June the guns were hitting their targets and the infantry was ready to move forward. The operation was planned in great detail, down to what each infantryman would carry in the assault: 200 rounds of ammunition, two grenades, and two sandbags. Quartermasters distributed a shovel for every three men to help dig in new defensive positions should the attack be successful and twenty sets of wire-cutters per company to clear unexpected obstacles. Finally, each company had three sets of trench floorboards to use as bridges over trenches and ditches.[88]

The bombardment was violent, and bombers entering the German trenches found machine-gunners still taking cover near their guns. The men had moved quickly, reaching their objectives before the enemy had an opportunity to recover from the shelling, and one officer managed to get a Lewis gun firing at the retreating enemy; machine guns were no longer used exclusively for defence. German artillery fired at the Canadians while they were consolidating their positions, and most of the casualties from the attack occurred during this bombardment. Having learned their lesson at St-Eloi, infantrymen installed telephone lines within five minutes of arriving at their objective. The entire assault had taken about an hour;[89] detailed planning, including the allocation of equipment, as well as excellent cooperation between artillery and infantry had helped make the day a success. There was, however, an element of luck in the infantry's advance coming so close behind the barrage; more sophisticated liaison between the two arms would come later, at the Somme.

At Mount Sorrel the Canadian Corps saw its first major success and the last of the Ross rifle. For over a year soldiers had thrown away the Canadian-made weapon and picked up the British Lee-Enfield instead. On 12 June 1915 the 1st Division had rearmed with the British rifle, but the other formations of the corps had retained the Ross.[90] Sir Charles's company was having difficulty producing weapons that could pass inspection; the rifle bolt came under special scrutiny, and in mid-April an inspector reported that of 2,300 bolts received, fully 85 per cent were of insufficiently hard steel. Attempts to reharden the metal fell short of success, since the quality of steel used in manufacture was not uniform throughout the bolt.[91] Rifle bolts continued to chip and shear, and army attempts to rectify the situation were badly mismanaged, relying on fatigue parties to carry out work requiring skilled labour.[92] A solution was soon forthcoming. On 3 June the chief inspector of arms and ammunition announced that modifications to the bolt stop prevented chipping and shearing, and that even soft bolts did not break. He expected deliveries to begin in six weeks to two months, though at the end of

June the Ross Rifle Company explained that the first rifles with the new bolt would not be available until the end of August.[93]

It was too late. The issue came to a head when a battalion of the 3rd Division, left unnamed, urgently requested rearmament with the Lee-Enfield after many of its Ross rifles jammed during the early German attacks at Mount Sorrel. Field Marshal Douglas Haig, French's replacement as commander-in-chief of British armies in France, agreed to launch an investigation. On 28 May he reported to the War Office: 'I have the honour to inform you that I have satisfied myself, after extensive inquiries carried out throughout the Canadian Corps, that, as a Service rifle, the Ross is less trustworthy than the Lee-Enfield, and that the majority of the men armed with the Ross rifle have not the confidence in it that is so essential they should possess.'[94]

The investigation did not end there, and Canadian commanders continued to debate the relative merits of the Ross and the Lee-Enfield. Major-General M.S. Mercer had often criticized the weapon before his death, but since Sam Hughes was a strong supporter of the Canadian rifle, and given that many high-ranking officers in the corps owed their positions to the minister of militia, the debate had serious political overtones. Major-General R.E.W. Turner, who had taken command of the 2nd Division in 1915 in spite of Lieutenant-General Alderson's misgivings,[95] favoured the Canadian weapon and presented evidence supporting its retention. According to his report to Lieutenant-General Sir Julian Byng, the 28th and 31st battalions, who had been most active in recent fighting, found the rifle satisfactory, and 'The Regimental Sergeant-Major of the 28th Battalion reports that he has heard no complaints whatever, despite the fact the firing was intense.'[96] Both battalions were part of the 6th Brigade, but not all the troops in that formation were happy with the Ross; since the previous September Private Donald Fraser of the 31st Battalion had complained, in his diary, of the weapon's deficiencies. In June censors intercepted a letter from T.W. Law which contained an unqualified condemnation of the Canadian weapon.

You ask about the Ross Rifle well darling it is a great shame to say that we are out in this country trying to do our bit and they will not give us the rifle that is the most use to us. I have seen darling when we were in action the boys kicking the bolts back and then having another shot and for the whole five rounds they had to do this. There is some talk of us getting Enfields and the sooner the better and give us a chance to fight for our lives for after the first ten rounds with the Ross it is only good to use as a club. Let us hope that the people of Canada will get wise to this.[97]

Brigadier-General E.S. Hoare-Nairne, a British artillery officer temporarily in command of the 3rd Division after Mercer's death at Mount Sorrel, had few doubts about what had to be done; 'In view of the clear and emphatic reports of the Battalion Commanders of the 7th Canadian Infantry Brigade, I most strongly urge that this Division be re-armed with the Lee-Enfield Rifle.'[98] Less than a week after the division commander's harsh appraisal, Brigadier-General F.W. Hill, commanding the 9th Brigade, reported on his formation's attitude towards the Ross, concluding: 'The men have not much confidence in it, and claim that it jams when firing rapid.'[99] The Canadian weapon was more accurate, of that there was no doubt, but even Brigadier-General Victor Odlum, one of the Ross's proponents, admitted that it 'was not suitable for trench warfare in every respect.'[100] Major-General Arthur Currie, a future corps commander, blamed the Ross for causing more unnecessary casualties than any other factor in the war. A weapon that jammed in combat was useless, and the Ross jammed often. Only the snipers liked it, and they did not have to rely on the weapon in the heat of battle. Furthermore, the rifle was too long and hindered men trying to make their way through the trenches.[101]

The worst mark against the Ross was that there was little place, aside from sniping, for an accurate rifle in trench warfare, since the rifle was giving way to the bomb. Major Allan Brooks, one of Victor Odlum's officers, summed up his views in a report to his commander: 'My own experience in this campaign has been that the Ross was much more liable to jam ... but except at Ypres we have had very little use for rifles apart from sniping. Subsequent actions were ones in which grenades were the chief factor.'[102] In June 1916 the Canadians in France turned in what were left of their Ross rifles and received Lee-Enfields in return, while the 4th Division in England retained the Ross until after it moved to France in mid-August. The Canadian Corps, soon to become a national symbol, had rejected Canadian technology in favour of imperial-manufactured weaponry.

Mount Sorrel marked the Canadian Corps's coming of age as a fighting formation. Planned and executed by the corps, the battle was its first real success of the war, applying lessons in infantry-artillery cooperation learned as far back as the disastrous attacks on Kitchener's Wood. The death of the Ross was also a coming of age of sorts; it demonstrated that an accurate rifle was no match for a temperamental bomb. In defence the rifle was useful only until it jammed, a frequent occurrence, and in assault the men preferred grenades. From Ypres to Mount Sorrel the tactics of the platoon developed in raids and attacks into a system of specialists and bombs, initiative and innovation, while battalion assaults became tied to the availability and accuracy of artillery that, at Mount Sorrel, had proved critical. Thus within the Canadian Corps, in both the battalion and the platoon, tactics were slowly changing to take into account the destructive potential of barbed wire, artillery, and machine-gun.

3

Struggles on the Somme

On 21 February 1916 the Germans attacked French lines near Verdun in an offensive designed to bleed French armies white. The British, who had been planning an offensive of their own (ever since the campaigns of late 1915 had petered out with little gain), were asked to accelerate their timetable to take pressure off their French allies. Others were also in need of aid; on the Eastern Front the Russians had been pushed out of Poland, while the Italians had made no headway in four offensives against Austria-Hungary. The British attacks on the Somme were supposed to be part of a concerted offensive located at the point the British and French fronts met; heavily committed at Verdun, however, the French had little to contribute, though their xxth Corps would participate.[1] On 1 July 1916 the offensive opened and the British lost 56,470 of their volunteer soldiers (the 1st Battalion, Newfoundland Regiment, was annihilated).[2] As with all First World War campaigns, the offensive was in fact a series of battles in which new technology and changing tactics were introduced to the field. The engagement at Courcelette from 15 to 22 September (in which Canadian troops were prominent), is worthy of note; for there the British used tanks for the first time, when General Haig sent them into the fighting in a last desperate bid to win the day. This particular battle deserves a close look to examine the role and usefulness of the new weapon.

British experiences on the Somme shed light on what happened to the Canadians when they arrived, since they had the advantage of having learned from British mistakes. Though British commanders of the First World War have often been presented as bumbling dolts, this is caricature. Admittedly, they knew little of the kind of war they were fighting, but British staff officers and commanders in the field examined each battle closely in order to derive from it what lessons they could. Their reports were circulated throughout the British armies, and hence to the Canadian Corps.

By the time the British armies in France began their preparations for the offensive on the Somme, they had undergone much change. Kipling's army, small to begin with, had left many of its troops dead and wounded on the battlefields of 1914 and 1915. The New Armies, or Kitchener Armies, raised from hundreds of thousands of volunteers in the two years before the Somme, were not the crusty professionals of old; rather, they were young men of differing backgrounds who had joined up for the duration of the war. Women in 1905 would rather have seen their sons go to prison than turn soldier; in 1915 they encouraged them to go to France.

Compared with their regular army predecessors, the soldiers arriving at the front in 1915 and 1916 were ill-trained novices with poor fighting and survival skills. General Headquarters, responsible for all British armies in France, felt that these troops were incapable of exercising local initiative, and in fact platoon training did not begin until the tenth and final week of the basic course, when troops learned to approach the enemy in lines until they were 200 yards from his trenches, and 'Then would come the crucial orgasm of the bayonet charge.'[3] After they arrived in France, these men had little time for training, and the British Expeditionary Force had few instructors with whom to train them.[4] Haig thought the Kitchener Armies were just a 'collection of divisions untrained for the Field.'[5] This attitude determined the tactics headquarters would lay down for the troops that were to begin the offensive on 1 July. On 8 May Haig issued 'Training of Divisions for Offensive Action,' which stated that 'officers and troops generally do not now possess that military knowledge arising from a long and high state of Training which enables them to act promptly on sound lines in unexpected situations. They have become accustomed to deliberate action based on precise and detailed orders'[6] – an accurate appraisal of how the New Army divisions had been prepared for battle. Assault columns, instead of working their way up communication trenches or rushing from shell-hole to shell-hole, would have to move above ground straight to their objective in successive waves or lines, maintaining a continuous flow of troops from the trenches. Notes on training from headquarters taught that 'a single line of men has usually failed, two lines have generally failed, but sometimes succeeded, three lines have generally succeeded, but sometimes failed, and four or more lines have generally succeeded.'[7] According to General Headquarters, an all-out attack 'must be driven home without intermission ... till the endurance of the enemy is broken down,' and 'Troops once launched must push on at all costs.'[8] With the French in desperate straits at Verdun, as Haig believed, there was little time to teach the men any other form of assault. Given that the 1914 *Infantry Training* manual suggested six months were required to prepare recruits properly for battle,[9] he was not far wrong. Battalions had to expect heavy casualties.

The main work of destroying the enemy would fall to the artillery, whose preparatory bombardment lasted eight days at a rate of 10,000 shells every hour. The task was not an easy one, as the British had realized at Loos the previous September; for the Germans, who were prepared to remain on the defensive for some time to come, excavated dugouts twenty to thirty feet deep to protect their troops during bombardments.[10] Haig, however, believed that the infantry would be left with no one to oppose it after the terrible pounding he had ordered, so he was not concerned with small-unit tactics. General Rawlinson, commander of the 4th Army, which carried out the attack, agreed with Haig on the artillery's expected effectiveness, and issued 'Fourth Army Tactical Notes' to all officers down to the rank of captain. Attacking in lines was the only formation it mentioned; use of rifle and machine-gun fire to cover the advance, which had been an important part of pre-war training, was conspicuous by its absence. The thirty-one-page pamphlet did not ignore the technology of destruction; each brigade now had Vickers machine-gun companies, and Rawlinson urged that brigadiers take advantage of the additional fire-power. He also noted the possible usefulness of bombs and trench mortars,[11] but the infantry that were to carry out the attack knew little of how to use these specialized weapons.

Shortly before the assault, the gunners fired an intensive barrage on the enemy's front trenches, infantry companies left their positions, and the barrage would lift and drop on the next trench, continuing in this manner to the objective. For the most part, this creeping barrage did little to help the infantry on 1 July, except on the right; for, lifting from objective to objective, it did not protect troops advancing across no man's land or between German trench lines. Major-General Ivor Maxse, the innovative commander of the 18th Division, ordered his men to lie out in no man's land close to their first objective so they could jump enemy defences the moment the standing bombardment ended. They then made their way to subsequent objectives by following the barrage as closely as possible. (The 7th Division used similar techniques.) The creeping barrage was probably the logical successor to the linear barrage, though its origin is subject to debate, since the French claimed to have used it first. In any case, it emphasized the return to covering as opposed to destructive fire, the artillery concentrating on protecting the infantry instead of killing the enemy. Though the 18th Division lost 30 per cent of its troops, it reached all its objectives on 1 July. By the time of the second offensive on 14 July the technique had become accepted as part of the solution to the problem posed by German defensive skill.[12]

For other formations 1 July was an unmitigated disaster. The British lost almost 60,000 men killed, wounded, missing, or captured, a battle that General Spears, a British liaison officer, described as a slaughter by shell fire.[13] He also described the difference in tactics between the British and the French moving forward on their right flank: 'my memory was seared with the picture of the French and British attacking together on the Somme ... the British rigid and slow, advancing as at an Aldershot parade in lines that were torn and ripped by the German guns, while the French formed tactical formations, quick and elastic, [and] secured their objectives with trifling loss. It had been a terrible spectacle.'[14] British inexperience was not the only reason for the disaster; generals could not send reserves to take advantage of success, and front-line troops could not call for additional artillery support, or even slow the barrage when they fell behind, because of the terrible state of communications. Signallers could not always keep telephones operating, as artillery shot out their lines, pigeons were easily confused by the noise of battle, and flags and lamps were often masked by dust kicked up by the shelling. Only runners proved consistently reliable, but many of them were killed or wounded.[15] The battle continued at a slackened pace for several days, with another major push on 14 July, a night assault that largely succeeded until the Germans, inevitably, counter-attacked. (Remarque noted the inherent frustration such tactics engendered in the German infantry, when his main character remarked: 'Oh, this turning back again! We reach the shelter of the reserves and yearn to creep in and disappear – but instead we must turn around and plunge again into the horror.')[16] Then followed months of attack and counter-attack, with casualties mounting on both sides.

The Canadians arrived in August and began rehearsing for their upcoming role in the offensive.[17] In the next two and a half months one or more Canadian divisions would fight several major and minor battles, eventually pushing two and a half miles, through Flers-Courcelette from

15 to 22 September, Thiepval Ridge from 26 to 29 September, Le Trans-loy Ridges from 1 to 18 October, Regina Trench several times between 1 October and 11 November, and Beaumont Hamel and Desire Trench from 13 to 18 November. As each Canadian division took its turn in the assault, the corps continued to search for ways to carry out its mission on the Western Front without disintegrating into lengthy casualty lists. Platoon tactics had evolved in trench raids and cooperation between infantry and artillery had made some progress, but these developments, even taken together, were not sufficient to ensure success at low cost in a major battle. German artillery was still, essentially, unassailable and thus able to shell Canadian troops before and during battle, often inflicting casualties before the soldiers could leave their trenches. Wire proved a serious obstacle difficult to remove; the British and Canadians tried to cut it with artillery, but shell fuses were not sensitive enough to detonate within the wire or just as they hit the ground. Thus shells exploded deep in the earth, where they did no more than move the wire obstacles around somewhat. Enemy machine-gunners, if they were quick enough, could take their positions after the barrage had lifted but before the assaulting infantry could reach them. Between them, artillery, wire, and machine-guns ensured that failure would be common and even limited successes would be costly.

The tools of war were many and varied. The infantryman of 1916 carried a heavy burden, with a load-to-weight ratio greater than that of a mule. Going into the assault he was at his lightest, but 220 rounds of ammunition, four bombs, a pick or shovel (or both), rations for a full day, a greatcoat for the cold or a waterproof sheet for the wet, sandbags, Very lights and other signalling equipment, a respirator, and a rifle made it difficult for a man to walk, let alone run, in an assault. The almost constant shelling turned the countryside into a morass, and the men were soon covered with mud, which itself could add several pounds to the weight of a soldier's equipment. All told, the common soldier weighed 120 pounds more with his clothing and equipment than he did standing naked.[18] Men thus walked into battle already tired from trudging through the mire with over 100 pounds of kit and mud on their frames.

To defend themselves and attempt to destroy the enemy Canadian infantry was now armed with the 1903-pattern Lee-Enfield. It was accurate as well as rugged and was far more likely to survive the mud of the Somme than the Ross. Complete with bayonet – and one always went into battle with the bayonet fixed – the weapon weighed nine pounds eleven ounces and was five feet two inches long, only a few inches shorter than the average infantryman.[19] The bayonet in effect turned the rifle into a spear, and the British Army expected troops to take trenches in hand-to-hand fighting. Canadian infantry, however, much preferred using bombs.

Machine-gunners carried slightly more than their infantry brethren, since their Lewis guns were heavier than the other soldiers' Lee-Enfields, though not so heavy as to keep them out of the assault. Also, operation of the Lewis was easier to teach than that of the complicated Colt. By September each battalion had twelve Lewis guns – so many that ammunition allocations had to be altered. Companies went into the attack with two guns apiece to give them direct support against German machine-gunners; two were required, since one could not maintain a steady rate of fire without overheating. Compared with the Vickers, the Lewis brought with it certain disadvantages: it was air cooled, with more easily broken parts and somewhat fragile magazines to hold ammunition. Its only advantage over the Vickers was that it was sufficiently light to carry into combat;[20] that was advantage enough.

The Lewis, firing in bursts from forty-seven-round magazines, shot off the same amount of Lee-Enfield ammunition as an infantry platoon. It was also hardier; with nine men in each Lewis team, it was necessary for the enemy to kill or incapacitate over half the crew before its volume of fire was reduced.[21] The gun was hindered, however, by this very ability to generate a high rate of fire; the gun team was large in order to have extra men available to carry ammunition, and at times Lewis gunners had to enlist riflemen to help them keep their guns supplied with bullets. A War Office pamphlet reminded officers that 'the mobility of a gun depends on the mobility of its ammunition,'[22] but if the gun could be kept supplied, it served well in the hands of the assaulting infantry. On the Somme, however, the Lewis, like the Lee-Enfield, did not come into play until infantry companies had captured their objective, when it was called upon to help defend against counter-attack.[23]

In the midst of these seesaw battles the 2nd Division's assault at Flers-Courcelette (part of a Fourth Army offensive on 15 September) stands out, mainly because tanks were allocated to help the infantry take its objectives. Also, though the latter's tactical formations had not changed, Courcelette marked a pivotal point in the war, where new technology was introduced but where tactics, now a year old, were retained. The Canadians captured the village in a two-phase battle. Six tanks accompanied them, three with the 4th Brigade on the right and the others with the 6th Brigade on the left; all six became casualties,[24] but not before some had done their work. After a fifteen-minute bombardment the infantry left its trenches at 6:15 in the morning and quickly captured the German front line. One soldier later wrote home: 'We then started out over open country for the sugar refinery which was our objective. We had the assistance of the tanks at this place. There was some stubborn fighting here, but the "land dreadnoughts" soon put the enemy machine-guns out of action and then "walked over" the remains of the refinery.'[25]

Lance-Corporal Donald Fraser also had the opportunity to see a tank in action that morning. Heading across no man's land, he was surprised to see the Germans firing their rifles at the attacking Canadians because artillery was supposed to have killed or wounded all of them. The assault wave moved forward, but the defences were too strong and the infantry dropped into shell-holes and started sniping. So far the attack had been a failure, but

Away to my left rear, a huge gray object reared itself into view, and slowly, very slowly, it crawled along like a gigantic toad, feeling its way across the shell-stricken field. It was a tank, the 'Creme de Menthe,' the latest invention of destruction and the first of its kind to be employed in the Great War. I watched it coming towards our direction. How painfully slow it travelled. Down and up the shell holes it clambered, a weird, ungainly monster, moving relentlessly forward. Suddenly men from the ground looked up, rose as if from the dead, and running from the flanks to behind it, followed in the rear as if to be in on the kill. The last I saw of it, it was wending its way to the Sugar Refinery. It crossed Fritz's trenches, a few yards from me, with hardly a jolt.[26]

When he entered the German trench, Fraser found it empty; he presumed the defenders had withdrawn at the sight of the tank.

The sugar refinery was short of the town; so that afternoon the 22nd and 25th Battalions attacked the defences of Courcelette proper, and the 45th Battalion's assault on the left was near-perfect demonstration of the nature of British tactics on the Somme. The battalion was formed in four lines on an 800-yard frontage with fifty yards between waves. The after-action report described the move across no man's land: 'As we started our advance we came under artillery fire almost immediately but this did not in the slightest degree check or confuse our men. They marched that distance of 2200 yards as though they were on a General Inspection Parade.'[27] Canadian and British artillery had been accurate and devastating, and the battalion moved into the German front line with thirty-four men killed, 191 wounded, and seventy-seven missing. Typically, it would suffer heavier casualties in the days that followed as the Germans shelled and counter-attacked the new Canadian positions without respite.[28] The 22nd Battalion also had the advantage of moving into German trenches heavily bombarded by Allied artillery. 'Une trentaine de minutes après le début de la bataille et après un violent corps à corps à la baionette, les 22e et 25e bataillons faisaient la jonction au milieu du village, s'emparaient des positions défensives a l'arrière de celui-ci et, avec l'aide du 26e bataillon, entreprenaient de se rendre maîtres du bourg qu'ils venaient d'emporter, et commençant par étouffer les nombreux nids de résistance ennemis que recelaient les ruines et caves du village.'[29]

Attacks to expand Canadian gains continued in the days that followed, while, to prepare for further advances, work parties built the necessary infrastructure to ensure supplies could get to the new front line. J.A. Brice witnessed this advance behind the advance at Courcelette: 'As quickly as a few hundred yards' advance is made, big working parties make new roads (and good ones, too), all running in the same direction. Before the road is half-done the guns have been brought up to new positions and the stream of ammunition wagons soon become unbroken.'[30] The week's fighting at Courcelette, from 15 to 22 September, cost the Canadian Corps 5,969 casualties, the great majority of them in the 2nd Division, which had been the most heavily engaged formation.[31]

In the months that followed the battle did not range every day, and, during lulls, men in reserve trained much as they had during normal trench routine. Emphasis, not surprisingly, was on the assault, and the tactics the men learned were still primitive. The infantry was trained to attack in waves, the experience of trench raids notwithstanding, in long straight lines at intervals of fifty or 100 yards. Commanders insisted on rehearsals before every battle, and Major-General Arthur Currie, commanding the 1st Division, blamed a disaster at Transloy Ridges on 8 October on the battalion commander's failure to rehearse his troops. There was little or no attempt to inculcate rigid drills; for commanders had come to accept that variations in terrain and the nature of German defences made it impossible to develop a standard drill appropriate for all attacks.[32]

Each Canadian battalion exercised as a unit by day or night, practising its soldiers' skills in mock battles and exercises. Machine-gunners and mortarmen participated in these manœuvres, learning to support the infantry as best they could. Artillery was not represented, but Canadian infantrymen learned to follow the creeping barrage as closely as possible, the curtain represented by mounted officers carrying flags. By mid-September battalions learned to cooperate not only with artillery but with aircraft as well, practising different methods of communicating their position to the airplanes, which could then inform headquarters of the infantry's progress (or lack of it), either by wireless or through the simple expediency of landing nearby.[33] The tactics of the assault were augmented by training in the use of bombs and Lewis guns; though the average infantryman could not be as proficient as the specialist who had spent weeks learning the art of mass destruction with a machine-gun, he could take a gunner's place should the latter become a casualty.[34]

Each of the Somme battles followed a similar pattern. First, with their equipment in their hands and on their backs, Canadian infantrymen moved into assembly areas, but before they could even begin their advance across no man's land, German artillery began to take its toll. The men were shelled on the roads as they marched up towards the front from the training grounds, in the trenches as they waited for the order to move forward, and as they crossed no man's land to come to grips with the enemy. Letters home related the dangers posed by the barrages and counter-barrages that characterized much of the fighting on the Somme. Lieutenant J.M. Walton wrote: 'The other day I was standing in a particularly hot spot when a large shell dropped thirty yards away, completely disintegrating an officer and sergeant-major, and wounding two men. It was Friday, 13th so I had "the wind up" for the rest of the day and it was some day. They shelled us increasingly with large stuff and finally gassed us that night. But we have the preponderance in artillery and in everything else, in fact, and we give them twenty shells to their one. How they live through our terrific bombardments is a wonder to me.'[35] He had probably not yet seen the German dugouts.

Shelling was almost continuous, so that Lieutenant Walton could refer to 'the eternal din of artillery and bullet.' At Thiepval Ridge in late September the 5th Canadian Mounted Rifles found themselves in the midst of an artillery barrage two or three minutes before they were scheduled to attack, and an extra platoon had to be brought up at the last minute to replace casualties. Some battalion commanders reported that their form-up trenches were constantly swept by artillery fire. Near the end of the campaign the Canadians had developed possible solutions, and before assaulting Regina Trench on 10 November the Canadians moved out into no man's land and dug in their start line 150 yards in front of their positions, effectively putting them on the German side of the enemy barrage and leaving them unscathed until it was time to attack.[36]

When the depleted Canadian ranks moved out into no man's land, they encountered almost cutter-proof barbed wire, which defeated all counter-measures troops could devise.[37] When on 30 September the 8th Brigade received the order to attack Regina Trench, it sent out scouts to locate gaps in the wire, but they could not find enough openings to get two battalions through the obstacle. Artillery was instructed to create more, and after severe shelling the gunners took a one-hour break while the scouts again examined the ground, after which wire cutting resumed. More was cut but it was still not enough, and the 4th Canadian Mounted Rifles tried to force themselves through the gaps available.[38] At times trench mortars were used, with some success, but failure was the norm and on the Somme barbed wire ruled the day. An assault on 8 October failed because the men could not find gaps in the barrier in the morning twilight, and though one battalion managed to work its way through the uncut wire, its troops were the only ones to do so that day. Almost all of the 13th Battalion was held up, half of the 16th got through, and the 3rd and 4th could find no gaps in spite of reports that the wire was weak or broken. At Ancre Heights the men encountered wire ten to twenty yards thick, undamaged by artillery. Again at Thiepval the 5th Battalion halted its advance because of barbed wire.[39]

If Canadian gunners lacked the technology and the knowledge to silence enemy guns or destroy the ubiquitous belts of barbed wire, they could still attempt to fulfil their primary role and support the infantry assault. Infantry tactics were based on the concept that 'The artillery conquers, the infantry occupies,'[40] or 'the plan is the artillery barrage.'[41] Artillery support could take several forms. Sometimes the bombardment was short and violent, and in one of the attacks on Regina Trench the shelling lasted only eight minutes in order to ensure the Canadians had the element of surprise while still disrupting German defences. At other times the barrage was long and deliberate, and in other battles for Regina Trench attacks were sent in whenever heavy artillery had two successful days of bombarding the enemy's trenches and wire, though how success was measured is unknown. Throughout, observers went as close to the Canadian front line as possible, though sometimes they were still too far back and could not tell when their shells dropped into friendly trenches.[42] One soldier, identified only as a Mr. J. Robinson, described the disastrous attack on Regina Trench on 25 October and the unfulfilled promises of artillery support:

I ... met the battalion in the trenches and ... and we were supposed to go over in the morning and we were told that this trench, we were told that our artillery would smash it all up and we got going over the top in the morning and there was nothing, you see, and they start falling around me like wheat and I lay in a shell hole all of one day with another fellow ... We got about 150 yards or so and the guys were dropping all around us. So we crawled into this trench and another guy crawled in and you know that by about seven o'clock there was seven of us in there. They were wounded. They all died except he and I and he was wounded and we laid there all day with our nose right to the ground and every time one of them jumped up to run back he'd be sniped and we lost about half the battalion.[43]

The gunners were still groping for a means of protecting infantry battalions as they advanced in the open against heavily defended positions.

The results were as haphazard as the methods. An attack on 9 September succeeded after a three-minute bombardment, since men left their trenches before it lifted and advanced almost into the middle of their own shells. German dugouts, not as well built as usual, disintegrated, the survivors crouching behind their parapets and surrendering when the Canadians arrived only seconds after the shelling stopped. The 4th Canadian Mounted Rifles, like the rest of the 8th Brigade, experienced both extremes; in an attack on 15 September the barrage was described as 'perfect,' while on 1 October many shells fell short because the observers were not far enough forward. The Canadians suffered casualties from their own artillery and then found the German trenches untouched; German machine-gunners put an end to the attack.[44]

The most successful approach to protecting the infantry while crossing no man's land was the creeping barrage, a refinement of the technique that had proved so useful for the 18th British Division on 1 July. In later Somme battles the British learned to create curtains of shell fire which moved across no man's land in hundred-yard lifts every three minutes instead of lifting from trench to trench.[45] The gunners thus made no attempt to destroy the enemy's defensive positions, which was mostly a matter of luck in any case, but concentrated on keeping defenders from their machine-guns and parapets until it was too late. The 5th Battalion described a rolling barrage of 26 September: 'As the barrage was moving forward very slowly the men would advance a short distance and then lie down and wait until it again lifted.'[46] In the assault on Ancre Heights of 1 October, the 22nd Battalion experienced some problems; troops followed the barrage too closely, suffering casualties from their own shells, but given that ammunition and fuses could never be perfect, this was taken as a sign that soldiers had kept up with their cover. More problematic, the second and third waves, farther back, were shelled by German artillery.[47] In the creeping or rolling barrage the Canadians had found the necessary technique by which the artillery could effectively protect attacking infantry, but they also had to discover some means of silencing German guns, or troops could find themselves caught between two fires.

Artillery was not the only arm trying to help the infantry across no man's land; Stokes mortars were used throughout most of the Somme assaults. By September 1916 the bomb was a simple cylinder with an 'all-ways' contact fuse, allowing greater versatility than time delay devices, each of which was preset to a specific range.[48] In December 1915 General Headquarters determined that these would be an infantry responsibility, and the decision was implemented in the following March, with each division incorporating a four-tube battery.[49] Before an attack began as many mortars as possible were installed, complete with ammunition caches, in the front trenches, where they helped to destroy barbed wire but, like artillery, were hampered by lack of sensitive fuses. When the infantry launched its attack, the mortars shelled enemy strong points, sometimes with good effect, but again, as the artillery found, results were mixed, principally on windy days. Sometimes they were not used at all, especially when units were in a hurry to begin an assault.[50]

Assisting trench mortars and artillery in setting up barrages were Lewis guns and machine-guns. If they could see the enemy's trenches, the gunners could cover the infantry advance by keeping down or unsettling enemy fire, or such was the theory, and the debate over the effectiveness of machine-gun fire in such a role lasted until well after the war. Firing further back in the German trench system gunners could delay the movement of reinforcements, while at Thiepval machine-guns fired over the heads of the attacking infantry, with Lewis guns following riflemen in the second and third waves to guard against counter-attacks (three or four Lewis guns remained in battalion reserve).[51]

If artillery, trench mortars, and machine-guns were effective, and if barbed wire was scanty, assaulting infantry could get within charging distance of the German trenches. While actually crossing no man's land, the troops moved in artillery formation, an open, vaguely diamond-shaped pattern that was supposed to ensure a single shell could not wipe out an entire section or platoon.[52] The battles that historians portray as arrows and lines on maps were actually made up of hundreds of skirmishes as Canadian and German soldiers attempted to destroy one another. The Canadians used the same weapons in these fights that they had brought with them on trench raids since 1915; so with rifle and bomb, Canadian battalions attempted to wrest the trenches from German hands, and bombs in particular came into their own when the distance between adversaries dwindled. When the 58th Battalion attacked the Ancre Heights, each company had its own bombing section, whose men entered the trenches, throwing bombs as they ran, until they had forced their way to their objectives, where they set up blocks and waited for counter-attacks. After capturing different parts of the German trench system, units bombed their way towards each other to form a continuous front. Bombs were so important that some actions were lost or broken off when the Canadians' supply ran out.[53]

If the infantry was successful in capturing its objectives, it then became necessary to hold them, and the main reason the Canadians carried so much kit was to enable them to consolidate newly won positions. The 4th Division used the rear platoon of each company to carry stores for this purpose, each man carrying a pick or shovel, ten pounds or more of barbed wire, and a screw picket to fasten it to. Men dug communication trenches back to their original lines so more troops and materials could be moved up; the shovel thus became one of the most important consolidation tools in Canadian hands. Lewis guns were sited diagonally to produce overlapping fire, while bombs, always important, were delivered as quickly as possible. All this work was usually carried out under enemy shelling.[54]

If infantry companies had enough men left after their losses during forming up, assaulting, and consolidating the position, the Canadians might be able to beat off German counter-attacks, which almost always followed a successful assault. Typically, the Germans started with a bombardment followed by the infantry's tossing bombs and attacking with machine-gun support, and the combination was sometimes successful in driving out the Canadians' depleted units. On 2 October elements of the 5th Canadian Mounted Rifles withdrew because they had too few men to hold off the Germans. Their right-hand company was completely destroyed, only three men returning to their original trenches.

One company of the 24th Battalion was annihilated on 1 October for the same reason; it did not have enough troops. Counter-attacks could sometimes be brought to a halt with Lewis guns or bombs, the latter so important one commander left the trenches in the midst of a German counter-attack to replenish personally his company's supply. Rifle grenades were also useful for breaking up German formations while they were still some distance away. At the Somme artillery was less valuable than it had been in the past in protecting new Canadian positions; for the Germans still had command of a complex trench system through which they could assault their old defences without exposing themselves. Even if artillery could have helped, sometimes gunners were unaware the infantry was in trouble, when signal rockets failed to function.[55]

One cannot exaggerate the difficulties of maintaining communications in the mud and confusion of the Somme. Telephones provided the quickest way to send messages, but signallers and their infantry labourers had to bury cables several feet deep to protect them from shelling. Keeping telephone lines open was a hazardous task for signallers, as Sergeant R.B. Gibson could testify:

My job is to see that telephone communication is kept up between the front line and brigade headquarters – a job that sounds easier than it really is. I remember one day in particular we had a stretch of line that was rather worse than usual. We had forty-three breaks in that small 300 yards in a day, and when anybody went out to fix same it was the last we expected to see of him ... I assure you repairing lines on that front was hardly what one would call safe. Linemen work practically sixteen hours a day and are under the most intense shell-fire during that period. But telephone communication has got to be kept up, for on it rests the success and co-operation of the whole attack.[56]

Headquarters feared moving, for they would have to leave their phone lines behind.[57]

Forward of battalion headquarters telephones could not be used, for the assaulting companies moved too fast to allow cable-burying parties to keep up. Supplementary means of carrying messages were needed, and in the fall of 1916 runners, pigeons, and visual devices such as lamps and flags were common on the battlefield. Runners proved best, being faster even than pigeons, making their way back with messages as soon as the leading platoons met with success or disaster, so the battalion commander could allocate reserves accordingly, though every man sent back was lost to the firing line. Experiments involving aircraft were not so successful; the Canadian Corps issued orders to its divisions stressing the importance of setting flares to identify the forward line's position to passing airplanes, but these measures did little to help improve liaison between the infantry and their contact aircraft. The latter often had to fly low – a hazardous manœuvre – to distinguish uniforms before they could report on the first wave's progress. The troops were given Very lights, rockets, and even white panels, the latter much stressed in instructions, to signal the planes, but mistakes were still common. In an attack on Regina Trench on 8 October aircraft reported that the 1st Canadian Division was on its objective when it was nowhere near.[58]

Compared with the first day's success at Courcelette, the battles that followed were brutal fights, characterized by heavy casualties. When the Somme campaign ended, 24,029 Canadian soldiers, or about a quarter of the corps's original strength, were dead, wounded, captured, or missing. Casualties for the corps were the worst to date, excepting Second Ypres. While in April 1915 the 1st Division lost 5,026 of its infantry, in September 1916 the three divisions the corps sent into the fighting each lost an average of 4,407 infantrymen, or over a third of their infantry strength.[59] Commanders soon began to seek alternative ways to fight battles and to determine what lessons could be gleaned from the carnage.

Before the Canadians moved to the base of Vimy Ridge, commanders began sending reports to their superiors at Corps Headquarters detailing their experiences and suggesting improvements. Many of these reports were concerned with the role of the battalion commander; as the 22nd Battalion phrased it succinctly, 'Once the attack is launched the Battalion Commander is practically impotent.'[60] It also noted that the company and the platoon were cut off from higher headquarters soon after the battle began, and they had to have specific objectives in mind when they left their trenches; how they captured these objectives would then be up to individual commanders. The battle, once the forward German lines were breached, became fluid and fighting was continuous; and, with positions changing daily or even hourly, only those on the spot could choose the necessary course of action to deal with the inevitable crises of battle. Soldiers, the report went on, should spend twenty-four hours in the line to get a good view of the objective and then spend another twenty-four hours in reserve so their tasks could be explained to them in detail. The bomb and the machine-gun had given the platoon enough fire-power to act on its own and it would soon be treated as an independent unit.[61]

What the infantry carried into combat did not pass without comment.

The staff of the 5th Canadian Mounted Rifles suggested means of reducing the soldier's load, which had proved such a hindrance in the Somme battles. The first wave should carry no tools but be limited to 120 rounds of ammunition, two bombs, two days' rations, and one rubber sheet per man. The 22nd Battalion also suggested eliminating tools from the front wave, since they were almost always thrown away during the assault.[62]

Major-General Arthur Currie, commanding the 1st Division, emphasized the importance of an adequate supply of bombs, mainly because barbed wire between defensive lines forced troops into the enemy's communication trenches, which then had to be captured in close combat, thus reducing the supply of bombs available to break up counterattacks. If barbed wire could be destroyed, these soldiers could move above ground straight to their objectives and leave the intermediary defences to the moppers-up. He also suggested the men get far more training in bombing.[63] Both the 1st and the 2nd Canadian mounted rifles agreed: the former insisted that the first two waves be liberally supplied with bombs, and the latter simply stated in its equipment list, 'All the bombs possible,' adding that Canadians should learn to use German grenades, since they were often captured in large numbers in the course of the fighting.[64] The 22nd Battalion noted that both Mills grenades and captured bombs and had been used to good effect.[65]

The Lewis gun had also proved useful. Company commanders insisted they have it under their control and that it be placed well forward in the attack; they could thus support platoon and company assaults at close range, adding their bursts of destruction to the infantry's bombs and rifles. The 22nd Battalion suggested sending Lewis guns with the second wave, with infantry helping to carry magazines; for each weapon required several boxes of ammunition. The larger machine-guns were far less mobile, but they could be used to cover the advance by firing at enemy trenches and, if within range, at German artillery. By the end of the Somme offensive the number of Lewis guns had been increased to one per platoon, or sixteen per battalion, controlled by company headquarters; so each company commander had four guns he could allocate as he wished.[66]

There was less consensus over the value of the Stokes mortar. The weapon had sometimes been useful in cutting wire and could be used to create a hurricane bombardment of the enemy's positions before the assault went in. The mortar's main disadvantage lay in its hunger for ammunition. It could not be brought forward, since there was no efficient means to carry the heavy bombs it needed, each of which weighed almost eleven pounds. There were several schemes to solve this problem, but none was wholly effective. Each man going to the front line could carry a single round, but infantrymen were already carrying a heavy burden. The bomb itself was useful for destroying deep dugouts and blocking tunnels, but the mortar was not necessary for fulfilling these tasks; moppers-up could simply toss bombs through doorways and other openings. Furthermore, the mortar was somewhat fragile, and one commander suggested that each tube be supplied with two breech mechanisms, since one was almost certain to break. In short, the trench mortar was most useful when the battlefield was static; it could cover the original assault against a new position but was not worth bringing forward until road construction allowed ammunition to move forward.[67]

Tanks also received mixed reviews. According to the staff officers of the Canadian Corps, they could be useful, but one had to take note of their inadequacies. Admittedly, the armoured vehicles had done well, considering that the Somme was their first battlefield test; where roads were available, they had proved their ability to take out strong points hindering the infantry advance, such as the skirmishes around the sugar refinery at Courcelette. They were undoubtedly good for morale, especially when they attracted shrapnel fire away from the much less-protected infantry. The Mark I tanks, however, had trouble moving across shell-pitted ground, were not impervious to high-explosive shells, and had a frustrating tendency to break down. (Haig would later be much maligned for using the tanks prematurely, but only through battlefield testing could such deficiencies be properly addressed.) Without prior training, infantry platoons found it difficult to advance at the tanks' pace, and vice versa, so coordination was impossible. Staff officers suggested that, if riflemen were in the lead, tanks could mop up behind them, and, if the tanks were ahead, they could break through German defences. Overall, the Canadians were not impressed with the new battlefield technology: 'No action of infantry should ever be made subservient to that of tanks. Tanks are a useful accessory to the infantry, but nothing more.'[68]

Having dealt with the weapons used in an assault, commanders examined the tactics of the day. Major General R.B. Stephens of the British 5th Division discussed the formation of a new platoon organization in an address to officers of the 4th Army; two rifle sections, each with two rifle grenadiers, a bomber section, and a Lewis gun section, would replace the four rifle sections that made up the platoons at the Somme. Tactics would concentrate on flanking manœuvres, especially since the Germans in the latter battles of 1916 had formed strong points instead of linear defences. The new organization would take advantage of the increased fire-power the rifle grenade and the Lewis gun gave the infantry.[69] If artillery was accurate and in touch with forward troops, the infantry could follow the creeping barrage across no man's land to within 100 yards of the enemy; soldiers could then crawl a further fifty yards and then wait for the barrage to lift before assaulting the enemy's trenches. It would then be a matter of reaching the parapets while the Germans tried to extricate themselves from their dugouts and take their positions. To ensure rapid consolidation each wave should be organized differently, using specialists, as had the groups going out on trench raids since 1915. The first wave, representing about half the force, would consist of riflemen, Lewis gunners, and bombers. Riflemen would stop at the objective while the gunners and bombers moved out further to set up outposts. The second wave would carry the necessary tools for consolidation and reinforce the first.[70]

There was some disagreement as to how objectives should be allocated to different waves. The 22nd Battalion recommended sending the first wave all the way to the final objective rather than have it halt at the enemy's front-line trench, where subsequent waves might bunch up. The 8th Brigade, on the other hand, thought it preferable to have the first wave stop at the first line and consolidate, while succeeding waves could go over their heads to the next objective; this leap-frog tactic was in fact adopted later.[71] It had the advantage of allowing the front-line troops, who bore the brunt of the fighting, to shift quickly into a consolidation and support role, while fresher troops could carry the battle further into the German trench system.

There was also much discussion as to how much spacing to put between the men as they crossed no man's land. If they were too close together they could be mauled by both machine-guns and artillery, and Lieutenant-Colonel Thomas Tremblay, commanding the 22nd Battalion, reported that 'On Oct. 1st, three waves of one man per 5 yards in an 800 yards advance in the open against a strong and practically undamaged trench like Regina was sheer suicide.'[72] The men had to spread out somehow and yet still have the numbers necessary to carry the position. The issue remained unresolved in the months after the Somme, and a solution would have to wait until 1917.

Mopping up was another problem. If the forward waves were to jump over lesser objectives, someone would have to ensure their rear was secure from snipers and other enemy troops; mopping-up parties thus served an important function on the battlefield. If the assault went well, they would follow the front waves as a matter of course, clearing trenches and dugouts as they moved along; if the attack bogged down, they supplied an immediate reserve which could be used to restore the situation. Battalion commanders felt that these groups should consist of about one man in the mopping-up platoons for every three men in the first wave. Thus one of the four companies in each of the lead battalions could serve as a mopping-up group.[73]

Holding captured positions was yet another challenge. The officers of the 1st Canadian Mounted Rifles suggested that a third wave follow the first two, ensuring that fresh troops would take on the task of consolidating the objective instead of leaving it to units that had just been bloodied in a fight.[74] Whoever was to defend any newly won position would need artillery support, and the Canadians had learned from their experiences at Ypres that gunners firing shrapnel could prevent German forces from counter-attacking by barring their way or breaking up their formations. At the Somme Canadian troops had found that strong-posts flung out in front of the position, to be joined up when opportunity allowed, offered a good defence against counter-attack by giving early warning and, with machine-gun and bomb, could force the enemy to take cover before he was within bombing range of the Canadian trenches.[75] Commanders and troops alike were well on their way to developing procedures to ensure that consolidation, the most difficult phase of the assault, was a success.

For the infantry to ensure that its artillery support had the necessary information to carry out its task, and for battalion and brigade commanders to know where to send reserves, reliable means of communication were necessary. Most units agreed that nothing surpassed the telephone for accuracy and speed; the 22nd Battalion did not even bother to use either visual signalling or pigeons to keep in touch with brigade headquarters (visual means were somewhat problematic anyway on a battlefield saturated with smoke and dust). Other units, like the 2nd Canadian Mounted Rifles, found that runners were often the only way to send messages to subordinate units. It was simply impossible to predict before the battle began which means of communication would work best; so the Canadians adopted all of them and were prepared to use whatever proved useful in the battles to come. This gave battalion commanders the choice between telephones (if these were not shot out by shelling), runners (if they could get through enemy fire), pigeons (if the smoke and noise of battle did not confuse them), and visual signalling (if dust and mist did not mask the signaller). Using airplanes had not been successful, and the infantry needed more training in signalling to their contact patrol aircraft.[76]

The Canadians at the Somme learned that they had not yet learned enough. Their success at Mont Sorrel with wave attacks and close co-operation between artillery and infantry was not repeated at Thiepval, Regina Trench, and the other engagements of the late summer and fall of 1916. Even Courcelette, later to be declared a Canadian victory, turned into a bloody see-saw of attacks and counter-attacks after the initial day's success. British developments on the Somme, however, would be important in Canadian battles to come. The rolling barrage would help ensure success at Vimy in 1917, while the tank would prove a useful support weapon in 1918. On the Somme, when the infantry met with success, it was because of the experience it had gained in training and in trench raids, experience that taught troops the use of the bomb as a weapon of both defence and attack. By the time the British opened the Battle of the Somme on 1 July 1916, the rifle had already begun to give up its place as the infantry's favoured weapon in trench warfare, and during the battle itself the Lewis gun saw greater use in the attack and would soon become an integral part of any as-saulting platoon. While artillery worked at becoming more accurate and more responsive to the infantry, the latter had already chosen the tech-nology it would use in upcoming battles: the bomb and the automatic rifle.

4

Towards Vimy

On the Somme the British had wrested a few square miles of occupied France from German hands, while at Verdun, the French had brought the German offensive to a halt. Unknown to both at the time, 1917 was to be a black year, in which the Russians would leave the alliance, French soldiers would mutiny, British and neutral losses in shipping would reach frightening levels, and the Italians would suffer their worst defeat of the war at Caporetto. The Allies, who would be joined by the Americans (one of the few rays of hope in an otherwise bleak year) had two options: either wait, until tank production increased and the United States built up its army; or launch an all-out offensive against Germany. In what was essentially a debate between politicians who preferred the first option and generals who favoured the second, those attending the Chantilly conference in November 1916 decided to try to knock Germany out of the war in the coming year. In January 1917 General Robert Georges Nivelle, hero of Fort Douaumont and Joseph Joffre's replacement as commander of the French armies, proposed a double offensive he insisted would end the war. First, the British and French, each with four armies, would attack near Arras to attract and 'fix' the enemy's strategic reserves; then, a fortnight later, the French Fifth Army would strike on the Aisne River front to take advantage of any breach in the German lines or thinning within enemy ranks.[1] The Canadian Corps's part in the Battle of Arras would be an assault against the solidly entrenched German defences on Vimy Ridge.

In the days between the Battle of the Somme and the assault on Vimy the Canadian Corps took stock of its successes and failures and set out to develop a system of tactics, based on available technology, that would allow the infantry to capture its objectives and hold them without the heavy casualties characteristic of earlier battles. Artillery, which had at times been woefully inaccurate on the Somme, set out to find ways to bring its shells down on target whenever they were needed, and at Vimy gunners achieved their major goals mainly because they had greater access to information about the enemy and a willingness to experiment with a wide range of technical developments. Both artillery and infantry needed information about the enemy's defences and dispositions before they could plan the attack, and the Canadian Corps gathered this intelligence in many ways: through aerial photographs, trench raids, and front-line observation, to name just a few. Some of this information was employed in devising full-scale replicas of infantry objectives to allow detailed rehearsals. Finally, many infantry battalions avoided enemy shell fire in their assembly areas by making their way to the front line in tunnels they had discovered, which the engineers then rebuilt and expanded. Taking into account a wide variety of factors – German defensive tactics, the Canadian search for a new way to attack, training, information-gathering, the tunnels, and artillery preparations – will lead to an understanding of the evolving relationship between the soldiers of the Canadian Corps and the technology of war.

In the spring of 1917 German defensive tactics were in a state of flux. Casualties on the Somme and at Verdun had been high, mainly because German regiments in defensive positions had been subjected to horrible punishment by the enemy's guns before each battle began. The first line often disappeared in a hail of shells and shrapnel or became incapable of defending itself; it was then left to the infantry of the second and third lines, and sometimes reserves further back, to recapture lost positions in counter-attacks, which were costly whether successful or not. Transferred from the Russian front, where he had enjoyed much distinction, General Erich Ludendorff of the General Staff suggested that the armies of the Western Front adopt a defence in depth. Instead of a forward line, German battalions would form outposts, with the main line 1,500 to 2,500 yards behind.[2] General Freiherr von Falkenhausen commanded the German Sixth Army, which was responsible for Vimy Ridge; he did not, however, implement these new tactics. On his right, where he faced the 3rd and 4th Canadian divisions, a defence in depth would have meant giving up the crest of the ridge and hence the best observation site the Germans had on that part of the front. On the left, however, the main German line would have run through Thélus, thus blocking any attack towards high ground. Perhaps von Falkenhausen was applying the same tactical principle to the ridge as a whole, treating it as a special feature inappropriate for defence-in-depth, though according to Jeffery Williams: 'A more elastic system was planned but work on it had not yet begun. In the face of increasing destruction caused by the British and Canadian guns and frequent alarms caused by infantry raids, the garrison could do little more than maintain their existing defences.'[3] No matter what his reasoning, the general's conservatism worked to the Canadians' advantage, because they faced defences similar to those on the Somme. To succeed, they had to silence enemy guns, create gaps in the wire, and isolate the dugouts and strong points that stood in their path.[4]

The most important link in the German defensive chain was the machine-gun, which had proved effective so often in the past. These nests were dug in immediately behind the forward defensive line in a chequer-board arrangement that allowed for mutual protection and overlapping arcs of fire. Some were concealed in hollows to hide them from air observation and make them almost impervious to shelling. The crews were well trained and determined; in the battle to come the Canadians would comment on the machine-gunners' skill and bravery as they fought until completely surrounded or killed. If German riflemen were forced to withdraw, their comrades with the machine-guns formed rearguards to cover the retreat and form small pockets of resistance to delay the enemy's advance.[5] Either artillery would have to discover some way to suppress German machine-guns, or infantry would have to devise some means to destroy or capture them.

British tactics evolved slowly. In the months following the Somme the official infantry handbook of 1914 changed in only one respect; missing were the words 'close with the enemy, cost what it may.'[6] The French, however, had learned much from the battles around Verdun, as their performance on the Somme had shown. As early as April 1916 General Joffre, commander of all French forces in France, issued a memorandum stating that 'Infiltration (advancing in driblets) is a good procedure during a battle whenever it is possible.'[7] This memorandum was issued to Canadian battalions, and in the days leading up to the attack on Vimy Ridge Canadian tactical thinking focused on small groups, as did that of other armies on the Western Front, allied and enemy alike. By March the 4th Division could send out memoranda insisting that 'Mobility of the platoon is the only method possible for dealing with the sudden discovery of a machine gun in an unexpected place.'[8]

To develop effective and less costly tactics, the Canadian Corps's British commander, Lieutenant-General Sir Julian Byng, sent one of his division commanders, Arthur Currie, to see how the French had fought their battles at Verdun. This information, added to the lessons of the Somme, would help the Canadians develop the attack techniques they sought. Currie learned much from the French and agreed with their emphasis on reconnaissance and information: 'I cannot lay too much stress on the importance attached by the French to this preliminary occupation of the line for reconnaissance purposes. Every man saw the ground over which he would have to attack; his objective was pointed out to him as well as the places where he might expect resistance and check.'[9] There were other sources of information; prior to any attack the French took innumerable air photos and distributed them to the officers of attacking units.[10] Both the Somme and Verdun had taught the Allies the importance of knowing where the enemy's strong points were and ensuring that such information reached the troops who would have to destroy or capture them.

Once sufficient information was available, the French chose their objectives and, unlike the British and Canadians, sent their troops to capture tactical features, such as hills or ridges, instead of German trenches. This was sound policy. The Germans sited their front line so as to dominate the land towards the Allies; capturing these positions in no way guaranteed that the Canadians would dominate territory in the enemy's direction. It was best, Currie felt, to aim at wresting from German hands features that could be used as bases for further attacks; capturing the enemy's trenches was a necessary condition for gaining these positions, but it should not be an end in itself.[11]

To ensure that the troops would reach their objectives, they had to be trained. Currie found that in many ways the French were far less prepared for their assaults at Verdun, not having dug jump-off trenches, than the Canadians had been at at the Somme; 'It must be remembered though, that the greatest preparation for an attack consists in the training of troops and in this regard I claim we have something to learn from our Ally.'[12] The divisions chosen to carry out a particular attack were trained especially for the tasks ahead of them, rehearsing on ground similar to the area over which the troops were to advance, as had the British at the Somme, but concentrating on platoon and company tactics. They practised any special movements – such as passing through those who had captured the first objective – until they became second nature. They also learned to use a variety of weapons, such as rifle-grenades, automatic rifles, and bombs. Currie concluded, 'The French attach the greatest possible importance to this special training of attacking troops, and in my opinion it is the greatest lesson to be learned from our visit to Verdun. I believe greater success would attend our attacks if those attacks were made by absolutely fresh troops who had been specially trained for the work in hand.'[13]

The focus of all this training was the platoon, which Currie believed could devise means of dealing with strong points left unscathed by artillery, using the weapons its soldiers carried with them. Year by year the platoon had gained in fire-power and hence in importance. The French, who were to prove a partial model for Currie's recommendations on tactical doctrine, noted the difference between the small units of 1914 and those of 1916. In the first days of the war the rifle and bayonet dominated the armaments of each company, with two machine-guns for each battalion. At Verdun the company organization included thirty-two bombers, sixteen rifle-grenadiers, eight Chauchat automatic rifles, eight machine-guns per three companies, and a 37-mm pom-pom per battalion. By late 1916 each company was composed of four platoons, each divided into half-platoons. The first was formed of a squad of eight bombers and another of seven fusiliers who fired the Chauchat; the second was made up of voltigeurs, or riflemen, and itself was divided into two squads. Edmund Blunden in early 1917 noticed the change in British tactics, where he as a platoon commander led his troops in outflanking manœuvres rather than forming waves conforming to a battalion plan. The restoration of the platoon organization within the British armies was important; at the Somme companies had been arbitrarily divided into platoons prior to going into an attack, in effect making the platoon commander and his second in command superfluous.[14]

The idea of concentrating on small-unit tactics was familiar to Currie, who had been a part-time officer in Canada's Active Militia before the war: 'It may be pointed out that there is nothing new in this system of training. Before the war we endeavoured to make the platoon a self-reliant and self-sufficient unit of battle. Owing to the demands for so many specialists, there grew up in our battalions a wrong system of organization and the development of the initiative of Company, Platoon, Section and Squad leaders were some-what neglected. It is necessary for us to revise our own training on the old lines.'[15] Again lessons learned on the Somme were reinforced by the French experience at Verdun; they were further reinforced by the experiences of Canadian officers themselves, many of whom had trained as members of small units in the year before the war when militia regiments were too small to do anything else.

Once the men were trained, it was necessary to see them properly equipped, formed up, and across no man's land. Currie learned nothing from the French about what the infantry should carry, since each division commander had his own list and discrepancies were common. Their formations were much the same as those of the British, with two companies out in front and one in reserve and two platoons per company leading the attack. The French were more flexible, however, about the number of waves they would send into an attack; the British held to the magic number eight. Again Currie found the French attitude more sensible, since the number of waves sent over the top should be determined by factors such as the depth of the attack, the strength of enemy resistance and the nature of hostile artillery shelling. (It should be noted that the word 'wave' no longer meant a line of soldiers moving forward as on parade but referred to those units that left the trenches at the same given moment.)[16]

Once the attack was launched, each platoon or company was responsible for reaching its allocated objectives, and all troops left the trenches at the same time in order to cross no man's land before German gunners could begin shelling them. Currie noted that at Verdun the French were often held up by German strong points, but, more often than not, they managed to remove the cause of delay. They used rifle-grenades or automatic rifle fire to keep the enemy's head down while parties of infantry rushed in or took the position from the rear. At all events, priority was on forward movement, the infantry confident that pockets of resistance left behind would be dealt with by mopping-up parties armed with knives, rifles, and incendiary bombs to fight at close quarters. The French also leap-frogged their units. In one attack they used six battalions forward with three following behind. The first six captured the first objective and paused for an hour. The three other battalions, following closely, formed up behind the first objective, under cover of their companions now occupying the German trenches, and attacked the final objective, which they then consolidated.[17]

Once the infantry had reached its goal, troops made some effort to press even further, though they did not rush forward until fatigue and German bullets put an end to them. The French sent out patrols to destroy enemy artillery and turn the German retreat into a rout; Currie learned what not to do from this approach, however, because casualties were high. Furthermore, morale suffered, since those wounded or trapped on these patrols were destroyed by their own artillery. None of the French division commanders with whom Currie spoke was in favour of this plan of exploitation,[18] and Currie, being an advocate of the bite-and-hold approach, would concentrate on consolidating newly won positions, not exploiting them.

In the context of the often heavy loss of life on the Western Front, the French attacks were successful without prohibitive casualties. Their assault of 15 December 1916 cost one division over 3,000 casualties and another 431 killed and 2,381 wounded, total French losses for that day amounting to 11–12,000; but they had captured 12,000 German prisoners, an indication that their tactics had completely overwhelmed the enemy's positions.[19] The French system could be termed a success, and Currie returned to the Canadian Corps prepared to suggest changes to Byng.

Lieutenant-Colonel A.G.L. McNaughton, Canada's best-known artillery officer, had far less success with the French. He had been sent out to find ways to increase the Canadian artillery's ability to destroy the enemy and otherwise support the infantry's advance, but unfortunately the lessons the French had learned from their experiences since 1914 differed according to the level of command one questioned. Army, corps, division, and brigade were isolated from one another and suggested contradictory solutions to McNaughton's problems.[20] Information had to come from elsewhere, and the gunner found it among British veterans of the Somme; Colonel A.G. Haig of the 5th British Corps was especially helpful. McNaughton, who would later become head of Canada's National Research Council, had an affinity for scientists and gadgets, and, according to his biographer, 'when the scientists arrived with an "eagerness to display their wares" they met a kindred spirit in Mc-Naughton, one who was only too willing to make the best use he could of this "rather amorphous mass of ability." '[21]

Various methods of locating enemy guns through sound-ranging had been under development for some time. Charles Nordmann, a French gunner who had been an astronomer for the Paris Observatory, appreciated in the autumn of 1914 that a gun's position could be pinpointed by measuring the difference in time required for the report to reach widely placed microphones. He teamed up with Lucien Bull, a French physicist, who fashioned the necessary equipment. By the autumn of 1915 British officers were intrigued by the idea, but it was not until June of the following year that microphones and measuring instruments

were developed that could operate under field conditions. By the time
McNaughton went to see Colonel Haig, the system was workable. Haig
and Sir William Bragg, a Nobel laureate after the war, produced instruments capable of determining the location of enemy guns with microphones placed at different locations along the front line. Each sound-
ranging battery consisted of a headquarters connected to six or more
microphones carefully placed along the front about 2,500 yards behind
the forward trenches. A listening post, well forward of the microphones,
started the ranging process as soon as the operator heard an enemy gun
firing and pressed a key that started a recorder at headquarters. Each
microphone in turn picked up the sound of the report, which registered
on the recorder. From the time intervals between the microphones staff
could determine the gun's location.[22] McNaughton remembered the
infantry's plight at the Somme: troops had found themselves subject to
shelling from the time they approached their jump-off trenches to the
moment survivors were relieved and sent back for rest and further
training; if enemy guns could be silenced, the infantry would suffer far
fewer casualties before, during, and after the assault. The sound-ranging
equipment the French and British had developed might help.

McNaughton learned much about the techniques of counter-battery
fire, interestingly enough, from Currie, whose trip to Verdun had supplied him with a wealth of information. Furthermore, Currie had been
in the garrison artillery years before and knew the importance of accurate
gunnery. (Field artillery before the war concentrated on swift movement
and speed in coming into action rather than on accuracy, while garrison
or coastal artillery, being anchored to a fixed site, worked at being as
accurate as possible.) The French insisted on every round's being observed, so its successor would fall on target, and, though Haig had insisted on just such a procedure before Neuve Chapelle, subsequent British
battles had relied on mass rather than on accuracy. The French continued to insist that there be no wild firing, which was often so wide of
the mark as to be useless, or worse, fell on friendly troops; and, like the
British, they relied on aircraft to spot shells aimed beyond the range of
ground observers. For counter-battery work they had gone so far as to
determine the amount of ammunition one had to expend to destroy a
hostile battery, 600 rounds of six-inch shells being considered sufficient.[23]

The French at Verdun went to great lengths to destroy the enemy's
defensive works before the infantry was sent into the attack. For the 15
December assault each division commander had 142 guns of various

calibers and twelve batteries of trench mortars at his disposal. With these he was expected to destroy all barbed wire, machine-guns, trenches, strong points, and enemy artillery within his zone of responsibility. If necessary, front trenches in close proximity to enemy lines were evacuated so heavy artillery could destroy German defensive works. In the days preceding the attack the gunners laid down barrages similar to those that would be used for the assault itself, thus allowing the infantry to gain tactical surprise, since the Germans would not know which barrage preceded the actual attack.[24] This was yet another lesson of the Somme reinforced at Verdun.

The artillery barrage did not cease when the infantry left their trenches. 'Accompanying fire,' like the creeping barrages on the Somme, moved forward at a prearranged rate until it reached the objective and formed a standing barrage. The wall of fire, however, was never brought back to help the infantry in case of delay; for platoon tactics and weapons were expected to solve unforeseen problems. If the delay was severe, the French waited until nightfall to attack the position from the rear. There was thus far less reliance on the guns during the actual assault, which made sense given the primitive state of communications at the time. Currie noted the contrast between French and British empire attitudes towards artillery: 'Too often, when our infantry are checked they pause and ask for additional preparation before carrying on. This artillery preparation cannot be quickly arranged for and is often not necessary. Our troops must be taught the power of manœuvre and that before giving up they must employ to the utmost extent all the weapons with which they are armed and have available.'[25] This implied a somewhat different relationship between artillery and infantry: rather than having the former conquer and the latter occupy, Currie proposed that infantry do the conquering and artillery play a supporting role. The platoon, not the battery, was the new focus of attack tactics.

Byng and his staff applied the lessons Currie and McNaughton had learned in formulating the plan of attack for Vimy Ridge. The objective was the ridge itself, from which the Canadians could dominate the area for miles around. The attack would evolve in two or four stages, depending on how far a given division had to advance, since the Canadian trenches were not parallel to the objective. A system of coloured lines was devised to mark the intermediate and final objectives for the entire corps: the Black Line consisted of the German forward defence zones, and the Red Line marked the final objective for the 1st and 2nd divisions; the 3rd and 4th divisions, having further to go, would advance

A practice platoon attack at Shorncliffe, September 1917. Soldiers are dispersed to limit the effectiveness of German artillery. The Lewis-gun section is near the centre of the front wave.

to the Blue Line, another intermediate objective, before moving on to the Brown Line, which would place them in commanding position at the top of the ridge. At each line fresh troops would take over from the attacking infantry and wait for the barrage to shift towards enemy positions before moving on. Every platoon was to have its own set of objectives, and battalions were to advance even if the units on their flanks were held up, though only for a time, thus ensuring that the front waves kept up to the artillery's curtain of fire.[26]

Before this plan could be implemented it was necessary to train the troops for the task ahead in accordance with the lessons of the Somme and Verdun. Also, many of the men with the corps had recently arrived to replace those killed or wounded in previous battles, and these inexperienced recruits had to be brought up to standard. The Princes Patricia's Canadian Light Infantry, for example, had only 150 men left of the original battalion that had been formed in 1914. The others had become casualties or had been sent to other duties in France, England, or Canada. The 31st Battalion saw its composition change as men came from units broken up in England to replace casualties. First, soldiers of the 56th Battalion were prominent, but after some time in the trenches the 82nd and then the 89th were better represented; as Vimy approached, the 135th (after being broken up) had more men in the 31st Battalion than any other reinforcing unit, and at Passchendaele the 202nd's men were in the majority.[27] The 31st was not alone, and the corps as a whole needed replacements for its battalions and training for its replacements; because of rapidly changing technology and tactics even veterans were in need of training to keep up with recent developments. Lieutenant F.G. Newton spoke for his comrades in a letter home on 25 March: 'War has become so revolutionized that the recruit regiments of the latest era have every right to expect to be able to do as much after a couple of months' seasoning as the oldest regiments of the line.'[28] The corps's instructional burden eased somewhat when Sir Richard Perley, of Canada's Overseas Ministry in London, adopted the War Office's training syllabus and demanded that every recruit arriving in the United Kingdom have a certificate to attest to his progress.[29]

Trench routine had not changed since 1915, and Canadian troops still spent much of their time out of the trenches relearning old skills, learning new ones, and teaching their reinforcements the art of survival in trench warfare. Fire and movement, neglected since 1914, was reinstated when Currie returned from the Verdun front in late 1916. The Canadian division commander was not, however, the only one learning from others' experiences. In February 1917 the British General Staff issued *Instructions for the Training of Platoons for Offensive Action*, which proposed a new platoon organization, taking advantage of the many weapons adopted by the infantry since 1914. Instead of being made up exclusively of riflemen, the new platoon would be formed of four sections, one each of bombers, Lewis gunners, riflemen, and rifle-grenadiers. Each of these groups, ideally, would have nine members, guided by a platoon headquarters formed of an officer, a senior non-commissioned officer, and two runners. According to the instructions, a platoon should have a minimum strength of twenty-eight men, since it could not act on its own otherwise. On the Vimy front, platoon assaults, company attacks, and various deployments were repeated over and over to drill them into the minds of the suffering infantrymen; they also performed mock attacks at the battalion level in which emphasis was placed on dealing with unforeseen contingencies like machine-guns and strong points. The men learned to advance in artillery formation, moving forward in long, spread-out platoon columns far less vulnerable to artillery fire than tight waves.[30]

The troops were also trained to use the tools of their trade. Bombing practices still caused some casualties, especially since the corps had begun to train all infantrymen in the art of grenade throwing. Lewis gunners learned to use German machine-guns as well as their own, and small groups from the infantry battalions sat through similar lessons. Snipers continued to practise their specialist trade on the rifle ranges, learning and relearning to fire in the open or through loopholes. Training did not neglect the importance of communications, and the infantry practised signalling to patrol aircraft with flares, lamps, or panels until they were deemed proficient. The artillery took advantage of any quiet time to practise the precise shooting that would be required when the barrages began.[31]

In February some units set up full-scale replicas of the ground over which they would be attacking. In March, a month before the scheduled assault on the ridge, engineers laid out a facsimile of the German trenches to be attacked, using tape to mark the various trench lines and strong points on ground similar to the corps's objectives. This kind of practice area was familiar to Canadian troops, who had rehearsed on similar training grounds before many of their raids. Currie, however, had seen the French using the technique on a much larger scale before their 15 December attack at Verdun, and the British had used it extensively before and during the Somme battles. Based on aerial photographs, the taped course became the final training ground for those who would be engaged in the attack; starting with platoons and working their way up to full divisions, the Canadians spent several weeks rehearsing their tasks.[32]

The course was elaborate. Trenches were marked with signboards bearing their German names, and all known emplacements were iden-

Two soldiers with gas helmets examining a rifle, March 1917. The pouches worn against the chest contained filters to remove toxic agents from the air in case of gas attack. They were worn only during an alarm, though here the soldiers have no doubt put them on for the photographer. By this time the Canadian Corps was armed with the Lee-Enfield.

tified in a similar manner. The weather was foul (it was the worst winter in decades) and hampered training, but all units, including the infantry, engineers, and artillery spotters, were put through their paces. Units were rotated through the line to see for themselves the ground the taped course was supposed to represent, and each platoon, when out of the line, practised capturing the specific objectives that had been denoted as its responsibility. Results were dramatic. The 1st Division's official report claimed that every man knew his place in the attack and what was expected of him, with or without his officers' leadership. Though many of the troops 'thought it very foolish and useless,'[33] they soon changed their minds. C.S. Burgess, a Lewis gunner with the 2nd Canadian Mounted Rifles, later evaluated his training: 'when we finally reached the top of the hill, we not only landed in exactly the right place, but we *knew* we were in the right section of those trenches we were supposed to be in.'[34] Colonel H.S. Cooper's experiences were similar; 'you've gone over it so often, and this is literally true, that when we went in the battle, I didn't have to look at my maps, to tell you the map location of where I was at that time.'[35] The taped course served its purpose well; the troops knew what was expected of them and what they could expect from others. At least one aspect of confusion that arises in battle, where to go and when to move, had been largely removed.

To update the taped course, ensure it reflected the true nature of German defences, and draw up a plan with a reasonable chance of success, the Canadians needed information. Aerial photographs, observation posts, and kite balloons proved useful in determining the enemy's movements and positions. Each battalion had an intelligence section made up of an officer, scouts, and snipers, the latter gaining information through their telescopic sights.[36] To these were added documents, maps, and the interrogation of prisoners of war captured on patrols and trench raids.

Patrols served two purposes: they were an attempt to dominate no man's land, thus preventing the Germans from sending out information-gathering patrols of their own; and they could be used to locate and evaluate the enemy's wire, advanced positions, and main line of defence. German machine-gunners often fired at patrols in the dark, with little or no chance of hitting them, but giving their positions away to the Canadians who had been sent out for just that purpose. Dominating the intervening ground between the two armies was no easy task; though the Germans were essentially on the defensive, they did not remain in their trenches and allow the Canadians to wander about as they pleased. From 2 to 21 December the Canadian Corps received reports of twenty-three hostile patrols, of which one had penetrated into Canadian trenches. The others led to skirmishes, and reports were punctuated with comments like 'Forced to retire to their trenches,' 'driven off by our bombers,' and 'were chased in.' The favourite weapon on both sides for this kind of work was still the bomb.[37]

Occasionally the Germans were even more aggressive and attempted to raid Canadian positions, themselves having learned the value of gre- nades, mortars, and other weapons of trench warfare. On 29 November 1916 German raiders managed to kill two infantrymen and wound five others in a brief raid lasting some fifteen minutes. On 21 February the enemy tried to reach the Canadian trenches but was forced back by bombers, Lewis-gun fire, and artillery. Six days later German raiders, following an accurate bombardment, bombed an outpost and captured two of its occupants, though their progress was halted by a Lewis gun that forced them back to their own lines. The local commander attrib- uted their success to a short hurricane bombardment of rifle grenades and trench mortars seconds before infantry rushed the doomed out- post.[38]

Such raids continued even as the Canadians became more active in trying to gain information for the upcoming offensive, though usually the Germans replied with artillery, and the Canadian Corps's heavy batteries were often called upon to answer SOS calls. On 13 March, for example, a small raid was driven off and German artillery was suc- cessfully silenced by the counter-battery office. The 2nd Division, how- ever, lost fifteen men in two well-organized enemy raids supported by heavy trench mortars and guns. Two days later about seventy-five Ger- mans attempted a raid but were forced away before any of them could enter the trenches, though one Canadian soldier was killed and two went missing from an outpost. The 263rd Reserve Infantry Regiment attempted another raid on 21 March but ran into heavy artillery, rifle fire, and bombs, leaving a prisoner in its withdrawal. The next day another Canadian outpost disappeared in a surprise attack carried out without artillery support.[39]

The Canadians, however, were preparing for a major offensive and put all possible effort into gaining the upper hand in no man's land, though Currie refused to sanction raids unless he felt they would bring tangible results rather than aim at German morale, almost impossible to measure in any case. One officer complained when the division com- mander cancelled a minor operation, because soldiers had trained hard for it and were very keen, but Currie, having received the information he wanted from another source, saw no point in sending the troops over.[40] He could still take satisfaction from successful raids, and he made entries in his diary like '3rd Bn carry out most successful raid,' '8th Bde pull off very fine day light raid,' and 'In afternoon 6 parties of 1st Bde went over in daylight, all but one got in, had a regular field day, drove Bosches out of their front line into their support, killed a good many and had only two casualties in 2nd Bn and about 10 in First, men got very keen and it was hard to hold them back.'[41]

Since early 1916 trench raiding had been a duty for all battalions, and in the winter of 1916–17 General Headquarters commanded that each division carry out two raids every week. Previously, high command had ordered them to gain identification and destroy trenches, though some units carried them out to prove their élite status; but by the time the Canadians began preparing for the assault on Vimy Ridge minor operations had become part of Haig's war of attrition. They also served a political role, since the commander-in-chief could point to the large number of raids if the French complained of British inactivity; from April to December 1916 there were 270 raids on the British front. From 29 October 1916 to 1 April 1917 over sixty Canadian raiding parties left their trenches to invest the enemy's positions, and of these four out of every five managed to enter German trenches. On many nights there were multiple raids, as on 27 November, when two raiding parties left their lines, or 9 December, when no less than three set out across no man's land. They might be composed of a handful of men, like the ten members of the Princess Patricia's Canadian Light Infantry who raided on 9 December or the nine men of the 42nd Battalion who left their trenches on 1 January; or whole battalions might be sent over, like the 422 men of the 1st Canadian Mounted Rifles who attacked the German trenches on 20 December or the 875 men from the 20th and 21st Battalions who, with engineer support, crossed no man's land on 17 January. Few men carried rifles, since they were allowed to bring their weapons of choice; bombs were the most popular, revolvers almost as favoured, and some men brought clubs. Raiders often used explosives; packed into a tube, they could be used to create lanes through the enemy wire; packed into a suitcase they could be tossed into dugouts with devastating effect. The Bangalore torpedo, or ammonal tube, proved very useful on a battlefiled criss-crossed with barbed wire obstacles. Developed in Bangalore, India, in 1912, it was meant to be a partial solution to the barriers that had been prevalent during the Russo-Japanese War. It consisted of six-foot-long tubes that could be locked together to form a torpedo of any manageable length; a hardwood conical nose fitted to the front allowed sappers to push the tube through most wire obstacles without snagging, while a detonator fitted into the rear set it off, creating a lane through the barrier wide enough for a raiding party.[42]

The pattern of small and large raids continued into 1917, right up to the eve of the attack.[43] In a raid carried out by the 1st Canadian Mounted Rifles, the battalion had learned that in broken ground full of craters troops could be assembled well forward and thus still retain the element of surprise in daylight. In his final report Major-General L.J. Lipsett, British commander of Canada's 3rd Division, suggested, 'I think this may be made use of for larger Operations, in conjunction with Tunnels.'[44] The lesson was not lost on the corps commander or his staff.

At the end of 1916 the Canadian Corps took a close look at the raids it had carried out since October. Barbed wire had proved a problem on many occasions, and ammonal tubes were in short supply; some effective means of getting through the wire would have to be devised. The use of an explosion as a signal for the artillery to begin a bombardment was hazardous; for many raids failed to enter the trenches when German observers, seeing shadows approaching in the dark, tossed grenades which the Canadian gunners mistook as the signal to open fire. As the shells poured in, the Canadians lost any opportunity for surprise and had to return to their trenches. Other raids had been an almost total waste of time, troops expending bombs and ammunition on abandoned positions. Finally, it was not enough to blow up German defences; the raids also were supposed to gather information, and the dugouts often contained documents such as maps and orders that would help in planning the upcoming battle. There were positive lessons as well. Artillery barrages went a long way towards protecting raiders, and the German policy of placing machine-gun posts behind the front line in chequer-board arrangement was in this case beneficial; for artillery could isolate these positions without hindering the raiders' foray into the German front lines. Stealth was important, since German rifles and machine guns had a much longer range than Canadian bombs and revolvers; it was thus critical that the battle not begin until the raiders were close enough to use their weapons to best effect.[45]

Adopting the lessons of late 1916, the Canadian Corps created a sequence of events, or a checklist, to help raid leaders prepare for their missions. The result was, on the surface, a complex affair, but one that tried to leave nothing to chance and made the best use of available resources. First, whoever called for the raid, whether the brigade or division or even corps commander, indicated the objective to the raid leader in precise detail, including the target's frontage and depth and any special tasks he wished carried out. The raid leader then conducted a personal reconnaissance of the objective, choosing routes in and out and positions from which friendly troops could give covering fire. Then followed a series of conferences in which the scouting officer, bombing officer, signal officer, and anyone else having a certain expertise could advise the raid leader on how his mission could be supported; he then drew up preliminary orders, so the operation could be prepared in detail. Artillery and trench mortars cut gaps through barbed wire as best they could; patrols went out into no man's land to verify the gunners' success and gauge enemy reaction, while officers and group leaders went out with these patrols if possible to get a good look at their objectives, preferably in daylight. Once these preparations were complete, the raid leader could draw up his final orders. These instructions specified what every man and gun would do at precise times; the gunners were given their targets and the times when they would engage them, and trench mortars and machine-guns received similar orders. Once all preparation was deemed complete, the raiders assembled in a prearranged jump-off position and moved out across no man's land.[46]

On 19 February the 78th Battalion carried out a raid, one of whose purposes was to thwart the enemy's attempts to gain the upper hand in the continuous underground war of tunnel and mine. The raiders carried mobile charges – haversacks or suitcases filled with explosive with an easily accessible external fuse to set them off. One party, engaged in demolishing dugouts and mine shafts, single-handedly destroyed a German tunnel system and demonstrated the power and usefulness of explosives for sabotage. The raid leader reported that one mine shaft

evidently contained either a Tunnelling Coy's Explosive Store or had a mine already laid, as simultaneously with the explosion of the Mobile Charges, a terrific explosion occurred, and a large crater was formed in the enemy's front line at that point. Some portions of earth which were thrown in the air appeared to be of several tons weight, and large quantities were thrown as far as our trenches.

The explosion evidently set fire to an extensive underground mining system, and will probably result in the cessation of any mining activity at this point for considerable time.[47]

Dugouts were treated in a similar manner, and the raiders withdrew with thirteen casualties.[48]

Throughout the early months of 1917 the raiding continued with similar results. The Canadians were not immune to disaster, however, and experiments with new technologies did not always have beneficial consequences. In late January the 4th Division planned a massive raid with two battalions, introducing a novel feature to Canadian minor operations – poison gas. As planned, specialists would release the colourless and odourless vapour, from cylinders placed in the forward trenches, ninety minutes before dawn; the infantry would then cross over to the enemy trenches in a wave, supported by strong patrols. Artillery would not open fire until the infantry began to withdraw.[49] Gas was different from all other weapons the Canadian Corps used on the Western Front in one important regard; unlike rifles, machine-guns, artillery, or even bombs, it could not be aimed but relied on the breeze to carry it to the enemy. It could be fired in artillery shells, but thousands of these were necessary to create a deadly cloud large enough to cover a front held by several battalions. On the night of 28 February – 1 March, something went terribly wrong; when the gas was released it drifted *parallel* to Canadian lines, inflicting casualties on the 75th Battalion before it could prepare to move out. When the men of the 54th and 75th battalions attacked at 5:30 in the morning, the Germans were ungassed and alert; both battalion commanders and many of their troops were mowed down in the battle that followed. The Canadians suffered 687 casualties for no gain.[50] The raid's failure demonstrated the dangers of experimenting with the technology of war, and subsequent minor operations returned to proven methods and relied on cover fire from artillery, mortars, and machine-guns to protect the infantry in no man's land.

One raid can serve to demonstrate the symbiotic relationship that had developed among all arms of the Canadian Corps in the days before Vimy. On 1 April the 42nd Battalion raided German lines. The time the infantry was to leave its trenches was, in accordance with staff procedures, designated as zero-hour. At zero minus one minute a battery of eighteen-pounders opened an intense shrapnel barrage on enemy front-line trenches, and at zero minus thirty seconds the infantry fired a volley of rifle grenades. Four small parties, totalling forty-one men, then moved out, three trench mortars each shelling a trench junction while machine-guns fired at a suspected assembly area for German reserves. Twenty rifle grenadiers continued their barrage of the front line while six rifle grenadiers and a Lewis gun took aim to the right of the objective to protect the raiders' flank.[51] When troops entered the enemy trenches under this complicated barrage, they used Mills grenades and Stokes mortar shells to destroy dugouts, and revolvers, rifles, and Mills bombs to fight. They chose their weapons for their effectiveness in trench warfare, and even the rifles had been cut down so their barrels would not jam into trench walls. The raiders charged down communication trenches right into their own barrage, which forced them to halt. After inflicting casualties and destroying several strong dugouts, one of which had eight entrances, the Canadian raiders returned to their lines with one man slightly wounded.[52]

Throughout this period, cooperation between artillery and infantry improved. The gunners often interrupted their systematic destruction of enemy trenches to support raids, especially in the last week of February and first week of March, when Byng pressed for more information from the infantry battalions. Raiders gathered information about German strong points, which the artillery could then attempt to destroy, and brought the enemy's reserves out into the open, where the guns could inflict casualties. In the last weeks before 9 April, troops went over the top every night to update information on German defences for the artillery barrage plan.[53]

While infantry and artillery carried out their respective and interlocking missions above ground, below them engineers carried out their usually silent and hidden war against the enemy's tunnellers. There were two ways to destroy the enemy's shafts; one, already discussed above, was to locate the entrances to the German tunnels from aerial photographs, prisoners, and captured documents and then send raiding parties to seal them up will mobile charges; the other was to dig one's way towards the sounds of the enemy's work.[54] After locating enemy tunnels and shafts, one could either blow them in with explosives or, more rarely, force openings into them and kill or harass enemy engineers with rifle fire. Allied tunnelling tactics were the same everywhere on the Western Front; attackers sometimes used smoke to force the enemy to evacuate underground works, but gas was avoided because it was too persistent.[55] The tunnellers worked in almost total isolation, and 'the Canadian tunnelling companies ... saw even less of their field and army troops compatriots than they did of daylight.'[56] They did, however, apply their detailed technical knowledge of mining and tunnelling to solve one of the corps's major problems: high casualty rates from German artillery while the troops were still forming up. At the Somme whole companies had been reduced to half strength, and both the artillery and the engineers found solutions, the first through counter-battery fire, which will be discussed in detail later, the sappers through tunnels.[57]

The engineers, under the direction of Brigadier-General William B. Lindsay, employed five tunnelling companies in excavating new tunnels and enlarging and revetting old ones left by the French and British. Soil conditions were excellent; Vimy's chalk required little reinforcement and could be chipped away quickly with pick and shovel. Elaborate subways appeared, some of them large enough to accommodate whole battalions, complete with lights and ventilation shafts. Eleven of these subways were eventually hollowed out of the chalk twenty-five feet underground, and caves used in quarrying operations going back several hundred years were used to house the troops in safety, if not in comfort.[58] For German shells, in whatever number, could not penetrate the thick, reinforced, overhead cover these subways afforded. Tunnels were important elements of siege warfare, an endeavour the engineers were more than qualified for. Nor could the enemy try to destroy the tunnels in raids; for after three years of bloody warfare on two fronts and the need to reinforce their Austro-Hungarian allies, the German armies in the west no longer had the numbers to carry out offensive operations on anything but a very small scale.

Vimy Ridge was, in no small part, an artillery battle, and the gunners began operations while the infantry was still training on the taped course. Guns were plentiful; in a battle where Byng hoped, as much as possible, to replace blood and muscle with explosive and steel, the Canadian Corps deployed 245 heavy guns and howitzers, 480 of the ubiquitous eighteen-pounders, and 138 4.5-inch howitzers. The British I Corps was also prepared to add 132 heavy pieces and 102 field guns. The Canadians thus had one heavy gun for every twenty yards of front and a field gun for every ten yards, twice the density available in the Somme battles.[59] Prior to z (zero-day) minus twenty days, corps policy was to harass enemy movement behind his own lines by day and night, and a considerable portion of the 4.5-inch howitzers fired barrages to destroy communication trenches. From z minus twenty to z minus seven many of these same batteries fell silent; in this same period each division relied on six eighteen-pounder batteries and two howitzer batteries to cut barbed wire, harass the enemy day and night, and bombard German defences. Meanwhile, gunners, infantrymen, and engineers could continue to build gun positions, roads, ammunition dumps, and observation posts. From z minus six to z-day about three-quarters of available guns broke their self-imposed silence to cut wire, destroy trenches, and harass movement. Not only was the corps expending more ammunition than ever before, it was doing so more accurately; adopting French principles, gunners observed each round in the preliminary phases of each bombardment, until batteries could get on target.[60]

At Vimy 16 Squadron of the Royal Flying Corps (RFC) lost three of its twenty-four aircraft from 1 to 13 April, observing the fall of shot for Canadian and British batteries. Spotting artillery rounds was not easy for the airmen, or the observers for that matter; for in order to avoid anti-aircraft fire the pilot had to keep making short turns, dives, or side-slips, while also operating the transmitter, if one was available. The observer had to keep an eye on his target through all this activity, record the fall of shot, and either send his report back by lamp or drop it over a headquarters if wireless was not available. Airmen also took photographs of the German lines for closer study, though the task was no easy one in a plane loaded down with heavy equipment at the mercy of German fighters. The squadron carried out its aerial photography missions with eighteen aircraft at a time, fifteen to defend the three that actually held the cameras. Technicians developed enough photographs and reprints to hand them out to junior officers as supplements for their maps, and, in the week ending 1 April, 9,101 reprints were issued.[61]

German aircraft were also busy, coming over in squadron strength to engage British and Allied pilots as the air war approached a climax, soon to be known to RFC flyers as 'Bloody April.' By 11 March the 2nd Division was reporting an abnormal incidence of German aerial patrolling; enemy aircraft operated with impunity, since the RFC, already hard-pressed to carry out its many tasks in the face of superior aircraft, was stretched to the limit. On 24 March the 3rd Division reported that German aircraft were flying very low, and on 28 March the 4th Division experienced severe bombardment while German observers flew close to the trenches. Every week from 7 March to 12 April corps headquarters reported an increase in German air activity;[62] there was little doubt the Germans knew what the Canadians were up to, though artillery preparations would have given away their intentions in any case.

With new technology and techniques, gunners began to shell neutral and enemy territory, a large area that can be separated into four main sectors. The first was just forward of the Canadian lines – the barbed wire obstacles similar to those that had caused so much trouble on the Somme; the second consisted of the German defences proper – the trenches, strong-points, and machine-gun nests the Canadian battalions were to attack; the third was actually behind the enemy's defences and consisted of his artillery position; and in the last area the gunners shelled roads, ammunition dumps, and assembly areas behind the German lines to hinder the movement of reserves, food, and ammunition to the front. This final task was also supposed to lower German morale by interfering with reliefs and preventing deliveries of hot food. Each presented its own particular problems and so was allocated its own artillery batteries chosen in accordance with their calibers and thus with what they could best achieve. Often, a few days of experimentation preceded particular tasks to determine which type of trench mortar, gun, or howitzer would obtain the best results.

In 1917 only artillery had the means to destroy the thick belts of wire that had caused so much trouble on the Somme, and gunners soon had access to the technology they needed to turn their shells into wire-cutters. General Shrapnel's eighteenth-century invention was a timer that could be placed in a shell so it would explode in the air, spreading bullets over a wide area; it was thus an anti-personnel weapon and proved useful in rolling barrages, the shells exploding above the heads of advancing infantry to spread destruction to their front. The timers were not sufficiently precise to detonate high-explosive shells within wire obstacles. Before Vimy, however, the 106 fuse appeared in British ordnance; based on the French *fusée instantanée allongée*, it had been under development at Woolwich since the fall of 1915 and was first used on a large scale during the Arras offensive. Using it, a shell exploded on impact; the principle was far more primitive than Shrapnel's but far more useful for cutting wire; for if the fuse was sensitive enough, it would set off the shell when it hit the wire or just as it struck the ground, in either case exploding within the barrier. The 106 fuse was not only sensitive, it added a mushroom-shaped cap that accelerated the detonation of the main charge, ensuring that it would go off in the obstacle, not deep in the ground.[63]

With the availability of the 106 fuse in large quantities, it became necessary to decide which of the corps's great variety of guns would be most effective at cutting wire. Since the eighteen-pounders were most plentiful, these batteries were the first to try; but results were far from satisfactory, since their shells packed too little explosive. Light mortars were next, since their high rate of fire, up to twenty rounds per minute, might saturate the barrier with ten-pound bombs; but patrols and raiders reported little damage. Finally, artillery officers decided to use bigger guns, whose large explosive charges would pulverize the belts of barbed wire if their fuses detonated them in the barrier. Thus from 9:00 a.m.

until 2:00 p.m. on 5 April the front trenches in some areas were cleared so 4.5-inch howitzers could fire at the German obstacles; results were finally judged satisfactory.[64]

The experiments were expensive; most of the ammunition expended from 2 to 5 April had been wasted. With still much of the wire left unscathed, the corps began to run out of 106 fuses, and in some areas the situation was aggravated by poor observation, because the Germans had placed wire not only in no man's land but also around strong points and in front of trenches in the second and third lines of defence. The artillery's observers could not always see these barriers, some of which were on the other side of the ridge's crest or in dead ground, but the gunners developed several expedients to bring their guns and howitzers to bear. The first was a simple matter of pushing observers far out into no man's land. To hit barriers far behind the front line, guns themselves were moved into temporary positions close to the Canadian forward trenches, while air observation called in the fall of shot on the other side of the ridge. It was not until 7 April, however, that divisional commanders, relying on reports from patrols, declared themselves happy with the results.[65]

Behind the wire barriers lay trenches, dugouts, strong points, and machine-gun nests. The gunners systematically pounded as many of these as infantry raids, aerial observation, and their own forward observers could find; trench mortars also joined in the destruction, though heavy winds blew their low-velocity shells off course and seriously decreased accuracy. The ammunition shortages of 1915 and 1916 were no more, and shells rained down on the German positions by day and night; mortars and guns alike fired at the front line, 'smashing it to bits.'[66] Communication trenches between the main lines of defence were also destroyed, an easier task, since in most cases they were enfiladed by Canadian artillery. German infantrymen exhausted themselves trying to repair the damage at night, often under artillery and machine-gun fire designed to hamper their work. Thus, destroying the trenches not only lowered the enemy's capacity to fight by removing some of his defences, it also tired him out.[67]

Using thermometers to take into account the ammunition's temperature, testing the muzzle velocity of each gun at frequent intervals, and watching each spotting round as it fell, the gunners took a heavy toll of German defences. Concentrating on tactical points instead of bombarding the whole front line at random, artillery achieved good results from the Canadians' point of view. For example, patrols and raids of the 1st Division reported only one trench unscathed in their area.[68] Thélus, one of the 31st Battalion's objectives, ceased to exist, though here weight of shell was more important than accuracy: 'The damage done to Thélus from our artillery fire is extraordinary. Buildings are demolished, trenches obliterated and wire smashed to atoms; there is hardly an inch of ground but bears witness to the tremendous effect of our guns.'[69]

On 27 January 1917 Lieutenant-Colonel A.G.L. McNaughton became the corps's first counter-battery staff officer.[70] His first task was to locate the German guns, and there was no dearth of means to do this. Air observation reports and photographs were sent immediately to the gunners who would bombard the targets, while forward observation officers noted what they saw through their field-glasses and snipers passed along information seen through their telescopes. Signallers decrypted and translated German radio messages and passed them on to McNaughton, while the infantry, in its continuous raiding, captured documents, maps, and prisoners. In identifying the regiments that faced them, the Canadians could determine how many there were and hence estimate how many artillery batteries supported them. It also saw some German artillery positions at close hand and could report on the type and calibre of guns located near the front line. Intelligence officers processed the information thus gathered or sent it directly to McNaughton's headquarters; the counter-battery officer also had his own sources of information in the sound-ranging batteries.

By all available means the Canadian counter-battery staff discovered 176 of the estimated 212 guns the Germans had available to defend themselves, an 83 per cent success rate. The results were dramatic, especially when seen in the light of normal trench warfare; in a few months Canadian counter-battery gunners gained partial mastery over the battlefield, a position they had never achieved before. In January 1917, before McNaughton's policies were implemented, artillery duels similar to those of 1915 were common, and battalions often complained of slow artillery responses to their sos calls and noted the accuracy of German barrages. In February, however, some battalions reported that their mortars had bombarded German positions under cover of the counter-battery units, with little or no retaliation. After the battle, artillerymen discovered that some of their positions had been under German observation, but not shelled, and some artillery brigades reported surprisingly low casualties.[71]

Behind the lines were roads and dumps the Germans needed to move up food and ammunition. Rifles and machine-guns need bullets, and the Canadians sought to use their artillery to diminish the effectiveness of German weapons and the men who wielded them by cutting off their supplies. As early as January the diarist for the 11th Artillery Brigade described an action designed to hamper a German relief operation: 'From information received by a prisoner captured by the 7th. Can. Inf. Bde., an enemy relief was expected in the evening. Accordingly the enemies (*sic*) main routes to the trenches as described by the prisoner were shelled periodically from 5:00 P.M. to 3.00 A.M. by 13 Pdrs, 18 Pdrs, 4.5, and 6, Howitzers.'[72] In the weeks before Vimy Canadian artillery and machine-guns performed the same kind of interdiction on a massive scale, while gunners and machine-gunners remained in close touch to ensure their fire overlapped for best effect. Most of the trench destruction was carried out by day, but harassing fire took place at night, when the Germans attempted to reinforce and resupply their front-line trenches. Some units went without proper rations for days at a time as roads and communication trenches were swept by artillery and machine-gun fire. The German official history titled its section on the period leading up to the assault 'The Week of Suffering.'[73]

Finally, beginning on 5 April, the guns fired creeping barrages for the last three or four hours before dawn. These, combined with harassing fire, ensured the Germans would become accustomed to increased artillery activity in the morning twilight hours. By practising the creeping barrage for several days over the same ground through which the troops would advance, the gunners sorted out problems of observation before they could interfere with the actual attack.[74]

By 8 April 1917 preparations were complete. The men were trained in the tactics of the platoon and the movements of the battalion, having learned or relearned the use of bomb, rifle, rifle-grenade, and machine-gun not only on the training ground but in raids against their entrenched enemy. Whole divisions had gone over the taped course time and time again until the men became somewhat disgruntled with their officers' silly games, but they had learned every detail of the job at hand. The gunners had practised cooperation with the infantry in one raid after another and were adopting new technology and practices to engage the enemy's wire, trenches, and guns. The engineers had made their direct contribution to the battle in constructing or reconstructing tunnels which sheltered those members of the Canadian Corps who would be the first to move across no man's land when officers gave the signal to begin the attack. In war, however, no amount of planning or preparation can guarantee success, and it remained to be seen how all these elements would work together in a full-scale corps assault.

5

Spring and Summer 1917:
Developing Fire and Movement

On 9 April 1917 the four divisions of the Canadian Corps successfully stormed German defences in a battle that soon became part of Canada's national mythology. Of greater importance here, it was a notable example of the Canadian Corps's use of the tools of war within a well-defined tactical system. It has already been seen how the men of the corps trained to use their weapons effectively over the taped course; during the battle proper they used every technological means at their disposal to take enemy-held territory. The artillery with its guns and howitzers and the infantry with its bombs, rifles, and Lewis guns worked together to bring both long-range and short-range weapons to bear on a heavily entrenched enemy; when battalions advanced, their movements were protected by artillery fire until their platoons were close enough to the enemy to use their own weapons. At Ypres, and sometimes on the Somme, courage had not been enough to achieve victory; at Vimy soldiers had the means to reach their objectives.

On 8 April artillery trench-destruction, wire-cutting, and harassment fire ended, and infantrymen braced themselves for the move across no man's land. The creeping barrage was about to come into its own; the British, French, and Canadians on the Western Front had discovered that it was not enough for artillery to shell German positions before an attack; the bombardment had to accompany the assault. Trench systems were far more difficult to destroy than anyone had imagined and deep dugouts, protecting machine-gun crews and riflemen, were notoriously immune from high explosive and shrapnel. There was no such thing as a perfect gun or shell, or a perfect knowledge of atmospheric conditions; so hitting a small target like a dugout was, to some degree, a matter of chance. The gunners, by firing on German positions until the last possible instant while simultaneously putting up a moving curtain of destruction a few hundred yards in front of the infantry, would ensure that German defenders would remain in their dugouts until attackers were close enough to use their own weapons. Support barrages involved massed machine-guns, and all together would ensure that fire would accompany, not simply precede, the assault.[1]

Each brigade had eighty machine-guns of various types; the brigade machine-gun company contained sixteen Vickers, and each infantry battalion had two Colts and fourteen Lewis guns. At Vimy and elsewhere these guns filled two roles. The heavier weapons, the Vickers and Colts, were a supplement to artillery, firing at German strong points, communication trenches, artillery positions, and crossroads. The Vickers was best adapted to the indirect fire role, since it was fitted with a locking mechanism that allowed gunners to set it at high elevations, so in the final barrage, 150 machine-guns were used this way. The use of automatic weapons to fire indirectly at the enemy's positions was the subject of some controversy. The main proponent of this tactic was Brigadier-General Raymond Brutinel of the Canadian Machine Gun Corps, who believed that his machine-guns could fire over the heads of the advancing infantry at targets the gunners could not see themselves. The machine-gunner argued that a constant stream of bullets was more effective than intermittent artillery fire in denying the Germans the use of an intersection, for example; but for the technique to work massive quantities of ammunition were necessary. Opponents, McNaughton among them, did not believe machine-gun bullets were anywhere nearly as effective as eighteen-pounders firing shrapnel.[2] Donald Fraser had problems of his own with the technique: 'Tonight I shot away a couple of thousand rounds of indirect fire. Indirect fire is not very satisfactory – you cannot see your target and, of course, do not know what damage, if any, is done. Besides, the belts have to be refilled and it is a blistery job forcing the shells in with the palm of the hand without protective covering.'[3] Putting machine-guns to such use may well have seemed paradoxical at a time when the artillery was insisting on every one of its own rounds being spotted.

Also in support of the infantry were trench mortars. For the assault of 9 April the Canadian Corps used between sixty-eight and ninety-six small two-inch mortars at different phases of the attack and twenty of the massive 9.45-inch trench mortars throughout the day. The latter laid smoke to mask German positions and give the attacking infantry an added element of concealment and surprise. Most of the smaller mortars, however, accompanied the infantry to take out strong points along the way; two went with each battalion, which needed a total of twenty men just to carry ammunition. They followed the last wave to protect flanks during the assault and break up counter-attacks during consolidation, and, though the mortars served their purpose well in some cases, silencing machine-gun positions with a few well-placed rounds, they were very difficult to operate and easy targets for German artillery. Their firing mechanisms broke if mishandled, and hauling the mortars across no man's land aggravated the problem. Worse was the mortar's propensity to use far more ammunition than the infantry could carry. Though the British Army's General Staff felt that the mortar was useful, even if only twenty or thirty rounds could be carried with it, these were only enough to engage one strong point or trench. The Stokes mortar, basically a three-inch water pipe, required eight soldiers to carry it and thirty bombs; the mountings were too heavy and so were often discarded, forcing the gunner to aim and fire by hand – an extremely inaccurate technique.[4] Unlike the Lewis gun, which fit neatly into the Canadian platoon organization, the trench mortar could be used by the infantry only with much expended effort, and it would take another year to develop techniques that took advantage of its potential.

Artillery support during the attack conformed to a complex plan made up of five different tasks: the first was the creeping barrage, formed of four dozen batteries of eighteen-pounders; the second was the standing barrage on the German front line, also formed of eighteen-pounders, though with only three dozen batteries; the third was a more powerful standing barrage with eighteen batteries of 4.5-inch howitzers; fourth was McNaughton's counter-battery work, now less important than the barrages, which would continue throughout the battle with four to eight batteries; and, finally, some guns stood by to engage targets of opportunity called in by forward observers. The program was orchestrated minute by minute for eight and a half hours.[5]

To understand the artillery plan's complexity, it would be best to follow the program laid out for a single brigade, in this case the 7th. With zero-hour as the moment when the troops would begin to advance, artillery from z to z plus four minutes would bombard the enemy's front line with an intense shrapnel barrage, under cover of which the infantry would creep as close to the German lines as possible. From z plus four to plus ten the curtain of fire would lift 150 yards and the first wave would move in to capture the position while mop-up parties made their way up communication trenches as close to the barrage as possible. At z plus ten the shelling would begin to move fifty yards per minute until it reached the first objective, where it would remain until z plus eighteen, assault troops clearing the trenches behind it. At z plus eighteen the barrage would lift again, beyond the first objective, so infantry could mop it up and consolidate their position; there it would remain for fifteen minutes, allowing time for the second wave to take its jump-off positions in front of the first objective. At z plus thirty-four the barrage would then move off at fifty yards per minute to a point 150 yards beyond the second objective, where it would remain for an hour to allow the third wave to form up. At z plus 110 the shelling would again continue until it reached the final objective, where it would remain until z plus 146, and then it would move beyond the crest.[6]

After the preliminary bombardments were completed and the gunners' plans were in place, it was time for the infantry, after weeks of training on the taped course and raiding the German lines, to form up and prepare to attack. The first assault would consist of about 15,000 men from the corps, all of whom had to be placed in jump-off trenches before zero-hour; the leading brigades had to make use of all available protective features. The 8th placed its first wave in the observation line and jump-off trenches, its second wave in the front line, its third in the support line, and its last in tunnels or caves. The 31st Battalion of the 6th Brigade used the tunnels to move forward towards its jump-off positions, assembling its troops without loss in spite of heavy shelling from German guns.[7] McNaughton's counter-battery gunners had not found all of them.

The men who took up their positions packed far less on their backs than they had on the Somme, carrying 120 rounds of ammunition, grenades, a rifle, a bayonet, and an entrenching tool; they had no blankets or packs, and some units left their greatcoats behind for ease of movement, in spite of the snow. Leather jerkins were supplied for those whose task was to fall on the barbed wire and allow their comrades to pass, box respirators in case either side used gas, and a ground sheet that served as blanket, poncho, or shelter. Men could also be assigned to carry wire-cutters, flares, empty sandbags, picks, shovels, and hedging gloves for working with barbed wire,[8] but they carried little in the way of rations, tools, or defensive stores like barbed wire and pickets. Still heavily loaded, with about forty pounds of equipment, they were at least capable of a quick walk or short run, instead of trudging through no man's land bent over from eighty pounds of kit.

At 5:30 on the morning of 9 April 983 guns and mortars began bombarding the German defences, each gun firing three rounds per minute. Howitzers worked their way up communication trenches, while every fire trench, sunken road, or suspicious area was bombarded up to the time the creeping barrage reached it, when the guns of the standing barrage would shift to points on the next objective. As troops moved forward, officers and sergeants tried to keep them as close to the creeping barrage as possible, shrapnel shells exploding above their heads to spread bullets towards the enemy; some rounds fell short, and the 31st battalion was forced to slow its advance when casualties began to mount.[9] William Green of the 4th Battalion was witness to men who fell to the creeping barrage: 'An incident that stands out in my mind was when one of our own shells which incidentally was a dud ... cut the head off a machine gunner and took the leg off a Lance Corporal beside him ... Bill Hopkinson also got a leg wound from our barrage.'[10] Had the shell actually exploded, shrapnel would have caused even more severe casualties.

To cross no man's land infantrymen adopted the formations they had learned on the taped course. Normally, a platoon advanced in two lines, with the riflemen and rifle grenadiers in front and the Lewis gunners and bombers following close behind, but variations were possible. One could keep the rifle grenadiers and Lewis gunners in the rear line, since their weapons were to be used to support attacks on German posts; each wave, then, would have two lines with mutually supporting weapons. The 28th Battalion placed riflemen and rifle grenadiers in the first line, bombers and Lewis gunners in the second, and moppers-up in the third. A section of riflemen advanced on each flank, while Lewis gunners and bombers moved up the centre, available to aid their comrades on either side – the bomb was to be the main trench-clearing weapon. Four or five yards separated each man from the next, with fifteen to twenty yards between lines and fifty to 100 between waves, though the latter could be bunched up to ensure rear waves were not caught by German shelling. Each company would advance in two waves, with two platoons forward and two back, while units bringing up the rear were to advance in artillery formation, or in columns instead of lines, which were easier to manage, since the troops did not have to check constantly to ensure they maintained their proper position but only had to follow the man in front. These columns would form into lines and waves when their turn came to leap-frog through their comrades and take over the advance (see figure 2).[11]

The Canadians did not necessarily follow these techniques to the letter; formations differed from battalion to battalion, given the circum-

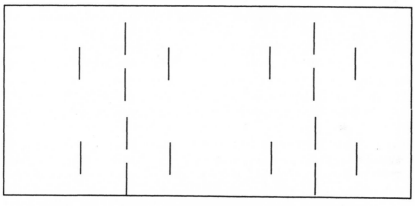

Figure 2

28th Battalion formations, Vimy Ridge. The figure shows one-half the battalion; the other half, which would have been advancing on its right or left, would have been identical.

Based on description in RG9, III, v.4142, folder 5, file 1, 28th Battalion, Order No. 162A, 7 April 1917 stances under which troops would have to move and fight. The 42nd Battalion, for example, moved with two companies forward, each with one platoon in front, while one mop-up party of about fifty men followed each company, with the other two companies of the battalion bringing up the rear, ready to leap-frog through their comrades at the intermediate objective. The 8th Brigade used similar tactics on a larger scale, crossing no man's land with three battalions forward and one back as a reserve, as ordered by Major-General L.J. Lipsett, commanding the 3rd Division. Each battalion would advance with one company in front, which was to capture a preallocated stretch of the German front line and support trenches, where the next company in line would leap-frog towards the second objective, where the third and fourth companies would form up to attack the ultimate objective at the crest of the ridge. The fourth company of each battalion was also to act as a reserve in case of unexpected turns in the battle (see figure 3).[12]

These units, then, would attack in depth instead of throwing all their companies at the front line in the hope of breaking through. It had become obvious that it was not necessary to inflict heavy casualties on an infantry battalion to force it to stop. Maintaining a steady pace behind the creeping barrage, fighting a series of small actions against machine-gun positions and strong points, only to move off to repeat the process at the next objective, was exhausting work. Companies eventually ground to a halt, with troops panting and sweating, having expended all their energy in what was essentially a war of movement – movement forward to capture the parapets before German riflemen and machine-gunners could prepare to defend themselves, and movement from position to position, taking cover as rifle grenades, bombs, Lewis gunners, or sometimes even artillery kept enemy defenders from returning effective fire, and then attacking with bomb and rifle. The only way to maintain momentum was to ensure companies would be replaced when they could go no further.

Advancing in formation also solved another problem posed by the modern battlefield – orientation. Powerful artillery pieces destroyed landmarks and even changed the ground's general features as villages, copses, and roads disappeared into the cratered fields; while on the day of the attack, mist, dust, and smoke made it difficult to pick one's way through no man's land and maintain direction. Though all armies on the Western Front used smokeless powder, many attacks, including some of the brigade assaults at Vimy Ridge, were accompanied by artillery barrages firing smoke shells at enemy positions to mask the advance.

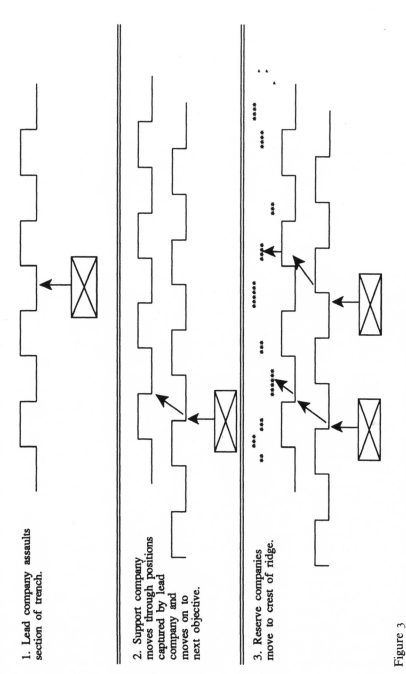

1. Lead company assaults section of trench.

2. Support company moves through positions captured by lead company and moves on to next objective.

3. Reserve companies move to crest of ridge.

Figure 3

Based on descriptions in RG 9, III, v.4163, folder 10, file 1, 8th Canadian Infantry Brigade to 3 Canadian Division, 9 February 1917, and 7th Canadian Infantry Brigade Operation Order No. 65, 7 January 1917

Also, the creeping barrage itself had smoke shells mixed in with the shrapnel so advancing troops could see and follow it more easily. Modern technology had rendered the battlefield faceless, grim, and dense with smog. Advancing in formations practised day and night on taped courses helped prevent individuals from getting lost as they followed section and platoon leaders navigating across the deadly landscape with maps, compasses, and air photos, trying to pick out landmarks that had not been destroyed or masked. Some units still became lost, but most managed to grope their way through the near-featureless terrain.[13]

In some areas the combination of standing and creeping barrages, added to the harassment fire of the previous weeks, had so shaken German regiments that they were in no condition to fight, and Canadian units had only to take over their trenches and send prisoners to the rear. Lieutenant M. Dunsford, writing to his fellow employees at the Canadian Bank of Commerce, explained afterwards: 'I expect you have read all about the big battle in the papers. There was not very much excitement where I was. I only saw two live Germans on the way [and] two dead ones until reaching our objective. I think our artillery barrage had chased them all down into their dug-outs and they afterwards came out in bunches and were taken prisoners.'[14] One of the soldiers with the 49th Battalion had a similar experience: 'We went out in the morning and started over the top. Oh there was some fighting but not too much, the Hun didn't stay loo long you know. The artillery bombardment prior to the attack was far in away the biggest we had ever put on ... there was still a few hadn't got out of their dugouts. But they were quite willing to when we got up there, they'd thrown up their arms and we just helped them back.'[15] The battalion lost about fifty all ranks from 9 to 13 April.[16]

Not all Canadian troops had such an easy time of it. Though gaps in the wire were common, and in some areas the wire had been destroyed altogether, it would have been overly optimistic on the part of the infantry to expect a perfect line of advance. Each platoon chose two men as wire-cutters, and gave them wire-breakers they could attach to their rifles; throughout the day these troops were called upon to cut their way through barriers that still stood here and there. The soldiers of the 4th Battalion found wire almost intact when they approached the crest of the ridge; so under cover of the now rare Colt machine-guns, firing from the original front line, three men cut lanes through the barrier.[17]

More dangerous than sparse barbed wire were German machine-guns: some of their crews made their way out of the dugouts in time to meet the Canadian attack, while others emerged after the first waves had gone by and fired upon Canadian reserves moving up to the front. Canadian artillery, for the most part, had kept German machine-gunners in their dugouts as long as possible, but the timetable was strict, and guns allocated to standing and creeping barrages could not be called upon to engage individual targets. Though there were extra guns available to the infantry in case particularly difficult positions held them up they rarely came into action, since advancing troops experienced the usual communications problems. In the 1st Division only one was used, when the 14th Battalion found itself under fire from an unscathed machine-gun post; within five minutes a 4.5-inch howitzer was turned onto the spot and destroyed the position.[18]

Otherwise, the infantry had to rely on the weapons in its own hands to destroy German machine-gunners. Though the corps had tanks and trench mortars to support the advance, the former broke down too quickly and the latter could not bring enough ammunition to be of any great help; so British tactics in such cases called for a Lewis-gun section to open fire and draw the defenders' attention while a rifle section worked its way around the flank to attack with rifle or bayonet. Rifle-grenades, the infantry's portable artillery, could support the final rush. Each strong point or machine-gun nest thus called for the platoon to use all its available resources and personnel. In one case the 14th Battalion, advancing as part of the 3rd Brigade, came under heavy fire from four machine-guns located in one of the major German trenches, the *Eisener Krenz Weg*. There was no artillery fire available, and communications were difficult in any case; so Lewis gunners advanced, firing from the hip to force German gunners to stay under cover. Two of the positions were destroyed with hand-grenades; one of the others was captured by Lieutenant B.F. Davidson, who shot the crew with his revolver; and the last was captured by the company sergeant-major, J.F. Hurley, who bayoneted the three men in the post. With McNaughton's counter-battery gunners effectively suppressing German artillery, machine-guns inflicted the great majority of assault casualties on Vimy Ridge.[19]

In the confusion and haze of battle, formations often broke down and tactics became a matter of instinct and initiative; and when platoons were separated or annihilated, small groups of individuals tried to carry on as best they could with the weapons at hand. When set-piece platoon assaults were impossible, the Canadians relied on bombs to break through enemy lines or silence strong points; the explosive devices were important enough for the 42nd Battalion to have six men from each company carry, in haversacks, 140 bombs and rifle-grenades among them. Each platoon had a bombing section, each thrower carrying ten grenades and each carrier twenty; they were also armed with revolvers. Each rifle-grenadier carried fifteen grenades and fifty rounds of blank ammunition to launch them.[20]

The Canadians used two main types of grenade: the Mills Number 5, which was thrown by hand, and the Mills Number 23, introduced in late 1916, essentially a Number 5 fitted to a rod so it could be fired from a rifle. (Using the same grenade in two different roles eased logistical burdens.) The Number 23 was the most successful of the British rodded-type grenades and could be attached to different lengths of rod to vary its range.[21] Each platoon had a section of bombers and another of rifle grenadiers, and both were very active on 9 April, the 1st Battalion noting that 'Rifle Grenades were used to overcome machine guns with marked success,'[22] while the 5th Battalion used its bombers and rifle grenadiers to destroy machine-gun nests blocking its way to the Red Line, and platoons of the 7th Battalion consciously broke up their formation so their bombers could fight their way up communication trenches and silence parties of German riflemen hiding in shell-holes. Private William Milne, who was to receive a posthumous Victoria Cross for his courage, destroyed a machine-gun nest by crawling on his hands and knees until he was close enough to toss a grenade into the position, while other members of Milne's battalion, the 16th, came across a machine-gun position made of concrete hidden in a haystack and forced the crew to surrender by scoring several direct hits on the bunker with rifle-grenades. At Bois de Ville members of the 6th Brigade captured enemy artillery by knocking out the guns with Mills Number 23s and routing the gunners in a bayonet charge.[23]

Lewis guns accompanied the infantry, one section per platoon. A Lewis-gun section was formed of nine men: a non-commissioned officer in command; the number 1, who carried and fired the gun; the number 2, who assisted him; and six others to carry ammunition, act as scouts, and help out should the leader or gunner become a casualty. Each gun needed thirty-two forty-seven-round drums of ammunition. Lewis-gun crews found that the German machine-guns in their trenches or strong points had a limited traverse; so a Lewis gun firing from an oblique angle forced members of the German crew to shift their weapon to defend themselves, allowing bombers, rifle-grenadiers, and riflemen to attack from the flank. The Canadians also used German weapons when possible, and battalions detailed men to search for ammunition on the battlefield and use it to bring captured machine-guns into action.[24]

The infantry at Vimy received little support from the other combat arms of the corps. Only the 2nd Division had tank support, with eight of the vehicles to help it through Thélus, but no one expected them to be of much use in the attack on the ridge. The staff officers of the corps had warned that 'The infantry must not rely on Tanks. The Tanks will cooperate with the infantry, but the absence of an expected Tank should in no way affect the Infantry programme.'[25] Cavalry did manage to engage the enemy but suffered heavy casualties from German machine-guns as it attempted to deploy along the roads behind enemy lines. The Canadian Light Horse captured ten prisoners, but itself was forced back by machine-gun fire.[26]

Keeping the infantry in touch with its own headquarters required effective communications; for troops could not advance far without reserves of men and supplies, and these reserves could not be sent where they were needed unless commanders knew what was happening at the front. To ensure messages got through, the corps relied on a wide variety of techniques. Linesmen, with the help of infantry work parties, buried twenty-one miles of cable and drove poles into the ground to within 2,000 yards of the front; when they were linked up, telephone conversations were possible between higher headquarters along a further sixty-six miles of cable. Wireless sets were distributed among brigade headquarters to allow them to send reports to their divisions, and the leading infantry carried power buzzers, of which more will be said later, which could send Morse code through the ground. Pigeons, lamps, flags, and runners were to take care of any other eventuality.[27]

After the Somme the communicators of the corps had worked out an efficient system of forward communications relying on the telephone. A division would have about four miles of trench available for burying – seven feet deep – twenty-five pairs of cable, six for the infantry, eighteen for the artillery, and one for the signal service. The Brigade Signal Section was responsible for laying wire down the middle of the formation's sector; so battalion signallers had but to tap their phones into this main line, which connected with a brigade report centre, which in turn held all possible means of communication needed to send messages to division headquarters or supporting artillery. Messages from battalions thus passed through brigade headquarters and then on to the artillery or division headquarters. The report centre was established as far forward as possible, a signal party leaving the forward trenches with the last wave of infantry, ten minutes after zero. At Vimy the tunnels were a great help, since they protected the miles of telephone wire that ran through them, but forward of the Canadian front trenches linesmen were kept busy repairing wire destroyed by the artillery of both sides.[28]

To maintain communications, the wire had to be kept whole, and according to Captain Duncan E. Macintyre, 'The trench telephones could be exasperating things at times, although signallers worked like heroes to maintain the lines under shell fire. When a line was hit, both ends would be flung far apart and a signaller would have to ... find the break and mend it. He could follow one end of the wire by letting it run through his hand as he walked, but the other end might be yards away, and he would have to locate and test it and then make the repair, often as not in darkness.'[29] To ensure further that telephones would remain in service, wire was laddered, with two parallel lines laid with crosspieces connecting them at regular intervals; British signallers developed the technique after the battles of 1915 had demonstrated telephone wire's vulnerability. If one line was cut between crosspieces, the system would continue to function; to sever communications it was necessary to cut both lines between crosspieces.[30] Results from all systems were mixed; whereas the 1st Division later reported that it had rarely used visual signals, wireless, or power buzzers because the telephones had worked so well, Brigadier-General Victor Odlum of the 11th Brigade had to go forward to check on the situation in the middle of the battle when communications failed completely.[31]

For units smaller than battalions telephone communication was out of the question; since companies and platoons were too numerous to supply with wire and moved too quickly and erratically to follow effectively with signal sections, the great variety of signalling techniques was mainly devised with the attacking companies in mind. Flags and lamps were sometimes useful, as long as they were visible. 'Carrier pigeons were tried, and indeed an extensive organization was built up for the purpose. Unfortunately it produced more jokes than useful results.'[32] Dogs did little better, for infantrymen adopted them as pets.

Power buzzers, or earth induction telegraph sets, were the most novel – though not necessarily most useful – technical means to accompany the assault on 9 April. The instrument evolved from listening devices developed in the late nineteenth century and was first used on a large scale during the Russo-Japanese War. A telephone functions by sending and receiving electrical impulses down a wire; they induce a magnetic field along the wire which can be picked up by enemy antennae, usually loops of wire, laid on the ground several hundred yards away. Such listening sets could also receive electrical impulses from a buzzer, a well-named device that produces an intermittent buzzing signal. By the end of October 1916, 500 power buzzer sets were available to the BEF, each made up of a transmitter with a hand-driven alternator, which produced a high-pitched buzz; a listening set acted as receiver and was able to pick up transmissions from as far as 2,000 yards away. Its main drawback was that the transmitter needed a steady supply of bulky accumulators – rechargeable electric cells – if it was to operate for any length of time. Signallers with the transmitters went in with the attacking infantry and operated in Morse code, while amplifiers were kept at Brigade headquarters. The device worked in only one direction, and ground conditions had to be just right; if the land was fairly level and not too torn up by snell holes and craters, the buzzer was the quickest way for the advancing infantry to report their position and any problems they may have encountered.

As in all prior battles, runners proved the most efficient means of getting messages to battalion headquarters, though the work was dangerous. Hand-carried messages were clear, and the runners got through more often than not.[33] On a battlefield where the pace of the advance was that of a slow walk and attackers often halted to regroup, runners were quick enough to keep headquarters apprised of the situation at the front.

Aircraft played an important role in following the infantry's progress at Vimy Ridge, and contact patrols went out at predesignated times to find out how far the Canadians had advanced and check on the enemy's defences. Forward units gave the aircraft their positions by lighting coloured flares, and the airplane's observer could then send back what he had seen over wireless or drop messages over headquarters. Soldiers could identify the brigade they belonged to with a two-letter code they flashed at the aircraft once they had gained its attention with flares. A typical flight would make its way to the front, where the pilot could identify the level of headquarters by emblems it displayed – brigade headquarters with a three-quarter white circle and battalion headquarters with a half-circle – and then fly towards the advancing infantry from the rear, flashing a white light. Forward troops could then give their position by lighting flares or flashing mirrors to denote their line of advance. They could add further messages by using a white ground-sheet to reflect the light from a lamp, sending the two-letter code that identified the brigade and another two letters to inform the pilot if the unit was short of bombs, held up by wire, short of ammunition, or held up by machine-guns. Other two-letter codes asked the artillery to lengthen its range or begin a barrage. Thus 'CB space O' meant that the 2nd Brigade's progress was barred by barbed wire and it wanted artillery support.[34]

The whole complex system of technology and technicians worked well. On the morning of 9 April the 1st and 2nd divisions reached the first trenches while defenders were still in their dugouts; by 1:18 in the afternoon the 1st, 2nd, and 3rd divisions were on the crest, having driven 4,000 yards through German defences and beyond. The 4th Division on the far left did not fare as well; its task, including the capture of Hill 145, a prominent feature that offered the Germans excellent observation, was not an easy one. Further, the 87th Battalion's attack failed, mostly because it had ordered a strong point left intact so it could make use of it after the assault – a serious error, since platoon tactics could not come into play until troops were within Lewis-gun and rifle grenade range of the enemy (about 100 yards), and to get there they needed artillery to pound strong points and keep defenders away from the parapets. Though units were willing to advance with insecure flanks, they would not consolidate a position if German artillery and machine-guns enfiladed it; so the 87th Battalion's failure forced partial withdrawals, which affected the entire division's operation. The strong point held out until just before dark.[35]

Historians have suggested other explanations for the division's failure. Desmond Morton and Jack Granatstein in *Marching to Armageddon*, Pierre Berton in *Vimy*, and E.L.M. Burns in *General Mud* contend that the 4th Division's difficulties can be traced to the disastrous raid of 1 March (when gas inflicted heavy losses). Though the division did suffer more casualties than any of the other three in the month preceding the assault on Vimy Ridge, the battalions involved in the raid did better on 9 April than the 87th, which had not been part of the 1 March operation. The 54th Battalion, which lost 226 men in the raid, including its commanding officer, captured all its objectives at Vimy, though it had to carry out a partial withdrawal because of the 87th's failure. The 72nd Battalion, which suffered eighty-eight casualties on 1 March, took three of its four objectives on 9 April. The 73rd lost 161 men in the raid but occupied its objectives within minutes of zero-hour at Vimy. Finally, the 75th Battalion, which lost 221 men, including its commanding officer, on 1 March, remained in its trenches on 9 April because the 87th Battalion, which it was supposed to follow in the assault, ran into trouble.[36] It thus seems clear that that disastrous raid had little effect on the operations of 9 April.

The battle did not end when the Canadians took the crest. As signallers laid wire to new positions and sappers dug communication trenches and built roads, the infantry on the hill sent out small groups to find the enemy and determine whether he intended to counter-attack. Many of these patrols captured guns the Germans had not been able to move away; others fired rifles and Lewis guns at the hard-pressed, retreating enemy. Moving along behind the front waves, machine-gunners struggled forward with their Vickers to stop counter-attacks with steady streams of bullets. Since three men were required just to carry the gun, tripod, and water, however, the Vickers had only a limited mobility and could not be used in the assault wave.[37] In many cases, Colts or Vickers arrived at the crest in time to harass the Germans, who could be seen for miles from the ridge.[38]

Nor was the day over for the gunners; many Canadian units had outrun their artillery support, which in any event could not fire effectively on the reverse slope of the ridge. Some howitzers were still within range but would not be if the Canadians continued their advance, and in the British Expeditionary Force it was dogma that all commanders should prepare for the next attack; so the guns had to move. Bridging parties, following closely on the heels of the attacking infantry, had already crossed no man's land, while engineers with infantry work parties filled craters with rubble and laid plank roads suitable for moving guns and ammunition. Like the infantry, though only after the assault was successful, artillery leap-frogged its way forward to ensure that at least some of the guns would be available if the Germans counter-attacked; for Canadians had often seen artillery break up infantry formations with shrapnel. As each battery found itself out of range, it began to move, and some were in action in no man's land by early afternoon. That so many guns were still functional is surprising; some batteries fired 500 or 600 rounds in eight hours, a few of them continuously, but only a handful of guns – for example, three in the 1st Division – were damaged by the end of the day, none of them seriously.[39]

The infantry set to work to maintain its positions on the ridge, and each battalion in its rear waves carried sixty-six picks and 130 shovels to dig trenches on and below the crest. The troops consolidated in depth; as they captured each feature they set upon it with their tools even if the next wave had already passed through. Since the 4th Division had been unable to take all its objectives, the 3rd prepared to defend its left flank as well as its front, all the way back to the start line.[40] Siege warfare followed the war of movement, and the tools appropriate to both crossed no man's land behind the advancing infantry; one party of fifty engineers from 7 Field Company carried twenty-seven spools of barbed wire with stakes, 200 sandbags, eighty-five shovels, ten picks, five axes, two sets of large wire-cutters, ten sets of small wire-cutters, fifteen pairs of hedging gloves, 6,000 rounds of ammunition, and 100 grenades.[41] Sappers built strong points as the infantry dug trenches, each redoubt made up of several short lengths of trench radiating about twenty-five feet from a common centre. A machine-gun was placed at each extremity, and the whole was circled by barbed wire so it could be defended from all directions; for the Canadians, whose attack tactics called for outflanking German strong points, took precautions to ensure that they themselves would not be outflanked. Barbed wire, as much as possible, was concealed in low ground.[42]

There was little interference during consolidation from the Germans, who limited themselves to the odd shell and long-range sniping with machine-guns. On 10 April intermittent shelling fell on some trenches, but the Germans were not well registered on their targets, and the Canadians had more to fear from their own artillery, which often retaliated against the German guns by bombarding their own front lines; the 42nd Battalion was shelled four times on 10 and 11 April.[43] With the battle over and the infantry on new ground, artillery needed time to register its guns properly.

While the Canadians consolidated, the Germans examined their options; von Falkenhausen retained his rear divisions, not wanting to waste them in counter-attacks against a difficult position. On 10 April Crown Prince Rupprecht accepted the loss of the ridge and withdrew his army a safe distance from observation and fire – the Germans were willing to give up difficult positions to save casualties. Meanwhile, on the left, Odlum's 11th Brigade was replaced by the 10th for the assault on the Pimple, or Hill 145. On 12 April the brigade assaulted with 100 field guns in support, found little opposition in the first two trench lines, but captured the defences on the left only after hard fighting. By the end of the day the Canadians were consolidating their positions on the hill,[44] and the entire ridge was now in Canadian hands.

As happened after the Somme, commanders and staff officers of the Canadian Corps tried to draw lessons from their experiences at Vimy. Major-General L.J. Lipsett, commanding the 3rd Division, attributed success to 'the care taken by the officers, N.C.O.s and men in studying, working out and practising all the details of the various Operations.'[45] Arthur Currie agreed: 'They had trained for this particular job, they had rehearsed the attack many times, and each and every man knew just exactly where he was going in the attack, and what he was going to do when he got there. Every feature of the German defense was studied, and definite plans made for the overcome of every obstacle, in so far as it is humanly possible to make such plans before an attack.'[46] Rehearsal of the movements and formations they would perform on the battlefield had been supplemented by an increased knowledge of the tools of war, and though Currie ascribed the victory in part to the men's confidence, perhaps their expertise with all the various weapons of trench warfare had been more important: 'That confidence was born of good training. The men knew how to shoot straight and how to use their bayonets ... They knew how to use the bomb, the rifle grenade and the machine gun, but best of all they knew the effective combination of these weapons.'[47] Technology requires technicians who know how to use it; at Vimy Ridge the gunners, infantrymen, signallers, and engineers had shown that they were capable of applying available technology to solve the tactical problems of the battlefield.

The price of victory, as always, had been high. In the first two days of battle, when most of the ridge was captured, the corps suffered 7,707 casualties, of whom 2,967 died, and by 14 April 10,602 members of the corps were out of action, of whom 3,598 were dead. Since losses were distributed among all four divisions of the corps, however, individual formations suffered less than they had in previous battles. The hardest hit was the 4th Division; 4,401 of its infantrymen became casualties, or about one in three, while on average each division lost 3,336 men from its infantry battalions, less than at Second Ypres, the first month on the Somme, or the battles for Mount Sorrel. Future battles would be bloodier. The Canadians had captured fifty-four guns, 104 trench mortars, 124 machine-guns, and 4,000 prisoners in a two-and-a-half-mile advance;[48] at the Somme the corps had suffered over 24,000 losses during two and a half months of arduous campaigning for similar gains. The artillery's counter-battery gunners, its insistence on accuracy and observation, and the sheer weight of fire-power at its disposal had helped the infantry get to its objectives; effective training in tactical formations and the intelligent use of bomb, rifle-grenade, rifle, and machine-gun had helped ensure that the infantry would capture the ridge.

Success became a common feature of subsequent Canadian Corps operations, at least in comparison with what was happening elsewhere on the Western Front. Vimy was part of the Battle of Arras; the British followed on 23–24 April with the Second Battle of the Scarpe, where the Canadian Corps attacked the Arleux Loop. The British official history's account of the assault was perhaps overglowing, but it showed that the tactics developed since December 1916 allowed the Canadians to break into, if not through, German defences: 'The Canadian Corps launched its attack on Arleux village with three battalions of the 2nd Brigade (1st Canadian Division) in most gallant and determined fashion, and achieved the only tangible success of the whole operation.'[49] The Third Battle of the Scarpe followed immediately, on 3–4 May, during which the Canadian Corps captured the village of Fresnoy. 'The capture of Fresnoy was the culminating point of the series of brilliant successes by the Canadian Corps during the Arras battles, and the relieving feature of a day which many who witnessed it consider the blackest of the war.'[50] For the time being at least, Canadian Corps tactics, based on British and French models, served the formation well.

After Fresnoy a break in the campaigning gave the Canadian Corps the opportunity to reflect on the Battles of April and May; two of its divisions, the 1st and 2nd, had fought three battles in a month, and it was time to take stock of the results. Technology and its use was a major focus of the various reports and memoranda commanders submitted to Sir Julian Byng and, after 9 June, to the new corps commander, Lieutenant-General Sir Arthur Currie. One of the most prolific of these reporters was Currie himself, supported of course, by the important contributions of his staff. Some of their suggestions were merely minor additions to an already large body of knowledge concerning the tools of war. Air photos, they found, could be used not only to supply the artillery with targets but to locate future positions for battalion head-quarters and report centres, which could be occupied as the advance progressed. The 106 fuse, recently brought into service, came under close scrutiny; gunners had found that thanks to its sensitivity it could be used to break up counter-attacks as well as cut wire, the shell exploding at ground level among unprotected troops.[51] Currie was more than satisfied with the role artillery had played in protecting Canadian soldiers: 'Throughout the operations from April 9th to May 3rd the co-operation between Artillery and Infantry had been the closest imaginable, and to the efforts of the Liaison Officers must be attributed no small share of the success.'[52]

The general was speaking only for the division under his command, which in fact had had excellent artillery support throughout the month-long campaign. The 2nd Division had not been so fortunate, as the events of 3 May demonstrated. At Fresnoy the barrage itself had been late, but worse, counter-battery fire had been totally ineffective, leaving the infantry to attack through a German artillery barrage. On 7 May Brigadier-General H.D.B. Ketchen, commanding the 6th Brigade, complained bitterly that he still could not get a proper response to enemy shelling from his own artillery: 'I wish to draw attention to the most unsatisfactory response to requests from the Infantry for retaliation by our Heavy Artillery. Three different requests were made between 7.30 a.m. and 9.30 a.m. today for Artillery retaliation on enemy trenches, for concentrated and heavy bombardment of our new trenches. The response to these requests was most feeble, and in two instances absolutely NIL.'[53] Though the tactics and technology the heavy artillery used to support both formations was identical, their experiences were different, which is not surprising. Major-General Sir E.W.B. Morrison's Canadian Corps Heavy Artillery, responsible for retaliating against enemy shelling, was hard-pressed to keep up with the infantry's demands. On 1 May it was heavily engaged in bombarding Acheville and Fresnoy, with some shelling of Avion, Chez Bontemps, and La Coulotte; it also carried out a feint barrage at dawn, and trench and wire destruction shoots in the Fresnoy area. Retaliation was not always possible while guns were allocated to such programs. A tactical and technical system that works does not work all the time and, if there was one lesson to be learned from the 2nd Division's experience, it was that gunners needed time to prepare themselves whenever they moved or took on a new task.

Other problems, easier to pin down and solve, cropped up between the battles of Vimy and Fresnoy. At Vimy especially, but in the other battles also, artillery was required to support an attack designed to reach deep into German lines in a short time; at Vimy infantry advanced 4,000 yards, at Arleux 1,400 yards, and at Fresnoy 1,100 yards. Since the guns had to remain far back to begin with, so as to be out of range of German machine-gunners and trench mortars, it was necessary for them to move up as the battle progressed if they were to help the infantry defeat counter-attacks. On many occasions the guns were delayed because no one was available to build the roads they needed across no man's land; for the infantry needed engineers to build strong points on the new front line, leaving few (or none) to help the gunners. Almost anything else – ammunition, machine-guns, barbed wire, and so on –

could be soldier-packed if necessary, but the guns needed horses to pull them and a strong surface to prevent them from sinking into mud and earth they themselves had loosened with the creeping barrage. Currie suggested that each division would need two labour battalions for the sole purpose of building these roads, instead of continuing to take men off the line to do so, most of whom were exhausted from the fighting.[54]

The smaller weapons as well as the large guns were scrutinized. Commanders from Vimy to Fresnoy discovered something the troops had long known: Canadian soldiers rarely used their rifles. Currie insisted the men accept the importance of accurate musketry in warfare; even in dealing with snipers the infantrymen tended to rely on machine-guns rather than on their own weapons. Grenades were a different matter: bombs, or hand-grenades, were most useful for mopping up, since they did not have the range to be of any great use in the attack; thus the front waves in an assault should use rifle-grenades, while bombs were reserved for the closer fighting of the rear waves. Lewis guns, like the rifle-grenades, were important infantry weapons, and gunners at Vimy and after carried them in a sling so they could fire from the hip while moving forward. The trench inventors of the corps spent much time and effort improving the design, so gunners could pull the Lewis out quickly and thus fire while prone if necessary. Trench mortars were more disappointing: keeping them supplied with ammunition in an advance was still a problem; so they were retained near battalion headquarters and sent forward to deal with emergencies and help defend newly consolidated positions.[55]

As with the platoon weapons, so with the platoon. According to Currie, the organization adopted just prior to Vimy – splitting the basic unit into four sections: the Lewis gun, riflemen, bombers, and rifle-grenadiers – was a marked success and bore out the lessons learned at Verdun. (It lasted until the summer of 1918.) 'The new Platoon Organization was tested under battle conditions for the first time and proved ... a great success ... The training on these lines during the winter months had greatly increased the efficiency of the Division and enabled it to carry out its task so successfully.'[56] Mopping-up had been a problem at Fresnoy because of new German tactics that first appeared at Vimy, troops emerging from deep dugouts after the first wave had gone by to attack it from behind; but even then the platoon had held together. New bombs, which worked by concussion rather than by breaking up into bits of shrapnel, had proved very useful in clearing dugouts; there would thus be more bombers among the moppers-up.[57]

Commanders like Sir Arthur Currie learned much about communications, though many lessons were ambiguous. There was no doubt that the telephone was the most effective means of communication available to the Canadian Corps, but signallers had to expend much effort ensuring the lines from battalions to higher headquarters survived, and cable had to be buried seven feet deep and camouflaged, for it was a highly prized target for German artillery. Laddered lines had proved successful when there was too little time to bury the many miles of cable necessary for each division. Lamps and flags were useless in the opening hours of a battle, when the field was covered in mist, dust, and the smog of war, but they could be used later on to keep in touch with forward troops. Power buzzers and amplifiers were of dubious value; for not only did the ground have to be just right, but the buzzer's heavy accumulators inhibited movement. Wireless was useful in a big advance, but again it was too bulky. Pigeons had yet to prove themselves; they were slow to arrive at their destination, if they arrived at all, and there was no way advancing infantry could know if they got through or not. Runners were the most effective way to maintain contact between a battalion headquarters and its troops; they could return with replies and also fill in commanders on what they had seen, since they were eyewitnesses to events at the front. The job was hazardous, however, one of the few that the Canadian Corps could not replace with some modern technical marvel or a change in technique. Currie concluded one of his reports: 'It would seem advisable to concentrate on telephonic, visual and runner communication, wireless being used as a subsidiary,'[58] thus suggesting the corps weed out many of the ineffective alternatives it had used in the spring battles, though it would retain all available means of communication, proven or not, until the end of the war.

When in reserve the infantry trained, if not engaged in other work, and training was usually for half a day, the balance being filled with sports.[59] Fifty years later, W.A. West of the 7th Battalion remembered Vimy: 'Then we took training and the new recruits took musketry at the range. We trained ... probably for two weeks and then we went into the line for a certain number of days ... Then we were taken out of the line and we were on support work which brought up the ammunition and supply to the front line. Then we trained for Hill 70.'[60] As the summer progressed, the corps commander placed greater and greater emphasis on getting the troops ready for fresh assaults, and in spite of the increased importance of grenade warfare, after mid-May British and Canadian officers insisted the men train with the rifle and bayonet.

Haig's staff was adamant: 'As our operations approach more and more the standard of open fighting to which we were trained before the present war, it becomes more and more important that men should know how to use their rifles and that junior officers and N.C.O.s should be quick to seize opportunities of using rifle fire especially in stopping small local counter attacks on the flanks of the attack.'[61] The Canadian Corps commander followed suit the following month, which must have come as some surprise to troops accustomed to using almost everything but the rifle in attack and defence, but Currie's policy was clear: 'It is desired to promote by every means a general recognition by all ranks of the importance of the Rifle, which, together with the Bayonet, remains the principal weapon of the Infantryman in spite of the introduction of subsidiary weapons.'[62] Instructors related supposed incidents where British units had thrown away rifles and withdrawn when they ran out of bombs, such stories no doubt a didactic tool to stress the rifle's importance in stopping German counter-attacks. It was thus still mainly a defensive weapon, in the soldier's mind serving as an adjunct to bombs, rifle-grenades, and the Lewis gun.

The British First Army, of which the Canadian Corps was a part, opened its musketry camp in early May, the first course graduating on the 15th. Of forty-eight candidates three were deemed competent enough to teach at the school, twenty-one could instruct battalion classes of non-commissioned officers, eighteen were knowledgeable enough to teach the men, and six failed. It is noteworthy that one of the students 'admitted' to having used his rifle for firing grenades, making it unsuitable for musketry. After graduating from the school the men returned to their battalions to teach the troops rapid-loading, aiming, judging distances, and similar skills. Brigades organized and ran six-day courses, which included teaching the men to fire their rifles from the hip during an assault,[63] a technique combining fire and movement at the most basic level.

The rifle, naturally, was not to be the infantryman's only weapon. Currie made no move to change the platoon organization adopted just before Vimy, and the British General Staff felt that the men needed more work in fire and movement as well as on the combination of bayonet fighting and musketry, seeking to see the word 'specialist' eliminated as applied to Lewis gunners, bombers, and rifle-grenadiers. In some ways the Canadian Corps was ahead of its British colleagues, since it had long tried to cross-train its troops, and in May 1917 the corps ordered that the men be trained on all platoon weapons, though rifle and bayonet should be pre-eminent. Next in order of priority was the rifle-grenade, and training with hand-thrown bombs was less emphasized.[64]

From May to August the battalions of the corps practised the different aspects of fire and movement at the platoon level. Junior officers, who would lead platoons into battle, learned the intricacies of 'Habits of Command,' 'Habits of Observation,' and 'Personal Initiative,' while other ranks drilled, fired their rifles, learned and relearned the platoon organization and carried out specialist training – the Canadians had not eliminated the word.[65] Division commanders mulled over the ammunition requirements of an offensive and tried to break the problem down into the number of bombs, rifle-grenades, and bullets their formations would need to advance a given distance. They eventually calculated that a rifleman needed 170 rounds to advance 1,000 yards, including 'fire to cover movement.'[66] The extra fifty rounds would have added just slightly more than three pounds to a rifleman's load.

By the beginning of June troops began to practise their platoon tactics on progressively more detailed exercises. Each platoon commander was given his objective; he then pointed it out to his subordinates and issued orders detailing where and how and in what order the unit would move and fight to reach its goal. When the time came to start, platoons moved out in artillery formation, each section in column to make it easier to keep in touch with one another in spite of being spread out. Umpires placed surprise ambushes at different locations, and when the platoon came under such fire, it changed its formation to an extended line, advancing in section rushes, each covered by the fire of other sections, with bayonets fixed for the assault. Some exercises emphasized the use of the rifle, troops capturing positions with that weapon alone. Later, platoons practised with half a section covering the other; since everyone except for the gunner in the Lewis section had a rifle, this manœuvre showed some promise. To add realism, troops often shot live ammunition instead of blanks, though not at each other. Sections thus learned to work together, but reliance on the platoon's integral fire-power may have been overstressed, since the Canadians made little effort to train with tanks; on one exercise conducted on 6 June observers noted that there were too few troops to make it in any way realistic. Having seen the success of tactics developed in the winter of 1916–17, the Canadian Corps was unwilling to innovate in the direction of armour-infantry cooperation. Furthermore, tanks were simply not available in large numbers; for all three of the BEF's tank brigades were preparing for the offensive towards Passchendaele, due to begin on 31 July, where they would remain until October.[67]

Field practices concentrated on solving particular problems encountered in the previous few months' fighting, most important of which was the German propensity, during the Canadian advance, to keep in strong dugouts troops who could later emerge to cause havoc in the rear; and even strong points with light garrisons could cause trouble. The first wave's role was to reach its objective, and it could not pause to take out machine-gun nests or infantry strong points. Subsequent waves, including the mop-up parties, were supposed to keep up with the advance, since they were needed to replace casualties and help protect the final objective from counter-attack. If the bunkers, dugouts, or trench systems were too formidable, mop-up parties had to move on and leave them unscathed; so support waves, which followed some minutes after the main attack, took on the job of destroying and capturing these defences. Because it supported the front waves, artillery would be unavailable; so infantry platoons in the follow-up companies would have to supply their own in the form of rifle-grenades.[68] Whether such techniques would solve the problem remained to be seen.

The infantry also practised consolidating captured positions. Above all, instructors taught troops to act quickly, digging in and making use of any wire available to set up a hasty defence, and staff officers suggested two or three men from each platoon be trained extensively in rapid wiring. Aerial photographs taken in front of British assaults showed only light scratches in the earth, while the Germans had strong lines from which to launch counter-attacks. The Canadians learned to dig in immediately and post sentries as soon as they had taken the objective. Forward posts would give the alarm if the Germans counter-attacked, at which time all available rifles would be brought to bear; for training among junior officers and non-commissioned officers stressed control over the riflemen's rate of fire to make it as effective as possible. When a hasty defence was ready, the engineers would be responsible for laying out more elaborate defensive works. About 300 yards ahead of the main trenches infantry, sometimes accompanied by artillery observers, established posts to give advance warning of any counter-attack and otherwise keep an eye on enemy activity. Behind the line, troops deployed in depth, because German counter-attacks to that time had concentrated on obliterating the front trenches, forcing the Canadians to keep strong reserves. Barbed wire protected each line of defence, leaving only the communication trenches, easily blocked, and a few gaps, covered by

Lewis guns, to enter or leave. Corps staff officers noted that German counter-attacks against Canadian units had often succeeded when artillery was unable to reply to SOS calls; they concluded that it was not enough to count on the artillery, and that barbed wire was the best way to strengthen defences.[69]

In August 1917 the war entered its fourth year and the Canadian Corps prepared for yet another battle. While raiders attacked the enemy in accordance with Sir Douglas Haig's instructions, Currie's staff drew up plans to take Hill 70. The field marshal had originally called for the Canadians to capture the town of Lens, but the Canadian Corps commander insisted the hill had to fall first; it dominated the town and would allow unhindered German artillery to pour fire onto Canadian troops. The general concept behind capturing the hill was simple; infantry would advance in three stages, taking the front trenches and reporting when they had crossed two imaginary lines, Blue and Green, the latter being on the final objective. Currie expected the Germans to relinquish their forward positions, hold their secondary lines with machine-guns, and counter-attack with fresh troops, in accordance with tactics the Canadians had been encountering since Arleux. Canadian gunners were to prevent the counter-attacks from breaching the infantry's newly won positions, and in the words of G.W.L. Nicholson, 'As far as possible Hill 70 was to be a killing by artillery.'[70]

Supplementing the guns was Allied air power. All six German balloons within range of the Canadian lines were brought down on 9 August, an operation pilots found particularly hazardous, since these observation platforms were heavily defended by anti-aircraft artillery. Two days prior to the assault aircraft bombed railway junctions, aerodromes, and rest billets, though results are unknown. Number 16 Squadron was responsible for supplying contact patrols and artillery observation aircraft on the day of the assault. One innovation at Hill 70 was the establishment of forward airfields, temporary facilities used only to refuel and rearm, to allow pilots more time over the battlefield.[71]

As with every set-piece battle of 1917, the Canadians rehearsed extensively for the operations to come, including the eventual capture of Lens.[72] William Morgan kept track of the 24th Battalion's training in his diary: on 28 July they 'Went over the same ground again. One realises what a wonderful organization this is. We even know the names of the streets we are to march up and the actual houses we are to mop up.' The battalion went over the tapes on 6, 8, and 18 August;[73] the battle opened on the 15th. Artillery, trench mortars, and machine-guns opened fire to destroy wire and defences and keep the Germans in their dugouts, and the combination worked better than ever before, at least as far as the hill's crest, allowing the infantry to move across no man's land with few losses.[74] Some, however, had a difficult time; as J. Younie related to the CBC fifty years later:

it started to get daylight and they started to snipe and snipe – machine guns going and I was pretty near the trench, our objective – and it got pretty bad and there was a shell hole right in front of me and two guys in there so I made a run and got in between them, was about from here oh about 20 yards to the trench and this fellow was facing – this fellow on my side put his head up and he got it through the bean. And this fellow he put his head up and he got it through the bean. I said, to myself, this is no place for me. So I crouched down; I made one leap out of there and I got on top of that trench and down it in nothing flat, practically.[75]

German machine-gunners thus threatened to dominate the battlefield, and that they did not was thanks mainly to Canadian small-unit tactics. In some cases blind courage won the day, as when Company Sergeant-Major Robert Hanna of the 29th Battalion took an enemy machine-gun, using his rifle as a club, and then held on to the position; or when Private William Williams, with two scouts, crawled up to an enemy machine-gun and took it from five German soldiers in close fighting. For the most part, however, strong points fell to small infantry groups coordinating their movements and their weapons.[76] On Hill 70 the rifle-grenade again came into its own,[77] and Lewis guns went into battle with the infantry.[78]

The communications sections were especially important once the position fell; for if the battle was to be a 'killing by artillery' brigade and division commanders had to know where their troops were and where the enemy was assembling. Wireless sets had been steadily improving since 1914, and the one used in the coming battle, a continuous-wave model to replace the spark set, had a greater range requiring less power – and hence lighter batteries. Tuning was much sharper, allowing four times the number of sets to operate in a given area, and, though the new equipment had been in use since Vimy, it was particularly useful at Hill 70.[79] Mainly, however, success depended on the infantry's ability to throw off German counter-attacks; the men of the forward battalions had to turn their advance into a defence before the enemy could react and force them out of their precarious positions. Taking trenches that had been designed to keep the Canadians out and then reversing them, especially when shells had already destroyed revetting and parapets, was no easy task. Engineers from the field companies followed the assault waves from the Blue Line and began building strong points as soon as the infantry reached its objectives; working under German shell fire, sappers suffered casualties day and night. Meanwhile, pioneers dug communication trenches across no man's land and put up barbed wire in front of the new Canadian defences; a company of pioneers could carry enough wire to cover a brigade. With picks, shovels, wire-cutters, and other hand tools, engineers and pioneers worked to make Hill 70 more defensible.[80]

As the pioneers and engineers prepared defences, the Germans counter-attacked. Supported by artillery and machine-guns, infantry charged up the communication trenches to dislodge the Canadians from the hill, and ammunition soon ran low in the Canadian lines, German artillery having prevented some stores from reaching the front. Soldiers went back along the trenches collecting grenades and bombs, many of them German, to replenish their supply. During the night enemy patrols crept through the woods that faced some of the Canadian positions and got close enough to engage at close range; Sergeant Frederick Hobson of the 20th Battalion held off one counter-attack with his rifle butt and bayonet. The Germans were quick to use all the weapons at their disposal, and on 18 August flame-throwers swept the Canadian parapets with liquid fire. But the devices were not very effective and were easy targets for rifle and machine-gun; Canadian troops captured at least two of the weapons that day.[81]

For the most part Currie's plan succeeded, though some German units managed to get within close range of the Canadian infantry. Furthermore, before the gunners could begin breaking up counter-attacks, they had to get their guns laid on properly, a task much eased by the use of wireless-equipped air observers from Number 43 Squadron.[82] Mistakes, however, were not uncommon. Second-Lieutenant F.R. Darrow wrote home that on the 16th 'one of our 9.2 batteries took a fancy to our Company headquarters, an old half-ruined pill box, and two of their guns started pelting us.'[83] The company commander sent the young officer back to inform the gunners that 'we were receiving quite sufficient attention in the line from the German Guns,'[84] and the battery increased its range by a few hundred yards. The officer's courage was then rewarded with rum.[85]

As to the counter-attacks, even those that did not break up before they started resulted in very heavy casualties among the courageous but hard-pressed German infantry. An attack on 18 August was typical: 'At 4.30 a.m., the 4th Canadian Infantry Battalion, holding the Green Line, [was] strongly attacked by the enemy in force. Our barrage caught the attacking forces and inflicted heavy casualties, but a considerable number got through and continued to advance until reaching a point about 70 yards from our Green Line, when our machine guns opened on them, cutting them to pieces.'[86] Though Currie had wanted the artillery to do most of the killing, German counter-attacks failed because weapons at two different levels were coordinated in the defence; the artillery broke up attacks as they were forming up or in their early stages, while platoon weapons, mostly Lewis guns, killed or wounded advancing troops if they got through the barrage. In this manner the Canadians fought twenty-one German counter-attacks to a standstill from 15 to 18 August.[87]

The Canadian Corps suffered 3,527 casualties taking Hill 70: 1,056 dead, 2,432 wounded, and thirty-nine captured, but the battle was far from over. Haig wanted the Canadians to take Lens, and the hill's capture was only the first part of a larger plan. By the time the offensive came to an end on 25 August, the Canadians had suffered 9,198 casualties in eleven days,[88] fewer losses than at Vimy Ridge, but it must be remembered that only three divisions, the 1st, 2nd, and 4th, were involved. Furthermore, and more important, the bulk of all these casualties, 5,671, occurred after the most important physical feature in the area, Hill 70, had been taken. Fire and movement had brought about the hill's fall but had not kept down losses; Canadian tactics were a better guarantor of success than the haphazard rushes of 1915, but they did not ensure that individual units would survive intact. Furthermore, they demanded time for preparation and planning, and Vimy was a success because it was so set piece the corps had several months to get ready. Also, the lessons of Verdun and the Somme were easy to apply, since German defences were organized according to a familiar pattern; but, if time was not available or if the enemy changed his tactics, the results could be disastrous. Even if fire and movement kept men alive through the attack, once battalions had taken up static positions, artillery and counter-attacks drastically reduced their numbers and increased their suffering. The tactics of 1917 merely ensured that enough men would survive the assault to hold captured positions.

6

Bloody Passchendaele

If any battle the British fought on the Western Front could encompass all the horrors of that war, it must have been Passchendaele. Those who remembered it described hellish scenes and almost overwhelming misery; so it should come as no surprise that those who later wrote about it would render a harsh judgment of the battle that raged from July to November 1917. Bryan Cooper called the campaign 'the most useless disaster of them all,' in which during an average week 7,000 soldiers become casualties 'for not the slightest purpose or advantage.'[1] One in every four British soldiers to fall on the Western Front would lose life, limb, or freedom trying to capture the ridge, and the battle's futility would lead Leon Wolff to judge 1917 by 'the inability of the politicians to win a profitable peace, and the incapacity of the generals to win profitable battles,' and Third Ypres, the battle's official name, as 'one of many military cataclysms,' in which tactics amounted to 'pure and simple bludgeoning.'[2] Bidwell and Graham suggest that the battle would have been better fought as a protracted siege operation in which artillery and engineers could make a breach in German lines, rather than use infantry, with artillery support, to attempt a breakthrough to release a scourge of horsemen.[3] Bryan Gardner sees Passchendaele as the turning point in war literature; for, 'From then on the voice of those who found strength and interval enough merely for penning their visions was generally a cry,' while the idealism of Edmund Blunden, among others, was destroyed in the mud.[4]

After Hill 70 and the battles around Lens, the Canadian Corps settled into its now normal routine of trench life, characterized by mud, boredom, disease, and misery, sometimes punctuated by the excitement and terror of an occasional trench raid or artillery duel. Throughout the summer, while the Canadians trained, patrolled, or merely lived day to day, the British Fifth Army, commanded by Sir Hubert Gough, tried to crack German positions in Flanders, beginning on 31 July. Haig originally wanted to break through enemy defences and clear the channel ports of submarine bases, but the first assault failed to make any appreciable gains, and so did the next three. On 22 August the Fifth Army tried again, but without enthusiasm, and that day Sir Herbert Plumer's Second Army took over part of Gough's front and itself launched a series of attacks in August and September; a wood called Inverness Copse changed hands eighteen times. The British finally found some success on 20 September, on the Menin Road, when they advanced half a mile, and six days later they were similarly successful, at Polygon Wood, and yet again on 4 October. Then the advance bogged down. On 9 October the British failed to capture any of their objectives, three days later the New Zealanders were mauled, and on the 22nd Fifth Army and the French made little progress.[5]

Once again a war of movement proved unattainable and the war of attrition took its tool, and a small town sitting on a ridge, both called Passchendaele, eventually gave its name to the entire campaign. As on the Somme in the previous summer, the British were unable to cut their way through the enemy's strong defences and into the countryside beyond, and in the fall Haig needed reinforcements. The Canadians, though Arthur Currie was far from enthusiastic, made their way to the scene of battle, where they faced a constantly changing German tactical system, at the regimental level, that would not allow them to predict – as they had at Vimy – how the enemy would react when they assaulted his positions. For example, in September the Germans had used a thinly held advance zone which was quickly given up when the British attacked; counter-attacks followed, not immediately, but only after detailed preparation was completed, requiring about twenty-four hours. When this system failed to achieve its purpose, the Germans strengthened their front line but saw forward troops slaughtered in the British attack of 4 October. Their next experiment in defensive doctrine was again to use minimal resources and personnel in forward positions and to harass attackers with shrapnel as they moved to capture the more-distant defensive lines, but on 9 October a British attack got through. Crown Prince Rupprecht thus reverted to holding the front almost exclusively with machine-guns, keeping the bulk of the infantry further back to counter-attack; these tactics accounted for heavy British defeats in early and mid-October.[6]

Conditions were frightful. That summer was the wettest in thirty years, causing guns to sink out of sight and wounded men slowly to suffocate, and shelling made the situation steadily worse. Only for a few weeks in August did the ground dry. Mud seeped into everything from rifle bolts to food to water to the breeches of the great guns; it made trench-digging impossible, so that positions had to be built above ground. As James Page later remembered: 'we had our rough times and we had our good times there were some times you were pretty miserable. Take that Passchendaele stunt. That was something terrible that was all the experience I think that any human being could go through. I don't think they could be any worse than that. The fighting was no worse than the Somme or Vimy or anything else, [it was] the sea of mud.'[7] German defences were well organized, as British and Empire units discovered in the battles from July to September; for Colonel von Lossberg, the 4th Army's chief of staff, abandoned the tactics of the Somme. Instead of trying to stop British assaults in the front trenches, German divisions were deployed in depth. The trench gave way to the pillbox, a concrete structure capable of housing machine-gunners and riflemen and sited to give mutual support. For the British and then the dominion troops, it was no longer a matter of breaking through subsequent lines of defence while leap-frogging fresh troops into the assault; as troops attacked one pillbox they found themselves under fire from flanking positions. In October reconnaissance patrols discovered concentrations of machine-guns and a stronger system of defence generally in the forward areas designed to break up an attack before it could overwhelm the defenders. From other units the Canadians learned that the Germans had become even more aggressive in their defence, putting small units far forward in no man's land as soon as British artillery opened fire in order to place German troops on the Allied side of the barrage, where they could then inflict heavy casualties on attackers as they were leaving their trenches.[8]

Three brigades of tanks, with a front-line strength of 126 machines, tried to help the infantry forward, but the British soon found that armoured vehicles were close to useless in these conditions. Still, Haig insisted on sending them into battle until late September, but mud proved too much for them and they suffered heavily.'[9] In his memoirs Ludendorff admits that the tanks were inconvenient, but that German troops 'put them out of action all the same.'[10] Though the Germans feared the concrete bunkers might become tempting targets for artillery, in fact they were impervious to anything smaller than eight-inch shells, and the gunners could do no more than turn the muddy areas between pillboxes into a morass.

Chemical warfare had also taken a new turn. After the middle of

A heavy artillery piece stuck in the mud at Passchendaele. It had been placed on a wooden platform, which had collapsed. The mud of Passchendaele was reminiscent of Salisbury Plain, but in the training camp there was no enemy fire to make the situation worse.

October, just as the Canadians were arriving in the Passchendaele sector, the Germans began to use two complementary types of gas. First they would drop Blue Cross, or sneezing gas, which made respirators uncomfortable, tempting many soldiers to remove them. Then would come mustard gas, designed to disable by making breathing excruciatingly difficult and raising huge, painful blisters on the skin. Then of course there were the counter-attacks. On 11 October a report distributed through the British Second Army, of which the Canadian Corps was now a part, acknowledged that counter-attack had always been the Germans' best means of defence. At Passchendaele the Canadians could expect dozens of local counter-attacks in the course of an assault, now that the Germans had crowded their front line with riflemen and machine-gun units. German policy was to react while the British were still on the move, thus holding them to the forward line only.[11]

From Second Army the Canadians also learned which weapons were most effective against German defences. In attacks on 26 September and 4 October the British had found that those battalions most involved in the fighting had expended about seventy rounds per rifle, far below the 120 rounds or more each man carried. Lewis guns, however, showed a marked contrast; units that saw heavy combat used twenty-five forty-seven-round *magazines* for each gun in the course of an assault. Other weapons were far less useful, in contrast to their importance in earlier battles of the war. The Mills hand-grenade, for example, was practical only for the occasional strong point, and Second Army felt that one per man would be sufficient. Attacks still needed rifle-grenades, however, especially when German machine-guns fired from the roof of a pillbox or from a nearby position. Mortars could be just as effective if pushed forward with the attack; for, though direct hits brought no results, mortar bombs landing just outside the door could blow it in and force the garrison to surrender, as happened twice in the battles of 26 September and 4 October. How the mortars could be carried into battle through the mud of Passchendaele the report did not say.[12]

When the Canadians arrived in October, proposals on how to deal with battlefield conditions were soon forthcoming, but no one suggested major changes in Canadian tactics. The 31st Battalion recommended that artillery be more systematic in its bombardment of the forward areas, concentrating exclusively on occupied defences; not only would such shelling bring more destructive power to bear on the enemy's main positions, it would avoid turning dead ground and approaches into a bog. Protective barrages should not be static, the battalion insisted, but should continue past the newly captured position and then return at an appointed time to take on the next wave, when it would move forward again. The rolling barrage would thus shell the German defences three times and make it difficult for the enemy to judge when the actual attack would take place; it would also destroy more trenches and inflict further casualties, though breaking the ground in the process. Cooperating with artillery would be machine-guns placed to deal with defended areas before and during the infantry attack. Since the Germans had increased the depth of their defences, the battalion suggested that the first waves remain about the same but that the proportion of moppers-up be increased. Finally, in the mud of Passchendaele, commanders had to be especially careful to take the nature of the ground into account before choosing objectives.[13]

Reports and suggestions reached the Canadian Corps from many sources, including Australian, New Zealand, and British formations, and Currie's staff proceeded to refine Canadian tactics to suit the situation. To deal with German units that awaited the attack on the Canadian side of the barrage, corps staff proposed several solutions. The first was simply to pull the infantry back from the front trenches and start the initial barrage at the Canadian advance posts or even the front line. Another possibility was to patrol no man's land more aggressively and force any German units there to withdraw. Finally, forward battalions could push their outpost line right out to the barrage line, where they could use rifle grenades to keep the enemy at bay and at the same time warn the main body of any hostile troops in no man's land; the latter could then be forced out.[14]

While corps staff officers planned, soldiers prepared for the upcoming offensive. Unknown to anyone then, the Canadians had three major battles to fight, on 26 October, 30 October, and 6 November, with many near-forgotten but costly skirmishes in between. Long before they came under fire the Canadians found they had a more insidious enemy – mud. One battalion suggested that its men keep an eye out for clean German rifles in the assault and use them if they could.[15] Mud also had a dampening effect on artillery shells, since it absorbed their impact instead of transmitting shock waves. At least one Canadian, a Mr G. McKnight of the 26th Battalion, discovered mud's absorbing qualities to his benefit: 'There was one great advantage to us in Passchendaele. We thought the mud and the water there was [a] terrific thing to be up against but it saved an awful lot of casualties because the shells would land and go down in the mud and blow the mud sky-high but it wouldn't hurt anybody.'[16] Being on higher ground, many of the enemy's defences did not have the same advantage, if having to walk through waist-deep mud and face the possibility of drowning after one wrong step can be termed an advantage. P.E. Bélanger had a few words to say about both the mud and the enemy's positions: 'It was simply awful, it was muddy all over the place and then the shelling was terrible because, with their observation balloons, they could see everything so the least little move you were doing, they were opening fire right on your section with the whizbangs.'[17]

Mud caused the artillery no end of worry. On reporting to the major-general, Royal Artillery, of the Second Army, Major-General Sir E.W.B. Morrison found his work cut out for him. He discovered that he was to take command of about 250 heavy guns in twelve groups, including sixty-pounders, six-inch, 9.2-inch, and fifteen-inch batteries; but, while reconnoitering his gun positions, Morrison and his staff could locate only ten groups of heavy artillery. Of 227 guns eighty-nine were out of action, none of which had been sent back for repairs, and only seventeen of forty-eight sixty-pounders were able to fire, as were only six of twenty-six 9.2-inch howitzers. The fifteen field brigades seemed ample enough to cover a 3,000-yard front, but they were in worse condition; not half of the 308 eighteen-pounders were in action, 'and these were dotted about in the mud wherever they had happened to get bogged.'[18]

Fifty years later Colonel William Rae, who had been a staff officer at corps headquarters, remembered the pitiful condition to which the artillery had been reduced, and could well hint at the nightmarish conditions everyone – at the front – experienced.

I remember very well, at the beginning, there was a report by the [general officer commanding Royal Artillery, i.e, Morrison] on the condition of the artillery in the forward positions and it was quite shocking. Some of these batteries had been there without relief for five or six weeks. The guns were absolutely bogged down and, in many cases, only one or two out of the normal six guns in the field artillery batteries were serviceable and the men themselves were just exhausted and Currie insisted on these batteries being pulled out so that the men could be refitted and the guns replaced. The plain truth was that these batteries were practically ineffective owing to the exhaustion of the men and material ... And I was up, myself, in the forward artillery positions later on and, frankly, I was horrified at what I saw. I mean, I went up the duck boards there, carrying very little except a gas mask and a walking stick. I had to go, I was told to go forward. I was a General Staff Officer and I was told to go forward and get certain information and, by the time I got to the Field Battery position, I'd just had about enough of it. The Germans were shelling and I was up with our [commander, Royal Engineers]. We had to get off the duck board and tunnel through the mud which was just a mass of shell holes and dead bodies and so on and I got up to these field battery positions and, there they were as I say, with the guns almost up to the hubs in mud and what the position of the Infantry, about three thousand yards ahead, I just hate to think. Never got as far as that.[19]

And the battle had not yet begun.

A German pillbox. This one was photographed near Lens in December 1917; those at Passchendaele would have been of similar design, though they varied in size. Not only were they impervious to all but the larger artillery shells, but they could be easily camouflaged.

Planning creeping barrages and other support for the infantry was difficult, since it was not clear how much time troops needed to advance through the slime. The gunners relied on close liaison between artillery observers and attacking troops and hoped they would be flexible enough to make whatever modifications changing conditions required. Ammunition was another problem; to support a major assault the Canadian guns needed truckloads of shells, so many that British staff officers had been known to complain of the Canadians' spendthrift habits. To get the shells up to the front, engineers, pioneers, and infantry work parties, often under heavy shell fire, built or rebuilt roads and light railways throughout the muddy sector; over 1,500 of them became casualties. The guns themselves needed platforms, or the first shot fired would drive the cannon into the muck, forcing its crew to extricate and re-aim it each time.[20]

While engineers, pioneers, and others built roads and platforms, the gunners began to prepare the way for the upcoming infantry attacks. Wire entanglements disappeared thanks to the 106 fuse, and patrols were unable to find any serious wire obstacles after the artillery had finished its work. Howitzers rained shells on the enemy's defences, while heavy artillery sought out German batteries and answered the call whenever infantry or field artillery came under shell fire. As often happened in previous battles, many of the gunners' activities led to artillery duels. Meanwhile, observers prepared to go forward with wireless sets so they could call in corrections without relying on tenuous telephone lines.[21]

The infantry took care of its own preparations – mainly training. Those brigades destined to lead the assault left the line in early October and began a long succession of route marches, musketry practices, specialist training, and tactical exercises. Engineers reproduced the enemy's trenches and pillboxes on the ground, performing what had long before become a familiar task. Though the wet weather sometimes interrupted training, infantrymen went over the taped course to familiarize themselves with the operations to come; officers and their men paid special attention to map reading, writing messages, and patrolling as part of the usual battle rehearsals.[22]

While infantry trained, the artillery prepared to support the assault, with batteries firing 'preparatory bursts of fire' by day and night. Since the German defences were organized in depth, so were the Canadian barrages – this was of course nothing new: at Vimy the artillery's responsibility had been a large area, not just a line. Heavy artillery, field guns, and machine-guns co-operated to harass German infantry, gunners, and supporting troops; the 3rd Divisional Artillery, for example, expended between 3,200 and 3,400 shells each night. On the day of the attack artillery barrages covered the entire area of the enemy's defences. The guns supporting the 8th and 9th brigades, who would be attacking on 26 October, were disposed so that two-thirds of the eighteen-pounders fired on a predetermined line, while the other third fired 100 yards beyond. Batteries of 4.5-inch howitzers fired an additional 100 or 150 yards, and machine-guns kept their point of aim 100 yards farther still. Medium howitzers fired 100 yards farther on, and heavy howitzers 200 yards beyond that.[23] The barrage was thus 600 yards deep. Corps artillery had 128 eighteen-pounders for creeping barrages and standing protective barrages.[24]

At 5:38 on the morning of 26 October the Canadians attacked, with the 8th Brigade on the left, the 9th Brigade in the centre, both of the 3rd Division, and the 10th Brigade of the 4th Division on the right. According to Alex Strachan, 'It was really a miserable day, quite miserable. We were lying practically on the bed of the river which had been shelled all to pieces and it was just a marshy bog ... our company headquarters got blown to pieces ... before we started off ...'[25] When the attack did begin, heavy machine-guns allocated to the barrage opened fire; two minutes later artillery began to shell the enemy's defences and to lay down the creeping barrage, while simultaneously Stokes mortars fired eighty rounds at pillboxes and on some wire in front of the intermediate objective. The creeping barrage began to move in fifty-yard lifts every four minutes, much slower than usual because of the sea of mud the attacking infantry had to wade through. Unlike the artillery support at Vimy, this barrage was not a single curtain but contained seven lines created by everything from small field pieces to sixty-pounder guns.[26] The barrage was too complex and, ironically, too slow, at least for some units. The 10th Brigade, with the 46th Battalion on the far right, complained later that shells were too scattered and troops often found themselves within their own supporting artillery fire. Though no man's land was muddy, advancing soldiers could walk much faster than fifty yards every four minutes, and the longer they were in no man's land, the greater the chance that German artillery could shell them. In fact, enemy guns were registered on their own forward outposts, the 'forefield,' which their troops evacuated when the attack began. Casualties from German shells were heavy.[27]

German defensive tactics also took their toll; machine-gunners, known for their indomitability, emerged from their shelters after the leading waves had passed, firing to both their front and their rear. Canadian troops did their best to deal with the defence in depth; the 8th Brigade advanced with the 4th Canadian Mounted Rifles in the lead, two companies forward, two in support, and a company of the 1st Canadian Mounted Rifles following close behind. Men were felled by machine-gun and rifle fire as soon as they left their trenches, the Germans having posted men far forward of their front line. In what was described 'as particularly hard fighting' the brigade reached its intermediate objective and occupied it, though the Germans fought with machine-guns and rifles until bayoneted or bombed. After this initial success the brigade carried on towards its final objective but was forced to dig in and consolidate short of the mark because of German small-arms fire. The company of the 1st Canadian Mounted Rifles following close behind the main assault went forward to push through to the final objective, but even these relatively fresh troops could not force their way through German positions. Defence in depth had been at least partially successful; the 4th Canadian Mounted Rifles had taken only part of their objectives for the day and had suffered 321 casualties for their effort, out of a strength of 944.[28]

The 10th Brigade's experiences on that day were similar, German machine-guns causing heavy casualties. The 46th Battalion's report on the assault read: 'The attack was carried out most excellently by this Battalion, all objectives being quickly gained against very severe opposition and heavy machine gun fire. Severe casualties were caused this Battalion by the M.G. fire experienced, 70% of the attacking force becoming casualties.'[29] Again the Canadians paid a high price for the little ground they could wrest from the enemy; the pillboxes, almost impervious to shell fire, served the Germans well.

Tactics at the platoon level had not changed. Infantry sections diverted German machine-gun fire with rifle-grenades and Lewis guns while small parties made their way around to the blind side of enemy positions and threw their bombs. Heavy machine-guns sent forward with the attacking troops did little during the assault but were instrumental in breaking up counter-attacks when artillery, owing to a failure in communications, did not respond.[30] The Stokes mortars proved a disappointment, mainly because of resupply problems: 'Stokes Guns did not prove a success taken forward with the attacking force. Ammunition supply was extremely difficult owing to the heavy ground, parties eventually arriving with but a portion of their original load, and the actual transport of the gun and parts with the attackers was found very difficult. It was found to be more advisable to send the guns forward after the line had been consolidated.'[31] A weapon's usefulness in an attack or immediately afterward was therefore somewhat dependent on its weight; machine-guns and trench mortars might be heavy but could still be hauled across a muddy no man's land and serve to break up counter-attacks, and the two were similar in many ways. The Stokes could be broken down into three main parts: the base plate weighed twenty-nine pounds, the mounting thirty-five pounds, and the barrel, a considerable load for even the burliest soldier, weighed forty-nine pounds. The Vickers gun weighed 28.5 pounds empty and 38.5 pounds with its water jacket filled, but the tripod weighed forty-eight pounds, once again requiring a particularly muscular machine-gunner to carry it through the mud of Passchendaele. Ammunition presented similar problems; a Stokes mortar bomb weighed over 10.5 pounds, and a box of 250 rounds of .303 ammunition, ready for use, weighed twenty-one pounds. If mud made the Stokes and Vickers difficult to move, it could also make all weapons useless by clogging their barrels and breeches, and some machine-guns became little more than dead weight. The 46th Battalion, assaulting for the 10th Brigade, captured its objectives but ran into serious difficulties when the Germans counter-attacked, because rifles and Lewis and Vickers guns jammed. Artillery, too far back to see the battalion's SOS signal, did not respond for twenty minutes, by which time it was too late and the Canadians were withdrawing to a position just forward of their original outpost line.[32]

Communications were a problem throughout the day. Work parties had buried wire three feet deep, but that depth was insufficient to guard the cables from artillery fire. Forward of battalion headquarters, runners proved invaluable, as usual. They were also very much in evidence at higher headquarters; the 10th Brigade kept thirty-two soldiers to carry messages and wished it had forty. Communications between artillery and forward troops were non-existent, as flares sent up to warn of imminent counter-attack went unseen. After the battle an artillery officer from corps headquarters visited the 10th Brigade, whose trials and tribulations are related above, and made arrangements for signals to be relayed directly to artillery positions; but exactly what those arrangements were, and their usefulness, is unknown.[33]

On the evening of 26 October the 44th Battalion of the 10th Brigade, at the extreme right of the assault, attempted to take Decline Copse, which had eluded the 46th Battalion that morning. As it had done in the earlier battles, artillery inflicted some casualties, but it was small-arms fire that held up the assaulting troops. Zero-hour was fixed at 10 p.m., but while the assaulting company was waiting to move off, German artillery shelled its positions; isolated guns caused some casualties and gassed one platoon, but the attack got under way with little confusion. The hastily organized Canadian barrage was ineffective, since shells fell to the left of the objective and among the attackers. Pressing on regardless – it was, after all, safer in the German trenches – two platoons quickly reached their objectives, and only in the centre did heavy machine-gun fire prevent the Canadians from reaching the copse; but even this obstacle was overcome when rifle grenadiers worked their way around the position's flanks. Decline Copse fell a little after midnight; the Germans counter-attacked, but, in contrast to the experience of the 46th Battalion earlier in the day, the Canadians' sos signal brought down artillery fire that cleared the entire front.[34]

In the early morning of the 27th the battle ended, though counter-attacks, skirmishes, and patrol clashes continued to add to the casualty lists until the 29th. The 46th Battalion, having borne the brunt of the fighting for the 10th Brigade, had suffered 375 casualties of which thirty-seven were fatal, while the 44th Battalion, which was not engaged until evening, lost twenty-eight men at Decline Copse. The 10th Trench Mortar Battery, supporting the 10th Brigade, lost twelve men, and the 3rd Divisional Artillery lost twenty-four.[35] The figures show that the 26 October assault was no Somme; for even attacking battalions were still in condition to carry on operations – none was annihilated, and those who supported the main attack suffered light casualties. German artillery was therefore not as important a factor at the first assault on Passchendaele Ridge as it had been in previous battles. The great majority of those who fell were in assault battalions, and narratives concentrate on the dangers of enemy small-arms fire; thus the rifle and the machine-gun, used in accordance with German defensive tactics, were the deadliest weapons in enemy hands.

After the battle, time to take stock of the situation and apply lessons to the next push was very limited. Still, the 1st Division, which had not been involved in the attack, noted that on 26 October some units had to check their advance when enemy machine-gunners popped up behind them, firing against the front and support waves simultaneously, a tactic that had been causing trouble since Vimy. The division staff suggested not only that moppers-up be thoroughly familiarized with strong points and accompany each wave but that the distances between waves be shortened and that they should leap-frog more often. Though the operation would be more complex, it would better ensure that the advance would be secure from rear attacks. Information continued to come in from the British Fifth Army. In order to frustrate British tactics, which concentrated on working around to the rear of German pillboxes, the enemy in at least one instance had placed riflemen in a trench behind the position in such a manner as to enfilade any attacking infantry. The British offered two solutions: the first was simply to call for more artillery, though this could be a problem on a battlefield where communications were tenuous at best; while the second, and most promising, was for the attacking infantry to widen its flanking attacks to encircle entrenched infantry as well as the pillbox.[36] The search for a more effective means of breaking into the enemy's defences continued.

Preparations went forward for the next attack, even as skirmishing continued on some parts of the Canadian front. After the battle of the 26th, engineers, pioneers, and infantry work parties built more roads, fascines, plank tracks, and corduroy roads to take mule trains of 250 animals. There was time for some units to train, and grenade officers demonstrated new types of bombs to the 1st Battalion, while in the 7th Brigade small parties of all ranks left training to take a close look at the ground over which they soon would be attacking; the brigade intelligence officer and bombing officer often led these groups. The brigade hoped in this manner to avoid seeing any of its attacking units getting so lost and confused in the featureless terrain that they could not find their objectives.[37]

In the final days before the assault, to be launched on 30 October, units moved into position, some of them under German artillery fire. On the night of the 28th–29th many of the advance battalions of the 7th Brigade, ordered to attack between the 8th on the left and the 12th on the right, came under such fire. The Princess Patricia's Canadian Light Infantry and the 49th Battalion suffered casualties as they moved up the mule tracks to take over their portion of the battle front, but the two units reached their assembly areas in good order, and the form-up was complete at 5:30 on the morning of the 28th. Casualties continued to mount slowly, however, as German artillery shelled the assembly area. The 38th Battalion, which was to serve as a reserve for the 12th Brigade, suffered heavy losses when German artillery retaliated against a Canadian barrage. On the 29th the 49th Battalion lost troops under similar circumstances, while the night before the attack the 5th Canadian Mounted Rifles were also caught in an artillery duel, suffering numerous casualties.[38] Canadian counter-battery staff, having had very little time to gather information about the enemy's guns, could not silence them.

After the troops had taken up their positions, there was still time left for last-minute details; reconnaissance parties checked German defence works to verify that they had been destroyed, and some found new targets. On 29 October, for example, the 78th Battalion of the 12th Brigade reported movement at a ruined house, a suspected strong point; the unit requested heavy artillery to shell the area and the gunners complied, but the infantry observed no hits and the artillery concentration was deemed a failure. More successful were the observation officers, who went well forward and sent in valuable information; they remained with the attacking units throughout the battle, maintaining artillery support in spite of losing many of their number.[39]

Artillery, however, had not yet perfected the gunners' art of firing blind. They had had little time to register their targets, and this lack of preparation led to often inaccurate fire on the 30th, while time and time again Canadian troops suffered at the hands of their own gunners. The 78th Battalion reported one gun firing short, causing casualties during the morning barrage and the brief bursts of the afternoon, though, with so many guns firing at once, the infantry could not determine the direction from which the culprit was shooting.[40] Most complaints concerned the heavy guns, which the 49th Battalion reported 'were constantly short,'[41] though admittedly these same batteries inflicted severe losses on the enemy.[42] On the morning of the attack the 5th Canadian Mounted Rifles also reported shorts, but they were part of the creeping barrage, made up of shrapnel, and the shells bursting overhead propelled their metal balls and other fragments forward of the trenches.[43]

Gunners applied the lessons of the previous battle in ridding no man's land of skulking German infantry. Some units of the 7th Brigade withdrew from their assembly positions because the original barrage line was almost identical with their front trenches.[44] In some areas, however, preparation was poor, as the 49th Battalion reported: 'The Field Guns were given an almost impossible task – owing to the formation of the Line at zero hour the barrage could have only been successfully laid down after repeated practice, selected ammunition, and solid gun emplacements. As a result the barrage was short, irregular and ineffective in preventing enemy retaliation with rifle and machine-gun fire.'[45] The 5th Canadian Mounted Rifles, on the far left, suffered when their barrage sparked German retaliation a minute later; counter-battery fire on their front had obviously not been effective, and, worse, the battalion suffered casualties from its own guns before the men could leave their trenches.[46]

The 12th Brigade on the right presented a marked contrast; the rolling barrage at least was well coordinated, advancing 100 yards every eight minutes. The only problem the troops faced was in determining the exact location of the shrapnel barrage. Usually bullets propelled downward by mid-air explosions raised dust that indicated the barrage line, but the thick mud of Passchendaele hardly moved, and troops could not quite judge their distance from the creeping barrage.[47] Not everyone in the 12th Brigade had an easy time of it, as John Mackenzie of the 72nd Battalion later related:

The shell fire we had was absolutely intensive. And ... when the word came for over the top, we all went forward with shells flying around us in every direction. And we were told, and whether this is true or not I do not know, but we were told that they going to try something in the way of a new barrage. The barrage was going forward a hundred yards and then drop back two hundred with the expectation that the Germans might take their men, when the barrage opened up, might take their men out of their line, into no man's land, and follow our barrage to save their men. Whether that was true or not I do not know, but we got our own shells and we got the German shells. So we were caught in between the two of them.[48]

The 3rd Division, with the 8th and 7th brigades, attacked on the left, while the 4th Division, with the 12th Brigade, assaulted on the right as enemy machine-guns fired from protected positions.[49] Troops moved forward as best they could, and as they advanced the larger battle became a series of small skirmishes as each Canadian platoon and each German pillbox found itself fighting its own war. Rifle grenades proved their value in a battle where the infantry needed its own artillery to support the advance; men took cover in shell-holes and fired all they had at the pillboxes and trenches that barred the way to their objectives. Lewis guns, rifles, and rifle-grenades added to the destruction and noise, though bombs were almost useless, since the pillboxes forced the Canadians to fight from a longer range than they had experienced in previous battles or trench raids. Platoons avoided strong points and attempted to outflank them, and sometimes doing so involved long, sweeping movements. Crest Farm, named for its position on the ridge, was captured in this manner, as the forty men of the large garrison, completely surrounded and pelted with rifle-grenades and bullets, were killed or taken prisoner. The Germans used available ground as best they could, with small garrisons in small lengths of trench or in shell-holes, but flanking fire forced them to relinquish these positions or suffer death, wounds, or capture.[50]

On the left the 3rd Division was unable to capture all its positions, but on the right the 12th Brigade advanced quickly,[51] and whether or not battalions gained their final objectives, they had to prepare to meet counter-attacks.[52] Artillery, which on the left had been unable to support the assault adequately, came into its own across the entire front when the Germans tried to dislodge the Canadians from their new positions. At 8:12 a.m., soon after it had halted, the 12th Brigade received a message from its supporting artillery that the guns were shelling an enemy assembly area; the counter-attack the Germans were organizing never materialized, since communications were clear and the infantry had little trouble getting help. The problem consisted of trying to make the gunners stop, because shells often continued to fall long after the Germans had given up the assault; commanders later recommended that some means be found to sent an 'OK' signal to cancel the SOS. With support at hand the 12th Brigade managed to hold its positions. During the day heavy howitzers kept German assembly areas under fire, and when the enemy tried to launch a counter-attack at night, it was so broken up by shelling that German infantry hiding in shell-holes surrendered when the sun came up.[53]

After the assault of 30 October captured part of the ridge, there was some time to prepare for the next attack on 6 November. Scouts and patrols tried to map out the enemy's defences, commanders worked towards applying some of the lessons of the first few battles, and troops and junior leaders rehearsed. There was little definitive information on how the Germans were deploying their units; intelligence sections could assume only that each German battalion had placed three companies forward with one in close support. They did know that not all machine-guns were in concrete emplacements but could frequently be found in small sections of trench sheltered by pieces of canvas or corrugated iron. Having determined in some way how the enemy had set up his defences, leaders at all levels tried to find ways through them. In training, troops experimented with smoke bombs, only recently available, which produced a fog that could surround a pillbox or length of trench and prevent its occupants from seeing their attackers until it was too late.[54]

As for tactics, training followed the same road it had since Vimy. Battalion officers, non-commissioned officers, and many of the men went to Corps Headquarters to study the large relief map of the area, then each battalion went over the taped course while planners carefully briefed everyone on their objectives. After the battalion rehearsals brigades then trained on the course, practising mutual support, flank protection, and following the artillery barrage, represented by moving flags. Units tried to develop the best methods of capturing pillboxes, strong points, and machine-gun emplacements, and they relearned the techniques of fire and movement, of leadership and command. Training was capped with full-dress rehearsals.[55]

In the few short days prior to the assault the attacking battalions of the 1st Brigade on the left and the 6th Brigade on the right moved into their assembly areas, though German artillery and the mud of Passchendaele combined, as they had in the previous two battles, to make forming-up difficult. After operations on 30 October the 12th Brigade had suggested ways of cutting down on casualties among those who would go to the front: 'The necessity of keeping reserves well forward is emphasized. This is due partially to the almost impassable state of part of the ground in rear of the advance and also to the fact that the German fire was laid down on certain well defined localities of the support area.'[56] The 6th Brigade had only one duckboard track to make its way forward; the German bombardment was incessant, and the most careful arrangements were required to assemble the three attacking battalions on a 500-yard front. According to the brigade's after-action report, German artillery was the worst problem it had to deal with in the entire operation. After two days of observing enemy shelling, however, scouts determined that the best time to move was just before dawn, before the Germans fired their early-morning bombardment, and by moving troops at that time, battalions suffered only slight harassment. The 27th Battalion ran into the barrage none the less and suffered some casualties, though the brigade managed to assemble its troops within 150 yards of the enemy line without discovery, and outposts pushed to within forty yards of German positions. Lewis gunners and riflemen moved into them to protect the assembly from German counter-attack, and they also went undiscovered.[57]

The Canadians had complex instructions for their artillery and machine-guns. The 1st Brigade allotted thirty-two heavy machine-guns for the barrage, eight guns to accompany the infantry and help consolidate newly won positions and four guns to act as long-range snipers. The barrage on the 6th Brigade front included five batteries of heavy machine-guns, forty guns in all, whose role was to bolster the creeping and protective barrages. To reduce casualties they went into the line twenty-four hours before the attack and were to be removed forty-eight hours later, these movements attesting to the dangers machine-gunners faced in the front line, where German artillery, with its greater range, could harass them without their being able to retaliate.[58]

The barrage plan was overwhelming in its complexity. To give a small example, the 5th Brigade organized some of the artillery support for the 6th Brigade. At z to z plus four minutes, the infantry would use its own weapons to dominate the area 100 yards in front of the advance, and at 200 hundred yards, eighteen-pounders would fire a barrage, and a combination of eighteen-pounders and 4.5-inch howitzers would fire at targets 500 yards away. Machine-guns fired 700 yards in front of the advance, and the area 900 yards out was the responsibility of six-inch howitzers. Finally, heavy artillery, made up of sixty-pounders, eight-inch, and 9.2-inch guns, fired at targets 1,100 yards in front of the assault. Not all barrages lifted at the same time, to ensure that there would be some overlap at crucial stages in the advance; for example, when the machine-guns found that the attack had outranged them, they were to move forward while artillery ranged forward and back to cover the machine-gunners' zones. When the infantry reached its objective, all barrages would remain stationary for fourteen minutes, when the eighteen-pounders would increase their range by 400 yards and other batteries would lift to cover a 2,000-yard depth to discourage counter-attacks.[59] Whether or not artillery and machine-gun batteries could keep to such a complex plan remained to be seen.

The opening barrage was a complete success. According to G. McNight of the 26th Battalion: 'The barrage started at six in the morning and it was terrific. I remember turning around and looking back and all I could see for, it looked to be miles, everything seemed to be on fire. That was a terrific artillery barrage and we were mighty glad to have the support too.'[60] The Canadians advanced with a leading wave in two lines, generally two platoons, followed by sections in column. These small units were disposed to provide mutual support in case of hold-ups or small counter-attacks, while formations allowed troops to react quickly to machine guns or pockets of German infantry, and special parties were given the task of dealing with machine-guns, strong points, and pill-boxes. As G. McNight remembered:

They had these cement pill boxes all along the line and then these slits. They just fire out the slits, you see. They'd wave the machine guns back and forth and, if you ever got in front of that fire, there was no chance for you whatever, you see, but our main idea was to get around behind those pill boxes and put the Mills bombs in on them, you see, which we did successfully but those pill boxes, there was so much mud that they were sinking, they were right down low. There was just the top of them out of the mud, you see, and they were a hard thing to get at.[61]

When the operation was complete, McNight's company had only forty-one or forty-two of the 124 soldiers who had started out that morning.

Companies had precise objectives and leap-frogged their way forward,[62] but on this day artillery was by far the greater contributor to success. In the words of the 6th Brigade narrative:

Zero hour having been fixed for 6.00 a.m. of the 6th Novr our Artillery opened up with a tremendous burst, and all Units immediately 'jumped off' after the rolling barrage. The attack was a complete surprise to the enemy, for as soon as the 1st lift of the barrage was made he found himself confronted by our men, who had followed so closely upon our barrage that they were amongst the enemy front line garrison, and freely using the bayonet, before it was realized that such was the case. Four machine guns in the enemy front line were captured before they had time to open fire.[63]

Their defences having been overrun in the previous two battles, the Germans had to revert to older tactics based on the trench and the front-line machine-gun, because there had not been time to prepare pillboxes and more complicated positions. As it had done at Vimy, Canadian artillery was able to keep the Germans at the bottom of their trenches until it was too late to prepare an adequate defence.

The first objective fell quickly. The 6th Brigade reported the enemy's retreating from his main line, many riflemen having thrown away their weapons, and the 31st Battalion came across a number of houses, shattered by artillery and sheltering many of the enemy, though the Canadians were so close to the barrage that the Germans had little time to take up their positions. The 1st Brigade's 1st Battalion came across more bodies than live Germans, the guns having destroyed many of their defences; the garrison of Mosselmarkt, a small cluster of houses at the top of the ridge, had been for the most part killed in the cellars. The German barrage was rendered useless by the Canadians' rapid movement; enemy gunners began to fire three minutes after the attacking battalions moved off and their shells fell mainly behind the advance.[64]

Units carried on to subsequent objectives, but the advance began to slow; on the right the 27th Battalion met heavy opposition from machine-guns, and the 28th Battalion found itself mired in mud. The 31st Battalion ran into the now rare pillboxes on the outskirts of Passchendaele village, but eventually its troops managed to push on as, again and again, Canadian tactics succeeded in silencing strong points. Riflemen fired at the enemy, while rifle-grenadiers launched their bombs from the front and small groups worked their way around the flanks, and in the rush that followed the defenders either surrendered or were wiped out. German machine-guns tried to delay the 1st Battalion's advance, but they fell to the attackers. The Canadians supplied seven German machine-guns with captured ammunition and put them to use, and troops cleared a cluster of houses called Graf House with a Stokes mortar, one of which accompanied each battalion.[65] The battles against the pillboxes, however, demonstrated that Canadian tactics still, at times, had to rely on raw courage. Private J.P. Robertson of the 27th Battalion, while his companions fired rifles and machine-guns, rushed through a garrison's flank, bayoneting some of the German infantry and putting the others to flight. Lieutenant H. Kennedy of the 31st Battalion charged through the barrage and captured a pillbox with his revolver, taking thirty-seven prisoners. Corporal P.H. Lindsell of the 28th Battalion also rushed through the barrage and German machine-gun fire and captured a machine-gun at bayonet point, taking sixteen prisoners. It is important to note that many of the individuals who captured enemy positions on their own that day did so with the support of rifle, machine-gun, or artillery fire.

There were also threats from the air, however, as several times during the day German aircraft strafed the Canadians after they captured their objectives. When asked about the role of aircraft in the last three months of the war, W.D. Allen volunteered that 'Where we saw the most Heinie planes was at Passchendaele.'[66] Many were driven off with Lewis-gun fire, since they had to fly low in order to machine-gun the Canadians. During the assault, aircraft in support of the Canadian advance concentrated on flying contact patrols to pick up signals that would indicate how the attack was going; each platoon of the 31st Battalion, for example, chose six men to be flare specialists, whose task was to watch for the planes and signal to them, and throughout the battle the system worked well. In the latter stages of the Passchendaele offensive some squadrons began to specialize in ground-support work, though there was as yet no special training for them, and low-flying sorties often resulted in heavy losses. Aircraft also searched the ground for the enemy in counter-attack patrols; taking off an hour after the attack started, they were to warn Canadian gunners if the Germans seemed to be rallying.[67]

The contact patrols were part of a comprehensive system of communications. Brigades could contact each other with wireless sets, buried cable linked brigades to their battalions, and forward of battalion headquarters signallers used lamps and other visual devices to keep in touch with the front line. Runners served the same purpose, and on 6 November they were often the only means of communication available as smoke and shell explosions blocked visual signals. The assaulting battalions took with them power buzzers and amplifiers, though their usefulness was somewhat in doubt at this stage in the war. Interestingly, pigeons actually served some purpose on 6 November and often managed to carry messages through to their destination.[68]

The 1st and 6th Brigades soon reached their objectives and began to consolidate, companies preparing an outpost line on the ridge's forward slope. The attack was a 'bite-and-hold' operation, and according to G. McNight: 'We jumped off at six o'clock and, if I remember rightly, it was noontime before we consolidated and we only went two thousand yards but you couldn't go any faster. You'd go up to your knees in mud and you couldn't get out of the mud.'[69] These positions were organized in depth, using any wire that might be available, and the main line of defence was made up of continuous, long lengths of trench placed to allow crossfire from machine-guns and rifles and dug in behind the crest of the ridge so it would be hidden from enemy observation. Where possible the Canadians prepared a reserve line, and machine-guns moved from the positions they had hastily chosen in the minutes following the ridge's capture to those that would be more permanent and better placed. Trench mortars were a problem, since the mud made it difficult to move the weapons and their ammunition forward, though those that made it to the new defensive position were used to harass the Germans.[70]

The first German counter-attacks were hastily organized and half-hearted; artillery, Lewis guns, and rifle fire broke them up. One German battalion failed to counter-attack at all because its commander, visiting a friend at the front, had been captured in the assault. Barrages along the entire line helped discourage the Germans from assembling their men, and after nightfall, machine-guns prepared to fire at predetermined targets in the darkness to keep the enemy off balance. Though such tactics may have dissuaded counter-attacks, German snipers made life miserable for the consolidating troops. The ridge, however, remained in Canadian hands. That 6 November the Canadians lost 2,238 men, 734 of whom died. They took 464 German prisoners of war.[71]

The 2nd and 4th Brigades attacked on 10 November to gain the remaining high ground north of the village; they succeeded, suffering 1,094 casualties, 420 of them killed.[72] The attack was noteworthy in that enemy aircraft were more active than before in bombing and strafing Canadian troops, and they were exceptionally aggressive on the 11th and 12th, bombing rear areas and machine-gunning work parties, but bad weather put a stop to such activities for the next two weeks.[73] With that attack the battle ended; the Canadians had carried out Field-Marshal Haig's orders, but in taking the ridge the corps suffered a total of 16,041 battle casualties of which 3,042 were killed.[74] The Canadians had learned much in the process, and before each battle they tried to adopt some of the lessons of the last. Artillery altered barrage plans to eliminate German forward posts in no man's land, and to keep them out of reach of enemy artillery machine-gunners went into the line only when they were needed. Attacking companies were formed in greater and greater depth to cut through the deep defences of pillboxes and strong points, and the gunners also learned to fire in depth with a series of barrages, making use of any weapon with an adequate range. Everything, from machine-guns firing small .303-inch bullets to howitzers lobbing shells with a 9.2-inch diameter, joined in getting the Canadians close enough to the enemy to apply their tactics of flanking movements and mutual support. There had been serious errors, especially where artillery was concerned; for the gunners faced a new battle almost every time they entered the line, each time the Germans changed their defensive tactics, or the British chose a new objective. Mud made matters worse. Artillery registration and preparation were still time consuming, though at least by the time the gunners arrived at Passchendaele they were able to learn from their mistakes in days rather than weeks and to carry out their role effectively without sacrificing entire infantry battalions.

The tactics of the Canadian Corps, adopted prior to Vimy Ridge and developed in the battles of 1917, were effective in cutting through static positions of greater and greater depth, but casualties were still high. In one sense they were higher than they had been on the Somme; for in the three battles of Third Ypres involving the Canadian Corps the latter advanced only 2,000 yards, thus losing over 14,000 men for every mile gained, compared with under 10,000 per mile on the Somme. The war was to take a turn away from siege attacks against prepared defences leading to battles of attrition, however, since in 1918 the Germans broke the deadlock, if only for a time. In 1914 generals had sought a war of movement, and four years later a more limited form of that war came upon them in all its complexity. The Canadians spent the months between Passchendaele and the summer of 1918 preparing for the new style of warfare, one in which the entire corps, not just its infantry, had to move, and daily advances would be measured in miles rather than hundreds of yards.

7

Into 1918

In early 1918 the Canadian Corps, like the British Army as a whole, took time to absorb the lessons learned in the mud of Passchendaele. Field Marshall Sir Douglas Haig wanted to launch yet another offensive to breach German defences, in spite of Prime Minister Lloyd George's understandable doubts, and he expected major changes in the nature of combat on the Western Front. Haig and other officers of the British high command were convinced, as General Robert Nivelle had been a year before, that the next major battle would have to be more than an assault on an important geographical feature or economic centre; it had to be a campaign aimed at ending the war. Though the Eastern Front was moribund and the Germans were able to transfer troops to face the Allies, American involvement and the Royal Navy blockade warranted some optimism, and the break-in at Cambrai (to be discussed below), though short lived, was a good augury for the future. Open fighting, the generals believed, seemed a distinct possibility, and in early 1918 the Canadian Corps prepared for battles of manœuvre. In their training the Canadians relied heavily on reports from the British, whose army commanders kept the corps informed regarding German weapons and tactics as well as their own. When the Germans launched their offensive in March 1918, the stream of information continued, the Canadian Corps taking note of what the British and French learned in the first open fighting since 1914. The Canadians, who never felt the full brunt of the German attacks, were thus free to adapt to the new style of combat without losing whole battalions in the process.

The technology of war had changed little. The tank had first seen action on the Somme but with a maximum cross-country speed of two miles per hour could go no faster than a soldier could walk. On 20

November armoured vehicles were used en masse for the first time in an assault on Cambrai; the operation was a success, but only until a German counter-offensive forced the British off their gains. In effect Cambrai demonstrated that both sides could still launch offensives, but the British were able to determine how to put the armoured vehicles to best use to break in German positions, lessons important for the offensive at Amiens the following August. Gunnery also benefited from the lessons of Cambrai; with armoured vehicles to flatten German wire it was possible to retain the advantage of surprise by eliminating the preliminary bombardment, which previously had been necessary to blow gaps in German obstacles. The gunners did no ranging or registration but shot from the map the day of the attack, taking advantage of improved techniques of surveying and calibration that the Canadian Corps was also adopting.[1]

At Cambrai both sides learned of the tank's vulnerabilities. Martin Middlebrook, who interviewed German veterans for his book *The Kaiser's Battle*, found that 'Many men do mention the lessons learnt at Cambrai – how vulnerable a tank was to a brave man who could push a bundle of grenades under a tank track or to the field gunner who could destroy a tank by staying at his gun and firing over open sights.'[2] Tank casualties were high; at Flesquières on 20 November specially trained batteries of the German 54th Division destroyed twenty-six tanks without interference from the 51st Highland Division. By the end of the first day of the offensive 179 of 374 tanks were out of action, sixty-five from direct hits, seventy-one due to mechanical breakdown, and forty-three through ditching, and of the remainder many needed maintenance before they could carry on. Overall 56 per cent of the tanks became casualties on the first day, not including those damaged, and after a week's fighting the surviving crews were dead tired.[3] The tank, as a tool for breaking through German lines, had its limitations.

In November 1917, after the battle of Passchendaele had wound down and the British tank assault at Cambrai had come to a halt, the Canadian Corps issued its 'Notes on Training' to cover the next several months, and several aspects of these instructions are of interest here. Its authors, the staff officers of the Canadian Corps, insisted that soldiers must be prepared to go from trench warfare to open combat and back, though a constant mobile war was out of the question, since it was impossible to sustain a full-scale assault indefinitely. The notes implied that if it ever became possible to carry on an offensive of indeterminate length, the Germans would fold completely and the war would end. In any case, training soldiers for both phases of combat was not difficult, for they were very similar. Using parade-square drill as an analogy, the 'Notes on Training' stated that 'the principles of fighting are the same in both cases, the only difference is in the scale of time and space. In trench warfare we do things "by numbers" in open fighting we have to do the same things "in quick time." '⁴ The deliberate attacks of trench warfare would thus be replaced with quick assaults carried out under the command of junior leaders following already established tactical principles.

As in previous training periods, corps and army headquarters focused on musketry and support weapons to keep the platoon moving: 'A well-trained platoon should have complete confidence in its ability to cover its own advance by fire of its own weapons and thus to reach its objective even if the barrage has got far ahead of it.'⁵ There was nothing new in relying on the platoon to carry out an assault, but the 'Notes on Training' proposed to go a step further; referring to Passchendaele, it stated: 'A recent development in the method of attack has been the advance by Section rushes from cover to cover behind a slow-moving barrage (e.g. 8 minutes to 100 yards). This and also the advance by Section Columns over very broken ground should be thoroughly taught.'⁶ Sections would not be self-sufficient for combat but would move separately to avoid heavy casualties from artillery and machine-gun fire,⁷ though bringing the different sections of the platoon together to attack a strong point would require first-rate leadership abilities on the part of platoon commanders.

Training for the pursuit and consolidation phases of a battle remained basically the same. Should the enemy retreat, the Canadians were expected to advance from one tactical point to the next, units leap-frogging at pre-arranged boundaries. Scouts would lead, followed by advance platoons, themselves followed by the remainder of the company. As usual, troops were to advance under cover of rifle and Lewis-gun fire, and when the pursuit slowed to a crawl, they could consolidate their positions by digging in. To ensure soldiers could adopt defensive positions quickly, they would learn rapid wiring drills, so that everyone would become proficient at setting up barriers.⁸ The training notes did not consider solid lines appropriate for defence; rather, 'Troops must be trained to realize that the outpost line ... cannot be a continuous trench line but that the picquets must be dug in at the best tactical points available where the ground in front and flanks can be swept by machine gun fire.'⁹ Infantry would not stop counter-attacks by putting platoons in the enemy's path, but by keeping his routes of advance covered with automatic weapons.

In the months following the assaults on Passchendaele the gunners trained as they had in previous years, but they also had to fight the ongoing trench war. Diary entries like 'the usual artillery duels all day. Nothing of importance'[10] attest to the routine nature of barrage and counter-barrage on portions of the Western Front. G.G. Renison, in a letter home, related how 'Fritz was shelling a battery about half a mile from where I was. The bombardment could hardly be classed a success – about two out of every three shells were "duds." Where the gunners were I don't know, but after each dud lit a cheer floated across.'[11] Observers carried on in spite of the usual hazards: 'Went to front line this morning and began observing fire behind it. At noon they hit my house three times with 5.9s and altogether gave me a hell of a time for the 24 hours.'[12]

Since the beginning of the war artillery had steadily gained in importance, and by 1918 the Canadian Corps had far more guns than it had had three years previously. In its first year on the Western Front the Canadian contingent had had 6.3 guns for every 1,000 infantrymen; by early 1918 that ratio had doubled. Also, the gunners who came from Canada as replacements were already well prepared for their role, and time spent in England was mostly a refresher, though, once in France, new gunners joined units in a state of transition, preparing for open warfare. In the corps area at Auchel, eight miles west of Bethune, artillerymen spent their days in reserve grooming horses, going through physical exercises, riding, lectures, baths, and route marches. Batteries sent a section at a time for six weeks' instruction at the Canadian Corps Artillery School at Permes, then began training for open warfare, where gunners practised moving from position to position, often preparing their own sites before settling in to shoot. In late December the eighteen-pounder ceased to be the jack of all trades of Canadian artillery and was concentrated on use in barrages and sniping. As before, gunners learned gun maintenance and the proper selection of ammunition, but the need for increased accuracy meant they had to learn about the effects of atmospheric conditions as well.[13]

No amount of training could solve all the artillery's technical challenges. Shells were not entirely uniform, which was to be expected when they came off assembly lines in their millions from several countries on two continents. Shorts were a problem, though the gunners insisted that a round falling in no man's land could not be called a 'short'; only those that fell too close to Canadian posts could be considered a hazard, though what distance constituted 'too close' was never defined.[14] More dangerous to the gunners and anyone nearby were premature explosions, which occurred when the shell went off just before or a split-second after it left the barrel, and artillerymen in the 4.5-inch howitzer batteries often referred to themselves as 'suicide clubs'. Gunner R.P. Pangman described just such an incident: 'One of the chaps who had been on with me the night before, Stevens, went in to give the rest a hand with a little rapid fire, and I was just going in too, when I heard the order to fire, so waited at the door a second. The next think I knew there was a tremendous crash, and I ran in, and the whole gun had been blown to pieces. Stevens had been killed outright, and the rest pretty badly cut up.'[15] Luckily for gunner morale, such incidents were rare, but they served to remind artillerymen that the technology at their disposal was still imperfect.

To maintain communications between forward observation officers and their batteries, gunners still relied on the D3 telephone. It was far superior to its alternative, the power buzzer, since it allowed two-way communication between soldiers untrained in Morse code. SOS signals were still a problem: even forward observation officers had trouble distinguishing between actual assaults and enemy reconnaissance patrols; the 9th Brigade suggested using aircraft to signal the guns in case of a general attack. If the Germans shelled Canadian positions, it was sometimes difficult to call for an SOS to silence the enemy guns, since exploding shells usually cut telephone lines and it then became necessary to rely on rocket signals or runners. By 1918 the gunners were quick to reply and reasonably accurate with their shooting. An effective way to ensure artillery would react promptly was to place guns right in the front line, though circumstances had to be ideal; gunners could dig themselves in to one side of a strong point to help protect it from infantry assault. Wireless proved very useful, if the apparatus and trained operators were available, and Canadian signallers, far more than their British brethren, used the sets as auxiliaries to take up surplus traffic.[16]

Training for signallers was little different from that of a year before. Signal sections learned their trade on their own and on exercises with their battalions, setting up runner systems, with men on foot near the front and on bicycle further back; they were still the backbone of the communications system once an attack was under way. Men practised signalling with Lucas lamps, which were excellent if dust, smoke, or mist did not hinder visibility. Communication with aircraft could be tricky, but signallers were trained to use strips of cloth and panels to send simple messages to patrol airplanes. Flags, though of limited use, were also part of the curriculum. Finally, so signallers could find their way around the battlefield and report their positions accurately, they learned and relearned how to use compasses, telescopes, and binoculars – all this in addition to laying wire and operating telephones.[17] Ordinary battalion signallers seem not to have had access to wireless sets for training; useful as the devices could be, they were still within the realm of the specialist; tuning, maintaining, and operating the complicated apparatus was a full course in itself.

While trench life went on as it had for years, raids were common, and rifle-grenades continued to prove their worth. In a raid near Lens on 21 January 1918 members of the 58th Battalion rushed forward without artillery support; though eight guns covered part of the front line and twelve were ready to fire at the trench itself, they had orders to hold their fire until they were called for. They were not. The men advanced, each with the weapons he would need in the coming battle. The captain in charge of the raid carried a revolver, twenty-five rounds of ammunition, eight Number 23 rifle-grenades, a flare pistol, and six white flares; thus even the leader of the raid carried ammunition for the rifle-grenadiers. Each bomber carried a revolver and twenty-five rounds and a dozen Mills Number 5 hand-grenades. Scouts had their rifle and bayonet, fifty rounds of ammunition, twenty-five rounds of blank ammunition, and eight Number 23 rifle-grenades. Finally, the rifle grenadiers went through the gap with the same weapons and ammunition as the scouts. Thus the forward and rear elements of each section carried the most long-range weapons, one to cover the assault, the other to cover the withdrawal, while for such work the rifle-grenade was the weapon of choice, since by January 1918 it had more than proved itself in the eyes of the Canadian infantry. As one staff officer reported: 'The use made of the 23 Mills Rifle Grenade deserves consideration. In my opinion, the training in the use of this grenade, which enables us to out-range the German stick and egg grenades, is of great importance. It is interesting to note that the 58th Battalion carried out a very successful operation in almost the same place last September, through the intelligent use of the Mills Rifle Grenade. The value of this grenade is thus shown when used by a unit who correctly appreciate it.'[18] Captain Jucksch, the leader, credited the rifle-grenade for allowing his battalion to carry out the operation without casualties, though hand-grenades could still be hazardous to their users; the same Captain Jucksch, while waiting to move into a dugout, pulled the pin from a bomb, but the safety lever slipped out, and in the words of the report, 'he was compelled to throw it away.'[19]

The Germans had also – long before – recognized the need to develop tactics based on small units, and the squad was capable of manœuvring by itself by the end of 1915, and its leader became a key decision-maker on the battlefield. Such small-unit tactics using all available technologies gave the German infantry the means of crossing no man's land without suffering the kind of casualties it had experienced in its 1914 campaigns. In the opening phases of the Verdun offensive, specialized units spearheaded many of the attacks, and General Oskar Von Hutier, in an attack on Riga in the summer of 1917, kept his assault troops well back until the last possible moment, using a short, intense, preparatory bombardment to help clear the way for infantry moving forward in small infiltration units, each with its own artillery support. At Caporetto in November 1917 the Austro-Hungarian Army, with some German divisions using similar tactics, completely routed the Italians and made a 100-mile advance.

Then operation Michael began. On 21 March German formations using these innovative tactics forced their way through the understrength and badly organized Fifth British Army and threatened to break into the rear. Storm troops led the way, pushing forward as far as possible and leaving strong points to others. Meanwhile battle groups of more orthodox infantry in battalion or regimental strength followed, supported by machine-guns, mobile mortars, and field artillery to surround the strongest of the British positions. Behind them came fresh formations to maintain momentum. They had no tanks; instead, a brief hurricane bombardment prepared the way. With these tactics, the Germans kept the British and French reeling well into the summer, and they threatened Paris on 6 June. The Allies did not fully recover until mid-July, and even then it looked as if the war was to last indefinitely, since the Germans had proved their strength.[20] Events were to show, however, that they had also expended it.

Though Canadian positions were not part of the German objective, the Canadian front did not remain quiet. On 21 March the Germans carried out a well-supported raid against the 2nd Battalion, preceded by heavy and light trench mortars, whiz-bangs, and 4.1-inch guns shelling communication trenches as far back as battalion headquarters; the 2nd and 3rd companies took the full brunt of the assault. Canadians fired rifles and Lewis guns on all natural approaches from no man's land, while the 3rd Company used rifle fire and a heavy machine-gun to drive the Germans away from its positions. One of the company guns jammed after firing a single magazine, so infantry threw bombs while the gunner cleared the stoppage and got the gun working again. Outflanked, the Lewis gunner withdrew with his weapon under cover of bomb and rifle fire, while a Lewis gun belonging to another platoon fired into the Germans' flank. Yet another gun stopped a small German party directly to its front and swung around to cover the withdrawing Lewis; the enemy, however, succeeded in entering the trench. A staff officer with the 1st Brigade attributed the Germans' success to the gun's jamming. By the time the skirmishing ended, twenty-three Germans lay dead in the trenches, and the Canadians had lost twelve killed, thirty wounded, and four missing (probably taken prisoner). On 5 April the Germans launched another raid with about 100 men, but it failed to cross no man's land.[21]

As battalions relieved one another every four to six days, raids and counter-raids punctuated trench life for those at the front, while those in reserve continued to train. Troops sent over from Canada needed fourteen weeks' training before they went to France, though the corps had a large pool of trained reserves in England, if the 5th Division, with its 8,500 infantrymen, could be broken up.[22] According to one who served in the formation, Herbert A. Mowat, 'The ... 5th Division was the most thoroughly trained division that the Canadians had before it was in actual combat. They had a year of field training,'[23] including manœuvres in open warfare. Disbanded in February 1918, it kept the Canadians in France and Belgium up to strength while the British were cutting their divisions down from twelve to nine battalions each. Reinforcement drafts, which filed out the ranks depleted at Passchendaele, and veterans of previous battles had to learn the lessons of that muddy battlefield, while the corps altered its organization. A few months after the British reduced the size of their infantry divisions, Currie not only insisted on maintaining the same number of battalions per brigade but increased the strength of each by 100 men. In May 1918 each company still had four platoons and eight Lewis guns; platoon manœuvring was the keynote of operations, sections moving under cover of rifle, Lewis gun, and rifle-grenade. Fire control was critical; it was important that everyone engage the right targets on a battlefield where each platoon had its own objectives, so musketry was once again an important part of training. To make the whole organization work in an advance, training also stressed bold patrolling and reconnaissance, so commanders would know where they were in relation to their objectives. Troops were to practise rapid section deployment to avoid the effects of enemy fire as well as to encircle strong points and nests before they could react.[24]

It was some time before platoon organization was again standardized throughout the Canadian Corps. The 2nd Canadian Mounted Rifles, for example, had operated since November 1917 with five sections per platoon, consisting of a Lewis-gun section and four rifle sections, but such exceptions were rare and had been eradicated by the time the corps went on the offensive again. Each platoon was made up of thirty men: one officer, two sergeants, two corporals, two lance-corporals, and twenty-three privates, organized into two half-platoons, each under the command of a sergeant and each formed of two sections, one of Lewis gunners and another combining riflemen and rifle-grenadiers (figure 4). Corps staff believed that a half-platoon was a strong fighting unit in its own right, complete with Lewis-gun support and under the command of an experienced non-commissioned officer.[25] That a half-platoon of fifteen or twenty soldiers was considered a fighting unit in 1918 demonstrated the increase in fire-power available to the Canadian Corps in contrast to the situation of two years earlier, when it was considered impossible for a platoon of less than twenty-eight troops to function on the battlefield.

Physical training, wiring, bayonet fighting, gas drill, company close-order drill, musketry, specialist training for Lewis gunners, rifle-grenadiers, bombers, and others were the order of the day, as they had been for years. Within the general syllabus were a few additions based on lessons learned in previous battles. In February, for example, the 2nd Brigade had its battalions rehearse their companies in the attack in trench and semi-open warfare, with emphasis on how to stage counterattacks on short notice. One platoon per company practised stealth, raiding, and moving under artillery cover fire. Quick consolidation exercises vied with fifteen-mile route marches for the men's time; the soldiers also practised cooperation with tanks and airplanes.[26]

In the summer the German offensive began to peter out and the Canadians readied themselves for the battles to come. Brigadier-General Victor Odlum, commanding the 11th Brigade, ordered his subordinates to 'Make use of every hour available, subject only to the limitation that men must be allowed a reasonable proportion of rest,'[27] though whether his definition of 'reasonable proportion' was the same as the men's is somewhat doubtful. The Canadians followed the British lead in preparing for open warfare; as each brigade left the line to go into reserve,

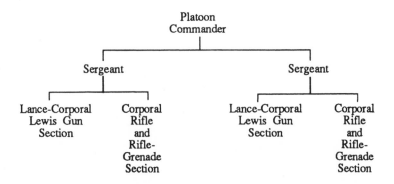

Figure 4
Platoon organization, 1918
Based on description in RG 9, v.4162, folder 9, file 3, '58th Battalion, Organi-
zation of a Platoon, 18 May 1918' and '3rd Division, 7 June 1918'

it trained as a unit for six weeks. The basic principle of operations was
for each platoon to be allotted its objectives and areas where it was to
fight the enemy; it would then proceed directly towards these fighting
areas, avoiding obstructions on the way, whether they be wire obstacles
or strong points, taking advantage of local topography and advancing
under cover of its weapons and those of nearby platoons. The Canadians
would thus advance by infiltrating through enemy defences, much as
the Germans had bypassed British strong points in March.[28]

   Though Currie had often pushed for a move away from specialization
within the infantry, insisting that every man know how to use a machine-
gun or rifle-grenade, his view of the corps as a whole was different,
especially where engineers were concerned: 'I am of the opinion that
much of the success of the Canadian Corps in the final 100 days was
due to the fact that they had sufficient engineers to do the engineering
work and that in those closing battles we did not employ the infantry
in that kind of work. We trained the infantry for fighting and used them
only for fighting.'[29] To lighten the infantry's burden and ensure that
the engineers would have the resources necessary to complete their tasks,
the latter were reorganized in the first week of May. The three field
companies per division were reformed and expanded into a single bri-

gade of three battalions, with its own headquarters, pontoon bridging, and transport unit. Each battalion, like the infantry, was formed of about 1,000 men, who were collected from the four disbanded pioneer battalions, the 1st and 2nd tunnelling companies, and the three field companies of the 5th Division. Thus, instead of dealing with the infantry brigades, engineer companies had their own chain of command, with their own personnel and logistical support to keep them going in the field and on the job.[30]

The new organization did not mean that the sappers could not act as infantry. To allow for this kind of transition, engineer battalions were organized like their infantry counterparts, with subsections broken down in the same manner as infantry platoons. Each subsection had a strength of about fifty men, with a headquarters composed of the commander, a sergeant, and the ubiquitous runners. The remainder was taken up with three subsquads of one non-commissioned officer and eleven riflemen, with two men told off as rifle grenadiers and bombers. There was also a Lewis-gun squad with a non-commissioned officer, six gunners, and three scouts, who could also act as riflemen. Their tactics were much the same as those of the infantry.[31]

Heavy machine-gunners, who operated the Vickers, also had their own organization within the Canadian Corps, under the command of Brigadier-General Raymond Brutinel. They supported advancing platoons but were not part of them. As the official history relates,

The machine-gun service was to be regarded as a distinctive arm, intermediate between the infantry and the artillery, and with tactics of its own. Though there were occasions when M.G. companies or batteries might be temporarily attached to infantry brigades or battalions for duty, machine-gun battalions were divisional troops, under the command and tactical control of a Divisional Machine Gun Commander, whose position was closely analogous to that of the CRA [Commanding Royal Artillery] of a Division with respect to artillery.[32]

The Canadian Corps agreed with Brutinel's appraisal, and staff officers added that machine-gun tactics were radically different from those of the infantry and approximated those of the artillery. There was no doubt that the main role of the machine-gun units, like that of the artillery, was to help the infantry survive on the battlefield.[33]

The formation of machine gun units proceeded apace. While aircraft were armed with the Lewis and tanks with the Hotchkiss, the British

Expeditionary Force retained the now-plentiful, and heavier, Vickers for land operations. Separating the Vickers from the infantry was made necessary by its lack of mobility. It was also inappropriate as an artillery weapon, since an eighteen-pounder firing six rounds per minute – its maximum rate was twenty – could splatter an area with over 2,000 bullets, compared with the Vickers' rate of 500 rounds per minute, so machine-guns had to be organized in batteries if they were to supplement the artillery's fire. Further, the eighteen-pounders outranged the Vickers by 6,200 to 2,500 yards. The machine-gun enjoyed two main advantages over artillery – it did not require roads to move forward and was available in great numbers, since thousands had already been manufactured. Organizing this technology and its technicians was an ongoing task, and in the spring of 1918 each Canadian division incorporated a complete machine-gun battalion of 1,558 all ranks and ninety-six Vickers machine-guns, and each infantry platoon received an additional Lewis gun.[34] Originally, each division had had only two machine-gun companies, but Currie ordered the formation of a third without waiting for the army commander's permission, though 'Official sanction can come later.'[35] Creating the third company required 2,400 men overall who were found by reallocating fifty of the 100 extra troops each battalion had recently received.[36] By the end of the war the Canadian Machine Gun Corps had a strength of 422 officers and 8,349 men,[37] or the equivalent of two infantry brigades. Though they were often useful in the battles of 1918, there would be some debate as to whether their contribution matched their numbers, and those who later insisted that the machine-gun dominated the battlefields of the First World War might have taken note.

These men had to be trained. Instructors judged machine-gunners, novices and veterans alike, by their ability to prepare their guns for action, rapidly select and occupy favourable positions, open fire according to previously issued orders, and maintain a high rate of fire as long as necessary. Brutinel's influence was obvious in the Machine Gun Corps's emphasis on indirect fire; he believed that in upcoming offensives such techniques might well by the only support machine-gun battalions could offer the infantry. Shooting at targets, either directly or indirectly, however, was only a small part of the machine-gunners' training. Improvised defences, open warfare, the advance after a breakthrough, the retirement after an enemy breakthrough, taking defensive positions behind the infantry, command, and liaison were also important subjects, and the focus of many a rehearsal or exercise. The machine-gunner's task, based as it was on the relationship between a technician and a complex piece of machinery, was not an easy one.[38]

Thus in addition to learning to shoot straight, machine-gunners had to adopt sophisticated tactics. Each section officer would move forward with the infantry battalion to which he was attached but would leave the guns behind to follow him by leap-frogging their way towards the enemy. In using machine-guns the British had learned much from the German spring offensives; whenever German infantry had been held up, they had called upon their artillery and machine-guns to fire at strong points while they attempted to move around the flanks. There was nothing new in this tactics, since the Canadian Corps had been practising just such manœuvres since before Passchendaele, but reports from the Canadian Motor Machine Gun Brigade, which had been attached to the British in their attempts to stem the German tide, confirmed that such moves could be very successful. It was critical, however, that enough machine-guns be available to keep the defenders' heads down.[39]

The trench mortar, less respected than the machine-gun, was none the less an important weapon in the Canadian Corps's arsenal, though no one felt the need to form a Trench Mortar Corps to parallel the Machine Gun Corps. The weapons were still allocated according to their calibre; each infantry brigade had under its command a light-mortar battery, equipped with the three-inch Stokes, and each divisional artillery had a battery of heavy 9.45-inch trench mortars, and two batteries of six-inch Newtons. As they had with machine-guns, the Germans had a preponderance of trench mortars, fifty per division as opposed to thirty-six carried by the British. Whether they would be useful in open in semi-open warfare was yet to be determined in early 1918, and the British organized a series of trials to see what the weapon could do. In May the 5th Canadian Divisional Artillery illustrated the trench mortar's potential by making it more mobile. Transportation had always been something of a problem, since the weapons were very difficult to carry, even when their crews had help from the infantry. The three-inch Stokes could be broken down, but even then its heaviest piece, the barrel, weighed forty-nine pounds, and ammunition was also a burden. The 5th Division gunners loaded the mortars on wagons, but ammunition was still limited; so crews had to concentrate on important targets, much as they had in the battles of 1917.[40]

Trench mortars, especially the larger six-inch and 9.45-inch versions, were most useful in static positions; between offensives they could help take pressure off the medium and heavy artillery needed for counter-battery work. They could also be used for counter-mortar work, or to retaliate against enemy rifle, grenade, or mortar attacks; or to shell observation posts, machine-guns, and strong points in the German forward positions. As far as the infantry battalions were concerned, the mortars' most important role was a retaliatory one; they were to fire at the German front line if enemy mortars shelled Canadian trenches, but keeping the mortars apprised of what was happening and passing orders to them required a complex system of communications, linking the mortars, infantry battalions, and artillery batteries (see figure 5). Keeping in touch with the situation at the front and calling for appropriate fire was a liaison officer at brigade headquarters, though his was not an easy task. Since mortars were still operating, in practical terms, in limbo between infantry and artillery, he had to keep informed of the plans and operations of both.[41]

To carry out their role effectively the trench mortars had to be accurate, or it would not be possible to destroy observation posts or machine-gun nests. The corps's General Staff was not happy with the 9.45; it was inaccurate and its ammunition often exploded prematurely, posing a serious hazard to its crews, and its only benefit was a heavy bursting charge which could destroy dugouts and trench mortar emplacements. The 1st Division recommended the 9.45 batteries be abolished and their personnel sent to other artillery units; for large howitzers, the twelve or fifteen-inch, could take on their tasks.[42]

Another problem the mortars had to deal with, like their artillery counterparts, were shorts. On 5 February, for example, Captain S. Macpherson of the 5th Canadian Trench Mortar Brigade reported that one six-inch and two 9.45-inch rounds had fallen short, one of the latter exploding in the Canadian barbed wire and the six-inch right in front of the Canadian trenches. Investigation into shorts of all kinds revealed three main problems: first, if the propelling charge was faulty, as was often the case in damp, wet, cold weather, it did not project the bomb as well and the round could fall short; second, the vanes, attached to the rear of the bomb and designed to keep it steady during flight, might break with the shock of discharge, allowing the shell's trajectory to become unstable; finally, there was always the possibility of human error, solved by carefully checking each lay before firing.[43]

In the winter and spring of 1918 Canadian Corps training included work with tanks; liaison was crucial, for armoured vehicles were useless if they went off on their own in ignorance of the infantry's needs. In the words of a British report: 'It must never be forgotten by Tank Com-

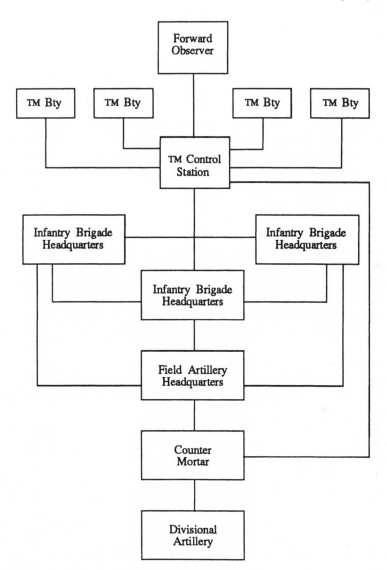

Figure 5

Mortar communications network, 1918

Based on description in RG 9, III, v.4033, folder 5, file 8, Canadian Corps, 30
January 1918, and 1st Canadian Division, 20 February 1918

manders that their role during an advance is not only to get their Tanks to the strong point, but to get the infantry there with them.'[44] Ideally, infantry platoons would get into position to make a final rush on a position, waiting for the tanks to create an opportune moment with their fire-power of six-pounders and heavy machine-guns, and, when the infantry rushed forward, the tanks would bring maximum fire to bear to support the advance. Alternatively, armoured vehicles could attack from a flank while the infantry entered behind them, then both could mop up together.[45] The tank was thus a weapon little different from the Lewis-gun section or the rifle grenadiers, though its proponents felt that it would be more effective in dealing with strong points than would vulnerable infantrymen.

Tank personnel and ground troops tried to develop communications systems that would maintain cooperation between the infantry and its armoured escorts. Flags were among the most successful; since the two arms had to remain within sight of each other anyway, visual signalling could well fit the bill. Inspired by the navy's signalling procedures (the tank had been developed by the British Admiralty), tanks carried flags to communicate with infantry platoons or each other. Those returning to the front line after a mission carried a tricolour, red, white, and blue, to denote them as British and avoid being fired upon by their own troops. A green and white flag was a signal to the infantry to 'Come on' and accompany the tank into as assault or an approach. A red and yellow flag denoted that the tank had broken down and accompanying platoons were to carry on without it. The infantry also developed signals to communicate with its armoured support; a helmet set atop a rifle and bayonet signalled 'Tanks wanted here,' though whether a dun-coloured helmet would show up clearly on a misty or dusty battlefield is somewhat doubtful.[46]

In training with tanks, the Canadians once again benefited from Allied developments, namely those of the French infantry training school at Sautrecourt. As they moved through no man's land, the tanks zig-zagged their way across to create more difficult targets for German artillery, to cover more ground, and to mop up any machine-guns the Germans may have placed forward of their positions. When they reached their objective, the tanks moved up and down the trench to kill its defenders or drive them to where they could be bunched together and forced to surrender. When crossing a trench, tanks halted momentarily to allow their gunners to fire into it. The infantry advanced in line, not in file, with waves about forty yards apart, while scouts linked the tanks to the infantry, and the two waves combined for the final rush. The tanks in the attack acted in groups of four, one to force its way to the Germans' rear, two to support the infantry, and another in reserve to deal with mopping-up or to replace casualties. As soon as the infantry consolidated new positions, the tanks withdrew around the flanks so as not to draw fire.[47]

Canadian training was not particularly methodical, however, though at least the infantry learned to avoid getting in the way of the mechanical monsters. During a tactical exercise in July, the tanks were held in reserve, owing to their limited numbers, ready to go forward and deal with strong points as moppers-up. On other exercises the infantry learned that in some things the tank was not sufficient in itself; for example, the tracked vehicles were supposed to flatten barbed wire, but Canadian soldiers soon saw that the gaps thus made were too narrow and acquired cutters to widen the lanes; passages through the wire had to be wide, or they would simply force infantry into ready-made milling zones for German machine-gunners and artillery.[48] Also in July the corps ordered that 'Every opportunity will be taken to carry out training Schemes for Infantry with Mk v Tanks,'[49] though staff officers thought that company exercises would be enough. This view is not surprising, since few saw the tank as a weapon that could be massed on a large scale to punch through to the enemy's rear; rather, it was considered an adjunct to the infantry, another way to deal with strong points, dugouts, and pill-boxes.[50]

Meanwhile, on 4 July the Australian Corps put its tank-infantry training to the test in a limited attack at Hamel. The previous April Brigadier-General Hugh Elles, commanding the Tank Corps, had convinced the Australians his arm could give them effective support; armoured vehicles would capture ground while infantry helped overcome strong points, mopped up defences, and consolidated any gains. Training was vital if infantry and armour were to work well together, and Lieutenant-General Sir John Monash, commanding the Australian Corps, insisted his troops carry out extensive rehearsals. He also insisted that on the day of the attack the tanks follow the creeping barrage as closely as possible, their armour rendering them nearly immune to the odd shrapnel shell that might explode short. The assault, one of many designed to slow the enemy's advance by threatening him on other sectors of the front, followed a pattern that would become familiar to colonial and imperial troops alike in the offensives to come. The Australian official history reported: 'when a tank was handy – as one generally was – the troops called for it; when none was there, they straightaway fought down the enemy themselves.'[51] The tanks and infantry went straight to their objective, leaving strong points to others, demonstrating not only the tank's potential but the possibilities offered by infiltration tactics.[52]

The Australian example is important, because it seems the Canadians did not follow suit, instead concentrating on making their artillery more mobile, practising quick-movement drills at length during the summer. Such training increased in scale, batteries, brigades, and whole divisions rehearsing their technique, and, finally, in June 1918, the guns joined the infantry, tanks, and aircraft on large exercises. It was not easy for the gunners to adapt to intensive mobile training; as Swettenham explained, 'The first manœuvres found batteries extremely awkward at the unaccustomed style of fighting. After long months and years of engaging the enemy from static sites, it was strange indeed to set out in the morning and take up three or four positions in succession, practising various methods of attack throughout a long, tiring day before returning to billets.'[53] The Canadians were already learning the importance fatigue could play in open warfare.

On 29 June N.W. Webster, the corps's brigadier general – general staff, issued instructions for an exercise in which Canadian soldiers would practise tactics, emphasizing fire and movement to penetrate machine-gun defences. Cooperation with tanks was a priority, as was cooperation between forward artillery and trench-mortar batteries. The exercise would also serve as a laboratory to test the efficacy of smoke laid by tanks or rifle-grenades.[54] After training for several months, however, troops had lost much of their eagerness. As Will Bird recalled of another exercise:

Some of the manœuvres were huge affairs. One nice morning we were disturbed by furious voices and saw the corps commander arriving with some of his staff. They did not seem pleased with our lack of enthusiasm, and our officers correctly implored us to show signs of action. At one point a village was designated as our battle ground. We were told to be prepared to make a wholesale attack and charged heartily – right into a Y.M.C.A. tent that was in our path. An enraged major ousted us from the place. He [the company commander] sent a platoon in one direction and when it vanished over the wrong hill, sent another after it. He left for a minute and returned to find his other two platoons had vanished. At night we lay around billets and laughed over the incidents of the day. It was a wonderful vacation.[55]

Liaison between airmen and infantry was still a subject for discussion and experiment. Flares were far from satisfactory; the Germans themselves used red and white flares, and green ones were almost invisible. Furthermore, infantrymen in action were sometimes too busy with the battle to light their flares when a plane called for them. In March 1918 the corps instituted a series of flights, weather permitting, over Canadian lines, so brigades and battalions could send practice messages and thus improve their liaison techniques with the Royal Flying Corps, which became the Royal Air Force on 1 April. Lamp parties remained in position for the same hours every day; so, when a passing airplane called for messages by sounding its klaxon, the infantry would reply by turning on lamps or exposing white panels. One brigade also experimented with mess tins, which soldiers could flash at oncoming aircraft.[56]

With the expanded role of the air force, it was important for both ground and air elements to know what was happening. On one exercise, the 12th Brigade sent aircraft to reconnoitre simulated enemy lines, locate centres of resistance, and practise bombing them; the brigade also instructed the planes to report on the progress of the attack by keeping a lookout for ground flares, still in use in spite of their drawbacks. Finally, the planes were to maintain communications between battalions and their brigade headquarters by passing on important messages. This multi-faceted role was hazardous, for soldiers, made nervous by enemy strafing and bombing attacks, often tried to shoot down their own planes, and in April Third Army investigated three cases where British aircraft were brought down by their own troops when they lost their way and fired on ground targets within friendly lines.[57]

Flyers and observers could certainly not expect better treatment from the Germans, as Flight Lieutenant P.R. Hampton related (Archie is anti-aircraft fire):

We went over the lines about a week ago to see what it was like, and we both saw and heard. The Hun let us get properly over when he opened up on us with some Archie ... batteries. He sent up a terrific barrage and his shooting was good, too; if it had been better it would have been too uncomfortable altogether. One cannot hear them come, but if they burst anywhere close one can hear the explosion. Of course with the noise of the engine, the explosion is very much deadened. Each shell leaves a small puff of black smoke, so that we could see the amount of stuff he was chucking at us. We could also see the flashes of the guns down below quite plainly. When we landed two out of the four machines had been hit, but nothing serious. I am sure I don't know how mine escaped.[58]

Not all escaped, as Lieutenant A.M. Kinnear could testify; in a letter home he described the effect of machine-guns on his wood and canvas aircraft: 'Perhaps you would be interested to know how I was wounded. Well, my observer and I had a job to do over in Hunland, and a rotten job it was too. I had to come down low to ascertain certain things, and 'Umpteen' machine guns started to shoot the bus to pieces.'[59] Many airmen did not return from reconnaissance missions, as enemy aircraft and anti-aircraft fire took their toll, and in the early summer the Fokker D-VII, one of the outstanding fighter aircraft of the war, which the Germans had introduced in January, ensured that casualties in the Royal Air Force would rise just as its pilots and observers prepared for the upcoming British offensive.[60]

While pilots concentrated on keeping their airplanes in the air, soldiers concentrated on learning to shoot them down. Canadians practised anti-aircraft fire often, and sometimes had the opportunity to fire at real enemy planes. Each battalion commander was responsible for defending his unit against all aircraft flying below 3,000 feet, and higher headquarters insisted that, when German airplanes flew low over Canadian position, every rifle, Lewis gun, and machine-gun should be brought to bear, in contrast with the policy of two years before that forbade the infantry from opening fire at all. Small-arms fire could force planes higher, where the Royal Flying Corps or heavy anti-aircraft guns could shoot them down or lacerate them with bullets, forcing the plane to go in for extensive repairs and taking it out of action for some time. It was important, of course, that the plane be within range: armour-piercing bullets, useless against tanks but deadly against aircraft, were in short supply, as were tracers, and they were not to be wasted on planes flying at a safe altitude. Staff officers informed all ranks that they should not fire at aircraft unless their markings were clearly recognizable and the struts visible to the naked eye; not only would planes thus be within range of anti-aircraft fire, but troops would be more likely to recognize, rather than shoot at, their own pilots.[61]

The British and Canadians continued to search for more effective ways of defending themselves against enemy aircraft. Following the German lead, the First Army discussed the possibility of using three-inch Stokes mortars against airplanes, and in May 1918 the 2nd Division carried out experiments to determine the mortar's effectiveness against low-flying aircraft. By altering the propellant charge, they could fire at four different altitudes: 500 feet, 1,000 feet, 1,200 feet, and 1,500 feet, with a time in flight of between eleven and nineteen seconds, all at an elevation of eighty degrees. That trench mortars could fire as anti-aircraft weapons had been demonstrated, but whether they shot down any planes was not mentioned. By April 1918 artillery pieces were already part of the front's anti-aircraft defences; if an infantry commander reported an air attack, one eighteen-pounder per battery would fire a burst 400 feet up, while successive fires would sweep the area and, with luck, force the aircraft away. By May the Canadians, with much British input, had developed and organized a thorough system of anti-aircraft defence. Behind the front were four lines of Lewis guns, in pairs, no more that 1,000 yards apart; the first two lines were 500 and 1,500 yards behind the front, and the other two followed the field artillery and heavy artillery lines.[62]

As the summer of 1918 neared its end, so did the last long interlude in the Canadian Corps's development. After Passchendaele the Canadians had continued to refine their tactics, and during the March offensive they applied lessons passed on to them by the hard-pressed British; they also learned to work with tanks more closely. Communications technology remained unchanged, but visual signalling proved useful in ensuring armour-infantry cooperation; telephones and wireless sets maintained communications between higher headquarters, and platoons and companies relied on runners and visual signalling to send back information or implore aid. In a sense, tactics in the summer of 1918 reflected the difficulties soldiers faced when trying to keep in touch with their commanders. Battalions had to move according to a detailed artillery timetable, since there was no way to guarantee communications would remain open to allow schedule changes should disaster or opportunity arise. For the same reason platoons needed their own fire support. Rifle-grenades and Lewis guns could fill this role, as could tanks if they were available. Thus fire and movement tactics combined rigidity at battalion level with initiative within the platoon to break into German defences and, it was hoped, into the countryside beyond.

8

The Final Offensives

In late July 1918 Germany's war effort was in a poor state. Its armies had almost spent themselves in a brilliant but costly campaign against the British and French which, however, failed to diminish their will to fight or their means of carrying on with the war. In the Second Battle of the Marne from 15–18 July, 500,000 French, African, and American soldiers, supported by 2,000 guns and 500 tanks, blunted the Germans' last attempt to capture Paris, and the initiative returned to the Allied camp; on that day the French managed to take their opponents by surprise and make substantial gains. The Germans were digging in once again, and the Allies, never hesitant to send their troops against enemy positions, were quick to launch an offensive. As early as 17 May Sir Douglas Haig had instructed General Sir Henry Rawlinson, commanding Fourth Army, to plan an attack east of Amiens. On 16 July the commander-in-chief confirmed that Fourth Army and the French First Army would carry out a large-scale assault; the Canadian Corps would move to that area of the front and, with the Australians, form the main body of the British attack.[1]

At Amiens the German Army, having learned from experience, prepared defensive positions that would prevent the events of 18 July from reccurring. Division fronts were narrow, so commanders would be responsible for less terrain and have more troops with which to defend it. Artillery was plentiful, and the Germans organized their trench systems in depth to absorb the shock of an assault and maintain a fresh reserve for counter-attacks. Field defences were not strong; there were no concrete pillboxes or deep belts of barbed wire to delay an advance. Rather, the main strength of the defence lay in the vast number of machine-guns hidden in great depth across the entire front; they would not reveal their positions until attackers were within range, thus avoiding deliberate shelling before the battle began.[2]

Canadians, however, had long before learned the value of cooperation between infantry and artillery and, to a lesser extent, between these two combat arms with tanks and aircraft. They had been rehearsing all summer, and, though the relationship between the four elements of the 1918 three-dimensional battlefield was far from perfect and in the case of the tanks the Canadian Corps seems to have neglected some of their potential, on the whole Amiens would demonstrate the importance of using weapons in combination and pooling technicians so their different skills could complement one another. The corps had spent several months training in open warfare and years practising small-unit tactics designed to make each platoon semi-autonomous with the weapons it needed to deal with strong points and machine-gun nests. Their training would be invaluable in the battle to come.

The gunners were also well prepared, with 646 guns of various calibers at their disposal. Canadian artillerymen left little to chance; for example, to check their guns for wear, gunners fired projectiles through two screens placed several feet apart; an electric circuit between them measured the shell's speed and allowed the gunners to calculate muzzle velocity and thus the gun's exact range. The artillerymen moved their guns into position under cover of darkness;[3] there was to be no lengthy shelling lasting several days and no target registration to give away Allied intentions; for, like the battle of Cambrai, this was to be a surprise attack preceded by a brief hurricane bombardment. The Canadians remained hidden until the very last instant, relying on the barrage and the tanks to take care of machine-guns and what little barbed wire the Germans had erected. Gunners received their counter-battery information from the Australians, who had previously occupied the position; counter-battery fire on the day of the attack would be crucial, since thousands of troops lay in the open waiting to assault, not having given themselves away with digging activity. Instructions to the artillery made its role very plain: 'During the phase in which Infantry ... are advancing to their first objective it will be necessary to subject all known and suspected hostile batteries to an intense neutralizing fire.'[4] The gunners would maintain this fire until the assaulting battalions were almost under the field artillery barrage or had advanced to a point where they could machine-gun enemy artillery. To make up for errors arising from the lack of preparation, guns from different batteries would fire at the same target, while guns from the same battery might fire at different targets;

so if one battery was inaccurate, others would compensate. The fire pattern thus created would, the gunners hoped, be effective enough to prevent the enemy from firing more than a few rounds.[5]

To update counter-battery information the Australians had given them, Canadian gunners relied on the intelligence-gathering system developed in late 1916 and early 1917. Aerial photographs, aircraft patrols, listening posts, observation posts, and sound-ranging batteries provided a picture of how German artillery was deployed, though, because the Canadians were not allowed to give away their positions, raids and patrols were out of the question. Having determined what the Germans were using and where they had placed them, the gunners then calculated the calibre of gun and number of rounds needed to isolate the enemy's artillery, or at least those batteries that posed a particular threat; knowing the number of rounds required led to determining the number of guns needed to carry out the shoot. Once staff officers had sent their instructions to the appropriate batteries, the gunners sited them, provided them with ammunition, and waited for the battle to start. Corps planners allocated six of nine heavy batteries to counter-battery work, and their counterparts at army level lent them four long-range siege batteries for the same purpose. The counter-battery officer, Lieutenant-Colonel A.G.L. McNaughton, and his staff gave each gun or group of guns specific tasks to be executed at precise times. For example, one gun could receive orders to fire at target A with 100 rounds over ten minutes, then switch to B with fifty rounds for twenty minutes, and so one. McNaughton had a further, very important responsibility: if it became obvious that the Germans had discovered the Canadians' positions and began to shell them, the counter-battery officer had the authority to retaliate and thus begin the battle. In the event, it was not necessary for McNaughton to do so.[6]

Behind Canadian lines gunners prepared the general barrage plan: field artillery, supplemented by many heavy guns, protect infantry battalions as they moved forward, as they had at Vimy and Passchendaele, and heavy artillery concentrated on all known strong points, lifting in accordance with a prearranged plan. Artillery was also to harass all approaches the Germans could use to ferry up reserves, ammunition, or supplies, and long-range guns were responsible for shelling detraining stations, rest billets, and similar facilities in the enemy's rear to disrupt his defences in depth.[7]

Meanwhile, tank crews readied themselves for battle. The Canadian Corps, with support from the 4th Tank Brigade, had more of the armoured, tracked vehicles than in any previous engagement, the brigade being formed of the 1st, 4th, 5th, and 14th Tank Battalions, each of which would be supporting one of the corps's divisions. At full strength, a tank battalion comprised forty-two machines, but the 1st Tank Battalion, understrength with only thirty-four, would remain in reserve with the 4th Division.[8] Battalion commanders were responsible for arranging all necessary details with the divisions to which they were attached,[9] forty-two tanks accompanying the first wave, six the second wave, and fourteen the third.[10]

Getting the armoured vehicles to the start line was the first order of business. They remained 1,000 yards in the rear until twelve minutes before the attack was supposed to begin, then moved forward. Their large, powerful engines and metal tracks made a terrible noise as they clanked their way down roads or across fields, and, since Amiens was to be a surprise attack, this noise had to be masked in some way; aircraft, which had been operating in the area for months and years and would not arouse suspicion, flew overhead as the tanks approached their form-up positions. The armoured vehicles drove in second gear, supposedly the most silent, though it made the ride even more uncomfortable than usual; fumes from the engine, always irritating in the tank's limited and badly ventilated space, were far worse as the vehicles rumbled along slowly. The 4th Tank Battalion, sent to support the 1st Division, reported that many of its crews were overcome by fumes, causing such delay that there was no time to rest at the start line, but at least none of the monsters broke down, and their engineers soon repaired those that suffered minor mechanical trouble. One tank in the 4th Tank Battalion was thirty minutes late after ditching itself.[11] British armies, and hence the Canadian Corps, were armed with the Mark v tank, with thicker armour and a far superior transmission than its predecessors. Steering the Mark iv had required four men: the driver, the commander – acting as brakesman – and two gearsmen, one to a side; but the Mark v could be steered by the driver alone. The new tank, however, was even more poorly ventilated than previous models had been.[12]

The infantry, like artillery and armour, made its preparations as surreptitiously as possible; camouflage and concealment were the watchwords of the day, and assembly areas behind the front were kept quiet in the time leading up to the attack.[13] During the night of 7–8 August thousands of men marched into position, like snails carrying everything they would need in the upcoming battle on their backs. Lieutenant R.J. Holmes described his experiences in a letter home: 'The night of the

192 / Surviving Trench Warfare

7th/8th August, 1918, we marched fourteen miles to get into battle
position, being loaded down more or less like Christmas trees with two
days' rations, two large water bottles filled, and a large pack, besides all
our battle equipment and steel helmet, glasses, compasses, gas respirator,
revolver, ammunition, and heaven knows what not, arrived in position
at 2.30 a.m., and went over the top at 4.20 a.m.'[14] All movement was
at night; soldiers hid during the day, brigades completing their form-up
with a minimum of interference from German artillery, and some narratives, like that of the 3rd Brigade, mention no shelling at all.[15] Preparations included filling the troops in on the job at hand; as Lieutenant-
Colonel W.H. Joliffe remembered: 'Prior to the attack, the commanding
officer of the battalion would have a conference with all officers and
explain to them what the object was and what each company was expected to achieve and, after that, the company commanders and platoon
commanders explained the situation to the men in their platoons so
that all ranks knew what the picture was.'[16]

On the morning of the attack the ground was covered in a thick mist
that masked most features and made orientation difficult. Troops moved
off, keeping direction with compasses, leap-frogging towards the Green,
Red, and Blue dotted lines. Three divisions, deployed in depth, each
launched the attack with one brigade forward; the 4th Brigade of the
2nd Division was on the left, the 3rd Brigade of the 1st Division moved
in the centre, and the 3rd Division's 9th Brigade advanced on the right.
Since 1915 artillery had learned the importance of sending gunnery
officers forward with the attack to ensure well-trained technicians could
call for artillery support, and these forward observation officers, usually
battery commanders, had instructions to observe enemy activity and
pick out targets of opportunity. In open warfare the guns, without which
infantry operations could become far too costly, had to move with the
rest of the corps; so artillery patrols, as they looked for points from
which to observe the battle, sought out future sites for their batteries
and looked for captured enemy positions they could turn to their own
use, though gun pits faced the wrong way. If the guns were still in them
and operational, however, the Canadians could use them to further
disorganize the enemy.[17] Artillery laid a smoke screen which, combined
with the mist, masked advancing troops, and the massed guns opened
fire with one great roar at 4.20 and 4.30 a.m. On the 3rd Brigade's front,
shorts caused twenty to thirty casualties among the 13th Battalion, but
other shells were right on target. Counter-battery fire was so severe and
accurate in some areas that German gunners never fired a shot, though

in others it was less effective and German crews toiled until the last possible moment and then destroyed their guns.[18]

Keeping all levels of command and all different elements informed of what was going on and what each other's needs were was a battle in itself, an often frustrating effort to keep communications open in spite of technical limitations and enemy intervention. As noted in the previous chapter, neither technology nor training for communications had changed much since Vimy Ridge; signallers, their helpers, and their commanders used every means available, and if there was any difference between Amiens and Passchendaele or Amiens and Vimy, it was that technology offered more ways to do the same thing. At Amiens telephones, lamps, flares, pigeons, message-carrying rockets, power-buzzer and amplifier sets, wireless telegraphy, runners, and contact aircraft all had a role to play in keeping communications open. After the battle some suggested that dispatch riders on motorcycles could maintain communications between battalions and higher headquarters if roads were suitable.[19]

Communication techniques differed from one level of command to the next. Brigade headquarters used runners, mounted orderlies, visual signalling, telephones, pigeons, wireless, and aircraft-signalling panels. Since the headquarters seldom moved, its signallers could use bulky equipment like the wireless. The brigade also had an advanced report centre close to the front, which had the same means of communicating both up and down the line except for wireless, because there were too few sets to allocate below brigade level. Battalion headquarters had the same communications organization as the advanced report centre. After the battle started, signallers followed closely behind the infantry and tanks, turning houses along the line of advance into nodes in the system, which was used to keep in touch with a given unit's flanks as well as its parent formation. As the advance progressed, signallers formed more advanced report centres and set up more battalion headquarters, and when the infantry and tanks reached their final objectives, patrols laid down telephone wire to keep the battalions in touch with their forward companies. In the course of the battle itself runners, as before, kept the battalions informed of what was happening.[20]

Though the experience of battle was not uniform from unit to unit, the progress of the centre division was sufficiently typical to serve as an example for the corps as a whole. Infantry companies moved forward under cover of mist, smoke, and artillery barrage in the formations they had practised during the summer, advancing by infiltrating their way past strong points and machine-gun nests directly to their objectives. Units of the 3rd Brigade attacked four objectives in depth at once, some of them hundreds of yards behind German lines, advance waves moving steadily on to their targets and leaving any trouble areas they found along the way to others. The 14th Battalion, advancing on the brigade's left, cleared the outpost line without difficulty and pushed on to a wood where troops found eight machine-guns; but gunners could do nothing, because, as the observer reported, 'I had perfect communication and direct observation, but was unable to use Artillery as the Infantry were steadily encircling [the wood].'[21]

One of the company's supporting tanks was stranded in front of the copse and the others passed by, moving on to other objectives, oblivious to the infantry's plight. A battery of eight machine-guns followed each company's attack and looked for positions from which to fire at German defences, and these heavy machine-guns proved useful in a battle where the enemy had hidden his support weapons. The 14th Battalion used L Battery, of the Canadian Machine Gun Corps, to good effect, breaking up concealed machine-gun posts as it continued to skirt the wood. The machine-guns followed closely and sometimes became involved in skirmishes in the mist, though their main role was to fire over the heads of attacking platoons at targets beyond. Gunners used the same tactics as the infantry; to move across no man's land they broke up into sections and advanced in artillery formation, keeping direction with compasses and air photographs. Like those of the infantry, their casualties mounted.[22]

Members of the 14th Battalion flanked the wood, which was not one of their objectives, and attacked the next position back. From there they moved on to a trench system, where the Germans surrendered when the Canadians subjected them to enfilade fire. The battalion's remnants then advanced again, reaching the Green Line according to schedule. Two trench mortars moving with the infantry faced a difficult task; for crews had to move six-inch mortars across rough terrain, keeping as close as possible to the advance. Each mortar was set up on a mobile platform, which also carried twenty bombs, pulled by two mules in tandem, and a wagon carrying thirty more rounds followed behind. They were under the command of the infantry whose assault they were supporting, and the 14th Battalion was very impressed with the potentials of the trench mortar, along with the heavy machine-gun, for destroying or capturing strong posts. When listing the lessons learned from its attack, the battalion officers replied: 'In assaulting Machine Gun nests our Heavy Machine Guns and T.M.'s can, and should be used with the greatest boldness. Volume of fire is the essential factor to allow Infantry to get to assaulting distance, [for] over flat country, a well placed enemy Machine Gun, manned by determined gunners is a considerable obstacle, and can hold an advance up at a range of 500 yards, thereby putting our rifle grenadiers out of range.'[23] When the attack reached the Green Line, machine-gunners set themselves up in defensive positions while other units leap-frogged their way to further objectives. Many of the heavy machine-guns, however, were under brigade command and returned to the rear to take positions behind the reserve line.[24]

Training in the summer had stressed the importance of tanks and infantry moving together, the only exceptions being the Whippets, small tanks armed with four machine-guns which were supposed to act as cavalry, using their greater speed, eight miles per hour on roads, to reconnoitre ahead of the main advance. Like cavalry, they not only sought information about the enemy's dispositions but fought to disrupt the forward movement of enemy food and ammunition, in the process inflicting many casualties.[25] When the 14th Battalion reached its objectives the Whippets were there. So were the Germans, with machine-guns pushed forward to hamper Canadian consolidation, and when the tanks went forward to destroy or capture the guns, the Germans kept well down in high grain and, with the exception of one crew, remained undetected. The Whippets were destroyed, though they were credited with keeping down enemy fire and so helping the Canadians prepare a proper defence.[26]

To the right of the 14th Battalion advanced the 13th, whose experiences were similar. Before the battle aircraft had taken photos to help guide ground troops to their objectives, since maps were useless in an area that had been badly mauled by previous artillery duels and the activities of preparing defences. Sometimes even the air photographs could be inaccurate if overhanging trees or light cloud helped hide obstacles; Major Ian Sinclair of the 13th Battalion was horrified when he and his company ran into a stream that appeared on neither the maps nor the air photos.[27] Generally, the battalion managed to keep direction, and it quickly captured Hangard Wood. 'Beyond here, heavy resistance was encountered from Croates Trench, were a large party of Huns held out, using Rifle Grenades and bombs effectively. Our men were at a disadvantage as they were but poorly equipped with grenades and bombs, but Lieut. Green of the Trench Mortars hurrying up with his two guns [sic] turned the tables and assisted in quickly reducing the garrison, who put up white flags.'[28] It was the only time the trench mortars appear in the battalion's narrative.

It had better luck with tanks. Regardless of whether German battalions were familiar with armoured vehicles, the surprise of seeing them emerge from the smoke and mist, which may have covered the sound of their engines as well as their movements, was enough to make some garrisons surrender. Infantry sections usually preceded the tanks, which moved ahead of their charges only when needed. After completing a task, such as destroying a machine-gun nest or clearing a section of trench, they returned to their positions behind the advancing infantry. The 13th Battalion found them most useful when, as it approached a wood, it came upon barbed wire, very rare at Amiens, and ordered a tank through it. Tanks moved in, encircling the wood while the rear company, with two more tanks, mopped up. The 4th Tank Battalion reported that its advancing armour completely demoralized the defenders by taking them unawares.[29]

The 16th Battalion's experiences were little different as it moved on the 13th's right. Troops met with light opposition in the first few copses they went through and found no one at all in the trench system they encountered along the way to their objective. At a crossroads, however, they suffered heavy casualties from German machine-guns but pushed the enemy back. Troops of the 16th had as much reason to appreciate tanks as their colleagues in the 13th had. After his unit had captured most of its objectives, the battalion commander sent a small infantry party forward; the group moved towards a quarry, where the Germans had placed a regimental headquarters, and came under heavy machine-gun fire, but a tank moved in and soon overwhelmed the position. The Canadians captured the regimental commander, equivalent to a colonel, and his entire staff. There were few left to defend Aubercourt Village, the unit's objective, and the battalion reached it without difficulty.[30]

So ended the first phase of the centre battle. In the second and third phases the infantry moved with whatever tanks had survived the first assault and enough additions, it was hoped, to bring tank companies up to full strength. Thus many tanks followed the advance the whole way, though already by the time they reached the Green Line (the first objective), which took several hours, their crews were weary of firing the guns, driving the machine, and inhaling exhaust fumes. Nevertheless, in the second phase of the advance the 1st Brigade left the Green Line with two additional sections of tanks, six in all, the tanks of B and C companies finally resting when they reached the Red Line (the intermediate objective). Upon arrival, the 2nd Brigade took over for the final part of the advance, heading for the Blue Dotted Line with all of A Company, composed of fourteen tanks, which had been closely supporting their colleagues in the first wave for the first 3,500 yards of the attack. The company moved forward with ten tanks in front and four in reserve.[31]

At the same time, along the entire front, artillery worked to ensure that the forward troops would not lose the support of their own guns, no matter how far the attack progressed; so batteries received orders to move as soon as the assault had advanced outside their range.[32] Gunners had to limber up their guns, load ammunition onto wagons and trucks, and load themselves up or prepare to walk. They then moved forward through areas that may not have been completely mopped up, located the positions laid out for them by artillery patrols, unlimbered the guns, and unloaded the ammunition. Finally, they had to lay on and prepare to fire. The 10th Battalion, which moved forward in the final phase of the 8 August attack as part of the 1st Division's assault, praised the gunners 'for the rapid manner in which they moved forward, and for their speed in taking up positions and coming into action.'[33] Unit officers afterwards suggested two eighteen-pounder guns be attached to each battalion headquarters to take on special targets.[34]

As the 10th Battalion advanced, it made a long detour around a wood that had become a target for heavy shelling; units did everything possible to avoid casualties until they reached their objectives, when there would be dead and wounded enough.[35] The battalion had little trouble with German machine-guns and captured or destroyed those it met along the way by outflanking and enfilading them. Though one company never saw the tank that headquarters had allocated to it, this did nothing to slow its advance; the company commander later discovered the vehicle had broken down.[36] The other companies were more fortunate, and the battalion later reported: 'The 2 Tanks which went forward with the Battalion to the Final Objective did excellent work, and too much credit cannot be given them for the valuable assistance they rendered, and the gallant manner in which they took on every obstacle which presented itself.'[37]

The tank crews faced a well-trained enemy. General Ludendorff, in effect commanding the German armies on the Western Front, after the war described how his soldiers prepared to engage British tanks in the early months of 1918.

In the artillery, especially in the case of the field guns and light trench mortars, training in direct individual fire at tanks was considered of decisive importance.

The allotment of special ammunition to the heavy machine guns was increased more extensively. Experiments in destroying tanks with multiple grenades were carried out, and all experience gained in fighting them was communicated to the troops, whose opinions were called for. Our positions were examined as to their liability to attack by tanks; traps and stops were made, barricades constructed, mines put down, and anti-tank guns dug in at many points.[38]

The Germans had a variety of anti-tank weapons. One was a large-calibre rifle, firing an armour-piercing bullet or small shell. Unlike an artillery piece, it was easy to conceal, and, though it was effective only at close range, the weapon sometimes pierced its target's armour and might even strike fuel or ammunition and turn the vehicle into a fireball. Tank crews had to be especially careful when these were about. If an armoured vehicle ran a track lengthwise into a trench and 'bellied,' it could no longer move and became an easy target for anti-tank weapons.[39] Eric Grinsdale described how effective artillery could be: 'I saw a very poor show – there was three tanks came up, supposed to be with us, and they came up in single file, one behind the other, and there was an anti-tank gun there which knocked over the whole three of them. The only survivor was one of the infantry scouts.'[40]

When the 10th Battalion reached its final positions for the day, the Whippets were late but still served to protect the unit's flank until troops came up to fill the gap. One patrol of three such tanks moved forward from the positions the battalion had captured and proceeded into Rosières.[41] The battalion commander was put off when his artillery liaison officer showed up six hours after his troops had taken the objective; he was supposed to have met up with them at zero-hour. The same unit also endured that always morale-shaking experience of being shot at by one's own guns, and officers claimed that 40 per cent of the unit's casualties occurred after the final objective had been reached and were due to their own field artillery's firing short. A 4.5-inch howitzer shelled battalion headquarters for about thirty minutes.[42]

Meanwhile, the 4th Division experimented with tanks as armoured personnel carriers. Each tank accompanying the 12th Brigade, for example, carried an infantry or machine-gun officer, an infantry scout, a runner, a Vickers gun with crew of five, and two Lewis guns with crews of three each; there were thus fourteen people packed into the tank or riding on top. The scout was to watch the advance while the others disembarked at the final objective to form strong points. Fumes from the engine, however, turned the experiment into a miserable failure, and the 12th Brigade simply reported that 'Infantry personnel should not be carried in the tanks, as they become sick from the petrol fumes.'[43] Professor A. Logan, who was then with the 4th Machine Gun Battalion, was more loquacious:

We had twenty-four guns in as many tanks for that show and they had instructions to go forward to the Blue [Dotted] Line and rest there. I think only one of the tanks got to the Blue Line; that was Billy McDonald's tank. So many of them were hit by direct fire from the German artillery and a great many of them had to unload their crews because the boys couldn't stand the fumes. One of the tanks unloaded and was carrying on, holding their ground, and they were surrounded by Germans and taken prisoner, the whole crew were taken prisoner.[44]

Rehearsing the technique during summer training might have avoided much heartache.

As night fell there was time to evaluate the events of the day; the Canadian Corps had advanced seven miles, and armour had done well. In the 4th Tank Battalion's A Company, thirteen of fourteen tanks left the start line with the infantry, three reached the Red Line and stayed there, halfway between the Germans' first and second lines of defence and 8,000 yards from the Canadian trenches, and a further six went on to the Blue Dotted Line, set at the German's outer defences. Two were knocked out with direct hits, three broke down, and two ditched themselves; in all, ten of fourteen rallied before daylight on 9 August. The casualties in B Company were similar; four tanks reached the Green Line, the primary objective 5,500 yards from the Canadian lines, and one of them went on to the Red Line. Four tanks were hit, three broke down, two lost their way and did not rejoin the battle, and three ditched themselves; nine tanks rallied before daylight on 9 August. In C Company it was the same story: eight tanks reached the Green Line, seven reached the Red Line, three were knocked out, three broke down, one ditched, and nine rallied next day. The 4th Tank Battalion lost fully a third of its tanks on the first day of battle but could still start the second day's fighting.[45]

As casualties mounted, however, the tanks found it progressively more difficult to support the infantry on the battle's second and third days. On the entire front, available tanks fell from 342 Mark vs on 8 August to 145 on 9 August, eighty-five on the 10th, thirty-eight on the 11th, by which time the crews were completely exhausted, and only *six* on the 12th.[46] Some infantry units came to appreciate the tanks' importance in their absence, or to wish that the tanks they had would get on with the job. Again, the centre battle, involving the 1st Division's 2nd Brigade, can serve as an example. The 8th Battalion prepared to attack on the morning of 9 August when the tanks came up, moving to the rear of the infantry assembly area. There, they drew the Germans' attention, and a violent bombardment fell on Canadian positions.[47] The 5th Battalion started the battle without tank support when the latter failed to show up at the start line, and German machine-gun nests held the advance to a slow crawl. When the tanks finally caught up with the infantry, however, the attack went far more smoothly; after capturing the village of Varvilliers, the battalion encountered more machine-guns, which it captured or destroyed with the tanks' assistance.[48]

Members of the 8th Battalion saw one tank cross the unit's front 800 yards ahead, where it was surrounded by the Germans and set on fire; infantry-tank cooperation was supposed to protect the tanks too, but tank tactics were still rudimentary at best and dangerous at worst. After the battle it was obvious that the armoured vehicles had moved forward too close together, for their hulks littered the countryside in clumps; furthermore, they did not make effective use of dead ground and left themselves open to enemy fire when they were silhouetted against the skyline.[49] The battalion narrative summarized the experience of the previous two days and the tank's importance in a short but revealing paragraph: 'During the first phase of the attack on the 8th August, our tanks, both light and heavy, did very effective work, but on the second day, they were not so effective. On the latter day they were late in getting into position and did not appear to know the correct direction of advance, thus delaying what might have been a much more rapid advance and a greater reduction in casualties.'[50]

On the second day the tanks were useful, but not omnipotent, especially against a German force still high in morale and fully equipped. With only one obstacle between it and its objective, the 5th Battalion ran into problems the tanks could not solve: 'The last belt of opposition was encountered in the taking of the final objective, which consisted of old elements of trenches, strongly garrisoned with six or eight machine guns. These machine guns did a considerable amount of execution. This strongly fortified position offered very stout resistance indeed, and all the efforts of our tanks, both light and heavy, were unavailing in subduing them; and it was not until towards dusk that our objective was reached.'[51] Once the Germans had recovered from the initial shock of a surprise assault, they were prepared to defend themselves against tanks and infantry alike. After the battle the commander of the 4th Tank Battalion commented, 'Once the enemy has taken a stand it is useless to push tanks against him, unless under a screen,'[52] and 'That unless surprise can be obtained Tanks are of only little assistance to the Infantry.'[53]

Artillery was a great help in some close assaults, demonstrating its ability to keep moving forward, at least for a time, to take advantage of the infantry's initial gains. The 8th Battalion had the undivided support of a complete field battery,[54] and on the whole the gunners managed to fulfil their role to the infantry's satisfaction. The 8th Battalion's experiences demonstrated the importance of artillery support; those machine-gun nests the gunners had shelled in the opening hours of the battle fell almost immediately, and those that had avoided shelling thanks to their concealed positions inflicted heavy casualties on Canadian troops.[55] The 5th Battalion reported similar success; though machine-gun crews held on tenaciously, after severe shelling they could not withstand the impetus of the battalion's attack.[56]

There was much activity in the air as German aircraft attempted to slow the advance or prepare the way for counter-attacks by machine-gunning rear areas during the day and dropping bombs at night. To defend their gains, brigadiers ordered that anti-aircraft Lewis guns be mounted at every stage of the attack, their main priority to protect transportation from machine-guns and bombs. Drivers dispersed their trucks and wagons to avoid forming the concentrated targets that so tempted German airplanes, for anti-aircraft gunners had few successes to celebrate. One shot down a German aircraft only after firing at various targets for two days,'[57] while the BEF's anti-aircraft gunners as a whole were damaging or destroying only about ten planes a week.[58]

The Germans did not have complete supremacy in the air. Squadrons of the Royal Air Force were an almost constant presence over Canadian lines, according to some units, keeping hostile planes at bay and flying low to fire into the retreating enemy. The aircraft, fulfilling part of the artillery's role, also carried out strafing missions against German troops, who seemed to be massing for counter-attacks. These missions were not haphazard but fit within an overall plan; for the first two days of the advance, for example, the 12th Canadian Infantry Brigade had enough aircraft support to form three infantry contact patrols to report on the attack's progress and three artillery contact patrols to act as spotters. On the first day a counter-attack patrol started two hours after the Canadians left their trenches and lasted until dark. Other aircraft sought to neutralize the anti-tank guns that were proving so dangerous, but problems with communications hindered such operations; their turn would come in future battles. The variety of aircraft missions demonstrated the possibilities of infantry-airplane cooperation as never before, and the 14th Battalion unwittingly looked into the future when it suggested that planes work even more closely with the infantry during the attack and drop bombs on strong points, headquarters, suspected woods, and other targets. Implementing such a close relationship on a large scale would have to wait for another army and another war, though British planes did support the advance of the 29th and 31st battalions by bombing and machine-gunning German posts.[59]

The Royal Air Force had a variety of roles to play in supporting the Amiens operation. Before the troops assaulted, it had to deny the area to enemy reconnaissance aircraft to maintain security and hence the element of surprise – so much more important than in the set-piece battles of 1917. The close cooperation already described was more intense than in any previous campaign, though the mist prevented it from being closer still. On 8 August Allied air power dominated the skies over the Amiens battlefield, though one major task that proved impossible was the destruction of bridges over the Somme to prevent the Germans from moving up reserves. Enemy airfields were within six miles of the targets, and on the afternoon of the 8th their main task was to keep the RAF from destroying the bridges. The intense air battles that followed, involving bombers and fighters, hindered the British extensively. They tried again on the 9th, the bridges now first priority, but on the 10th many of them were still open and reserves were pouring into the area. The ground offensive slowed, and thus one of the first attempts at interdiction through air power had failed, though not through lack of effort.[60]

The Allies continued to press forward until 18 August, advancing thirteen miles overall. Most of the fighting was on the 8th and 9th, by which time the Canadians had pushed forward almost ten miles, spectacular gains compared with the bloody snail's pace of the Somme or Passchendaele. In a CBC interview, Lieutenant-Colonel J.M. Morris, ex of the 42nd Battalion, described the first day of the Amiens offensive as

the most inspiring experience [for] till then it was trench warfare, and a few hundred yards was considered quite an advance whereas in the Battle of Amiens in the first day we went in eight miles and everything – we saw everything moving up. Even the observation balloons on their trucks moved up. Infantry, artillery, cavalry – the artillery very often stayed behind to cover advances and would be moved forward – they did not move as rapidly – the guns were brought forward and the whole army moved forward for eight miles on the 8th day of August.[61]

According to the official history, which measures casualties in relative terms, losses were light compared with the amount of ground captured, and, in fact, casualties were light when Amiens is compared with all previous Canadian battles. By the end of the first day 1,036 Canadians were dead, 2,803 were wounded, and twenty-nine were prisoners of war. The total for 8 August, 3,868, was lower than for Vimy Ridge, the Canadian Corps's most spectacular battle to that time, were 7,707 men became casualties, of whom 2,967 died, in the two days necessary to capture their main objectives. The second day at Amiens, casualties mounted by 2,574, while the corps advanced three miles (one-tenth the number of soldiers lost on the Somme while capturing about the same amount of ground). Casualties for the entire battle, from 8–20 August, totalled 11,725, similar to the 10,602 of Vimy Ridge.[62]

The British Expeditionary Force learned much in its campaigns of early August, mainly about tanks, and most especially about their vulnerability. It had been evident even before the battle that the tank's main enemy on the battlefield was the artillery piece, able to pierce the vehicle's armour and kill its crew. Staff officers in the British Army suggested that the best way to avoid destruction at the hands of German artillery was to keep moving as quickly as possible and not stop until forced to do so, but tanks could manage no more than two miles per hour cross country, and blind movement would have the further disadvantage of leaving the initiative to the enemy, who placed obstacles and anti-tank guns along likely approach routes. Another suggestion made far more sense and merely repeated what infantry and tank crews already knew, that they had to remain in close touch for mutual protection. On 24 August First Army circulated suggestions gleaned from the British experience which stressed the importance of reconnaissance; for German defences included hidden positions and traps. Advance guards should ascertain the locations of defended localities and machine-guns, then tanks and enveloping tactics could capture or destroy them. Tanks themselves should not move forward until the infantry had completed such reconnaissance.[63]

The British and, after Hamel, the Australians placed more emphasis

Armour-infantry tactics. These soldiers are in training near Arras, in October 1918. They remain dispersed behind the tank because it could attract shrapnel fire in an assault. Note the anti-ditching beam on the tank's upper rear, to aid in getting it free should it jam itself sideways into a trench.

on tank tactics than did their Canadian colleagues. British 'Notes on Lessons Learned' advocated using heavy tanks to break through German lines and follow them up with Whippets and armoured cars to force the enemy to keep retreating and to wreak havoc with his lines of communication. To achieve this goal, tanks would be kept within their own units, not allocated piecemeal, and would breach the German line at several points. In the battle leading up to the breach the tanks could support the infantry advance, even if some of the objectives were in terrain the tanks could not negotiate, such as forests; for if they could not penetrate into woods, the armoured vehicles could still fire their six-pounder guns or machine-guns to keep the Germans' heads down. The British did not view the tanks as omnipotent, however, and insisted that, should the Germans knock them out or mud bring them to a halt, the infantry must push on regardless and capture its objectives. In the British view then, the tank was a useful tool when used en masse but was vulnerable to German artillery at close range and was not to be wholly relied upon to reach one's objectives.[64]

The Canadians came out of Amiens with lessons of their own, most of them confirmations of what the corps already knew. Trench mortars and heavy machine-guns, for example, were useful if they could be made available when they were needed, but moving them across difficult terrain was a problem. In fact the commander of the 78th Battalion was not at all impressed with the heavy machine-guns, mainly because their crews could not move them quickly. Trench mortars as large as the six-inch were carried on the battlefield at Amiens, but once again there was no way to guarantee they would be at the right place at the right time, because they were too heavy to move with any speed.[65] Other weapons also came under scrutiny, including the lowly bayonet; for bayonet fighting had been part of the soldier's training schedule since the beginning of the war, when commanders still believed battles would be decided with hand-to-hand fighting. Training with the weapon consisted of a series of drill manœuvres, such as thrust, parry, and slash, but, as the 78th Battalion's commander pointed out, 'I doubt if much attention is paid to drill movements when the moment comes for the man to use it.'[66] Thus the weapons with the greatest rate of fire or potential for destruction, the machine-gun and the trench mortar, were not as mobile as the infantry they were supposed to support, while the weapon easiest to carry was almost never used. Somewhere in between lay the Lewis guns, rifles, bombs, and rifle-grenades the Canadians had been relying upon for years.

Artillery adapted well enough to the war of movement, though it had needed to move on only two different days, 8 and 9 August, and whether it could continue to transfer its guns from position to position over several days or weeks remained to be seen. All in all, the tactics of infiltration supported by tanks, artillery, and other weapons worked well in a summer campaign where the ground was dry enough to allow the quick movement of tracked vehicles, lorries, and horses, and where there was no mud to slow the infantry to a crawl. Though neither soldiers nor their commanders knew it, ahead lay over two more months of campaigning during which the Canadian Corps would rely heavily on the tactics of Amiens to fulfil its role in maintaining pressure on the German Army and force it to an armistice.[67]

After the battle ended, there was little time to apply any lessons learned, for the Canadian Corps had only a few days until its next attack, which – as the Battle of the Scarpe – began near Arras on 26 August. Tank losses at Amiens led the corps to use them cautiously, and armoured vehicles were ordered to remain behind the infantry except to take on specific strong points.[68] The fighting lasted until the 30th and paved the way to the Drocourt-Quéant Line, and the battle to break those defences lasted from 30 August to 3 September. The first order of business was to capture jump-off positions, and on 30 August the 1st Brigade took Upton Wood and the Vis-en-Artois switch. On the 31st the 2nd Brigade captured Ocean Work, and on 1 September the 2nd and 3rd brigades brought preliminary operations to a close in taking the Crow's Nest.[69] The gunners had a difficult time playing their supporting role, as Lieutenant-Colonel J.L. Hart, then with the 46th Battalion, later related: 'the artillery were supposed to have cut the wire for us out here in front of Drury and they didn't get it cut, because we were going so fast that the artillery couldn't be brought up and keep in touch and they were not getting a chance to set their guns, just shooting, encountering a lot of shorts weren't too pleasant, we had some casualties from our own shorts but that was part of war.'[70] The Canadians spent three days working their way towards a line from which they could reach their main objective in one swift action, rather than try to batter their way through the Drocourt-Quéant from their initial positions.

The main battle to capture the Dorcourt-Quéant took place in a single day, on 2 September, the 4th Division's 10th and 12th Brigades advancing on the left while the 1st Division's 2nd and 3rd Brigades moved forward on the right. Artillery, as always, played an important role in the battle, and in fact the 1st Division captured its jump-off line so the guns could deploy far enough forward to put down a rolling barrage through the Drocourt-Quéant proper.[71] German artillery was also very much in evidence, since there has been little or no time to lay down effective counter-battery fire, and German guns harassed the Canadians whenever they tried to form up for an attack.[72] Formations and tactics were the same the troops had practised in the summer; battalions assaulted with two companies forward, each company putting two platoons in front.[73] In the battles of the last three months of the war leap-frogging gained in importance as the Canadian Corps, like the British, French, American, and other Allied troops, attempted to make impressive gains while the Germans were still recovering from the battles of the summer and suffering under the British blockade. With the pace of combat thus accelerated, units in support often found themselves replacing battalions too exhausted to continue, sometimes in the midst of counter-attacks. Discipline and experience were of crucial importance in carrying out such movements.[74] Canadian tactics also aimed at platoon autonomy; it was especially important for small units to operate on their own when there was very little time for the corps to gather information on German defences and dispositions.[75]

At Drocourt-Quéant the pattern set at Amiens repeated itself; the tanks were successful in the first hours of combat but ran into more and more trouble as German defences hardened. The 1st Canadian Division summarized the tank's usefulness in the battle: 'The Tanks worked well and assisted the Infantry very materially in capturing the Drocourt-Quéant Line, breaking paths through the wire and reducing the enemy's resistance. Upon the cessation of the protective barrage however, all the Tanks became casualties, and were unable to assist in the subsequent advance, where they would have been most useful – especially against the Buissy Switch.'[76] The tanks operated best when they could count on some artillery protection, and at Drocourt-Quéant the Canadians used them as an adjunct to infantry; for, while the latter often carried on without the tanks and captured its objectives, the former never operated alone and were very vulnerable to German anti-tank fire if neither artillery or infantry was available to protect them.

Capturing the line did not silence the machine-guns, which as usual the Germans had placed in depth. Arriving at the Red Line, the first of two report lines, Canadian troops found themselves under fire from machine-guns further on, notably from the town of Villers les Cagnicourt, in the Buissy Switch trench system. One such strong point fell when a lance-corporal worked forward with his Lewis gun and opened

fire from short range; after the Canadians captured Dury, another machine-gun nest fell to a barrage of rifle grenades. (Lewis guns from the
flank often forced machine-gunners to surrender.) Behind the machine-
guns was German artillery, which in a fluid battle such as those of 1918
often found itself under Lewis-gun fire; on 2 September, when emerging
from a village it had just captured, the 14th Battalion found itself facing
a German artillery battery galloping into view. A Lewis-gun fusillade
brought it to a halt.[77] Such tactics left the Drocourt-Quéant line in
Canadian hands by the end of the day, and the corps advanced to the
Canal du Nord on 3 September.[78]

The pace of operations did little to improve communications, and
forward of the start line they were intermittent at best. Behind the front,
telephone lines remained open for the most part, though after the battle
battalion commanders stressed the importance of keeping copious
amounts of cable on hand to repair breaks caused by friendly and enemy
artillery. Some units used pigeons, with the usual mixed results. Visual
signalling with the forward troops was often a problem on a battlefield
where many strong points were left behind and could act as snipers, for
lamps made excellent targets. All in all communications were patchy,
though it did not seem to make much difference as long as infantry
platoons could carry on with scheduled artillery support. Though battalion commanders and their superiors wanted to know what was happening at the front, by 1918 they had very little input in the battle's
progress. Thus the nature of communications reflected the nature of
war in general: long periods of inactivity punctuated by crisis whenever
front-line troops needed artillery or other support.[79]

After Drocourt-Quéant the Canadian Corps had a few weeks to wait
before beginning operations against the Hindenburg Line. It was to these
defences that the Germans had withdrawn in 1917 and from them that
they had launched their March offensive, and now they had retreated
again. The British first began to attack the line on 12 September, but
it was not until the 27th that the Canadian Corps became involved, its
objective the Canal du Nord, a wide ditch blocking the way to Cambrai.
German defences, locked into natural features, were impressive; the
canal itself was 100 feet wide, and the Germans had flooded the marshes
on their flanks and placed machine-gun posts close to the canal, so
crossing it would be most difficult. The main German defences, the
Marquion Line, were a mile past the canal, and air photographs showed
that the line's main strength lay in its dense wire barricades, though the

trenches themselves did not seem strong enough to give much protection against heavy bombardment.[80]

The 1st Division would advance on the left while the 4th Division attacked on the right. When the Canadians assaulted, they used the same tactics and formations they had used at Amiens and Arras, but one aspect of operations at the canal was somewhat unique, the need for engineer bridging parties. The bridges were crucial if ammunition, artillery, tanks, and other combat necessities were to keep up with the infantry. Where the canal was filled with water the troops themselves needed bridges to get over the obstacle; first, platoons that had crossed in dry areas swung around and captured a bridgehead, then the engineers put up foot bridges, made of cork slabs baled with wire netting, to allow units like the 42nd Battalion to make their way to their assembly areas on the other side of the canal.[81] The engineers' second task would then be to prepare crossings for field guns and transport, using pontoon or prefabricated trestle bridges. Finally, they would assemble prefabricated Inglis bridges for the larger guns and trucks, while the tanks would be ramped across the dry portion of the canal in the southern area of the corps front.[82]

When the creeping barrage began to move forward, sappers followed directly behind assaulting troops to repair roads and canal crossings,[83] the 3rd Battalion being the busiest of the engineer units that day. Its A Company helped the 1st Divisional Artillery get its guns forward, with one subsection attached to each of the four forward batteries. For example, the 3rd Sub-Section, accompanying the 5th Battery, bridged a small stream, crossed the canal at a site prepared by other engineers, and cut a passage through barbed-wire obstacles. B Company built two crossings for the guns to move forward, though one crew working on a pontoon bridge was hampered by machine-gun fire. C Company was closest to the fighting, since it put four infantry foot bridges across the canal for the 15th Battalion; after the first was in place, sappers rushed across to capture a machine-gun so the next three could be built, and the company was also responsible for six light transport bridges made of prefabricated materials called Weldon Trestles. Wagons brought materials forward, often under machine-gun fire. D Company build a heavy bridge for the tanks, starting construction six hours after the operation began.[84]

Sir Arthur Currie was pleased with overall results. In a letter to Sir Robert Borden he gave the engineers much credit for the attack's success:

'The work of our engineers in bridging the Canal immediately after the
infantry had crossed was of such a character as to win the special praise
of the Commander-in-Chief, and the press commented most favourably
on it. Let me tell you that those bridges were begun not only under shell
fire, but under machine gun fire, and yet nothing could deter the work
of our men.'[85] The operation was a foreshadowing of the next war, when
engineers in many theatres would be hard-pressed to keep tanks, artillery, and truck-borne infantry moving over rivers and rough terrain.

Canadian artillery faced a difficult task, because the front widened
from 2,600 to 15,000 yards in the course of the advance, and the depth
of the attack, especially on the 4th Division's front, required batteries
to move forward into captured ground.[86] In the fighting from 27 September to 1 October Canadian gunners used 'relay' barrages to maintain
support for the advancing infantry and armour. Of ten brigades supporting the 4th Division, only six fired the barrage up to the first objective, while the other four moved forward. Eight brigades fired the
barrage to the second objective, four from their original locations plus
the four that had just moved forward. Meanwhile, two brigades joined
the latter, and these six then fired the barrage to the third objective.[87]
As one would expect, results were mixed, some batteries having difficulty negotiating their way across the canal and through pock-marked
terrain. For example, in capturing Bourlon Wood, a copse 2,000 yards
deep and the main objective for many units, the 38th Battalion quickly
reached its objectives and declared itself satisfied with its artillery support,[88] while the 87th Battalion lost about 150 men completing its tasks
and made no mention of its supporting gunners, usually an indication
of success, since infantrymen took their artillery support for granted.[89]
The 102nd Battalion suffered heavier casualties but also made no com-
plaint;[90] but the 1st and 13th Battalions, attacking on the left, had a
more difficult time, the former later stating that 'From the outset the
attacking infantry were at a disadvantage due to the ragged barrage,'[91]
and German machine-gunners took a heavy toll.

After the battles of August and early September it had become obvious
that artillery had a major role to play in the new style of fighting. Since
infantry battalions needed support, they were allocated artillery sections;
and, since anti-tank guns made armoured operations particularly hazardous, artillery went forward to counter them. Accuracy was critical,
since a field-gun crew could take only 176 rounds into the advance.
Naturally, such units needed protection, so Lewis gunners moved with

them to guard against local counter-attacks.[92] At Canal du Nord, however, late in the first day and in the days to follow battalions missed their supporting guns. Many small actions were stand-up battles between Canadian machine-guns and rifles advancing from cover to cover and German infantry and machine-gunners in defensive positions sometimes protected by barbed wire. Even when targets were within range of artillery fire, cooperation between gunners and infantry was far from optimal. The 10th Battalion, repeating the role it had filled at Amiens by advancing with the final assault of the day, ran into thick wire obstacles. When the gunners suggested that the troops withdraw so they could cut a gap through the wire, the battalion commander refused; for he did not want to give up ground so dearly taken. When on the next day, the 28th, the unit received orders to attack again, it found that the line for the creeping barrage coincided with what the battalion was holding; fifty men were lost in the withdrawal to reach an area safe from their own artillery. On the 29th, the 1st Canadian Mounted Rifles captured the village of St-Olle, on the outskirts of Cambrai, but they were forced to leave precipitously when a flanking unit ordered the village shelled. The artillery liaison officer with the battalion halted the barrage, but not before the unit sustained casualties. In this case it was communication between infantry units that had broken down.[93]

Gunners were still capable of some notable successes. On the 29th the 102nd Battalion reported that 'The enemy continued to put in reinforcements in the low ground about Bantigny and considerable work was enabled to be put in against these and against machine guns around Blécourt by two forward guns of the 4th C.D.A. and also the 4th C.D.A. 6, Trench Mortars.'[94] Obviously, some artillery units did better than others, depending on their ability to get forward to support the infantry, and inconsistency should have been expected under such circumstances. That some battalions complained when the gunners were not available was symptomatic of the infantry's continued dependence on guns and howitzers to protect its advance until it could bring its own weapons to bear.

Many infantry commanders came to appreciate the kind of work the tanks could do for them. Each of the 1st and 4th divisions attacking on the 27th was accompanied by eight tanks of the 7th Tank Battalion, which crushed wire entanglements and destroyed machine-gun posts, five of the sixteen becoming casualties. Officers of the 78th Battalion wished they had had tank support for their attack but none was available.[95] Whether the heavy, tracked vehicles could have negotiated the muddy fields in that area is unclear, though there were no reports of any of them becoming stuck.

Since they left the Somme in October and November 1916, the commanders and staff officers of the Canadian Corps had been searching for a way to break into German defences without prohibitive losses. At Canal du Nord they succeeded, but the tactical system devised in early 1917 and revised in the summer of 1918 could still break down. One of the more unfortunate units of the 27 September attack was the 13th Battalion, for which everything went wrong. First, its infantry companies captured their first objective in the Arras-Cambrai Road.

D Coy then started its advance on Marquion but at once ran into heavy belts of wire, quite untouched by shell fire. Four tanks, which on paper were to have been with us from the start, now appeared and matters looked much brighter, but the tanks merely advanced to the wire, turned around and departed in the direction of Sains, despite the 'Come to our help' signal from the Company, and personal requests from Lieuts. R.A.C. Young and J.E. Christie. As the barrage had passed well in advance of the company, the German gunners were able to shoot down many of the men, while cutting their way through the wire and one tank going in advance through the wire, would have cut our casualties to a quarter. Both our Stokes guns had been knocked-out previously and the enemy machine guns were up a bare slope out of range of our rifle grenades ... Field guns could have cleared up the situation at once, but we had no Liaison Officer with us. The first Artillery Officer seen reported soon after 1.00 pm and he was not in direct communication with his battery.[96]

Such difficulties, however, translated into heavy but not prohibitive casualties; the battalion lost 225 officers and men in the battle, most of them on the 27th. The battalion captured Marquion the next day.[97]

Operations to capture Cambrai lasted until 11 October and brought the other two divisions of the Canadian Corps into the battle. With the Hindenburg Line behind them, the Allied and Associated Powers pressed on towards the German border, while their enemies, ill fed and low on ammunition, tried to prepare defensive positions as best they could to keep the war from reaching their home soil. The Canadians would fight in their last set-piece battle of the war at Valenciennes, the key to the Canal de l'Escaut Line. Planning began on 27 October; between the Canadian Corps and the town was the canal, and to the north flood waters made movement impossible; to the south was Mount Houy, where the Germans had placed their artillery. The 51st Highland Division was ordered to capture the hill to provide the 4th Canadian Division with a jump-off line for its assault on the town.[98]

Mount Houy held out against two attacks, so the 10th Brigade relieved the 154th Infantry Brigade on 31 October[99] and began another assault the following day. The brigade moved north through the outskirts before investing Valenciennes itself, while the 38th and 72nd Battalions of the 12th Brigade attacked directly across the Canal de L'Escaut and into the town, though all units were understrength after the autumn's fighting and the usual depletions caused by illness and injury.[100] The artillery plan was a simple one, to saturate every known German artillery position, every possible approach for German troops, and every likely assembly area for German reserves.[101]

As they had at Amiens, the gunners did not preregister but relied on their maps, the science of calibration, and the skill of survey sections in gathering information and of battery officers in fixing gun positions, lines of fire, and targets.[102] The Canadians had 104 heavy artillery pieces alone, with seventy-six six-inch howitzers, five eight-inch howitzers, eighteen sixty-pounders, and two six-inch Mark XIX guns, the latter among the most modern in the British Army. Field artillery contributed twenty-four batteries for the 10th Brigade's creeping barrage alone, which meant that 144 eighteen-pounders and forty-eight 4.5-inch howitzers would be firing, or one eighteen-pounder for every seventeen yards of front.[103] The infantry requested a slow rate of advance and the artillery complied; platoons were then able to manoeuvre around buildings, secure behind a dense wall of shrapnel, smoke, and dust. The smoke by itself was a complete success, blown by the wind into German positions, blinding them. In the course of the advance the 3rd Brigade – Canadian Field Artillery, followed the infantry to supply close support as soon as it had completed its barrage tasks.[104]

Supply conditions for the artillery were far better than they had been in previous campaigns; for senior Canadian gunners sensed that the war was nearing its end and did not baulk at expending vast quantities of ammunition. There was much talk of peace in the air, and the gunners knew it. 'It was therefore the proper time to neglect economy and to exert every possible effort by means of supporting mechanical weapons to break down the enemy's resistance and thus, as far as possible, minimize the infantry casualties.'[105] Ammunition expenditures were phenomenal; eighteen-pounders and 4.5-inch howitzers combined fired 56,200 rounds, or 620 tons of shell, and heavy artillery fired 31,500 rounds, or 1,520 tons, for a grand total of 87,700 rounds, or 2,140 tons.[106] McNaughton compared the bombardment with the 2,800 tons of shell fired by both sides in the Boer War and the thirty-seven tons fired at Waterloo, exclaiming that 'there had been nothing like it the whole history of war for intensity.'[107]

Infantry went into the attack accompanied by machine-guns and trench mortars, as before. Nine batteries, or seventy-two machine-guns, thickened the artillery barrage in the early stages of the assault, many placing themselves on the Canal de L'Escaut, firing at German positions until Canadian troops moving across their front were almost upon them. A battery of eight guns accompanied each attacking battalion and took up defensive positions after the objectives fell, and a few six-inch Newton mortars followed the battalions as well. In one case two mortars fired eighty rounds in twenty minutes, destroying or silencing several machine-gun posts. The Canadians controlled the battlefield, though they could do little to prevent the Germans from using gas, which caused some of the Canadian casualties on 1 and 2 November. All in all, the 10th Brigade, which bore the brunt of the fighting, lost sixty men killed, 380 wounded, and sixty-one missing of the approximately 1,200 available for the battle.[108]

Conditions were ideal and Canadian artillery, machine-guns, mortars, and infantry were capable of taking advantage of them. As A.W. Strudwick remembered: 'The main thing about that – there wasn't much fighting – heavy fighting going on I remember ... When we got near there [Valenciennes] they were surrendering in droves. We knew then that the enemy was practically breaking up, beginning to break up.'[109] Soon after, there was some controversy as to whether artillery or machine-guns had paved the way to success. Brutinel pointed to Valenciennes as proof of the machine-gun's dominance of the battlefield in attack as well as defence; he had long advocated using machine-guns to fire indirectly at distant targets and to set up barrages to pave the way for the infantry. McNaughton ordered his intelligence crew to interview prisoners of war to determine which had been most important in their defeat, the machine-gun or the artillery piece. As it turned out, no one from the German counter-attacking battalions mentioned machine-guns, but most volunteered that artillery had broken up their assaults.[110] Though the interviews may have been biased, it should be pointed out that whenever a Canadian assault went wrong, infantry tended to point to ragged or ineffective artillery barrages as the cause, proof of their reliance on the big guns.

After Valenciennes the pursuit continued. Battles became skirmishes between platoons – between Canadian forward patrols and German rear guards. The enemy, with almost no resources left to fight a war, was unable to prepare strong defences, in spite of a countryside laced with streams and dotted with villages. For the last nine days tactics were far less important than logistics and shells far less important than bridges. The Canadians crossed into Belgian territory on 7 November; cavalry came into its own once again, pushing patrols forward to find roads and locate the enemy, reaching some four miles beyond Mons by the time of the armistice. Fighting continued until 11 November – then the war ended. As the last Canadians fell near Mons, total casualties for the Canadian Expeditionary Force on the Western Front, for the period 1915 to 1918, rose to 212,688, 53,216 of whom were dead or dying.

In the last three months of the war the advances made by the Canadian Corps were spectacular compared with previous battles, including Vimy. The combination of artillery, machine-guns, and infantry weapons, wielded by men for the most part trained, and in many cases well trained, proved capable of breaking into German defences, albeit usually with heavy casualties. In 1918 the Germans turned the battlefield into open warfare with their offensives of spring and summer but could not sustain the pace, owing to the British blockade and the concomitant lack of supplies. The Allied and Associated Powers had the necessary war materiel to support an offensive, even though the tactics of fire and movement required shiploads of shells and bullets.

The cost of war is always too high, but the Canadian Corps's last battles on the Western Front were less costly than the disaster at Ypres or the massacre on the Somme. In the cold-blooded calculus of war one trades lives for territory, or perhaps even the lives of one's own troops for those of the enemy; in either case the tactics of fire and movement proved themselves. At Amiens alone the corps advanced further than it had in any previous battle, and on only two of the last ten days of the war did it advance less than a mile. As for casualties, German prisoners of war often outnumbered total Canadian losses. Only once, however, did technology come close to replacing flesh and blood, at Valenciennes, although two divisions suffered their worst month of the war in the campaign, the 3rd losing 4,716 infantrymen in August while the 4th lost 7,352 infantrymen in September.[111] Even in the last three months the evolving technology of war could not drastically reduce casualties; it could only change the ratio between losses and gains. Perhaps, however, costly victories were better than costly defeats.

Conclusion
The Canadian Corps:
Tactics and Technics in the
Industrial Age

The conflict that engulfed Europe from 1914 to 1918 was not the first of the world's industrial wars; the mobilization of mass armies whose clashes led to severe loss of life was also characteristic of the American Civil War, the Franco-Prussian War, and the Russo-Japanese War. Nor were the battles that took place in France, eastern Europe, or northern Italy necessarily the bloodiest of such conflicts. Though almost 20,000 British soldiers died in only a few hours on the first day of the Somme offensive, as many or more Japanese were incinerated in the first instant after the atomic bomb exploded over Hiroshima, and the Russians, who bore the brunt of the fighting in the Second World War, saw 20 million of their people die (possibly 26 million, according to recent Russian estimates). The First World War, however, was a watershed; for from it rose an important communist nation and a powerful western state which would eventually seek to spread their conflicting ideologies through the rest of the world and would push the development of the tools of war to the point where, for a time, any major conflict could well have been the last. In the First World War a large offensive was, in the words of Prime Minister Briand of France, 'nothing less than a great industrial organization,'[1] but it was left to the next industrial war to mass-produce death.

One of several issues that arises from studying the history of the Canadian contingent and the Canadian Corps from 1914 to 1918 is the evolution of tactics within Canadian combat arms. At Second Ypres the Canadian contingent relied on the most basic tactics to come to grips with the enemy during its many counter-attacks, notably at Kitchener's Wood and Mauser Ridge. Industrial warfare was new to everyone, so troops marched or charged at the enemy as best they could, every man a rifleman, the gunners little more than witnesses to the carnage that followed as soldiers pitted their own bodies against German defences. Three years and four months later, however, the Canadians were part of a huge offensive that brought the war to an end. What role tactics played in the German defeat is difficult to assess, but what is important here is that changing tactics were symptomatic of an evolving relationship between the tools of battle and those called upon to use them. In the last three months of the war, in marked contrast with the Canadian contingent's first three months on the Western Front, the Canadian Corps fought a fluid battle, battalions moving forward under an artillery umbrella and sections advancing with the support of tanks and their own weapons. Each soldier was a specialist with a specific role to play in battle, whether it be as Lewis gunner or rifleman, but he was also a jack of all trades, ready to use bomb, rifle-grenade, Lewis gun, or rifle if need be. The Canadian Corps thus moved away from the concept of the citizen-soldier who could ride and shoot to an army of technicians which, even in the infantry battalions, specialized in particular aspects of fighting battles.

Another issue to arise from studying the Canadian Corps's evolution is the relationship between tactics and casualties, or the calculus of death, especially given that Julian Byng and Arthur Currie advocated replacing flesh and blood with shell and bullet. When a country's leaders decide to make war they accept that lives will be lost, and military leaders make similar decisions when planning their campaigns. A commander may be willing to give up lives to capture ground, or he may aim at a battle of attrition, hoping to take even more lives from among the enemy's soldiers. Almost all the battles the Canadian Corps fought from 1915 to 1918 fall into the first category – lives for ground. From the counter-attacks around Ypres to the final push of the war the commander's main goal was to force the enemy to abandon his positions and move back either towards his own borders, or at least away from important strategic and tactical features.

Attrition rarely figured in Canadian Corps operations, not because the Canadians valued human life any more than did the French or British, but because their role was to break into German positions in accordance with Haig's often touted but never-achieved goal of shattering the deadlock on the Western Front. There were times, however, when a battle was aimed to some extent at wearing down the enemy; Hill 70 is the most obvious example, when Currie decided to capture the position not only to push the Germans from a hill where they could dominate Canadian assaults towards Lens but also to force them to wear themselves out in one counter-attack after another. The final battles of the war were also aimed to some extent at wearing the enemy down, keeping the Germans off balance to force them to accept a difficult armistice. In either case, the tools of war served both to protect friendly soldiers and to kill or wound enemy soldiers, and the tactics that determined how the tools were used may well have helped determine the number and nature of casualties on both sides. There were other factors of course, which together may have been more important, such as fatigue, illness, the availability of medical care, the amount and quality of food and water, weather, topography, and no doubt many more; but this is not to deny that there was a close link between tactics, gains on the battlefield, and casualties.

At Ypres, Festubert, Givenchy, St-Eloi, and Mount Sorrel the Canadians, with the British and French, sought ways to break the deadlock of trench warfare. During its long tour in the line at Ypres, from 15 April to 3 May, the 1st Division lost 5,976 men, the great majority of them in a defensive battle where gains were minimal or non-existent as the Canadians fought to hold or regain lost ground.[2] The experience at Festubert was similar, as the corps attacked German defences for five days and advanced only 600 yards on a one-mile front, suffering 2,323 casualties.[3] Givenchy was no better. At St-Eloi the Canadians suffered 1,428 casualties and lost ground the British had captured a few days before.[4] At Mount Sorrel the corps once again tried to regain lost ground after the Germans had captured the hill, and some 9,383 soldiers fell,[5] but troops demonstrated that they were able to attack and capture a heavily defended tactical feature. Thus, up to the Somme offensive, the Canadian Corps, though slowly adopting changing British tactics and developing some of its own, suffered more loss than gain. Tactics and training did not match soldiers' courage.

The campaign on the Somme was made up of several battles where the Canadian Corps saw a few successes and many setbacks, always at a high price in casualties. In their first week, from 15 to 20 September, the Canadians lost about 7,230 men in the battles of Flers-Courcelette and the fighting for Fabeck Graben and Zollern Graben,[6] advancing over a mile in some places and taking important positions like Mouquet Farm, the sugar factory, and large sections of German trench. Though their tactics could not guarantee light losses, better-prepared artillery and infantry were able to press forward against strong German defences. At Thiepval Ridge, from 26 to 28 September, Canadian assaults were successful, but troops often had to fall back under pressure of German counter-attacks, though without relinquishing everything they had captured, and some units managed to advance 1,000 yards. The attack on Regina Trench that followed on 1 October was mostly a series of reverses punctuated by the odd success, and casualties from 26 September to 1 October were high; brigades became battalions and companies disappeared altogether. The 5th Brigade went from 1,717 to 773 men, while the 9th Brigade, on 8 October, lost 941 men with nothing to show for it, and the 4th Division required from 21 October to 11 November to capture the trench system.[7] The Canadians still sought means to bring success more readily within their grasp without sacrificing whole battalions in each attack.

The assault on Vimy Ridge ended with a different balance between cost and results. In six days the corps advanced 4,500 yards, captured an important tactical feature, seized fifty-four guns, 104 trench mortars, 124 machine-guns, and took 4,000 prisoners, for a total loss of 10,602 men, 3,598 of whom died. Casualties were not low, since 16 per cent of those involved in the battle were killed or wounded, but such losses were a marked improvement over the Somme, which lasted much longer and where 31 per cent of those engaged became casualties.[8] At Arleux, casualties were high, the 2nd Brigade losing 1,000 men and capturing 450, but in the centre the brigade advanced 1,500 yards and took the town of Arleux-en-Gohelle.[9] At Fresnoy gains were similar, and the 1,259 casualties there were distributed among three brigades.[10]

In capturing Hill 70 on 15 August the 1st and 2nd divisions suffered heavy losses but took the most important feature in the area, while from 16 to 18 August the Germans counter-attacked repeatedly but inflicted less than 1,000 casualties, though losing heavily themselves.[11] To the right of Hill 70 lay Lens, where on 21 August the 10th and 11th brigades lost 1,154 men capturing the outskirts of town, the advance continuing with high losses until 25 August, and casualties in the last fortnight of that month were almost the same as at Vimy, with 10,011 Canadians killed, wounded, captured, or missing.[12] Once again the Canadians were successful in capturing an important tactical feature and inflicting heavy casualties on the enemy, and once again about one man in eight paid the price for success.

At Passchendaele the Canadians faced a new German tactical doctrine, and the advance on the ridge and village was slow, with attacks on 26 October, 30 October, and 6 November. The first moved the line forward some 500 yards and cost 2,481 casualties divided between the

3rd and 4th divisions;[13] the second attack saw gains of up to 1,000 yards
with 884 men killed, 1,429 wounded, and eight taken prisoner;[14] the
final assault took the village and the ridge and left 420 killed, and total
losses for that last day, among the troops of the 1st and 2nd Divisions,
were 1,094.[15] Total battle casualties in the Canadian Corps for the campaign that ended on 10 November amounted to 16,404, or 20 per cent
of those engaged, with gains less spectacular than those at Vimy.[16] The
Canadians had captured their objectives with what was becoming clockwork regularity, but changes in German defensive tactics slowed the
Canadian advance and inflicted heavier casualties, which at Passchendaele amounted to one man in five.

The Canadian Corps continued to develop its tactics during the summer of 1918, preparing for open warfare. During its first battle of the
final offensive, at Amiens from 8 to 20 August, there were rapid advances totalling fourteen miles on a front of 7,500 to 10,000 yards, or
an area of sixty-seven square miles. They liberated twenty-seven villages, captured over 9,000 prisoners, 200 guns, and over 1,000 machineguns and trench mortars. Casualties were highest in the first few days,
when gains were most spectacular; some 3,868 men were killed, wounded,
went missing, or were captured on the first day, and casualties totalled
9,074 for the first four days. By 20 August the Canadian Corps had lost
11,725 men, over 1,000 more than at Vimy Ridge but with far more
impressive results, while only 13 per cent of those engaged in the battle
became casualties, compared with the 16 per cent who fell taking Vimy
Ridge.[17] Advances from 1 to 3 September were also impressive, including a break through the German defences at Drocourt-Quéant, but
more important was the fact that the Canadians captured 6,000 unwounded prisoners from 1 to 4 September while losing 5,662 men.[18] In
the Arras-Cambrai battle, from 26 August to 11 October, the Canadian
Corps advanced twenty-three miles against the elements of thirty-one
German divisions, who fought hard in spite of supply shortages. At
Arras, where they pierced the Drocourt-Quéant line, 14,349 men were
killed, wounded, or went missing; at Cambrai, where they captured
Bourlon Wood, 14,849 men became casualties; meanwhile they captured
18,585 prisoners, 371 guns, and almost 2,000 machine-guns, and liberated fifty-four towns and villages and 116 square miles of French
territory. In the last battle the Canadian Corps fought in the war, Valenciennes fell, with eighty men killed and 300 wounded. In the three
months from 8 August to 11 November the corps took 31,281 prisoners
while suffering 45,835 casualties.[19]

TABLE 1

	Combatants engaged (approx.)	Casualties	Percentage lost (approx.)
Ypres, 1915	16,500	6,104	37
Somme, 1916	77,000	24,029	31
Vimy, 1917	81,000	13,477	16
Passchendaele, 1917	81,000	16,404	20
Amiens, 1918	91,000	11,725	13
Arras, 1918	46,000	6,836	15
Drocourt-Quéant, 1918	46,000	7,218	15.5
Canal du Nord, 1918	68,500	13,672	20

In studying the relationship between gains and losses, the war can be roughly separated into two periods. From 1915 to the end of the Somme campaign attacks often met with bloody failure, and even successes were costly. From Vimy Ridge to the end of the war the relationship changed; successes were common, and even at Passchendaele casualties amounted to almost 10,000 less than those on the Somme, as table 1 indicates.[20] It is interesting to note that piercing the Canal du Nord in 1918 was as costly in terms of the percentage of soldiers lost as taking Passchendaele. Furthermore, the 3rd and 4th divisions suffered their worst infantry losses of the war in August 1918 and September 1918, respectively. If one measures infantry casualties as an average per division engaged in any given month, April 1915, the month of Second Ypres, still stands as the worst, with 5,026 infantrymen of the 1st Division killed, taken prisoner, missing, or wounded severely enough to require evacuation. But the second-worst figure is for September 1918, when the 1st, 3rd, and 4th divisions lost an average of 4,914 riflemen, Lewis gunners, and rifle-grenadiers. In September 1916, the only full month the corps spent on the Somme, the 1st, 2nd, and 3rd divisions each suffered an average of 4,407 infantry casualties, and August 1918 was only slightly better, each of the corps's four divisions losing an average of 4,397 infantrymen. Battles were still bloody, but the corps made far greater gains for its losses, an exchange favourable in the eyes of the higher command and perhaps in the eyes of some of the troops. Thus changes in technology or in the use of familiar technology did have some impact on the relationship between the Canadian Corps's potential for success and the number of men it lost in each battle.

To the military commander soldiers are a resource to be used and husbanded in the best interests of the nation they are supposed to serve. This attitude is an important part of the calculus of death that forces commanders, sometimes, to justify casualties; at the time of the Somme Haig claimed that the heavy losses the British Expeditionary Force was incurring were justified by the even heavier losses it was supposedly inflicting on the Germans. Currie rarely, if ever, tried to justify heavy losses, though he never expected the battles he and his staff planned to be bloodless. Soldiers in the Canadian Corps were not to be squandered or wasted; as much as possible battalions were to be given everything they needed in the way of weapons or support to get them to their objectives with as few losses as possible. The Canadian Corps was less a glorious institution of soldiery than a gathering of technicians. These soldiers and their managers sometimes agreed on common means to different ends, the technicians to keep their skins and the managers to achieve their mission. That the soldiers also wanted to achieve victory certainly helped; the Russian debacle demonstrated what could happen when troops and officers had completely different goals.

The Canadian Corps's relationship with the tools of war changed markedly between 1915 and 1918. At the beginning of the war the combat arms of the Canadian Expeditionary Force could be separated into infantry, artillery, and cavalry, though there was very little of the latter. Each infantryman carried out the same job, runners being an exception; companies or even battalions attacked en masse in an attempt to overpower the enemy, and though regiments could have different titles and uniforms, such as highlanders or grenadiers, on the battlefield they had exactly the same role. As with the infantry, so with the artillery, at least as long as all gunners worked on the same type of gun, whether it be the thirteen- or eighteen-pounder. As the war progressed, both infantry and artillery became more specialized; by the end of 1916 a platoon was made up of several sections, each armed with its own weapons and having its own role to play; in the artillery, different guns carried out different jobs, with eighteen-pounders firing the creeping barrage while 4.5-inch guns destroyed the trenches and heavier guns concentrated on counter-battery fire. The Canadian Corps fought several successful battles in the course of 1917 and 1918 thanks to tactics that took advantage of available technology.

From the turn of the century to 1918 Canadian soldiers saw dramatic changes; from peace to world war, from siege warfare to open fighting, from parade-square drill to the fire and movement tactics of 1918. Their inventory of tools expanded to include bombs, rifle-grenades, Lewis guns, bangalore torpedoes, and a host of others. Those that were wholly inappropriate, like the Ross rifle, they rejected; those that were of dubious utility, like the Colt machine-gun, they criticized (that Lee-Enfields and Vickers were in short supply was, of course, outside their control); others, like the rifle-grenade, they accepted, adapted, and used extensively. Technology does not evolve or change by itself but requires those who invent and those who adapt, and, if necessity is the mother of invention,[21] then the Germans can take much of the credit for most of the technological developments the Canadians adopted; for it was mainly in reaction to their enemy's defensive techniques, not through any intuitive perception of technology's usefulness, that the Allies brought increasingly complex tools to the battlefield. By the end of the war, technology in all its forms had turned combat into a three-dimensional enterprise requiring literally an army of specialist technicians to handle them. Inventors, mainly civilians whose work was named after them, such as the Stokes mortar, the Mills bomb, the Hales rifle-grenade, the Newton mortar, and the Lewis gun, developed or redeveloped tools of war that the War Office then tested. Once they were adopted, staff officers organized training so that knowledge of how the tools could be used was communicated to units at the front. But the process of technological diffusion did not end there, as trench inventors produced their own bombs, cut the stocks of their rifles, or developed slings for Lewis guns. Canadian soldiers were less sheep led to the slaughter than thinking people who set their minds to the challenges of survival and, in the process, contributed to the defeat of a well-trained and well-motivated enemy.

In the Canadian Corps soldiers sometimes had influence on the tools they were expected to use, and sometimes they did not. Throughout, it was their task, determined by others, to storm hills, hold villages, and destroy their enemies. Whether those enemies deserved to be destroyed has been a subject for debate ever since, and in recent years consensus has been that the gains of the First World War, ephemeral in any case, were not worth the cost. But still, we must remember the soldier, who had to face shelling and machine-gun fire and barbed wire, who carried out his task the best he could, unable to have any impact on the policy-making and decision-making that had put him on the battlefield, but who was sometimes able to affect his own destiny through his choice of tools and his ability to learn.

Appendix A

Canadian Corps Organization 1915–1918

When the two orders of battle that follow are compared, it becomes evident that the corps grew not only in size but in complexity. The addition of motor transport companies, the increase in artillery, the formation of engineer battalions, and the reorganization of signal services are just some of the changes that attest to the growing specialization on a large scale that was mirrored within the platoons themselves. The formation of an anti-aircraft searchlight company is a clear sign of the importance of aerial warfare on the Western Front from the point of view of the troops on the ground.

OCTOBER 1915: CANADIAN CORPS ORDER OF BATTLE

Headquarters, Canadian Army Corps
Headquarters, Signal Company, Royal Engineers
Headquarters, Canadian Cavalry Brigade
   Royal Canadian Dragoons
   Lord Strathcona's Horse
   2nd King Edward's Horse
Headquarters, 1st Canadian Mounted Rifle Brigade
   1st Regiment, CMR
   2nd Regiment, CMR
   3rd Regiment, CMR
Headquarters, 2nd Canadian Mounted Rifle Brigade
   4th Regiment, CMR
   5th Regiment, CMR
   6th Regiment, CMR

42nd Canadian Infantry Battalion
49th Canadian Infantry Battalion
Composite Infantry Detachment
Canadian Field Troop, Royal Engineers
Special Detachment, Canadian Engineers
Canadian Corps Troops Supply Column
1st Canadian Division Supply Column
2nd Canadian Division Supply Column
Canadian Corps Ammunition Park
1st Canadian Ammunition Sub-Park
2nd Canadian Ammunition Sub-Park
Royal Canadian Horse Artillery Brigade
1st Canadian Motor Machine Gun Brigade
Borden Motor Machine Gun Brigade

1st Canadian Divisional Headquarters
1st Canadian Divisional Mounted Troops
  Cyclist Company
  Cavalry Squadron
1st Canadian Divisional Artillery
  1st Canadian Artillery Brigade
  2nd Canadian Artillery Brigade
  3rd Canadian Artillery Brigade
  118th Howitzer Brigade, Royal Field Artillery
  1st Canadian Division Ammunition Column
1st Canadian Divisional Engineers
  1st Field Company
  2nd Field Company
  3rd Field Company
1st Canadian Divisional Signal Company
Headquarters, 1st Canadian Infantry Brigade
  1st Canadian Battalion
  2nd Canadian Battalion
  3rd Canadian Battalion
  4th Canadian Battalion
Headquarters, 2nd Canadian Infantry Brigade
  5th Canadian Battalion
  7th Canadian Battalion
  8th Canadian Battalion
  10th Canadian Battalion

Headquarters, 3rd Canadian Infantry Brigade
   13th Canadian Battalion
   14th Canadian Battalion
   15th Canadian Battalion
   16th Canadian Battalion
1st Canadian Divisional Train
   Headquarters Company
   No. 2 Company
   No. 3 Company
   No. 4 Company
1st Canadian Field Ambulance
2nd Canadian Field Ambulance
3rd Canadian Field Ambulance
No. 1 Sanitary Section
1st Canadian Motor Ambulance Workshop Unit
1st Canadian Mobile Veterinary Section

2nd Canadian Divisional Headquarters
2nd Canadian Divisional Mounted Troops
   Cyclist Company
   Cavalry Squadron
2nd Canadian Divisional Artillery
   1st West Lancs Artillery Brigade
   2nd West Lancs Artillery Brigade
   3rd West Lancs Artillery Brigade
   4th West Lancs Howitzer Brigade
   4th Canadian Artillery Brigade
   2nd Canadian Divisional Ammunition Column
2nd Divisional Engineers
   No. 4 Field Company
   No. 5 Field Company
   No. 6 Field Company
2nd Canadian Divisional Signal Company
Headquarters, 4th Canadian Infantry Brigade
   18th Battalion
   19th Battalion
   20th Battalion
   21st Battalion
Headquarters, 5th Canadian Infantry Brigade
   22nd Battalion

24th Battalion
25th Battalion
26th Battalion
Headquarters, 6th Canadian Infantry Brigade
27th Battalion
28th Battalion
29th Battalion
31st Battalion
2nd Canadian Divisional Train
   No. 5 Company (Headquarters Company)
   No. 6 Company
   No. 7 Company
   No. 8 Company
4th Canadian Field Ambulance
5th Canadian Field Ambulance
6th Canadian Field Ambulance
No. 2 Sanitary Section
2nd Canadian Motor Ambulance Workshop Unit
2nd Canadian Mobile Veterinary Section

NOVEMBER 1918: CANADIAN CORPS ORDER OF BATTLE

Headquarters, Canadian Army Corps
Corps Cavalry
   Canadian Light Horse
   Royal North West Mounted Police
Headquarters, Corps Heavy Artillery
1st Brigade, Canadian Garrison Artillery (CGA)
   3rd Canadian Siege Battery
   7th Canadian Siege Battery
   9th Canadian Siege Battery
   1st Canadian Siege Battery
2nd Brigade, CGA
   1st Canadian Heavy Battery
   2nd Canadian Heavy Battery
   2nd Canadian Siege Battery
   6th Canadian Siege Battery
   4th Canadian Siege Battery
   5th Canadian Siege Battery
3rd Brigade, CGA
   10th Canadian Siege Battery

11th Canadian Siege Battery
8th Canadian Siege Battery
12th Canadian Siege Battery
'E' Canadian Anti-Aircraft Battery
  No. 1 Canadian Section
  No. 2 Canadian Section
  No. 3 Canadian Section
  No. 4 Canadian Section
  No. 5 Canadian Section
8th Army Brigade Canadian Field Artillery (CFA)
  24th Battery, CFA
  30th Battery, CFA
  32nd Battery, CFA
  43rd Battery, CFA
  8th Army Brigade C.F.A. Ammunition Column
5th Canadian Divisional Artillery
13th Brigade, CFA
  52nd Battery, CFA
  53rd Battery, CFA
  55th Battery, CFA
  51st (Howitzer) Battery, CFA
14th Brigade, CFA
  60th Battery, CFA
  61st Battery, CFA
  66th Battery, CFA
  58th Battery, CFA
Other Artillery
  V5C Heavy Trench Mortar Battery
  X5C Trench Mortar Battery
  Y5C Trench Mortar Battery
  5th Canadian Divisional Artillery Ammunition Column
Canadian Corps Cyclist Battalion
Engineers
  Canadian Corps Survey Section
  1st Tramways Company
  2nd Tramways Company
  Permanent Base Engineer Company
  3rd Tunnelling Company
  1st, 2nd, 3rd, 4th, 5th Army Troops Company
  AA Searchlight Company

Corps Signal Troops
  Canadian Corps Signal Company
  No. 1 Canadian Motor Airlines Section
  No. 2 Canadian Motor Airline Section
  CE, CF, CG, CH Cable Sections
  Wireless Sections
  Signal Sections Canadian Corps Heavy Artillery
  Signal Subsection 1st Brigade, CGA
  Signal Subsection 2nd Brigade, CGA
  Signal Subsection 3rd Brigade, CGA
  Signal Subsection 8th Army Brigade, CFA
  5th Canadian Divisional Artillery Signal Detachment
Canadian Machine Gun Corps
  1st Canadian Motor Machine Gun Brigade
  2nd Canadian Motor Machine Gun Brigade
Canadian Army Service Corps
  Canadian Corps Troops Motor Transport Company
  1st Canadian Division Motor Transport Company
  2nd Canadian Division Motor Transport Company
  3rd Canadian Division Motor Transport Company
  4th Canadian Division Motor Transport Company
  5th Canadian Division Motor Transport Company
  Canadian Engineer Motor Transport Company
  Canadian Motor Machine Gun Motor Transport Company
  8th CFA Brigade Park Section
  5th Canadian Division Train Detachment
Army Service Corps (British)
  Canadian Corps Siege Park
Labour
  Canadian Corps Permanent Base Officers Establishment
  Headquarters Canadian Labour Group
  1st, 2nd, 3rd, 4th Canadian Infantry Works Companies
  5th Canadian Area Employment Group
  6th, 7th, 8th, 9th Area Employment Companies
Canadian Ordnance Corps
  Nos 81 and 82 Light Ordnance Mobile Workshops
  No. 83 Medium Ordnance Mobile Workshop
Canadian Army Veterinary Corps
  Canadian Veterinary Evacuation Station
Reinforcement Formations
  Canadian Corps Reinforcement Camp

Canadian Corps Labour Reinforcement Pool
Schools
    Canadian Corps Infantry School
    Canadian Corps Lewis Gun School
    Canadian Corps Signal School
    Canadian Corps Machine Gun School
    Canadian Corps Gas School
Medical
    1st, 2nd, 3rd, 4th, 5th, Canadian Sanitary Sections
    14th Canadian Field Ambulance
    Canadian Corps Dental Laboratory

1st CANADIAN DIVISION

1st Canadian Infantry Brigade
    Headquarters
    1st Canadian Battalion
    2nd Canadian Battalion
    3rd Canadian Battalion
    4th Canadian Battalion
    1st Canadian Trench Mortar Battery
2nd Canadian Infantry Brigade
    Headquarters
    5th Canadian Battalion
    7th Canadian Battalion
    8th Canadian Battalion
    10th Canadian Battalion
    2nd Canadian Trench Mortar Battery
3rd Canadian Infantry Brigade
    Headquarters
    13th Canadian Battalion
    14th Canadian Battalion
    15th Canadian Battalion
    16th Canadian Battalion
    3rd Canadian Trench Mortar Battery

Divisional troops
Headquarters
    Headquarters 1st Canadian Division
    Headquarters Divisional Artillery

1st Brigade, CFA
  1st Battery, CFA
  3rd Battery, CFA
  4th Battery, CFA
  2nd (Howitzer) Battery, CFA
2nd Brigade, CFA
  5th Battery, CFA
  6th Battery, CFA
  7th Battery, CFA
  48th (Howitzer) Battery, CFA
Other Artillery
  V1C Heavy Trench Mortar Battery
  X1C Trench Mortar Battery
  Y1C Trench Mortar Battery
  1st Canadian Divisional Ammunition Column
1st Brigade, Canadian Engineers
  Headquarters
  1st, 2nd, and 3rd Battalions, Canadian Engineers
  1st Pontoon Bridging Transport Unit
Other Divisional Troops
  1st Canadian Divisional Signal Company
  1st Canadian Divisional Train
  1st, 2nd, 3rd Canadian Field Ambulances
  1st Canadian Mobile Veterinary Section
  1st Canadian Divisional Employment Company
  1st Battalion Canadian Machine Gun Corps

2nd CANADIAN DIVISION

4th Canadian Infantry Brigade
  Headquarters
  18th Canadian Battalion
  19th Canadian Battalion
  20th Canadian Battalion
  21st Canadian Battalion
  4th Canadian Trench Mortar Battery
5th Canadian Infantry Brigade
  Headquarters
  22nd Canadian Battalion
  24th Canadian Battalion
  25th Canadian Battalion

26th Canadian Battalion
5th Canadian Trench Mortar Battery
6th Canadian Infantry Brigade
  Headquarters
  27th Canadian Battalion
  28th Canadian Battalion
  29th Canadian Battalion
  31st Canadian Battalion
  6th Canadian Trench Mortar Battery

Divisional troops
Headquarters
  Headquarters 2nd Canadian Division
  Headquarters Divisional Artillery
5th Brigade, CFA
  17th Battery, CFA
  18th Battery, CFA
  20th Battery, CFA
  23rd (Howitzer) Battery, CFA
6th Brigade, CFA
  15th Battery, CFA
  16th Battery, CFA
  25th Battery, CFA
  22nd (Howitzer) Battery, CFA
Other Artillery
  V2C Heavy Trench Mortar Battery
  X2C Trench Mortar Battery
  Y2C Trench Mortar Battery
  2nd Canadian Divisional Ammunition Column
2nd Brigade, Canadian Engineers
  Headquarters
  4th, 5th, and 6th Battalions Canadian Engineers
  2nd Pontoon Bridging Transport Unit
Other Divisional Troops
  2nd Canadian Divisional Signal Company
  2nd Canadian Divisional Train
  4th, 5th, and 6th Canadian Field Ambulances
  2nd Canadian Mobile Veterinary Section
  2nd Canadian Divisional Employment Company
  2nd Battalion Canadian Machine Gun Corps

3rd CANADIAN DIVISION

7th Canadian Infantry Brigade
  Headquarters
  Princess Patricia's Canadian Light Infantry
  Royal Canadian Regiment
  42nd Canadian Battalion
  49th Canadian Battalion
  7th Canadian Trench Mortar Battery
8th Canadian Infantry Brigade
  Headquarters
  1st Canadian Mounted Rifles Battalion
  2nd Canadian Mounted Rifles Battalion
  4th Canadian Mounted Rifles Battalion
  5th Canadian Mounted Rifles Battalion
  8th Canadian Trench Mortar Battery
9th Canadian Infantry Brigade
  Headquarters
  43rd Canadian Battalion
  52nd Canadian Battalion
  58th Canadian Battalion
  116th Canadian Battalion
  9th Canadian Trench Mortar Battery

Divisional troops
Headquarters
  Headquarters 3rd Canadian Division
  Headquarters Divisional Artillery
9th Brigade, CFA
  31st Battery, CFA
  33rd Battery, CFA
  45th Battery, CFA
  36th (Howitzer) Battery, CFA
10th Brigade, CFA
  38th Battery, CFA
  39th Battery, CFA
  40th Battery, CFA
  35th (Howitzer) Battery, CFA

Other Artillery
  v3c Heavy Trench Mortar Battery
  x3c Trench Mortar Battery
  y3c Trench Mortar Battery
  3rd Canadian Divisional Ammunition Column
3rd Brigade, Canadian Engineers
  Headquarters
  7th, 8th, and 9th Battalions Canadian Engineers
  3rd Pontoon Bridging Transport Unit
Other Divisional Troops
  3rd Canadian Divisional Signal Company
  8th, 9th, and 10th Canadian Field Ambulances
  3rd Canadian Mobile Veterinary Section
  3rd Canadian Division Employment Company
  3rd Battalion Canadian Machine Gun Corps
  3rd Canadian Division Train

4th CANADIAN DIVISION

10th Canadian Infantry Brigade
  Headquarters
  44th Canadian Battalion
  46th Canadian Battalion
  47th Canadian Battalion
  50th Canadian Battalion
  10th Canadian Trench Mortar Battery
11th Canadian Infantry Brigade
  Headquarters
  54th Canadian Battalion
  75th Canadian Battalion
  87th Canadian Battalion
  102nd Canadian Battalion
  11th Canadian Trench Mortar Battery
12th Canadian Infantry Brigade
  Headquarters
  38th Canadian Battalion
  72nd Canadian Battalion
  78th Canadian Battalion

85th Canadian Battalion
12th Canadian Trench Mortar Battery

Divisional troops
Headquarters
   Headquarters 4th Canadian Division
   Headquarters Divisional Artillery
3rd Brigade, CFA
   10th Battery, CFA
   11th Battery, CFA
   12th Battery, CFA
   9th (Howitzer) Battery, CFA
4th Brigade, CFA
   13th Battery, CFA
   19th Battery, CFA
   27th Battery, CFA
   21st (Howitzer) Battery, CFA
Other Artillery
   V4C Heavy Trench Mortar Battery
   X4C Trench Mortar Battery
   Y4C Trench Mortar Battery
   4th Canadian Divisional Ammunition Column
4th Brigade, Canadian Engineers
   Headquarters
   10th, 11th, and 12th Battalions
   4th Pontoon Bridging Transport Unit
Other Divisional Troops
   4th Canadian Signal Company
   4th Canadian Division Train
   11th, 12th, and 13th Canadian Field Ambulances
   4th Canadian Mobile Veterinary Section
   4th Canadian Division Employment Company
   4th Battalion Canadian Machine Gun Corps

Casualties of the Canadian Contingent and Canadian Corps

January 1915	1st Canadian Division Losses: Nil
February 1915	1st Canadian Division Losses: 52
March 1915	1st Canadian Division Losses: 320
April 1915	1st Canadian Division Losses: 5,240
May 1915	1st Canadian Division Losses: 2,567
June 1915	1st Canadian Division (Under IV British Corps) Includes Canadian Cavalry Brigade without 2nd KEH Strength, 1 June: 14,859 Losses: 1,164 Reinforcements: 1,684 Operations – Cooperated on attack in Givenchy Sector
July 1915	1st Canadian Division (Under III British Corps) Includes Canadian Cavalry Brigade without 2nd KEH Strength, 1 July: 15,004 Losses: 275 Reinforcements: 1,648 Operations – Situation normal

August 1915	1st Canadian Division (Under II British Corps) Includes Canadian Cavalry Brigade without 2nd KEH Strength, 1 August: 16,395 Losses: 202 Reinforcements: 1,832 Operations – Situation normal
September 1915	Canadian Corps (1st and 2nd Divisions and Cavalry Brigade) Strength, 1 September: 17,736 Losses: 316 Reinforcements: 2,050 Operations: Situation normal
October 1915	Canadian Corps (1st and 2nd Divisions and Cavalry Brigade) Losses: 984 Operations: Enemy exploded five mines on St-Eloi front.
November 1915	Canadian Corps (1st and 2nd Divisions and Cavalry Brigade) Strength, 5 November: about 52,000 Losses: 937 Operations: Trench raids by 5th and 7th Battalions on 17 November
December 1915	Canadian Corps (1st and 2nd Divisions and Cavalry Brigade) Losses: 753 Operations: Trench raids by 5th Battalion
January 1916	Canadian Corps (1st, 2nd, and 3rd Divisions) Strength, 2 January: 53,241 Losses: 658 Operations: Trench raids
February 1916	Canadian Corps (1st, 2nd, and 3rd Divisions) Strength, 4 February: 54,733 Losses: 553 Operations: Trench raids
March 1916	Canadian Corps (1st, 2nd, and 3rd Divisions) Strength, 4 March: 60,087 Losses: 764 Operations: Situation normal

April 1916	Canadian Corps (1st, 2nd, and 3rd Divisions)
	Losses: 2,900
	Operations: Active in St-Eloi crater area
May 1916	Canadian Corps (1st, 2nd, and 3rd Divisions)
	Strength, 5 May: 66,557
	Losses: 3,119
	Operations: Situation normal
June 1916	Canadian Corps (1st, 2nd, and 3rd Divisions)
	Strength, 4 June: 70,207
	Losses
	1 to 7 June: 5,838
	8 to 15 June: 2,630
	1 to 30 June: 11,468
	Operations: Loss and recapture of Mount Sorrel and Observatory Ridge
July 1916	Canadian Corps (1st, 2nd, and 3rd Divisions)
	Losses: 2,430
	Operations: Situation normal
August 1916	Canadian Corps (Four Divisions)
	Strength, 4 August: 73,000
	Losses: 2,177
	Operations: Situation normal
3 September to 16 October	Canadian Corps
	Includes casualties of 1st Division, 1–2 September
	Strength, 25 August: 94,152; 13 October: 82,848
	Losses: 19,423
	Operations:
	Somme front, captured territory at Courcelette, Mouquet Farm, Fabeck Graben, Zollern Graben, Zollern, Hessian and Kenora trenches
	4th Division subsequently took Regina and Desire trenches under II British Corps.
September 1916	Canadian Corps
	Losses: 13,906
	Operations: Somme front
October 1916	Canadian Corps
	Losses: 7,887
	Operations: Somme front to 20 October

November 1916   Canadian Corps
Strength, 3 November: 69,030
Losses: 1,167
Operations: Situation normal

December 1916   Canadian Corps
Losses: 1,073
Operations: Situation normal

January 1917   Canadian Corps
Losses: 927
Operations: Trench raids

February 1917   Canadian Corps
Losses: 1,118
Operations: Trench raids

March 1917   Canadian Corps
Losses: 1,776
Operations: Trench raids

9 April to
3 May   Canadian Corps
   Strength, 7 April
   Including attached units: 172,486
   Excluding attached units: 97,184
Losses: 16,649
Reinforcements: 9,459
Operations: Vimy Ridge, Gavrelle, Fresnoy

April 1917   Canadian Corps
Losses: 14,301
Operations: Lens-Vimy front

3–31 May 1917   Canadian Corps
Losses: 6,913
Operations: Minor ops and trench raids

June 1917   Canadian Corps
Losses: 3,675
Operations: Trench raids

July 1917   Canadian Corps
Losses: 2,828
Operations: Trench raids

August 1917   Canadian Corps
Strength, 4 August: 119,056
Losses: 10,607
Operations: Capture of Hill 70

September 1917   Canadian Corps
Losses: 2,196
Operations: Trench raids

1–11 October   Canadian Corps
Losses: 356
Operations: Trench raids

12 October to
15 November   Canadian Corps
Strength, 27 October: 130,685
Losses: 12,404
Operations: Capture of Passchendaele

October 1917   Canadian Corps
Strength, 27 October: 130,685
Losses: 7,052
Operations: Passchendaele

November 1917   Canadian Corps
Strength, 30 November: 88,632
Losses: 9,901
Operations: Passchendaele

December 1917   Canadian Corps
Strength, 29 December: 97,586
Losses: 665
Operations: Situation normal

January 1918   Canadian Corps
Strength, 31 January: 99,640
Losses: 680
Operations: Trench raids

February 1918   Canadian Corps
Strength, 24 February: 103,324
Losses: 737
Operations: Trench raids

March 1918   Canadian Corps
Strength, 23 March: 101,505
Losses: 2,075
Operations: Trench raids

April 1918   Canadian Corps
Excludes 2nd Division detached from Corps
Strength, 27 April: 122,876
Losses: 2,881
Operations: Lens front

May 1918   Canadian Corps
Excludes 2nd Division detached from Corps
Strength, 4 May: 104,901
Losses: 1,427
Operations: In army reserve from 7 May

June 1918   Canadian Corps
Excludes 2nd Division detached from Corps
Strength, 1 June: 82,343
Losses (2nd and 3rd Divisions): 1,043
Operations
   1st and 2nd Divisions in reserve
   2nd and 3rd Divisions with 3rd Army

July 1918   Canadian Corps
Excludes 3rd Division detached from Corps
Strength, 20 July: 91,970
Losses: 1,233
Operations: Trench raids

August 1918   Canadian Corps
Strength, 7 August: 102,372
Losses (8 to 22 August): 11,725
Sick: 2,006
Reinforcements: 12,652
Losses (August): 19,644
Operations: Battle of Amiens

26 August to
9 September   Canadian Corps
Strength, with attachments, 1 September: 148,090
Strength, Canadian Corps, 25 August: 101,599
Losses: 14,349
Sick: 1,228
Reinforcements: 12,768
Operations: Battle of Arras, Drocourt-Quéant
   Line

27 September to
12 October   Canadian Corps
Strength, including attachments, 23 September:
   118,194
Strength, Canadians, 25 September: 98,790
Losses: 14,849
Sick: 1,808
Reinforcements: 10,881
Operations: Bourlon and Cambrai

September 1918   Canadian Corps
                     Strength, 9 September: 115,504
                     Losses: 18,811
                     Operations: Bourlon Wood and Cambrai

12 October to
11 November   Canadian Corps
                     Strength including attachments, 14 October:
                        128,820
                     Strength of Canadian Corps, 1 October: 98,835
                     Losses: 4,912
                     Sick: 3,475
                     Reinforcements: 10,673
                     Operations: Douai and Mons

October 1918   Canadian Corps
                     Strength, 21 October: 118,151
                     Losses: 8,432
                     Operations: Douai and Mons

November 1918   Canadian Corps
                     Strength, 11 November: 105,868
                     Losses: 1,745
                     Operations: Douai and Mons

A Note on Sources

In studying the various elements that made up the Canadian Corps and supporting formations – infantry, artillery, communications, the air component, and engineers – one can refer to a large body of literature amassed since the end of the war. Official histories, regimental histories, monographs, collections of letters and reminiscences, and several theses have appeared, and they are important in setting the stage on which the details of this work are presented. For a more complete list covering the wide variety of books and printed sources on the subject, see O.A. Cooke, *The Canadian Military Experience 1867–1983: A Bibliography*, the section dealing with land forces in 1914–18, which contains over 700 entries; or C.H. Dornbusch, *The Canadian Army 1855–1965: Regimental Histories and a Guide to the Regiments.*

Two official histories of the Canadian Expeditionary Force were prepared in the years after the war. The first was Fortesque Duguid's *Official History of the Canadian Forces in the Great War, 1914–1919*, but its title is misleading; for only the first volume, ranging from August 1914 to September 1915, was ever prepared, since the project was interrupted by Canada's declaration of war in 1939. Published in 1938 the tome is a useful introduction to the early days of the Canadian Corps, including the training of the first contingent at Valcartier as well as in England. It recounts in some detail the second battle of Ypres, in which the Canadian Expeditionary Force was first bloodied. More important for the preparation of the present work is appendix 111, which gives an indepth discussion of the history of the Ross rifle, one of Canada's first and least successful attempts at producing the weapons its soldiers would use in battle.

The second official history of the Canadian Corps is G.W.L. Nicholson's *Canadian Expeditionary Force 1914–1919*, which was published in 1962. Making an effective use of primary and secondary sources, Colonel Nicholson put together a chronological history of the corps which concentrates on the battles it fought and the periods of organization and reorganization that punctuated its life. The author's battle descriptions strive for accuracy and concentrate on larger formations, such as brigades or divisions, though sometimes Nicholson follows the trials of smaller units, battalions, even companies and recounts the exploits of those individuals who won the Victoria Cross. Not only is this official history useful in putting events in order, but also it presents casualty statistics that help determine the success or failure of different tactical systems. Technology as such very rarely emerges in the narrative, though Nicholson, like Duguid, includes a section discussing the problems of the Ross rifle. He also has a two-page section dealing with tank and air support at Amiens.

Useful for comparison is C.W. Bean's official history of the Australian imperial forces, each volume of which has a separate title. The author was a journalist during the war and collected much in the way of interesting material. As a multi-volume history of a formation no larger than the Canadian Expeditionary Force it is very detailed. To help place Canadian operations into context one can turn to the British official history, also a multi-volume work, by several authors, of whom James E. Edmonds and Cyril Falls are of greater interest here, since between them they produced those volumes dealing with the Western Front.

Other works dealing with the activities of the Canadian Corps include Sir Max Aitken's *Canada in Flanders*, first printed in January 1916 in an attempt to publicize Canada's contribution to the war. As such it is somewhat propagandistic in nature. J. Castell Hopkins's *Canada at War: A Record of Heroism and Achievement 1914–1918*, published in 1919, is similar in tone but covers the entire war. A separate essay by Robert John Renison titled 'A Story of Five Cities,' describes the battles of the last offensives. Similar in tone is Colonel George G. Nasmith's *Canada's Sons and Great Britain in the World War*. Colonel Nasmith was a member of the Canadian Machine Gun Corps and participated in many of the corps's battles. J.F.B. Livesay, in *Canada's Hundred Days*, presents an enthusiastic account of Canadian participation in the last battles of the war. Far more critical is the *Report of the Ministry: Overseas Military Forces of Canada, 1918*, which discusses a wide variety of activities, including those of ancillary units such as the Canadian Railway Troops and the Canadian Forestry Corps. It is an excellent source for anyone interested in the administration and logistics of the Canadian Expeditionary Force in its final year. Sir Andrew McPhail's *The Medical Services* accompanies Duguid's official history, and, as its title implies, it is concerned with the administrative and operational aspects of Canada's medical services, which experienced advances as revolutionary as did the troops in the field.

Since the activities and technologies of ancillary units are important in determining the relationship between soldiers and the tools of war, the histories of the artillery, the corps of signals, and the engineers have helped shed some light on the evolution of these services. G.W.L. Nicholson's *The Gunners of Canada*, published in 1967, describes the development of Canadian artillery from earliest times. The chapters dealing with the First World War not only provide a narrative of the artillery's activities but also at times discuss questions of organization and technology that are crucial to the present work. John Moir's *History of the Royal Canadian Corps of Signals*, which became available in 1962, also provides several chapters dealing with the First World War. Though Professor Moir does not provide as much detail about the technology of communications as does Nicholson vis-à-vis the gunners, he provides some information about specific technologies and their success and also discusses the many changes in organization. *The History of the Corps of Royal Canadian Engineers* is similarly written. Prepared by A.J. Kerry and W.A. McDill, like all the corps histories listed here it presents a narrative of the events through which its subjects passed over a long period, and like *Gunners of Canada* and *Signals* it details changes in organization throughout the war. It also provides some important information on gas warfare not available in any of the other secondary sources. For information concerning Canada and the air war, one can turn to S.F. Wise, *Canadian Airmen and the First World War*, which discusses in great detail the relationship between air power, technology, and the land battle. Taken together, then, the above works help one follow the Canadian Expeditionary Force from battle to battle and from one reorganization to another.

Many of the battalions that participated in the war were perpetuated afterwards. The Royal Canadian Regiment existed before, and the Royal 22e Régiment and the Princess Patricia's Canadian Light Infantry still exist as part of Mobile Command. Other battalions replaced their numbers with regimental names and remained as part of the Militia. Almost all have regimental histories that describe their adventures from the day they were formed to the 1950s, 1960s, and even the present. C.E. Dornbusch, in *The Canadian Army 1855–1965*, provides a bibliography for Canadian units, but they are listed in alphabetical order by the regiment's current name, and it is difficult to find material on First World War battalions without knowing the units that perpetuated them, and not all were perpetuated. Some works deal exclusively with the histories of infantry battalions from 1914 to 1919, such as E.S. Russenholt's *Six Thousand Men*, a history of the 44th battalion, Joseph Chabelle's *Histoire du 22e Battalion canadien-français 1914–1919*, H.C. Singer's *The History of the 31st Canadian Infantry Battalion, C.E.F.*, H.R.N. Clyne's *Vancouver's 29th*, D.J. Corrigall's *History of the 20th Battalion*, L. McLeod Gould's *From BC to Baisieux; being the Narrative History of the 102nd Canadian Infantry Battalion*, Joseph Hayes's *The Eighty-Fifth*, D.G. Scott's history of the 28th, G. Chalmers Johnston's *The 2nd Canadian Mounted Rifles*, James L. Williams and R. James Steel's work on the 46th, *The Suicide Battalion*, Bernard McEvoy's book on the 72nd, W.W. Murray's history of the 2nd, H.M. Urquhart's work on the 16th, R.C. Fetherstonhaugh's *The Royal Montreal Regiment, 14th Battalion CEF, 1914–1925*, C. Beresford Topp's *The 42nd Battalion*, and F.B. MacDonald and John J. Gardiner's *The Twenty-Fifth Battalion*.

Others follow the history of their chosen unit for a hundred years or so and cannot devote much space to detail, especially since their regiments, excepting the RCR, PPCLI, the Royal 22nd Régiment, and some of the cavalry units, did not operate as such in the First World War. Their historians were thus more interested in the second of the great conflicts. Those devoting a chapter or so to the experiences of the First World War include Douglas Harker's *The Dukes*, Reginald Roy's *Sinews of Steel: The History of the British Columbia Dragoons*, Paul Hutchinson's *Canada's Black Watch 1862–1962*, Douglas How's *The 8th Hussars*, G.T. Service and J.K. Marteinson's *The Gate: A History of the Fort Garry Horse, Cent ans d'histoire d'un régiment canadien-français, les Fusilliers Mont-Royal 1869–1969*, G.R. Stevens's *A City Goes to War*, V.G. Quigley's *A Century of Rifles 1860–1960, the Halifax Rifles, A History of the First Hussars Regiment 1856–1980*, A.F. Duguid, *History of The Canadian Grenadier Guards 1760–1964*, Jacques Castonguay et Armand Ross's *Le Régiment de la Chaudière*, Jeffery Williams's *Princess Patricia's Canadian Light Infantry*, H.M. Jacksons's *The Princess Louise Dragoon Guards*, D.J. Goodspeed's *Battle Royal: A History of the Royal Canadian Regiment of Canada 1862–1962*, R.C. Fetherstonhaugh's *The Royal Canadian Regiment 1883–1933*, Brereton Greenhous's *Dragoon: The Centennial History of the Royal Canadian*

Dragoons, 1883–1983, Jean-Yves Gravel's *Histoire du Régiment de Trois-Rivières 1871–1978,* H.M. Jackson's *The Sherbrooke Regiment, Little Black Devils: A History of the Royal Winnipeg Rifles,* and *Histoire du Royal 22e Régiment.*

Many historians and enthusiasts have turned their attention to the Canadian Corps. John F. Meek in *Over the Top!* provides a pictorial and statistical history of the Canadians overseas. Herbert F. Wood's *Vimy!,* D.E. Macintyre's *Canada at Vimy,* D.J. Goodspeed's *The Road Past Vimy,* and Pierre Berton's *Vimy* all discuss the events leading up to what was perhaps the most important battle the Canadian Corps was to fight in the war, the capture of Vimy Ridge just after Easter in 1917. All provide reminiscences of some of the men who were there, and Macintyre's book is autobiographical. These reminiscences are useful in coming to grips with how technology was applied in practice rather than how doctrine determined it should be used. Daniel G. Dancocks has prepared three books in recent years dealing with the Canadian Corps. *Welcome to Flanders Fields, the First Canadian Battle of the Great War: Ypres, 1915, Legacy of Valour: The Canadians at Passchendaele,* and *Spearhead to Victory: Canada and the Great War,* are straightforward narratives of Canadian Corps operations at Second Ypres, Passchendaele, and the final offensives respectively. Desmond Morton and J.L. Granatstein, in *Marching to Armageddon,* discuss Canada's war experience as a whole – the trials, tribulations, and successes of the Canadian Expeditionary Force being one of their major themes. Stephen J. Harris's seminal *Canadian Brass: The Making of a Professional Army 1860–1939,* devotes a large section to the First World War and its impact on Canadian military professionalism, while Jean-Pierre Gagnon, in his important work, *Le 22e Battalion (canadien-français) 1914–1919: Etude socio-militaire,* is concerned with the background and experiences of all those involved with Canada's only Francophone unit to fight as such on the Western Front.

John Swettenham's *To Seize the Victory* follows the victories and vicissitudes of Sir Arthur Currie and his troops as they adjust to the new style of warfare. It gives some insight into the nature of innovation within the Canadian Corps and so helps to explain changes in tactics that took place under Byng and Currie. Swettenham's book is a combination of biography and military narrative. Many authors have chosen to concentrate on Currie himself. Hugh M. Urquhart's *Arthur Currie: The Biography of a Great Canadian,* is laudatory to say the least, but provides a reasonably accurate portrayal of the man who helped the

Canadian Corps innovate doctrine and make it successful. H.M.J. Hyatt's PH D dissertation, 'The Military Career of Sir Arthur Currie,' concentrates, as its title implies, on the war years of Currie's life, presenting an examination of the general's attempts, usually successful, to break the tactical deadlock on the Western Front. It was later published as a short book, *General Sir Arthur Currie: A Military Biography*. Daniel G. Dancocks, in *Sir Arthur Currie: A Biography* covers the general's entire life but devotes the bulk of his study to the period 1914–20. Other biographies include Ronald Haycock's *Sam Hughes: The Public Career of a Controversial Canadian, 1885–1916*, and John Swettenham's *McNaughton*, a three-volume study of the corps's most important innovator in the realm of artillery, especially in counter-battery work. The latter provides even more detail about artillery technology than does Nicholson in *The Gunners of Canada* and spends about half a volume discussing the First World War. E.L.M. Burns, in his autobiography *General Mud*, provides much that is useful concerning the world of communications, especially the application of new organizations and technology. *Ghosts Have Warm Hands*, Will R. Bird's autobiographical account of the war, contains much detail about life in and out of battle.

Many organizations have published collections of letters, reminiscences, and similar documents. *Thirty Canadian V.C.s* is a compendium of narratives describing why individuals were awarded the decoration, and it is interesting to note that many of these awards were given to men for destroying machine-gun nests. In the 1920s the *Canadian Defence Quarterly* presented many accounts of battles written by veterans. In 1920 the Canadian Imperial Bank of Commerce collected letters written to branch offices by employees who were serving overseas and published them as *Letters from the Front*. These, like the reminiscences in Wood, Macintyre, Goodspeed, and Berton, help separate theory from practice, since many of the writers described, sometimes in detail, what their jobs involved as machine-gunners, riflemen, bombers, communicators, or runners.

Some collections were compiled long after the war had ended, and relied on the memories of their subjects to provide insight into how the war was fought. The Canadian Broadcasting Corporation, in the early to mid-1960s, interviewed several hundred veterans. These interviews provide some insight into the minor changes private soldiers and their immediate superiors made to doctrine to suit the situation. Gordon Reid's *Poor Bloody Murder: Memoirs of the First World War*, was published in 1980, when most of his subjects were in their seventies and eighties. The bulk of their reminiscences deal with, to them, the more important issues of leave, food, and mud, but interspersed are accounts of small actions or large battles in which the subject gives a personal evaluation of the technology then present. William D. Mathieson's *My Grandfather's War* is similar – Canadian veterans recounting their experiences – and some excerpts were taken from Gordon Reid's work. A different and more sophisticated approach, can be seen in Reginald Roy's *The Journal of Private Fraser, 1914–1918*, in which the editor limited himself to correcting dates and names, in the process reproducing one of the great rarities of military narrative, the complete diary of a private soldier. Like other reminiscences it offers the opportunity to see what actually transpired when technology reached the hands of the soldiery. It also offers the advantage of following changes in the soldier's attitude over time.

One short thesis to come out of the University of New Brunswick, W.F. Stewart's 'Attack Doctrine in the Canadian Corps, 1916–1918,' is worthy of note here. The work is an in-depth study of the evolution of doctrine, including detailed discussion of the role of artillery in breaking the deadlock in some battles on the Western Front. Though the author does not deal with the situation below battalion level, he does an excellent job of describing the changes made at the top, which are of critical importance in understanding how the theory of warfare developed in the last three years of the war. Other recent university works that are important in following the evolution of the Canadian Corps are William Beahen, 'A Citizen's Army: The Growth and Development of the Canadian Militia, 1904 to 1914' (PH D thesis, University of Ottawa, 1979); M.V. Bezeau, 'The Role and Organization of Canadian Military Staffs 1904–1945' (MA thesis, RMC, 1978); Kenneth Eyre, 'Staff and Command in the Canadian Corps: The Canadian Militia 1896–1914 as a Source of Senior Officers' (MA, Duke University, 1967); Stephen Harris, 'Canadian Brass: The Growth of the Canadian Military Profession, 1860–1919,' (PH D thesis, Duke University, 1979) (later published as a book); Ronald Haycock, 'Sir Sam Hughes: His Public Career, 1892–1916' (PH D thesis, University of Western Ontario, 1976); and A.M.J. Hyatt, 'The Military Career of Sir Arthur Currie' (PH D thesis, Duke University, 1964).

Some works deal in depth with the relationship between technology and war but not with the Canadian Corps. John Keegan's *The Face of Battle* devotes one of its five chapters to the first day of the Battle of the Somme, 1 July 1916, a campaign in which Canadian troops would be involved later. Some sections deal exclusively with the use – or misuse – of artillery, the battles of infantry against machine-guns and those of infantry versus infantry. These are very detailed and allow much insight into the nature of First World War combat on a small scale. W.H. McNeill, in the *Pursuit of Power*, paints with a much wider brush. He concentrates on the bureaucratization of warfare that became necessary when technology became more and more complex, and he allocates much of his last chapter to the First World War. Kenneth Macksey, in *Technology and War: The Impact of Science on Weapon Development and Modern Battle*, begins his discussion in 1763 and covers the subject in short, well-illustrated sections. Richard A. Preston and Sydney F. Wise, in *Men in Arms: A History of Warfare and its Interrelationship with Western Society,* Theodore Kopp, in *War in the Modern World*, and Robert L. O'Connell, in *Of Arms and Men: A History of War, Weapons, and Aggression*, cover thousands of years of military history, touching on the technology and tactics that dominated warfare at different times. Ronald Haycock and Keith Neilson, in *Men, Machines, and War,* have collected essays dealing with the subject at issue here, among them 'Men, Machines, and War,' by William H. McNeil, 'Technology and Tactics in the British Army 1866–1900,' by Howard Bailes, and 'Observations on the Dialectics of British Tactics,' by Dominick Graham, among others.

John Ellis, in *The Social History of the Machine Gun*, discusses its development and use from the Gatling gun to the weapons of the First World War. It is his contention that the weapon dominated the battlefield in that war until the tank, a countervailing technology, was invented to end that dominance and create a new one. That may not have been the case, since the Canadian Corps found ways to cross no man's land in the face of machine-gun fire without using armoured vehicles, and German tactics in March 1918 did not rely on tanks. E.E. Morison's *Men, Machines and Modern Times* includes four essays on how armed forces in the mid- to late nineteenth century reacted to technological change and posits that with the bureaucratization of war and the inculcation of military or naval tradition technological change can take place only with some difficulty, because the decision-makers of the army or navy are less interested in increasing efficiency or destructive power than they are in preserving a way of life. Morison's views apply well to the First World War, where French, British and Russian officers proved reluctant to make drastic revisions either to their doctrine or to their arsenals.

Other works that do not study technology and war or technology and warriors are none the less useful in their approach to general questions surrounding the relationship between people and their machines. A.P. Usher's *A History of Mechanical Inventions* concentrates on the machine itself from Greece to the interwar period and discusses the nature of the process of mechanical invention, which he sees as arising out of economic necessity. In studying clocks, the inventions of Da Vinci, printing, textiles, and machine tools, the author postulates that new machines arise out of necessity and of necessity change the way people live. The first part of this proposition applies well to the Western Front. The tank, though not a necessary countervailing machine to automatic weapons, needed the latter as an impetus for its invention. The same could be said of other developments and redevelopments of trench warfare, such as the bomb, rifle-grenade, and mine. The contention that machines necessarily change the way people live is well supported. They do not, however, change the way they fight. Doctrine is developed by those who have no hand in the fighting, which allows them to ignore the opportunities offered by new technologies.

Sources for such a project as this abound, most notably at the National Archives of Canada. The main bulk of information for this project can be found in Record Group 9, documents pertaining to the Canadian Militia and including the First World War. The aim of this work is to study war at the lowest level possible, and the war diaries, prepared by individual battalions, are complete from the time they arrived in France between 1915 and 1916 to the occupation of Germany in 1919. They offer the opportunity to examine daily events, including training while the unit was in reserve, and artillery duels, patrols, and similar activities when the troops were in the trenches. The diaries are far less useful, however, in studying the course of different battles. Prepared in haste, they offer only an outline of events and do not provide much detail. It must be remembered that they were rarely updated, only corrected, so the diarist could not add information to an account gathered after the fact.

Of far greater utility in describing the activities of soldiers in combat are the after-action reports and narratives prepared by battalion headquarters, often by companies. Using field messages, oral reports, testimony from other units and similar sources of information, these documents pieced together the events of each day. Some go so far as to give a minute-by-minute account of parts of the battle. They also included appendices describing lessons learned and evaluations of different pieces of equipment. Anything from a raid carried out by a dozen men to the battle of Vimy Ridge was treated in this manner, supplying the historian with a rich source for studying the application of doctrine, or lack of it, in actual combat. These after-action reports form the bulk of information used in the present work.

The files in Record Group 9 also include documents discussing the technical qualities, usefulness, and difficulties surrounding different pieces of equipment. These include multitudinous files on the Ross rifle, incorporating questionnaires sent to battalion commanders to solicit their opinion of the controversial weapon. Bombs, trench mortars, rifle-grenades, signalling equipment, and other tools of trench warfare receive similar treatment. Though the great majority of these files deal with problems that do not figure in this work, such as how best to load trench mortars on ships and trains, there is much that is useful, most especially technical information giving some indication of the instrument's performance in battle. Also of some use are the periodic revisions of doctrine sent to the Canadian Corps from the British Army. In comparing these documents with after-action reports and war diaries, it is possible to note the difference between established thinking at the War Office or in the headquarters of the commander-in-chief and the manner in which front-line troops actually carried out their job. The contrasts are sometimes striking.

Other document collections proved useful. Record Group 24, containing files pertaining to the Department of National Defence, provides information similar to that available in RG 9. Though there are far fewer reports in RG 24, they serve as a a useful adjunct. Many of the files found in the records of the Department of National Defence are copies of those in the records of the Militia, which decreases the number of useful documents considerably. For example, no less than eighteen files titled 'Minor Operations' contain identical copies of the same report. The collections in RG 24, therefore, though they cannot be dispensed with, are far less useful than those of RG 9.

The Manuscript Division of the National Archives of Canada also has much to offer for a project of this nature. Individual narratives, reminiscences, and accounts are an important part of the present work, and many can be found in the personal papers of Canadians deposited in Manuscript Group 30. The collection provides not only the diaries and other papers of Sir Arthur Currie, H.D.G. Crerar, A.G.L. Mc-Naughton, Victor Odlum, and other high-ranking officers of the Canadian Corps, but also correspondence and journals deposited at the archives by veterans, their relatives, or friends. Diaries, if legible, can provide some insight into how weapons were or were not used. Some officers retained reports and other official documents that can also prove useful for a project of this nature. The main disadvantage of using these collections is the necessity of examining large bodies of material to retrieve just a few pieces of information.

Other individual accounts are available in Record Group 41, the records of the Canadian Broadcasting Corporation. They consist of interviews the CBC carried out with veterans in the early to mid-1960s for a radio series titled *Flanders Fields*. Though the questioners do not seem to have been interested in the tools of war, except perhaps for poison gas, it is interesting to note how old soldiers volunteered information about their jobs as machine-gunners or artillerymen while answering questions on other topics. As with the personal papers in MG 30, however, it is necessary to pore over hundreds of pages of transcript before one can find anything of value for a project in the history of technology.

The Directorate of History at National Defence Headquarters has in its collection training pamphlets that help to determine how doctrine was inculcated in the common soldier. Though the information provided is scanty, the documents are short and give good synopses of established thinking on subjects such as the infantry in the attack or the role of artillery. Though there is no way to determine with any certainty that the training laid down in the official publications was actually carried out, they are the best source available of the methods by which policy-makers hoped to implement their ideas.

The present work, then, has relied on official published accounts, nationalist writings, military documents, personal papers, war diaries, biographies, and studies of the nature of combat and technology in an attempt to discern the relationship between the soldiers of the Canadian Corps and the tools of war. There is nothing new or revolutionary in this approach, but then there is nothing new in studying battle, a topic that has interested historians since Herodotus and poets since the creator of the epic of Gilgamesh.

Notes

INTRODUCTION

1 Erich Maria Remarque, *All Quiet on the Western Front* (Greenwich 1958), 83
2 John Ellis, *Eye-Deep in Hell* (London 1976), 82
3 Georges Blond, *Verdun* (Paris 1963), 47
4 Siegfried Sassoon, *Memoirs of an Infantry Officer* (London 1930), 167
5 Edmund Blunden, *Undertones of War* (London 1928), 73
6 Sassoon, *Memoirs*, 147
7 W. Baring Pemberton, *Battles of the Boer War* (London 1964), 199
8 H.M. Tomlinson, *All Our Yesterdays* (Toronto 1930), 278
9 Tony Ashworth, *Trench Warfare 1914–1918; The Live and Let Live System* (London 1980), 14
10 Directorate of History (DHist), 78/289, *Infantry Training (4-Company Organization) – 1914*, 1914
11 DHist, FN 63, *Platoon Training –1918*
12 George Coppard, *With a Machine Gun to Cambrai: The Tale of a Young Tommy in Kitchener's Army, 1914–1918* (London 1969), 107

CHAPTER 1 The Learning Process Begins

1 Stephen Harris, *Canadian Brass* (Toronto 1988), 22–3
2 Desmond Morton, *The Canadian General: Sir William Otter* (Toronto 1974), 171
3 Canada, Department of Militia and Defence, *Supplementary Report:*

Organization, Equipment, Despatch and Service of the Canadian Contingents during the War in South Africa 1899–1900 (Ottawa 1901), 12

4 Ibid.
5 Morton, *Canadian General*, 203
6 Department of Militia and Defence, *Supplementary Report*, 12
7 Shelford Bidwell and Dominick Graham, *Fire-Power: British Army Weapons and Theories of War, 1904–1945* (Winchester 1985), 2, 22; Michael Howard, 'Men against Fire: Expectations of War in 1914,' *Internatinal Security* 9 (Summer 1984), 46
8 Thomas Packenham, *The Boer War* (London 1979), 361–2
9 Ian V. Hogg. *The Guns 1914–18* (New York 1971), 12
10 Frederick Myatt, *The Soldier's Trade: British Military Developments 1660–1914* (London 1974), 57–9; G.W.L. Nicholson, *The Gunners of Canada* (Toronto 1972), 2: 55
11 Bidwell and Graham *Fire-Power*, 2; T.H.E. Travers, 'The Offensive and the Problem of Innovation in British Military Thought, 1870–1915,' *Journal of Canadian History* (July 1978), 531, 546
12 DHist, 83/538, *Infantry Training*, 1905, 123
13 DHist, 71/149, 'The Ross Rifle,' 2
14 Ibid.
15 National Archives of Canada (NAC), RG 24, v.5942, HQC 516-3, 'Proceedings of adjourned meeting of the Committee to inquire into, and report upon the merits of a Rifle invented and submitted by Sir Charles Ross, held at Quebec on 15th, 16th, 17th, and 19th August, 1901'
16 Ibid.
17 Ibid.
18 NAC, RG 41, v.7, 4th Battalion, Lieutenant-Colonel N.M. Young
19 Harris, *Canadian Brass*, 6, 37, 79, 82, 88–9
20 DHist, 77/140, *Field Artillery Training*, 1902, 17
21 Ibid., ii
22 Ibid., 10–12
23 Ibid., 12
24 Ibid., 13
25 Nicholson, *Gunners of Canada*, 1: 190
26 Sir Ian Hamilton, *Report on the Military Institutions of Canada* (Ottawa 1913)
27 T.H.E. Travers, 'Learning and Decision-Making on the Western Front 1915–1916: The British Example,' *Canadian Journal of History* (April 1983), 96; T.H.E. Travers, 'Technology, Tactics, and Morale: Jean de Bloch, the Boer War, and British Military Theory, 1900–1914,' *Journal of*

Modern History (June 1979), 264; Bidwell and Graham, *Fire-Power*, 29; T.H.E. Travers, *The Killing Ground* (London 1987), 43

28 R.F.H. Nalder, *The Royal Corps of Signals: A History of Its Antecedents and Development (circa 1800–1953)* (London 1958), 51, 53

29 Travers, *Killing Ground*, 42, 54, 70, 71; Bidwell and Graham, *Fire Power*, 26, 27

30 Dominick Graham, 'Sans Doctrine: British Army Tactics in the First World War,' T.H.E. Travers and Christon Archer, *Men at War: Politics, Technology, and Innovation in the Twentieth Century* (Chicago 1982), 75–6

31 James E. Edmonds *Military Operations, France and Belgium, 1914* (London 1933), 6–7, 9, 13

32 Henry Borden, ed., *Robert Laird Borden: His Memoirs* (Toronto 1938), 1: 457–8

33 (NAC), RG 9, v.4143, folder 8, file 1, 'Lecture Given at N.C.O.'s School of Instruction, 2nd Army.'

34 *Canadian Annual Review* (1914), 20

35 NAC, RG 41, v.7, 4th Battalion, Interview with Vick Lewis

36 John Swettenham, *To Seize the Victory: The Canadian Corps in World War I* (Toronto 1965), 38; Archer Fortescue Duguid, *Official History of the Canadian Forces in the Great War, 1914–1919* (Ottawa 1938), 89

37 Swettenham, *Seize the Victory*, 38

38 DHist, 71/149, 'Ross Rifle,' 24

39 DHist, 78/289, *Infantry Training*, 1914, 224–30

40 Swettenham, *Seize the Victory*, 38

41 G.W.L. Nicholson, *Canadian Expeditionary Force* (Ottawa 1962), 26; Duguid, *Official History*, 79

42 DHist, 78/289, *Infantry Training*, 1914, 134

43 Duguid, *Official History*, 81; Bidwell and Graham, *Fire-Power*, 22

44 NAC, MG 30, E157, Crerar Papers, v.15, 'Personal Diary,' 9

45 NAC, RG 24, v.1832, GAQ 8–15d, 'Historical Record of the 1st Brigade, C.F.A.'

46 Nicholson, *Gunners of Canada*, 1: 198–9

47 John Swettenham, *McNaughton* (Toronto 1968), 1:35

48 NAC, MG 30, E237, Pte Alex Sinclair Papers

49 NAC, RG 41, v7, 2nd Battalion, Interview with Lieutenant-Colonel George Patrick

50 Nicholson, *Gunners of Canada*, 1: 237–8

51 Nicholson, *Canadian Expeditionary Force*, 27, 38; Harry Howland, a member of the 7th Battalion, exchanged his Oliver equipment for web

equipment some time in 1914, quite possibly while still at Esquimault, NAC, MG 30, E204, Harry Howland, 'March With Me,' (1972), 18–19; William Aldldritt reported that, on 20 January 1915, while his unit, the 8th Battalion, was in England, orders were posted informing officers that they would wear web equipment as well as the men. On a 'web equipment parade' on 28 January he 'Found the web equipment very easy to carry,' MG 30, E1, William Alldritt Papers, 3–4

52 Duguid, *Official History*, 130–1; Nicholson, *Canadian Expeditionary Force*, 37

53 NAC, RG 9, War Diary, v.4912, 1st Battalion, November 1914

54 Duguid, *Official History*, 130; NAC, RG 9, War Diary, v.4912, 1st Battalion, February 1915

55 NAC, RG 9, War Diary, v.4912, 1st Battalion, December 1914

56 NAC, RG 9, v.4049, folder 14, file 1, '2nd CIB to HQ Canadian Contingent, 14 January 1915;' 'Programme of Training (Machine Gun Section) of 8th Canadian Infantry Battalion (90th Rifles) 2nd Infantry Brigade (Western Canada) for week ending January 9th 1915, January 16th 1915, January 30th, 1915'; RG 41, v.17, 5th Canadian Mounted Rifles Battalion, Interview with Joe Cusack

57 NAC, RG 24, v.1832, GAQ 8–15d, 'Historical Record of the 1st Brigade, C.F.A.'; Nicholson, *Gunners of Canada*, 1: 195, 202, 209

58 Nicholson, *Gunners of Canada*, 1: 204; Swettenham, *McNaughton*, 1: 37, Nicholson, *Canadian Expeditionary Force*, 37

59 Swettenham, *McNaughton*, 1: 49: Herbert F. Wood, *Vimy!* (Toronto 1967), 23–4

60 Henri Castex, *Verdun, années infernales: La vie du soldat au front d'août 1915 à septembre 1916* (Paris 1980), 103–4

61 Harris, *Canadian Brass*, 113–14

62 Bidwell and Graham, *Fire-Power*, 72

63 NAC, RG 9, War Diary, v.4912, 1st Battalion, January 1915; April 1915; v.4916, 5th Battalion, December 1914

64 NAC, RG 9, v.4033, folder 3, file 1, 'An Example of Instructions Issued Regarding Local Attacks When the Opposing Forces Are at Close Quarters,' 2; RG 41, v.12, 29th Battalion, Interview with Lieutenant-Colonel W.S. Latta

65 NAC, MG 30, E157, Crerar Papers, v.15, 'Personal Diary,' 32; RG 9, v.4033, folder 5, file 10, 'Example of Instructions Issued Regarding Local Attacks,' 1

66 Swettenham, *McNaughton*, 1: 50

67 Bidwell and Graham, *Fire-Power*, 96–7
68 Denis Winter, *Death's Men* (London 1978), 81
69 D.E. Macintyre, *Canada at Vimy* (Toronto 1967), 58
70 NAC, MG 30, E113, George Bell, 'Back to Blighty,' as told to Lee Fuller, preface
71 John Terraine, *The Smoke and the Fire: Myths and Anti-myths of War* (London 1980), 56
72 Tom Wintringham, *The Story of Weapons and Tactics from Troy to Stalingrad* (Freeport 1978), 172
73 Ellis, *Eye-Deep in Hell*, 77
74 NAC, RG 9, War Diary, v.4912, 1st Battalion, 18 February 1915; v.4916, 5th Battalion, 6 April 1915; v.4912, 1st Battalion, 30 March 1915; RG 41, v.7, 4th Battalion, Interview with Vick Lewis
75 Winter, *Death's Men* 81, 107, 90
76 Ibid., 87
77 NAC, RG 9, War Diary, v.4912, 1st Battalion, 9–13 March 1915
78 Charles Lyons Foster and William S. Duthie, eds, *Letters from the Front: Being a Record of the Role Played by Officers of the Bank in the Great War, 1914–1919* (n.p. 1920), 95–6
79 NAC, MG 30, E157, Crerar Papers, v.15, 'Personal Diary' 65
80 Ibid., 55, 78
81 Ibid., 61
82 Ibid., 63, 80, 83–4; S.F. Wise, *Canadian Airmen and the First World War* (Toronto 1980), 343–4
83 Nicholson, *Canadian Expeditionary Force*, 51
84 Nicholson, *Gunners of Canada*, 1: 213–14; Ian V. Hogg, *Barrage: The Guns in Action* (New York 1970), 13; Gerard J. De Groot, *Douglas Haig, 1861–1928* (London 1988), 188
85 NAC, MG 30, E113, George Bell, 'Back to Blighty,' as told to Lee Fuller, 15–16
86 DHist, Biog File, L'Abbé, Michael Howard
87 NAC, RG 41, v.9, 16th Battalion, Interview with H.H. Oddaker
88 NAC, RG 9, War Diary, v.4916, 5th Battalion, 22 April 1915
89 J.E. Edmonds and G.C. Wynne, *Military Operations, France and Belgium, 1915* (London 1927), 1: 188
90 NAC, RG 9, War Diary v.4919, 10th Battalion, 22 April 1915
91 NAC, RG 24, v.1822, GAQ 5-29, 'J.A. Currie to 3 Brigade, 6 May 1915'
92 NAC, RG 9, War Diary, v.4919, 10th Battalion, 22 April 1915
93 Ibid.

94 NAC, RG 9, War Diary, v.4925, 16th Battalion, 22 April 1915
95 John Moir, ed., *History of the Royal Canadian Corps of Signals, 1903–1961* (Ottawa 1962), 12
96 NAC, RG 9, War Diary, v.4919, 10th Battalion, 22 April 1915
97 Ibid., 23 April 1915
98 Nicholson, *Canadian Expeditionary Force,* 66
99 NAC, RG 9, War Diary, v.4919, 10th Battalion, 23 April 1915
100 Ibid.
101 NAC, RG 9, III, War Diary, v.4912, 1st Battalion, Appendix A, 'Narrative of Operations 23rd to 30th April 1915'; v.4915, 4th Battalion, 23 April 1915
102 Gordon Reid, ed., *Poor Bloody Murder: Personal Memoirs of the First World War* (Oakville 1980), 81–2
103 Swettenham, *McNaughton,* 1: 43, 45
104 NAC, MG 30, E157, Crerar Papers, v.15, 'Personal Diary,' 6 May 1915; Nicholson, *Gunners of Canada,* 1:223
105 Moir, *History,* 12
106 NAC, RG 9, III, War Diary, v.4917, 7th Battalion, 24 April 1915
107 NAC, RG 9, III, War Diary v.4916, 5th Battalion, 25 April 1915
108 Moir, *Signals,* 9–10
109 NAC, RG 24, v.1874, 22(5)
110 NAC, MG 30, E300, Victor Odlum Papers, v.16, 'Report of Narrative of Events: Ypres April 22nd/26th 1915, No. 1 Company, 7th Battalion,' 6
111 Ibid.; RG 9, War Diary, v.4924, 15th Battalion, 24 April 1915
112 NAC, RG 9, War Diary, v.4916, 5th Battalion, 24 April 1915
113 R.C. Fetherstonhaugh, *The 13th Battalion Royal Highlanders of Canada, 1914–1919* (Toronto 1925), 41–54; Urquhart, *The History of the 16th Battalion (The Canadian Scottish) Canadian Expeditionary Force, in the Great War, 1914–1919* (Toronto 1932), 53–72
114 W.W. Murray, *The History of the 2nd Canadian Battalion (East. Ontario Regiment) Canadian Expeditionary Force, in the Great War, 1914–1919* (Ottawa 1947), 53–4
115 DHist, 71/149, 'Ross Rifle,' 29
116 Desmond Morton, *A Peculiar Kind of Politics: Canada's Overseas Ministry in the First World War* (Toronto 1982), 41
117 DHist, 71/149, 'Ross Rifle,' 29
118 NAC, RG 24, v.1866, file 9
119 Ibid.

CHAPTER 2 The Road to the Somme

1 NAC, RG 9, V.4049, folder 14, file 1, 'Headquarters, 2 C.I.B. to 1st Can Div HQ, May 7th 1915 – Report on Machine Guns,' 1

2 Ibid., 'Suggested Equipment for Machine Gun – "Colt" as used by Canadian Division. Establishment for One Battalion'; DHist, FN 45, *Guide for the .303" Vickers Machine Gun*; FN 06 *Handbook of the Lewis Automatic Machine Gun Model 1914*

3 NAC, RG 9, V.4049, folder 14 file 4, 'Headquarters, 2 C.I.B. to 1st Can Div HQ, May 7th 1915. Report on Machine Guns,' 1

4 *The Register of the Victoria Cross* (Cheltenham 1988), 28

5 NAC, RG 9, V.4049, folder 14 file 4, 'Headquarters, 2 C.I.B. to 1st Can Div HQ, May 7th 1915. Report on Machine Guns,' 2

6 NAC, RG 9, V.4049, folder 14, file 1, 'B.M. 56, HQ 2 C.I.B. to 1 Can Div, May 1915 – Replacement of Colt Automatic Machine Gun by the Maxim,' 1

7 Ibid.

8 NAC, RG 41, V.20, M.G. Corps, John Lundie, 4th Machine Gun Battalion

9 NAC, RG 24, V.2538, HQC-1843, V.1

10 Ibid.

11 NAC, RG 24, V.5942, HQC 516-1-25, 'Minister of Defence to Department of Militia, 1 July 1915'; 'Director of Musketry to Chief Inspector of Arms and Ammunition, 5 July 1915'; Colonel Grevilly Harston to Lt-Col R.A. Helmer, 7 July 1915'; 'Minutes of Meeting of the Standing Small Arms Committee, 8 July 1915'; 'R.A. Helmer and Charles Winter to Minister, 8 July 1915'; 'Chief Inspector of Arms and Ammunition to Major-General of Ordnance, 9 August 1915

12 NAC, RG 9, V.4011, folder 15, file 8, '5th Canadian Battalion – Narrative of Operations'

13 NAC, RG 9, V.4011, folder 15, file 8, 'Orders to 2nd Canadian Infantry Brigade,' 1

14 Ibid.

15 Ian V. Hogg, *Grenades and Mortars* (New York 1974), 70–5

16 NAC, RG 41, V.20, 2nd Division Mortar Battalion, Lieutenant Bud O'Neil

17 NAC, RG 9, V.4011, folder 15, file 8, '5th Canadian Battalion – Narrative of Operations'

18 NAC, RG 9, V.4011, folder 15, file 8, 'Orders to 2nd Canadian Infantry Brigade,' 1

19 G.W.L. Nicholson, *The Gunners of Canada* (Toronto 1972), 1: 209; Shelford Bidwell and Dominick Graham, *Fire-Power: British Army Weapons and Theories of War, 1904–1945* (Winchester 1985), 97

20 NAC, RG 9, V.4011, folder 15, file 8, 'Report on Action – May 20th 1915; Locality of Orchard M.9,' 1

21 Ibid.

22 NAC, RG 9, V.4011, folder 15, file 8, 'Diary of Operations, 3rd Canadian Infantry Brigade from May 17 to May 31, 1915,' 1

23 NAC, RG 9, V.4011, folder 15, file 8, '14 Battalion Report of Operations, May 18th–20th, 1915,' 1

24 NAC, RG 9, V.4011, folder 15, file 8, 'Diary of Operations, 3rd Canadian Infantry Brigade from May 17 to May 31, 1915,' 2

25 NAC, RG 41, V.7, 1st Battalion, Interview with M.C. McGowan, 1; RG 9, V.4011, folder 15, file 8, 'Diary of Operations, 3rd Canadian Infantry Brigade from May 17 to May 31, 1915,' 2; RG 9, War Diary, V.4916, 5th Battalion, May 1915, Appendix A, 1

26 NAC, RG 41, V.7, 1st Battalion, Interview with M.C. McGowan

27 Charles Lyons Foster and William S. Duthie, eds., *Letters from the Front: Being a Record of the Role Played by Officers of the Bank in the Great War, 1914–1919* (n.p. 1920), 105

28 NAC, RG 9, V.4011, folder 15, file 8, 'Diary of Operations, 3rd Canadian Infantry Brigade from May 17 to May 31, 1915,' 2; '5th Canadian Battalion – Narrative of Operations,' 2; War Diary, V.4916, 5th Battalion, May 1915, Appendix A, 2

29 M.V. Bezeau, 'The Role and Organization of Canadian Military Staffs 1904–1945,' MA thesis, Royal Military College, Kingston, 1978, 48–49

30 NAC, RG 24, 1886, AHS 82, Commands and Staff, Canadian Corps

31 NAC, RG 24, V.1885, AHS 71, 1 Division Commands and Staffs

32 NAC, RG 9, V.5073, 'Artillery, Festubert May–June 1915'; italics in original.

33 Ibid.

34 NAC, RG 9, V.5069, 2nd Corps, OTS 1-5-15 to 31-8-15, 2nd Corps to 5th, 28th, and 46th Divisions, 17/6/15

35 Ibid.

36 NAC, RG 30, E236, Paul Villiers Papers, Diary, June 1915

37 Tony Ashworth, *Trench Warfare 1914–1918: The Live and Let Live System* (London 1980), 27, 36, 72–3; John Ellis, *Eye-Deep in Hell* (London 1976), 76

38 Siegfried Sassoon, *Memoirs of an Infantry Officer* (London 1930), 27

39 Edmond Blunden, *Undertones of War* (London 1928), 73

40 NAC, RG 9, V.4106, folder 23, file 2, 'Summary of Small Offensive Opera-

tion Carried Out by the 5th and 7th Canadian Battalions, November 16th–17th 1915,' 1

41 Ibid., 2

42 Ibid., 2–3

43 Ibid., 4

44 Ian D. Skennerton, *The British Service Lee: The Lee-Metford and Lee-Enfield Rifles and Carbines, 1880–1980* (London 1982), 259–60

45 NAC, RG 9, v.4106, folder 23, file 2, 'Summary of Small Offensive Operation Carried Out by the 5th and 7th Canadian Battalions, November 16th–17th 1915,' 4

46 Ibid., 7

47 Ibid., 5–6

48 Ibid., 7

49 NAC, RG 9, War Diary, v.4912, 1st Battalion, 4 April 1916; 26 April 1916

50 NAC, RG 9, War Diary, v.4936, 31st Battalion, No. 4

51 NAC, RG 9, War Diary, v.4931, 24th Battalion; RG 9, v.4076, folder 5, file 1, 'Headquarters 3 C.I.B. to 1 Canadian Division'; v.4936, 31st Battalion, 15 October 1915

52 NAC, RG 9, War Diary, v.4916, 5th Battalion, 9 July 1915

53 NAC, RG 9, War Diary, v.4916, 5th Battalion, 18 March 1916

54 NAC, RG 9, War Diary, v.4938, 42nd Battalion, 11 January 1916

55 NAC, RG 9, v.4160, folder 1, file 12, 'Canadian Corps to 1 Canadian Division, 12 February 1916'

56 Hogg, *Grenades and Mortars*, 81–2

57 NAC, RG 9, v.4202, folder 14, file 2, 'Report on Trench Mortars during Operations around March 2nd 1916'

58 NAC, RG 9, War Diary, v.4916, 5th Battalion, 29 October 1915

59 NAC, RG 9, War Diary, v.4931, 24th Battalion, 18 November 1915

60 NAC, RG 9, War Diary, v.4912, 1st Battalion, 19 December 1915

61 NAC, MG 30, E438, F. Lacey Papers, 18 August 1916

62 NAC, RG 9, War Diary, v.4938, 31st Battalion, 11 January 1916

63 NAC, RG 9, v.4158, folder 1, file 3, '1st Canadian Division Artillery Memo 203, 10 January 1916,' 1–2

64 NAC, RG 9, v.4201, folder 11, file 11, 'Second Army, G.568, 29 March 1916'; v.4141, folder 4, file 9, 'First Army No. 568 (G) – First Army Instructions for S.O.S. Signals, 8 February 1916,' 1–2; v.4140, folder 1, file 3, 'Second Army G.12 – Responsibility as between Infantry and Artillery Commanders, 9 March 1916'; v.4140, folder 1, file 3, 'Canadian Corps G 457/1 to 2 Division, 10 March 1916'; Guy Hartcup, *The War of Invention: Scientific Developments 1914–1918* (London 1988), 79

65 NAC, MG 30, E155, Roger F. Clark Papers, v.1, Diary, 24 June 1916

66 NAC, MG 30, E113, George Bell, 'Back to Blighty,' as told to Lee Fuller, 77; Hartcup, *War of Invention*, 79–80

67 G.W.L. Nicholson, *Canadian Expeditionary Force* (Ottawa 1962), 137; NAC, RG 9, War Diary, v.4931, 24th Battalion, 6 December 1915; v.4912, 1st Battalion, 7 December 1915; D.J. Goodspeed, *The Road Past Vimy: The Canadian Corps, 1914–1918* (Toronto 1969), 60; D.E. Macintyre, *Canada at Vimy* (Toronto 1967), 34

68 Donald Fraser witnessed a bomb run in February 1916. Reginald Roy, *The Journal of Private Fraser 1914–1918, Canadian Expeditionary Force* (Victoria 1985), 96

69 NAC, RG 9, v.4099, folder 1, file 3, 'O.B./147 Instructions for Firing at Aeroplanes with Rifles and Machine Guns'; S.F. Wise, *Canadian Airmen and the First World War* (Toronto 1980), 321

70 Stephen Harris, *Canadian Brass* (Toronto 1988), 107

71 Roy, *Journal of Private Fraser*, 23

72 Harris, *Canadian Brass*, 109–13

73 NAC, RG 41, v.9, 13th Battalion, Interview with Lieutenant-Colonel T.S. Morrissey, 3–4; v.13, 44th Battalion, Interview with Mr W.G. Marshall; A.J.L. Kerry and W.A. McDill, *The History of the Corps of Royal Canadian Engineers: Volume I, 1749–1939* (Ottawa 1962), 97

74 NAC, RG 9, War Diary, v.4916, 5th Battalion, 8–10 May 1915; v.4936, 31st Battalion, 24–25 September 1915; v.4938, 31st Battalion, 29 December 1915

75 NAC, RG 9, v.4201, folder 12, file 1, 'Syllabus of Instruction in Musketry Subjects: 2 December 1915'

76 NAC, RG 9, v.4057, folder 35, file 3, '1st Canadian Division to 2 C.I.B. 12 January 1916'; '1st Canadian Division to 2 Bn C.M.R. 25 November 1915'

77 NAC, RG 9, War Diary, v.4912, 1st Battalion, 17 October 1915; v.4916, 5th Battalion, 11–14 June 1915; v.4931, 24th Battalion, 7 October 1915; v.4936, 31st Battalion, 2 November 1915; RG 9, v.4158, folder 1, file 2, 'Instructions Regarding the Formation of the Brigade Grenade Schools of the Canadian Corps Troops,' 1–2; Hogg, *Grenades and Mortars*, 18–19; RG 9, v.4160, folder 1, file 12, '8 C.I.B. to all Battalions, 27 February 1916; RG 41, v.17, 116th Battalion, Interview with General Pearkes,' 2

78 NAC, RG 9, War Diary, v.4916, 5th Battalion, 10–14 June 1915; RG 9, v.4049, folder 14, file 2, 'HQ 2 C.I.B. to O.C. 5, 7, 8 Battalions, 25 October 1915'; v.4049, folder 14, file 3, '1st Can Div to 1, 2, 3 Brigades, 10 January 1916'; George Coppard, *With a Machine Gun to Cambrai: The Tale of a Young Tommy in Kitchener's Army, 1914–1918* (London 1969), 66

79 NAC, RG 9, v.4049, folder 14, file 1, '2nd Army G941 to G.H.Q. – Machine Guns, 1 August 1915'; file 2, 'HQ 2 C.I.B. to HQ 1 Can Div, 19 November

1915'; HQ 2 C.I.B. to HQ 1 Can Div, 6 November 1915'; RG 41, V.17, 5th CMR, Interview with Mr Joe Cusack, 7; RG 9, V.4049, folder 14, file 3, 'O.B./1362. Issue of Additional Lewis Guns to Battalions – Organization of Lewis Machine Gun Sections, 20 February 1916'

80 James E. Edmonds, *Military Operations, France and Belgium, 1916* (London 1932), 177–8

81 NAC, RG 9, V.4694, folder 56, file 7, 'Report of Major Daly's Gallant Stand'; folder 55, file 5, 'Bombing Section to O.C. 28th Battalion, 10 April 1916'; 'Report from Captain Styles to O.C. 28th Battalion, 10th April 1916'

82 Roy, *Journal of Private Fraser*, 121

83 Peter Mead, *The Eye in the Air: History of Air Observation and Reconnaissance for the Army 1785–1945* (London 1983), 66; Wise, *Canadian Airmen* 362; Nicholson, *Canadian Expeditionary Force*, 146–7

84 NAC, RG 9, V.4141, folder 4, file 10, '2nd Canadian Division, 12th April 1916'

85 Ibid.

86 Ibid.

87 Hartcup, *War of Invention*, 68; NAC, RG 9, V.4162, folder 7, file 2, 'Canadian Corps A.S.R. A.Q. 1/7, 17 February 1916'; RG 41, V.18, PPCLI, Interview with Hugh W. Macdonald, 8

88 Nicholson, *Canadian Expeditionary Force*, 151–2; NAC, RG 9, V.4690, folder 47, file 6, 'Account of the Attack by 3rd Battalion – June 13th 1916'

89 NAC, RG 9, V.4690, folder 47, file 6, 'Account of the Attack by 3rd Battalion, June 13th 1916'; Nicholson, *Canadian Expeditionary Force*, 153–4

90 NAC, RG 24, V.1883A, file 25, Ross Rifle, 1916, 'General Officer Commanding-in-Chief, British Armies in France to War Office, 28 May 1916'

91 NAC, RG 24, V.2538, HQC-1843, 'George P. Murphy to Maj-Gen MacDonald, QMG, 18 April 1916'

92 NAC, RG 24, V.2538, HQC-1843, 'Lt H.R. Northover to Lt-Col B.C. Whyte,' 16 April 1916

93 NAC, RG 24, V.2538, HQC-1843, 'Chief Inspector of Arms and Ammunition to Major-General of Ordnance,' 3 June 1916'; 17 June 1916; 'Ross Rifle Co to H.W. Brown, 28 June 1916'

94 NAC, RG 24, V.1883A, file 25, Ross Rifle, 1916, 'General Officer Commanding-in-Chief, British Armies in France to War Office, 28 May 1916'

95 Desmond Morton, *A Peculiar Kind of Politics: Canada's Overseas Ministry in the First World War* (Toronto 1982), 40

96 NAC, RG 9, III, V.3825, folder 2, file 36, 'Major-General R.E.W. Turner to Canadian Corps, 9 June 1916'

97 NAC, RG 24, v.1883A, file 25, Ross Rifle, 1916, 'T.W. Law to Miss R.G. Gallacher, c. June 1916'
98 NAC, RG 24, v.1883A, file 25, Ross Rifle, 1916, 'Brigadier E.S. Hoare-Nairne to Canadian Corps, 11 June 1916'
99 NAC, RG 24, v.1883A, file 25, Ross Rifle, 1916, '9 Bde to 3 Div, 19 June 1916'
100 NAC, MG 30, E300, Victor Odlum Papers, v.18, 'LCol Odlum to General Carson, 1 April 1916'
101 NAC, MG 30, E100, Arthur Currie Papers, v.1, 'Canadian Corps HQ to Captain Alistair Fraser, 7 December 1918'; RG 41, v.13, 44th Battalion, Interview with W.G. Marshall, 7; v.15, 58th Battalion, Interview with Mr Macdonald White, 11; RG 9, v.4197, folder 1, file 3, 'O.C. 58 Battalion to 'A' and 'B' Companies, 3 May 1916'; MG 30, E300, Victor Odlum Papers, v.18, 'LCol Odlum to General Carson, 1 April 1916'; details of the myriad modifications made to the Ross to make it field-worthy can be found in Archer Fortescue Duguid, *Official History of the Canadian Forces in the Great War 1914–1918: Chronology, Appendices and Maps* (Ottawa 1938) appendix 111.
102 NAC, MG 30, E300, Victor Odlum Papers, v.18, 'Major Allan Brooks to Col. Odlum, 3 April 1916'

CHAPTER 3 Struggles on the Somme

1 James E. Edmonds, *Military Operations, France and Belgium, 1916* (London 1932), 1–15
2 G.W.L. Nicholson, *The Fighting Newfoundlander: A History of the Royal Newfoundland Regiment* (London 1963), 274
3 Denis Winter, *Death's Men* (London 1978), 39
4 Edmonds, *Military Operations, 1916*, 290
5 John Terraine, *Douglas Haig, Educated Soldier* (London 1963), 203
6 Edmonds, *Military Operations 1916*, 289–90
7 Ibid., 290
8 Terraine, *Douglas Haig*, 203
9 DHist, 78/289 War Office, *Infantry Training, 1914*
10 Ian V. Hogg, *Barrage: The Guns in Action* (New York 1970), 25; T.H.E. Travers, 'Learning and Decision-Making on the Western Front 1915–1916: The British Example,' *Canadian Journal of History* (April 1983), 88
11 Edmonds, *Military Operations, 1916*, 288, 292–3; Terraine, *Douglas Haig*, 203

12 Shelford Bidwell and Dominick Graham, *Fire-Power: British Army Weapons and Theories of War, 1904-1945* (Winchester 1985), 83–5
13 John Terraine, *The Smoke and the Fire: Myths and Anti-myths of War* (London 1980)
14 Terraine, *Douglas Haig*, 204
15 Terraine, *Smoke and Fire*, 118; R.F.H Nalder, *The Royal Corps of Signals: A History of Its Antecedents and Development (Circa 1800–1953)* (London 1958), 114
16 Erich Maria Remarque, *All Quiet on the Western Front* (Greenwich 1958), 72
17 NAC, RG 41, v.7, 4th Battalion, Lieutenant-Colonel W.H. Joliffe
18 NAC, RG 9, v.4089, folder 20, file 11, '5 Canadian Infantry Brigade – Report on Operations on the Somme, 17 November 1916'; v.4690, folder 46, file 18, '2 Battalion Report on Operations, September 9–10 1916'
19 DHist, 80/280 *Field Service Pocket Book, 1916*
20 NAC, RG 9, v.4199, folder 6, file 7, '58 Battalion to O.C. 9 Brigade, 10 October 1916'; v.4049, folder 14, file 3, 'O.B./896. Reserve Army, 26 September 1916,' 'W.O. 3312. Some Notes on Lewis Guns and Machine Guns, September 1916'
21 NAC, RG 9, v.4049, folder 14, file 3, 'W.O. 3312. Some Notes on Lewis Guns and Machine Guns, September 1916'
22 Ibid.
23 E.L.M. Burns, *General Mud* (Toronto 1970), 20
24 G.W.L. Nicholson, *Canadian Expeditionary Force* (Ottawa 1962), 169
25 Charles Lyons Foster and William S. Duthie, eds, *Letters from the Front: Being a Record of the Role Played by Officers of the Bank in the Great War, 1914–1919* (n.p. 1920), 187
26 Reginald Roy, *The Journal of Private Fraser, 1914–1918, Canadian Expeditionary Force* (Victoria 1985), 207–8
27 NAC, RG 9, v.4693, folder 53, file 18, 'Lt Col E. William's Report on 25th Battalion Capture of Courcelette on Sept 25th 1916'
28 Ibid.
29 Jean-Pierre Gagnon, *Le 22e bataillon (canadien-français) 1914–1919: Etude socio-militaire* (Quebec 1986), 102
30 Foster and Duthie, *Letters from the Front*, 166
31 NAC, RG 9, War Diary, v.4813, Canadian Corps, Appendix VI, 'Canadian Corps Summary of Operations'
32 NAC, MG 30, E100, Arthur Currie Papers, v.35, file 159, '1st Canadian Division to Canadian Corps, 12 October 1916'; RG 9, v.4089, folder 20, file 11, '5 Canadian Infantry Brigade – Report on Operations on the Somme,

17 November 1916'

33 NAC, RG 9, v.4237, folder 3, file 1, 'Notes on the Somme Battle, undated Memorandum, 1916, 78th Battalion'; War Diary, v.4943, 78th Battalion, 11 October 1916, 11 November 1916

34 NAC, RG 9, v.4237, folder 3, file 1, 'Notes on the Somme Battle, undated Memorandum, 1916, 78th Battalion'; v.4162, folder 9, file 6, '4 CMR, Lessons Learnt from Operations on the Somme, 14 November 1916'; RG 9, War Diary, v.4943, 78th Battalion, 23 October 1916

35 Foster and Duthie, *Letters from the Front*, 172–3

36 NAC, RG 9, v.4162, folder 9, file 6, '8 Canadian Infantry Brigade, Report on Operations from September 27th to October 3rd, 1916'; MG 30, E100, Arthur Currie Papers, v.35, file 159, '1st Canadian Division to Canadian Corps, 12 October 1916'

37 John Swettenham, *McNaughton* (Toronto 1968), 1: 61

38 NAC, RG 9, v.4162, folder 9, file 6, '8th Canadian Infantry Brigade – Report on Operations from September 27th to October 3rd, 1916'

39 Gordon Reid, ed., *Poor Bloody Murder: Personal Memoirs of the First World War* (Oakville 1980), 114; NAC, MG 30, E100, v.35, file 159, '1st Canadian Division to Canadian Corps, 10 October 1916'; '1st Canadian Division to Canadian Corps, 12 October 1916'; RG 9, v.4199, folder 6, file 7, '58th Battalion to O.C. 9th Brigade, 10 October 1916'; War Diary, v.4916, 5th Battalion, 26 September 1916

40 E.L.M. Burns, *General Mud*, 19

41 NAC, RG 41, v.16, 75th Battalion, Interview with Mr E. Baker

42 NAC, MG 30, E300, Victor Odlum Papers, v.19, '11 Brigade: Operations Order No. 27, 10 November 1916'; RG 9, v.4089, folder 20, file 11, '5 Canadian Infantry Brigade – Report on Operations on the Somme, 17 November 1916'

43 NAC, RG 41, v.13, 44th Battalion, J. Robinson

44 NAC, RG 9, v.4690, folder 46, file 18, 'Notes on Attack by 2nd Canadian Battalion, 9 September 1916'; v.4162, folder 9, file 6, '4 CMR, Lessons Learnt from Operations on the Somme, November 1916'

45 A.H. Farrar-Hockley, *The Somme* (London 1964), 84

46 NAC, RG 9, War Diary, v.4916, 5th Battalion, 26 September 1916

47 NAC, RG 9, v.4089, folder 20, file 11, 'B.M.L. 330, 5 Brigade, Summary of Operations, 26th–27th September to 1st–2nd October, 1916'

48 Ian V. Hogg, *Grenades and Mortars* (New York 1974) 85–7

49 Edmonds, *Military Operations, 1916*, 61–2

50 NAC, RG 9, v.4089, folder 20, file 11, '5 Canadian Infantry Brigade – Re-

port on Operations on the Somme, 17 November 1916'; v.4162, folder 9, file 6, '4 CMR, Lessons Learnt from Operations on the Somme, November 1916'; '8th Canadian Infantry Brigade – Report on Operations from September 27th to October 3rd 1916'; MG 30, E300, Victor Odlum Papers, v.19, '11 Canadian Infantry Brigade to HQ 4 Canadian Division, 19 September 1916'

51 NAC, RG 9, v.4690, folder 46, file 18, 'Report on Operations, September 9th–10th 1916'; v.4049, folder 14, file 3, 'W.O. 3312. Some Notes on Lewis Guns and Machine Guns, September 1916'; Nicholson, *Canadian Expeditionary Force*, 176; v.4089, folder 20, file 11, '5 Canadian Infantry Brigade – Report on Operations on the Somme, 17 November 1916'

52 Edmund Blunden, *Undertones of War* (London 1928), 125

53 NAC, RG 9, v.4199, folder 6, file 7, '58th Canadian Battalion to O.C. 9th Canadian Infantry Brigade, 10 October 1916'; v.4690, folder 46, file 18, 'Report on Operations, September 9th–10th 1916'; v.4162, folder 9, file 6, '8th Canadian Infantry Brigade – Report on Operations from September 27th to October 3rd 1916; MG 30, E100, Arthur Currie Papers, v.35, file 159, '1st Canadian Division to Canadian Corps, 12 October 1916'

54 NAC, RG 9, v. 4237, folder 3, file 1, 'Notes on the Somme Battle, undated Memorandum, 1916, 78 Battalion'; v.4690, folder 46, file 18, 'Report on Operations, September 9th–10th 1916'; v.4017, folder 34, file 11, 'Report, Major A.T. Powell, 14th Battalion to LCol R.P. Clark, 29 November 1916'; v.4049, folder 14, file 3, 'W.O. 3312, Some Notes on Lewis Guns and Machine Guns, September 1916'; MG 30, E100, Arthur Currie Papers, v.35, file 159, '1st Canadian Division to Canadian Corps, 12 October 1916'

55 NAC, MG 30, E100, Arthur Currie Papers, v.35, file 159, '1st Canadian Division to Canadian Corps, 12 October 1916'; RG 9, v.4162, folder 9, file 6, '8th Canadian Infantry Brigade – Report on Operations from September 27th to October 3rd, 1916'; v.4089, folder 20, file 11, 'Report on Operation – 1st October 1916, 24th Battalion'; v.4162, folder 9, file 6, '8 C.I.B. – Report on Operations from Sept 27th to October 3rd, 1916'; v.5690, folder 46, file 18, 'Report on Operations, September 9th–10th 1916'; MG 30, E100, Arthur Currie Papers, v.35, file 159, '1st Canadian Division to Canadian Corps, 10 October 1916'; '1st Canadian Division to Canadian Corps, 12 October 1916'

56 Foster and Duthie, *Letters From the Front* 174–5

57 NAC, MG 30, E100, Arthur Currie Papers, v.35, '1st Canadian Division to Canadian Corps, 12 October 1916'; RG9, v.4089, folder 20, file 11, '5 Ca-

nadian Infantry Brigade – Report of Operations on the Somme, 17 November 1916'; v.4162, folder 9, file 6, '4 CMR, Lessons Learnt from Operations on the Somme, November 1916'; Foster and Duthie, *Letters from the Front*, 174–5

58 NAC, MG 30, E300, Victor Odlum Papers, v.19, '11 Canadian Infantry Brigade Operation Order No. 27, 10 November 1916'; RG 9, v.4099, folder 1, file 3, 'Canadian Corps G.692'; v.4690, folder 46, file 18, 'Report on Operations, September 9th–10th 1916'; Nicholson, *Canadian Expeditionary Force*, 185

59 NAC, RG 24, v.1844, GAQ 11–11B, 'Casualties'; v.1883, file 27, 'Return of Killed, Wounded and Missing (by Months) for All Canadian Units in France.'

60 NAC, RG 9, v.4089, '22nd Battalion 22–75'

61 NAC, RG 9, 4237, folder 3, file 1, 'Notes on the Somme Battle, undated Memorandum, 1916, 78 Battalion'; v.4162, folder 9, file 6, '4 CMR, Lessons Learnt from Operations on the Somme, November 1916'

62 NAC, RG 9, v.4162, folder 9, file 6, '5 CMR, Lessons Learnt from Operations on the Somme, 20 November 1916'; RG 9, v.4089, '22nd Battalion 22–75'; 4237, folder 3, file 1, 'Notes on the Somme Battle, undated Memorandum, 1916, 78 Battalion'

63 NAC, MG 100, E100, Arthur Currie Papers, v.35, file 159, '1st Canadian Division to Canadian Corps, 12 October 1916'

64 NAC, RG 9, v.4162, folder 9, file 6, '1 CMR, Lessons Learnt from Operations on the Somme, 20 November 1916'; '2 CMR, Lessons Learnt from Operations on the Somme, 14 November 1916'; italics in original.

65 NAC, RG 9, v.4689, folder 20, file 11, '22nd Battalion, 22–75'

66 NAC, RG 9, v.4689, folder 20, file 11, '22nd Battalion, 22–75'; v.4237, folder 3, file 1, 'Notes on the Somme Battle, undated Memorandum, 1916, 78 Battalion'; v.4162, folder 9, file 6, '8th Canadian Infantry Brigade, Resumé of Some of the Special Points Dealt with by Battalion Commanders in Their Reports on Lessons Learned from Operations on the Somme, 23 November 1916'; '1 CMR, Lessons Learnt from Operations on the Somme, 20 November 1916'; '2 CMR, Lessons Learnt from Operations on the Somme, 14 November 1916'; '5 CMR, Lessons Learnt from Operations on the Somme, 20 November 1916'; Bidwell and Graham, *Fire-Power*, 122

67 NAC, RG 9, v.4689, folder 20, file 11, '22nd Battalion, 22–75'; v.4237, folder 3, file 1, 'Notes on the Somme Battle, undated Memorandum, 1916, 78 Battalion'; v.4162, folder 9, file 6, '8th Canadian Infantry Bri-

gade, Resumé of Some of the Special Points Dealt with by Battalion Commanders ...; '1 CMR, Lessons Learnt from Operations on the Somme, 20 November 1916'; '2 CMR, Lessons Learnt from Operations on the Somme, 14 November 1916'; '5 CMR, Lessons Learnt from Operations on the Somme, 20 November 1916'

68 NAC, RG 9, III, War Diary, v.4813, Canadian Corps, September 1916, Appendix VII, 'Report on Operations of Tanks, 21 September 1916'

69 Bidwell and Graham, *Fire-Power*, 120–2

70 NAC, RG 9, 4237, folder 3, file 1, 'Notes on the Somme Battle, undated Memorandum, 1916, 78 Battalion'

71 NAC, RG 9, v.4689, folder 20, file 11, '22nd Battalion, 22–75'; v.4162, folder 9, file 6, '8th Canadian Infantry Brigade, Resumé of Some of the Special Points Dealt with by Battalion Commanders ...

72 NAC, RG 9, v.4689, folder 20, file 11, '22nd Battalion, 22–75'

73 NAC, RG 9, v.4689, folder 20, file 11, '22nd Battalion, 22–75'; v.4237, folder 3, file 1, 'Notes on the Somme Battle, undated Memorandum, 1916, 78 Battalion'

74 NAC, RG 9, v.4162, folder 9, file 6, '1 CMR, Lessons Learnt from Operations on the Somme'

75 NAC, RG 9, 4237, folder 3, file 1, 'Notes on the Somme Battle, undated Memorandum, 1916, 78 Battalion'

76 NAC, RG 9, v.4689, folder 20, file 11, '22nd Battalion, 22–75'; v.4237, folder 3, file 1, 'Notes on the Somme Battle, undated Memorandum, 1916, 78 Battalion'; v.4162, folder 9, file 6, '2 CMR, Lessons Learnt from Operations on the Somme, 14 November 1916'; '5 CMR, Lessons Learnt from Operations on the Somme, 20 November 1916'

CHAPTER 4 Towards Vimy

1 Leon Wolff, *In Flanders Fields: The 1917 Campaign* (New York 1958), 44; C.E.W. Bean, *The Australian Imperial Force in France – 1917* (Sydney 1935), 2–3; Bernadotte E. Schmitt and Harold C. Vedeler, *The World in the Crucible 1914–1919* (New York 1984), 166–7

2 G.W.L. Nicholson, *Canadian Expeditionary Force* (Ottawa: 1962), 239–41; C.R.M.F. Crutwell, *A History of the Great War 1914–1918* (London, 1982), 440

3 Jeffery Williams, *Byng of Vimy: General and Governor-General* (London 1983), 149

4 Herbert F. Wood, *Vimy!* (Toronto 1967), 27, 77; Nicholson, *Canadian Expeditionary Force*, 246

5 NAC, RG 9, V.4049, folder 14, file 4, 'O.B./1782/A. Notes on Dealing with Hostile Machine Guns in an Advance. Issued by G.S. April 1917'; V.4026, folder 11, file 5, 'Report on Operations Carried out by the 1st Canadian Division – April 7th–May 5th, 1917.'

6 Denis Winter *Death's Men* (London 1978), 40

7 NAC, RG 9, V.4236, Notes on Oerations, 5-4-16 to 8-3-17, 'Memorandum Relating to the Experience Gained from the Verdun Actions, 5 April 1916'

8 NAC, RG 9, V.4236, folder 2, file 3, '4th Division to 11th, 12th, and 13th Brigades, 8 March 1917'

9 NAC, RG 9, V.4142, folder 6, file 2, 'Notes on French Attacks, North-East of Verdun in October and December 1916,' 3

10 Ibid., iii

11 Ibid., 10

12 Ibid., 4

13 Ibid., 3–4

14 NAC, RG 9, V.4940, folder 159, file 10, 'Interior Organization of Companies and Proceedings of Offensive Warfare for Small Units'; Edmund Blunden, *Undertones of War* (London 1928), 199–200; Shelford Bidwell and Dominick Graham, *Fire-Power: British Army Weapons and Theories of War, 1904–1945* (Winchester 1985), 126

15 NAC, RG 9, V.4142, filder 6, file 2, 'Notes on French Attacks, North-East of Verdun in October and December 1916,' 13

16 Ibid., 12, 4, 6

17 Ibid., 5, 4

18 Ibid., 11–12

19 Ibid., 14

20 John Swettenham, *McNaughton* (Toronto 1968), 1: 68, 85

21 Ibid., 77

22 Ibid., 72; Guy Hartcup, *The War of Invention: Scientific Developments 1914–18* (London 1988), 68–71

23 NAC, RG 9, V.4142, folder 6, file 2, 'Notes on French Attacks, North-East of Verdun in October and December 1916,' 8

24 Ibid., 6, 14, 7

25 Ibid., 5

26 Nicholson, *Canadian Expeditionary Force*, 247–8; NAC, RG 9, V.4141, folder 4, file 9, 'Preliminary Instructions for the Offensive No. 3, 30 March 1917,' 4

27 Reginald Roy, *The Journal of Private Fraser, 1914–1918, Canadian Expeditionary Force* (Victoria 1985), 92

28 Charles Lyons Foster and William S. Duthie, *Letters from the Front: Being a Record of the Role Played by Officers of the Bank in the Great War, 1914–1989* (n.p. 1920), 196

29 Stephen Harris, *Canadian Brass* (Toronto 1988), 128

30 DHist, FN 06, *Instructions for the Training of Platoons for Offensive Action, 1917* (February 1917), 6; NAC, RG 9, War Diary, v.4912, 1st Battalion, 11–24 March 1917

31 NAC, RG 9, War Diary, v.4943, 78th Battalion, 28 March 1917; v.4049, folder 14, file 4, 'HQ 2 C.I.B. to HQ 1 Can Div, 20 February 1917'; War Diary, v.4916, 5th Battalion, 13 March 1917; v.4166, folder 19, file 9, 'No 1/6, HQ 2 Btn CMR to G.O.C. Can Corps, 15, December 1916'; War Diary, v.4912, 1st Battalion, 13 February 1917; Swettenham, *McNaughton*, 1: 80

32 NAC, RG 9, War Diary, v.4943, 78th Battalion, 14 February 1917; A.J.L. Kerry and W.A. McDill, *The History of the Corps of Royal Canadian Engineers: Volume I, 1749–1939* (Ottawa 1962,) 132; Nicholson, *Canadian Expeditionary Force*, 250

33 Herbert F. Wood, *Vimy!* (Toronto 1967), 147

34 Ibid.

35 NAC, RG 41, v.7, 3rd Battalion, Interview with Colonel H.S. Cooper

36 NAC, RG 41, v.11, 27th Battalion, Interview with Mr. L.R. Fennel, 4

37 NAC, RG 9, v.4033, folder 4, file 5, 'Notes for the Guidance of Battalion Officers during Operations'; v.4076, folder 5, file 1, 'Can Corps I.G. 22 December 1916'; v.3866, folder 102, file 1, 'Patrol Report – 14th Battalion, 23 December 1916'

38 NAC, RG 9, v.4017, folder 47, file 11, 'HQ 14 Battalion to G.O.C. 3 C.I.B., 29 November 1916'; War Diary, v.4916, 5th Battalion, 21 February 1917; v.4017, folder 35, file 22, 'HQ 14 Battalion to 3 C.I.B., 27 February 1917'

39 NAC, RG 9, III, War Diary, Canadian Corps, v.4814, 2–22 March 1917

40 NAC, RG 41, v.7, 3rd Battalion, Colonel H.S. Cooper

41 NAC, MG 30, E100, Arthur Currie Papers, v.52, Diary, 9 December, 20 December, 5 April

42 Tony Ashworth, *Trench Warfare 1914–1918: The Live and Let Live System* (London 1980), 98, 181–5; NAC, RG 9, v.4158, folder 2, file 7, 'Raids Carried out by the Canadian Corps – 1916'; MG 30, E100, Arthur Currie Papers, v.35, file 160, 'Raids Carried out by Canadian Corps during Period from 1st January to 16th February, 1917'; RG 24, v.1826, GAQ 5–90, 'Summary of Raids by Canadian Corps during the Period Nov 1st 1916– April 1st, 1917'; RG 41, v.17, 1 CMR, Interview with W. Thow, 1, 5

43 NAC, RG 9, v.4158, folder 2, file 7, 'Raids Carried out by the Canadian Corps', 3

44 Ibid.

45 NAC, RG 9, v.4158, folder 2, file 7, 'Raids Carried out by the Canadian Corps,' 7; RG 9, v.4209, folder 1, file 12, 'Detailed Sequence for Raid Preparation'

46 NAC, RG 9, v.4209, folder 1, file 12, 'Detailed Sequence for Raid Preparation'

47 NAC, RG 9, v.4231, folder 25, file 3, 'S.G.2/G./165, Report on Daylight Raid Carried out by 78th Canadian Infantry Battalion, 12th Canadian Infantry Brigade on 19th February 1917,' 2, 4

48 Ibid., 4

49 NAC, MG 30, E300, Victor Odlum Papers, v.19, '4th Canadian Division G52–9, 31 January 1917,' 1

50 Nicholson, *Canadian Expeditionary Force*, 234; E.L.M. Burns, *General Mud* (Toronto 1970), 40

51 NAC, RG 9, v.4148, folder 14, file 16, 'Report on Raid by 42nd Canadian Battalion on Enemy Front and Second Line Trenches in Rear of Longfellow Crater, April 1st 1917,' 1–2

52 Ibid., 2–3

53 NAC, RG 9, v.4026, folder 11, file 5, 'Report on Operations Carried out by the 1st Canadian Division – April 7th–May 5th, 1917' 38; v.4163, folder 10, file 1, '3rd Canadian Division, G.944, to Brigades, CRE, CRA, 26 February 1917'

54 NAC, MG 30, E155, Roger F. Clark Papers, v.1, file 4, Diary, 28 October 1916

55 NAC, RG 9, v.4163, folder 10, file 1, '3rd Can Div to Canadian Corps, 21 February 1917'

56 Kerry and McDill, *History of the Corps*, 123

57 Ibid., 123, 126

58 Ibid., 131; NAC, RG 9, v.4026, folder 11, file 5, 'Report on Operations Carried out ...,' 7; Nicholson, *Canadian Expeditionary Force*, 250

59 Nicholson, *Canadian Expeditionary Force*, 248; Swettenham, *McNaughton*, 1: 76

60 NAC, RG 9, v.4026, folder 11, file 5, 'Report on Operations Carried out ...,' 41, 43–4

61 DHist, 75/413, 'Royal Flying Corps Headquarters Communiqués 81 and 82'; Foster and Duthie, *Letters from the Front*, 197; NAC, RG 9, v.4140, folder 1, file 3, '6 CIB, 26 March 1917'; v.4026, folder 11, file 5, 'Report Operations Carried out ...,' 7; III, War Diary, Canadian Corps, v.4814, Appendix IV, 'Intelligence Summaries,' 1 April 1917

62 NAC, RG 9, III, War Diary, Canadian Corps, v.4814, 6 to 28 March; Ap-

pendix III, 'Summaries of Operations rendered to First Army,' 7 March to
12 April
63 Hartcup, *War of Invention*, 57–9
64 NAC, RG 9, v.4026, folder 11, file 5, 'Report on Operations Carried out ...,'
7, 44–6; DHist, 87/191, *Light Mortar Training, June 1918*, 9
65 NAC, RG 9, v.4026, folder 11, file 5, 'Report on Operations Carried out ...,'
45
66 Foster and Duthie, *Letters from the Front*, 181
67 Ibid., 178; NAC, RG 9, v.4026, folder 11, file 5, 'Report on Operations Carried out ...,' 6, 45
68 NAC, RG 9, v.4026, folder 11, file 5, 'Report on Operations Carried out ...,'
7, 46
69 NAC, RG 9, v.4141, folder 4, file 11, '31st Canadian Battalion to 6th Canadian Brigade, 11 April 1917'
70 Swettenham, *McNaughton*, v.1, 66, 68, 72–4, 79; Nicholson, *Canadian Expeditionary Force*, 249
71 Nicholson, *Canadian Expeditionary Force*, 251; NAC RG 9, War Diary, v.4943, 78th Battalion, 2 January 1917; War Diary, v.4916, 5th Battalion, 8 February 1917; v.4026, folder 11, file 5, 'Report on Operations Carried out ...,' 43
72 NAC, MG 30, E133, McNaughton Papers, v.2, file 14, '11 Brigade CFA War Diary, 2 January 1917'
73 NAC, RG 9, v.4026, folder 11, file 5, 'Report on Operations Carried out ...,'
5, 21, 45; DHist, SGR II 202, 'Translated Exerpts from *Reichsarchiv*'
74 NAC, RG 9, v.4026, folder 11, file 5, 'Report on Operations Carried out ...,'
5, 46–7

CHAPTER 5 Spring and Summer 1917

1 NAC, RG 9, v.4026, folder 11, file 5, 'Report on Operations Carried out ...,'
48; v.4141, folder 4, file 9, 'Instructions for the Offensive No. 2, 2nd Canadian Division, 27 February 1917'
2 NAC, RG 9, v.4049, folder 14, file 4, 'Monthly Machine Gun Report for 2nd Canadian Infantry Brigade, 21 March 1917'; '1 Cdn Div to 2 C.I.B., 6 February 1917'; v.4163, folder 10, file 1, '7 C.I.B. Operation Order No. 65, 7 January 1917'; v.4026, folder 11, file 5, 'Report on Operations Carried out ...,' 6; III, v.4146, folder 9, file 2, '3rd Canadian Division: Narrative of Operations in Connection with the Attack and Capture of the Vimy Ridge, Appendix A, Report of 7th Brigade,' 4

3 Reginald Roy, *The Journal of Privat Fraser, 1914–1918, Canadian Expeditionary Force* (Victoria 1985,) 251

4 NAC, RG 9, v.4163, folder 10, file 1, 'Cdn Corps to 3 Cdn Div, 7 February 1917'; v.4026, folder 11, file 5, 'Report on Operations Carried out ...,' 6, 16, 20, 44; v.4141, folder 4, file 9, 'Preliminary Instructions for the Offensive No. 3, 30 March 1917'; folder 4158, folder 2, file 5, '42nd Battalion, Operation Order No. 116'; v.4142, folder 5, file 1, '28th Battalion Order No. 162A, 7 April 1917'; v.4049, folder 14, file 4, 'General Staff, Notes on Dealing with Hostile Machine Guns in an Advance, April 1917'; Jeffery Williams, *Byng of Vimy: General and Governor-General* (London 1983), 149

5 NAC, RG 9, v.4026, folder 11, file 5, 'Report on Operations Carried out ...,' 51–2

6 NAC, RG 9, v.4163, folder 10, file 1, '7th Canadian Infantry Brigade, Operation Order No. 65, 7 January 1917'

7 NAC, RG 9, v.4163, folder 10, file 1, '8th Canadian Infantry Brigade, G/80/8 to 3rd Division, 9 February 1917'; v.4141, folder 4, file 11, '31st Battalion to 6th Brigade, 11 April 1917'

8 D.E. Macintyre, *Canada at Vimy* (Toronto 1967), 103; NAC, RG 9, v.4158, folder 2, file 5, '42nd Battalion, Operation Order No. 116'

9 G.W.L. Nicholson, *Canadian Expeditionary Force* (Ottawa 1962), 253; NAC, RG 9, v.4026, folder 11, file 5, 'Report on Operations Carried out ...,' 52; v.4237, folder 3, file 3, '12th C.I.B. Operation Order No. 60, 3 April 1917'; Macintyre, *Canada at Vimy*, 79; 9, v.4141, folder 4, file 11, '31st Battalion to 6 C.I.B., 11 April 1917'

10 NAC, MG 30, E450, William Green Papers, 4

11 NAC, RG 9, v.4141, folder 4, file 9, '2nd Division G.S. 1494/453, 27 February 1917'; v.4142, folder 5, file 1, '28th Battalion, Order No. 162A, 7 April 1917'; 'O.B./1919/T. Commander in Chief, 14 February 1917'; v.4026, folder 11, file 5, 'Report on Operations Carried out ...,' 19

12 NAC, RG 9, v.4158, folder 2, file 5, '42nd Battalion, Operation Order No. 116.'; v.4163, folder 10, file 1, '8th C.I.B., G80/8. to 3 Cdn Div, 9 February 1917'; '7th C.I.B. 'Operation Order No. 65, 7 January 1917'

13 NAC, RG 9, v.4199, folder 7, file 11, 'First Army No.1227 (G), 9 May 1917'; v.4163, folder 10, file 1, '8 C.I.B. to 3 Cdn Div, 9 February 1917'

14 Charles Lyons Foster and William S. Duthie, *Letters from the Front: Being a Record of the Role Played by Officers of the Bank in the Great War, 1914–1919* (n.p. 1920), 208

15 NAC, RG 41, v.14, 49th Battalion, Interview with Mr W.B. Frame, 11

16 NAC, RG 9, III, War Diary, v.4940, 49th Battalion, 13 April 1917

17 NAC, RG 9, v.4188, folder 5, file 6, '9th C.I.B. 28/186, 19 February 1917'; v.4026, folder 11, file 5, 'Report on Operations Carried out ...,' 20

18 NAC, RG 9, v.4026, folder 11, file 5, 'Report on Operations Carried out ...,' 18, 52

19 NAC, RG 9, v.4163, folder 10, file 1, '7 C.I.B. Operation Order No. 65, 7 January 1917'; '8 C.I.B. to 3 Cdn Div, 9 February 1917'; v.4049, folder 14, file 4, 'General Staff, Notes on Dealing with Hostile Machine Guns in an Advance, April 1917'; v.4026, folder 11, file 5, 'Report on Operations Carried out ...,' 15; War Diary, v.4916, 5th Battalion, file 363(1), 9 April 1917

20 NAC, RG 9, v.4158, folder 2, file 5, '42nd Battalion, Operation Order No. 116, Schedule B and E, 5 April 1917'

21 Ian V. Hogg, *Grenades and Mortars* (New York 1974), 19; Ian Skennerton, *The British Service Lee: The Lee-Metford and Lee-Enfield Rifles and Carbines, 1880–1980* (London 1982), 263

22 NAC, RG 9, v.4026, folder 11, file 5, 'Report on Operations Carried out ...,' 19

23 Ibid., 16–17

24 NAC, RG 41, v.12, 31st Battalion, Interview with Mr G.E. Bain, 6; RG 9, v.4158, folder 2, file 5, '42nd Battalion, Operation Order No. 116, Schedule B, 5 April 1917'; v.4237, folder 3, file 3, '4 Cdn Div, I.G. 24–2, 3 April 1917'; v.4142, folder 5, file 1, '28th Battalion, Operation Order No. 162A, 7 April 1917'; v.4049, folder 14, file 4, 'General Staff, Notes on Dealing with Hostile Machine Guns in an Advance, April 1917'

25 NAC, RG 9, v.4199, folder 6, file 8, 'Notes on Conference Held at Canadian Corps H.Q. on 3rd March 1917'

26 Nicholson, *Canadian Expeditionary Force*, 258, Macintyre, *Canada at Vimy*, 110; NAC, RG 9, III, v.3846, folder 51, file 5, 'Canadian Corps, Vimy Ridge, Operations Narrative,' 16

27 Herbert F. Wood, *Vimy!* (Toronto 1967), 123; Macintyre, *Canada at Vimy*, 90; Nicholson, *Canadian Expenditionary Force*, 250; NAC, RG 9, v.4141, folder 4, file 9, 'Preliminary Instructions for the Offensive No. 3, 30 March 1917'; III, v.3846, folder 51, file 5, 'Canadian Corps, Vimy Ridge, Operations Narrative,' 6–7

28 E.L.M. Burns, *General Mud* (Toronto 1970), 41–2; NAC, RG 9, v.4026, folder 11, file 5, 'Report on Operations Carried out ...,' 71

29 Macintyre, *Canada at Vimy*, 90

30 NAC, RG 9, v.4026, folder 11, file 5, 'Report on Operations Carried out ...,' 71

31 Ibid.; Wood, *Vimy!* 156

32 Burns, *General Mud*, 41
33 John Moir, ed., *History of the Royal Canadian Corps of Signals, 1903–1961* (Ottawa 1962), 27; Guy Hartcup, *The War of Invention: Scientific Developments 1914–1918* (London 1988), 70–1, 76–8; NAC, RG 9, v.4026, folder 11, file 5, 'Report on Operations Carried out ...,' 71; Macintyre, *Canada at Vimy*, III, v.4146, folder 9, file 2, '3rd Canadian Division: Narrative of Operations in Connection with the Attack and Capture of the Vimy Ridge, Appendix A, 7th Brigade Report,' 5; R.F.H. Nalder, *The Royal Corps of Signals: A History of Its Antecedents and Development (Circa 1800–1953)* (London 1958), 123, 130
34 NAC, RG 9, v.4158, folder 2, file 5, '42nd Battalion, Operation Order No. 116'; 'Communication Between Infantry and the Royal Flying Corps'; v.4033, folder 4, file 7, '1st C.I.B. Operation Order No. 133, 6 April 1917'; v.4142, folder 5, file 1, '28th Battalion Order No. 162A, 7 April 1917'
35 NAC, RG 9, III, v.4859, 4th Division War Diary, Appendix B
36 NAC, RG 9, III, v.4942, War Diary, 54th Battalion, 1 March and 9 April 1917; 72nd Battalion, 1 March and 9 April 1917; v.4943, 73rd Battalion, 1 March and 9 April 1917; v. 4859, 4th Division War Diary, Appendix B
37 George Coppard, *With a Machine Gun to Cambrai: The Tale of a Young Tommy in Kitchener's Army, 1914–1918* (London 1969), 37–8, 49
38 NAC, RG 9, v.4026, folder 11, file 5, 'Report on Operations Carried out ...,' 17, 19–21
39 Ibid., 51–3
40 Ibid., 18; III, v.3846, folder 51, file 5, 'Canadian Corps, Vimy Ridge, Operations Narrative,' 16; Nicholson, *Canadian Expeditionary Force*, 256
41 NAC, RG 9, v.4158, folder 1, file 5, '42nd Battalion, Operation Order No. 116, Schedule B, 5 April 1917'
42 NAC, RG 9, v.4158, folder 2, file 5, '7 Brigade, Orders'; Kerry and McDill, *History of the Corps*, 133; v.4033, folder 4, file 5, 'Notes for the Guidance of Battalion Officers during Operations'
43 NAC, RG 9, v.4026, folder 11, file 5, 'Report on Operations Carried out ...,' 22; v.4258, folder 2, file 5, 'Narrative of Operations, 42nd Canadian Battalion – In Connection with Capture of Vimy Ridge 5th/6th to 11th/12th April 1917'; III, v.3846, folder 51, file 5, 'Canadian Corps, Vimy Ridge, Operations Narrative,' 17
44 NAC, RG 9, III, v.3846, folder 51, file 5, 'Canadian Corps, Vimy Ridge, Operations Narrative,' 17
45 NAC, RG 9, v.4199, folder 6, file 9, 'C.O. 3rd Division – Circular Memorandum, 29 July 1917
46 NAC, MG 30, E100, Arthur Currie Papers, v.1, '1 Cdn Div to H.C. Brewster, 31 May 1917'

47 Ibid.
48 Nicholson, *Canadian Expeditionary Force*, 261, 265; NAC, RG 24, v.1883, file 27, 'Return of Killed, Wounded and Missing (by Months) for All Canadian Units in France'
49 Cyril Falls, *Military Operations: France and Belgium, 1917* (London 1940), I: 423
50 Ibid., 450
51 NAC, RG 9, v.4026, folder 11, file 5, 'Report on Operations Carried out ...,' 79–80
52 Ibid., 60
53 NAC, RG 9, v.4140, folder 1, file 3, '6 C.I.B. to 2 Cdn Div, 7 May 1917'
54 NAC, RG 9, v.4026, folder 11, file 5, 'Report on Operations Carried out ...,' 81
55 Ibid., 77–9
56 Ibid., 77
57 Ibid., 79
58 Ibid., 73–4
59 NAC, RG 9, War Diary, v.4913, 1st Battalion, file 351(1), General
60 NAC, RG 41, v.8, 7th Battalion, W.A. West
61 NAC, RG 9, v.4199, folder 7, file 11, 'First Army No. 1227(G), 9 May 1917'
62 NAC, RG 9, v.4064, folder 15, file 3, 'Canadian Corps G.14-5-265, 12 June 1917
63 NAC, RG 9, v.4064, folder 15, file 3, '1st Cdn Div G.7-207, 15 May 1917'; 'Headquarters, 2 C.I.B. 15 May 1917'; MG 30, E300, Victor Odlum Papers, v.20, '11 C.I.B. 1377/128, Syllabus – Six Day Course, Charles Y. Harrison, 109
64 NAC, MG 30, E300, Victor Odlum Papers, v.20, 'First Army No.1127(G) to Cdn Corps, 18 June 1917'; RG 9, v.4033, folder 5, file 10, 'Canadian Corps, Notes on the Attack, 21 May 1917'
65 As late as early September the nominal roll for the 14th Battalion listed officer, other ranks, and Lewis gunners separately. R.C. Fetherstonaugh, *The Royal Montreal Regiment 14th Battalion CEF, 1914–1925* (Montreal 1927), 173
66 NAC, MG 30, E300, Victor Odlum Papers, v.20, '11 C.I.B. 8539/128, 22 May 1917'; RG 9, v.4064, folder 15, file 3, 'Canadian Corps G.869/14-3, 10 August 1917'; v.4033, folder 5, file 10, 'Canadian Corps G.14-3-940, 3 June 1917'
67 NAC, RG 9, v.4033, folder 5, file 10, 'Demonstration of an Infantry Field Practice Held near Aux-le-Chatham at 3 p.m. June 2nd, 1917'; B.H. Liddell-Hart, *The Tanks* (London 1959), 1: 112, 119

68 NAC, RG 9, V.4033, folder 5, file 10, 'Canadian Corps, Notes on the Attack, 21 May 1917'; III, v.3867, folder 107, file 11

69 NAC, RG 9, V.4033, folder 5, file 10, 'Demonstration of an Infantry Field Practice Held Near Aix-le-Chatham at 3 p.m. June 2nd, 1917'; 'Canadian Corps, Notes on the Attack, 21 May 1917'; v.4199, folder 7, file 11, 'First Army, 9 May 1917'

70 Nicholson, *Canadian Expeditionary Force*, 287

71 S.F. Wise, *Canadian Airmen and the First World War* (Toronto 1980), 421–2; NAC, MG 30, E100, Arthur Currie Papers, v.35, file 161, 'Report; 2 CIB Action of August 15,' 10, 13–14

72 A.J.L. Kerry and W.A. McDill, *History of the Corps of Royal Engineers: Volume I, 1739–1939* (Ottawa 1962), 137; Nicholson, *The Gunners of Canada* (Toronto 1972), 275; NAC, MG 30, E133, McNaughton Papers, v.1, file 10, 'E. Ford, Lt Col, A.D. Sigs, Cdn Corps, to Cdn Corps "A" Branch, 24 August 1917'; E100, Arthur Currie Papers, v.35, file 161, 'Report; 2 C.I.B. Action of August 15, Capture of the Enemy's Positions on Hill 70 and Subsequent Operations, August 16th, 17th, and 18th,' 32; Moir, *Signals*, 29; John Swettenham, *McNaughton* (Toronto 1968), 1:102

73 NAC, MG 30, E488, William C. Morgan Papers, Diary

74 NAC, MG 30, E100, Arthur Currie Papes, v.36, file 161, 'Report; 2 C.I.B. Action of August 15,' 28–9

75 NAC, RG 41, v.8, 5th Battalion, J. Younie

76 Canada, *Thirty Canadian VCs: 23rd April 1915 to 30th March 1918* (London 1918), 49; NAC, MG 30, E100, Arthur Currie Papers, v.35, file 161, 'Report; 2 C.I.B. Action of August 15,' 10, 13, 15; RG 9, v.4693, folder 53, file 10, '24th Canadian Infantry Battalion, "A" Company, Notes on Attack, N.W. Lens, August 15th 1917'

77 NAC, MG 30, E100, Arthur Currie Papers, v.35, file 161, 'Report; 2 C.I.B. Action of August 15,' 13–14

78 Ibid., 13, 15; RG 9, v.4693, folder 53, file 10, '24th Battalion, Notes on Attack, N.W. Lens, 15 August 1917'

79 NAC, MG 30, E100, Arthur Currie Papers, v.35, file 161, 'Report; 2 C.I.B. Action of August 15,' 14; Swettenham, *McNaughton*, 1: 102; John D.R. Rawlings, *Fighter Squadrons of the RAF and Their Aircraft* (London 1969), 116

80 NAC, MG 30, E100, Arthur Currie Papers, v.35, file 161, 'Report: 2 C.I.B. Action of August 15,' 25–6

81 Foster and Duthie, *Letters from the Front*, 232; NAC, MG 30, E100, Arthur Currie Papers, v.35, file 161, 'Report; 2 C.I.B. Action of August 15,' 23;

Foster and Duthie, *Letters from the Front,* Second Lieutenant F.R. Darrow, August 1917, 241; Canada, *Thirty Canadian VCs,* 52; D.J. Goodspeed, *The Road Past Vimy: The Canadian Corps, 1914–1918* (Toronto 1969), 105

82 Swettenham, *McNaughton,* 1: 102; Rawlings, *Fighter Squadrons,* 116
83 Foster and Duthie, *Letters from the Front,* 241
84 Ibid.
85 Ibid.
86 NAC, MG 30, E100, Arthur Currie Papers, v.35, file 161, 'Report; 2 C.I.B. Action of August 15,' 27
87 Nicholson, *Canadian Expeditionary Force,* 292
88 Ibid., 297

CHAPTER 6 Bloody Passchendaele

1 Bryan Cooper, *The Ironclads of Cambrai* (London 1970), 4
2 Leon Wolff, *In Flanders Fields: The 1917 Campaign* (New York 1958), viii, xix, 71, 83, 260, 178, 180, 182
3 Shelford Bidwell and Dominick Graham, *Fire-Power: British Army Weapons and Theories of War, 1904–1945* (Winchester 1985), 99
4 Bryan Gardner, *Up the Line to Death: The War Poets 1914–1918* (London 1966), vii
5 Wolff, *In Flanders Fields,* 141–99
6 Ibid., 226, 247–8, 187, 195
7 NAC, RG 41, v.13, 42nd Battalion, James Page
8 NAC, RG 9, v.4142, folder 6, file 2, 'Report of 31 Battalion, 22 October 1917'; v.4033, folder 3, file 3, 'Canadian Corps G 923/2520-1, 23 October 1917'
9 A.J. Smithers, *A New Excalibur: The Development of the Tank 1909–1939* (London 1986), 126
10 Erich von Ludendorf, *Ludendorff's Own Story* (Freeport 1971), 2: 488
11 John Terraine, *The Road to Passchendaele, The Flanders Offensive of 1917: A Study in Inevitability* (London 1977), 304; Daniel G. Dancocks, *Legacy of Valour* (Edmonton 1986), 114; Denis Winter, *Death's Men* (London 1968), 122; NAC, RG 9, v.3989, folder 4, file 14, 'Second Army Intelligence, Enemy's Probable Counter-Attack Policy, 11 October 1917'
12 NAC, RG 9, v.4210, folder 1, file 11, 'Second Army, Further Notes on Operations, 26th Sept. and 4th Oct., 1917'; DHist, 89/843, *Method of Instruction in the Lewis Gun, May 1917,* 9

13 NAC, RG 9, V.4142, folder 6, file 2, 'Report of 31 Battalion, 22 October 1917'

14 NAC, RG 9, V.4033, folder 3, file 3, 'Canadian Corps G.23/2520-1, 23 October 1917'

15 NAC, RG 9, V.4125, folder 6, file 1, '31 Battalion, Notes on Operations, No. 1'

16 NAC, RG 41, V.11, 26th Battalion, Interview with G. McNight

17 NAC, RG 41, V.11 22e Bataillon, Interview with P.E. Bélanger

18 NAC, MG 30, E81, Morrison Papers, V.2, 'Operations of the Canadian Corps during October, 1917'

19 NAC, RG 41, V.22, Canadian Corps Headquarters, Colonel William Rae

20 John Swettenham, *McNaughton* (Toronto 1968), 1: 112, 114; G.W.L. Nicholson, *Canadian Expeditionary Force* (Ottawa 1962), 313

21 NAC, RG 9, V.4033, folder 3, file 3, '1 Battalion, Narrative of Events, Passchendaele'; V.4238, folder 4, file 2, '78 Battalion, Report Covering Operations 1.20 a.m. Oct. 29th to 10.20 p.m. Nov. 2nd 1917'; MG 30, E100, Arthur Currie Papers, V.36, file 162, '3rd Canadian Divisional Artillery, Report on Operations Leading to the Attacks of October 26th and October 30th upon and the Capture of Part of the Passchendaele Ridge,' 3; 'Operations of 8th Canadian Infantry Brigade from 20th October 1917 to 3rd November 1917, 10 November 1917,' 4

22 A.J.L. Kerry and W.A. McDill, *The History of the Corps of Royal Canadian Engineers: Volume I 1749–1939* (Ottawa 1962), 139; NAC, RG 9, War Diary, 1st Battalion, V.4913, 23 October 1917; MG 30, E100, Arthur Currie Papers, V.36, folder 162, 'Report on Operations Carried out by the 7th Canadian Infantry Brigade from the Night of 28/29th October 1917, to the Night of 3rd/4th November 1917, Both Inclusive.'

23 NAC, MG 30, E100, Arthur Currie Papers, V.36, file 162, '3rd Canadian Divisional Artillery. Report on Operations Leading up to the Attacks of October 26th and October 30th upon and the capture of the Passchendaele Ridge'

24 Ibid., 4

25 NAC, RG 41, V.13, 43rd Battalion, Alex Strachan

26 NAC, MG 30, E100, Arthur Currie Papers, V.36, file 162, 'Operations of 8th Canadian Infantry Brigade from 20th October 1917 to 3rd November 1917, 10 November 1917'; Swettenham, *McNaughton*, 1: 114

27 NAC, MG 30, E100, Arthur Currie Papers, V.36, file 163, '10th Canadian Infantry Brigade Report on Operations in the Passchendaele Sector October 21st to 28th 1917'

28 NAC, RG 9, V.4033, folder 3, file 3, '1st Canadian Division, 27 October

1917'; MG 30, E100, Arthur Currie Papers, v.36, file 162, 'Operations of the 8th Canadian Infantry Brigade from 20th October 1917 to 3rd November 1917, 10 November 1917,' 2; D.J. Goodspeed, *The Road Past Vimy: The Canadian Corps, 1914–1918* (Toronto 1969), 118; RG 9, III, War Diary, v.4947, 4th CMR, October 1917, Appendix, 'Narrative of Events of the Action of October 26th, 1917'

29 NAC, MG 30 E100, Arthur Currie Papers, v.36, file 163, '10th CIB Report on Operations in the Passchendaele Sector, October 21st to 28th 1917'

30 Ibid.

31 Ibid.

32 DHist, 87/152, *Handbook for the .303-In Vickers Machine Gun, 1917*; DHist, 87/191, *Light Mortar Training, June 1918*; NAC, MG 30 E100, Arthur Currie Papers, v.36, file 163, '10th CIB Report on Operations in the Passcendaele Sector, October 21st to 28th 1917'

33 NAC, MG 30 E100, Arthur Currie Papers, v.36, file 163, '10th CIB Report on Operations in the Passchendaele Sector, October 21st to 28th 1917'

34 NAC, RG 9, v. 4695, folder 58, file 14, 'Report on Tour by 44th Canadian Infantry 25th/26th to 28th/29th October 1917'

35 NAC, MG 30, E100, Arthur Currie Papers, v. 36, file 163, '10th CIB Report...'; file 162, '3rd Canadian Divisional Artillery, Report on Operations Leading to the Attacks of October 26th and October 30th upon and the Capture of Part of the Passchendaele Ridge'

36 NAC, RG 9, v.4033, folder 3, file 3, '1st Canadian Division, 27 October 1917'; v.4033, folder 3, file 3, 'Fifth Army, 29th October 1917'

37 NAC, RG 9, War Diary, v.4913, '1st Battalion, 30 October 1917; MG 30, E100, Arthur Currie Papers, v.36, file 162, 'Report on Operations Carried out by the 7th C.I.B. from the Night of 28th/29th October 1917 to the Night 3rd/4th November 1917, Both Inclusive,' 1–2

38 NAC, MG 30, E100, Arthur Currie Papers, v.36, file 162 'Report on Operations Carried out by the 7th C.I.B. ....,' 2–3; RG 9, v.4238, folder 4, file 2, '12th C.I.B. Report on Operations October 28th to November 2nd 1917 on Passchendaele Ridge,' 6; MG 30, Arthur Currie Papers, v.36, file 162, 'Report on Operations Carried out by the 7th C.I.B. ...,' Appendix 8 (1), '49th Battalion to C.O. 7 C.I.B., 4 November 1917'; RG 9, v.4707, folder 87, file 19, '5th C.M.R. Summary of Operations, 30–31 October 1917,' 3

39 NAC, RG 9, v.4238, folder 4, file 2, '78th Battalion, Report Covering Operations 1.20 a.m. November 29th to 10.20 a.m. November 2nd 1917'; MG 30, E100, v.36, file 162, '3rd Canadian Divisional Artillery, Report on Operations Leading to the Attacks of October 26th and October 30th upon and the Capture of Part of the Passchendaele Ridge,' 6

40 NAC, RG 9, v.4238, folder 4, file 2, '78th Battalion, Report Covering Operations 1.20 a.m. October 29th to 10.20 p.m. November 2nd 1917'

41 NAC, MG 30, Arthur Currie Papers, v.36, file 162, 'Report on Operations Carried out by the 7th C.I.B. ...,' Appendix 8 (1), '49th Battalion to C.Q. 7 Brigade, 4 November 1917,' 5

42 Ibid.

43 NAC, RG 9, v.4707, folder 87, file 19, '5th C.M.R. Summary of Operations, 30–31 October 1917,' 3

44 NAC, MG 30, E100, Arthur Currie Papers, v. 36, file 162 'Report on Operations Carried out by the 7th C.I.B. ...,' 3–4

45 Ibid., Appendix 8 (1), '49th Battalion to C.O. 7 Brigade, 4 November 1917,' 1

46 NAC, RG 9, v.4707, folder 87, file 19, '5th C.M.R. Summary of Operations, 30–31 October 1917,' 3, 11

47 NAC, RG 9, v.4238, folder 4, file 2, '12th C.I.B. Report on Operations, October 28th to November 2nd 1917 on Passchendaele Ridge,' 3

48 NAC, RG 41, v.16, 72nd Battalion, John Mackenzie

49 NAC, MG 30, E100, Arthur Currie Papers, v.36, file 162, 'Report on Operations Carried out by the 7th C.I.B. ...,' 3, 5; RG 9, v.4707, folder 87, file 19, '5th C.M.R. Summary of Operations, 30–31 October 1917,' 4, 11

50 NAC, MG 30, E100, Arthur Currie Papers, v.36, file 162, 'Report on Operations Carried out by the 7th C.I.B. ...,' Appendix 8 (1), 5; RG 9, v.4238, folder 4, file 2, '12th C.I.B. Report on Operations ...,'

51 NAC, RG 9, v.4238, folder 4, file 2, '12th C.I.B. Report on Operations ...,' 4, 6

52 NAC, RG 9, v.4707, folder 87, file 19, '5th C.M.R. Summary of Operations, 30–31 October 1917,' 6, 7–8, 11

53 NAC, MG 30, E100, Arthur Currie Papers, v.36, file 162, 'Report of Operations Carried Out by the 7th C.I.B. ...,' 4, 14; RG 9, v.4238, folder 4, file 2, '12th C.I.B. Report on Operations ...,' 6

54 NAC, RG 9, v.4032, folder 2, file 7, '1st Canadian Brigade Instructions for the Offensive for 1 November 1917'; War Diary, v.4916, 5th Battalion, 3 November 1917

55 NAC, RG 9, v.4125, folder 6, file 1, 'HQ, 6th C.I.B. Narrative Report of Operations for the Capture of Passchendaele,' 1–2

56 NAC, RG 9, v.4238, folder 4, file 2, '12th C.I.B. Report on Operations ...,' 11

57 NAC, RG 9, v.4125, folder 6, file 1, '6th C.I.B. Narrative Report of Operations for Capture of Passchendaele,' 3–5

58 NAC, RG 9, v.4033, folder 4, file 7, '1st C.I.B. Operation Order No. 181, 4 November 1917,' 3; v.4125, folder 6, file 1, '2nd Canadian Division M.G. Battalion Operation Order No. 56.'

59 NAC, RG 9, v.4125, folder 6, file 1, '5th C.I.B. Operation Order No. 180, 2 November 1917,'

60 NAC, RG 41, v.11, 26th Battalion, G. McNight

61 Ibid.

62 NAC, RG 9, v.4125, folder 6, file 1, '6th C.I.B. Narrative Report of Operations for Capture of Passchendaele,' 2–3, 8

63 Ibid., 5–6

64 Ibid., 6; v.4694, folder 56, file 9, '31 Battalion, Narrative of Operations – Passchendaele Attack November 1917,' 1; v.4033, folder 3, file 3, '1 Battalion Narrative,' 3; v.4033, folder 3, file 3, '1 Battalion Operations Order No. 121, 6 November 1917'

65 NAC, RG 9, v.4125, folder 6, file 1, '6th C.I.B. Narrative ...,' 3, 6–7; v.4033, folder 3, file 3, '1 Battalion Narrative,' 3, 5; v.4694, folder 56, file 9, '31st Battalion, Narrative ...,' 2

66 NAC, RG 41, v.15, 50th Battalion, W.D. Allen

67 NAC, RG 9, v.4694, folder 56, file 9, '31st Battalion, Narrative ...,' 2; v.4125, folder 6, file 1, '6th C.I.B. Narrative ...,' 3, 8; v.4125, folder 6, file 1, '31st Battalion, Notes on Operations, No. 1,' 3; v.4033, folder 4, file 7, '1st C.I.B. Operation Order No. 181, 4 November 1917,' 4. 'He had hundreds of planes up and they certainly cut the boys to ribbons,' NA, MG 30, E351, Claude C. Craig Papers, Diary, 6 November 1917; S.F. Wise *Canadian Airmen in the First World War* (Toronto 1980), 434–5

68 NAC, RG 9, v.4125, folder 6, file 1, '6th C.I.B. Narrative ...,' 3, 8; v.4694, folder 56, file 9, '31st Battalion, Narrative ...,' 5

69 NAC, RG 41, v.11, 26th Battalion, G. McNight

70 NAC, RG 9, v.4125, folder 6, file 1, '6th C.I.B. Narrative ...,' 3, 8–9

71 Ibid., 7, 9; '2nd Canadian Divisional M.G. Battalion, 5 November 1917'; v.4694, folder 56, file 9, '31st Battalion, Narrative ...,' 3

72 Nicholson, *Canadian Expeditionary Force*, 326

73 NAC, RG 9, III, War Diary, Canadian Corps, v.4816, November 1917, Appendix IV, 'Intelligence Summaries'

74 NAC, RG 24, v.1874, file 22(5); RG 24, v.1844, GAQ 11–11B, 'Casualties'

CHAPTER 7 Into 1918

1 Wilfrid Miles, *Military Operations, France and Belgium, 1917: The Battle*

of Cambrai (London 1948), 10–15; Leon Wolff, *In Flanders Fields: The 1917 Campaign* (New York 1958), 254–5

2 Martin Middlebrook, *The Kaiser's Battle: 21 March 1918: The First Day of the German Spring Offensive* (London 1978), 60

3 Shelford Bidwell and Dominick Graham, *Fire-Power: British Army Weapons and Theories of War, 1904–1945* (Winchester 1985), 138; Bryan Cooper, *The Ironclads of Cambrai* (London 1970), 121; John Terraine, *The Smoke and the Fire: Myths and Anti-myths of War* (London 1970), 154

4 NAC, RG 9, v.4064, folder 15, file 6, 'Canadian Corps, Notes on Training – November 1917. Issued with Canadian Corps G.882/14–3, 27 November 1917,' 6

5 Ibid., 1

6 Ibid., 2

7 Ibid., 5

8 Ibid., 2–3

9 Ibid., 3

10 NAC, MG 30, E389, W.J. O'Brien Papers, Diary, 26 February 1918

11 Charles Lyons Foster and William S. Duthie, *Letters from the Front: Being a Record of the Role Played by Officers of the Bank in the Great War, 1914–1919* (n.p. 1920), 251

12 NAC, MG 30, E389, W.J. O'Brien Papers, Diary, 9 December 1917

13 G.W.L. Nicholson, *The Gunners of Canada*, (Toronto 1967), 209, 321–2; Foster and Duthie, *Letters from the Front*, 245; NAC, RG 9, III, v.4301, folder 9, file 18, 'Notes of Training, 2nd Canadian Divisional Artillery, 14th December 1917'

14 NAC, RG 9, III, v.4237, folder 1, file 4, 'HQ 12 CIB, 25 Apr 18'

15 Foster and Duthie, *Letters from the Front*, 280

16 NAC, RG 9, v.4057, folder 35, file 6, 'Canadian Corps, Instructions Governing the Use of Telephones in the Forward Area, 1 February 1918'; v.4201, folder 11, file 11, '9 C.I.B. 3 April 1918'; War Diary, v. 4913, 1st Battalion, 18 February 1918; v.4199, folder 7, file 12, 'Canadian Corps, Extracts from Notes on Recent Fighting, 23 April 1918,' 1

17 NAC, MG 30, E100, Arthur Currie Papers, v.37, file 167, '11 C.I.B. Training Instructions, 5 May 1918,' 2

18 NAC, RG 9, v.4028, folder 17, file 14, 'Canadian Corps, 28 January 1918,' 1–4

19 Ibid.

20 Bruce I. Gudmundsson, *Stormtroop Tactics: Innovation in the German Army, 1914–1918* (New York 1989), 43; T.N. Dupuy, *A Genius for War:*

The German Army and the General Staff, 1807–1945 (Englewood Cliffs 1977), 171–2; Larry H. Addington, *The Patterns of War since the Eighteenth Century* (London 1984), 150; Middlebrook, *Kaiser's Battle,* 55; Erich Ludendorff, *Ludendorff's Own Story* (Freeport 1971), 2: 202; John Toland, *No Man's Land: 1918 – The Last Year of the Great War* (New York 1980), 160

21 NAC, RG 9, V. 4690, folder 46, file 23, '1st C.I.B. Report on Enemy Raid, 21 March 1918'; War Diary, v.4913, 1st Battalion, 5 April 1918

22 NAC, MG 27, II D9, Kemp Papers, v.142, F4, 'Perley to Prime Minister, 3 November 1917'

23 NAC, RG 41, v.8, 8th Battalion, Herbert A. Mowat

24 NAC, MG 30, E351, Claude C. Craig Papers, Diary, 30 April 1918; Will R. Bird, *Ghosts Have Warm Hands* (Toronto 1968), 128–9; RG 9, v.4188, folder 5, file 6, '58th Battalion, Organization of a Platoon, 18 May 1918'; '3rd Division, 22 April 1918'; '58th Battalion to 9th Brigade, 4 May 1918'; '116th Battalion, 25 April 1918'; MG 30, E100, Arthur Currie Papers, v.37, file 167, '11 C.I.B. Training Instructions'

25 NAC, RG 9, v.4162, folder 9, file 2, 'Headquarters 2nd Canadian Mounted Rifles to 8 Brigade, 9 November 1917'; '58th Battalion, Organization of a Platoon, 18 May 1918'

26 NAC, RG 9, War Diary, v.4913, 1st Battalion, 2 February 1918; v.4064, folder 15, file 4, 'Headquarters, 2 C.I.B., 2 February 1918'; 'Headquarters, 2 C.I.B., 24 February 1918'

27 NAC, MG 30, E100, Arthur Currie Papers, v.37, file 167, '11 C.I.B. Training Instructions, 5 May 1918,' 1

28 Ibid.

29 G.W.L. Nicholson, *Canadian Expeditionary Force* (Ottawa 1962), 384

30 A.J.L. Kerry and W.A. McDill, *The History of the Corps of Royal Canadian Engineers: Volume I 1749–1939* (Ottawa 1962), 159–67

31 NAC, RG 9, v.4188, folder 5, file 6, '3rd Division, Engineer Sub-Section Organization, 5 June 1918'

32 Nicholson, *Canadian Expeditionary Force,* 383

33 NAC, RG 9, v.4049, folder 14, file 4, 'Notes for the Information and Guidance of all Officers Regarding the Organization of Machine Gun Battalions and Their Employment, 30 April 1918'

34 D.E. Macintyre, *Canada at Vimy* (Toronto 1967), 54; Nicholson, *Canadian Expeditionary Force,* 383

35 NAC, RG 9, v.4198, folder 2, file 4, 'Canadian Corps, 10 April 1918'

36 Ibid.

37 *History of the Canadian Machine Gun Corps* (Ottawa 1919), 1: 220

38 NAC, RG 9, v.4049, folder 14, file 4, 'Notes for the Information and Guidance of All Officers Regarding the Organization of Machine Gun Battalions and Their Employment, Canadian Corps G.126/3–6,' 4; v.4032, folder 1, file 13, 'First Army, Orders, 26 July 1918'

39 NAC, RG 9, v.4198, folder 3, file 4, '3rd Division, 17 May 1918'; v.4199, folder 6, file 12, 'Tactical Notes on Operations on the Somme, March and April, 1918, Obtained from Canadian Motor Machine Gun Brigade, 1 May 1918'

40 Nicholson, *Canadian Expeditionary Force*, 363; NAC, RG 9, v.4202, folder 14, file 2, 'First Army, 17 May 1918,' 1–2

41 NAC, RG 9, v.4033, folder 5, file 8, 'Canadian Corps, 30 January 1918'; '1st Canadian Division, 20 February 1918'

42 NAC, RG 9, v.4033, folder 5, file 8, 'Message – Captain S. Macpherson, 5th C.T.M. Bde to Bde Maj. 1 C.I.B. 5 February 1918'; '1st Division, 3 July 1918'

43 NAC, RG 9, v.4033, folder 5, file 8, 'Message – Captain S. Macpherson 5th C.I.M. Bde to Bde Major 1 C.I.B. 5 February 1918'

44 NAC, RG 9, v.4239, folder 8, file 15, 'Notes on Experience Gained and Lessons Learned during the Recent Training with the French Infantry at Sautrecourt. Attack on a Strong Point, 7 June 1918,' 2

45 Ibid.

46 NAC, RG 9, v.4201, folder 11, file 11, 'VI Corps, 30 June 1918'

47 NAC, RG 9, v.4239, folder 8, file 15, 'Notes on Experience Gained and Lessons Learned during the Recent Training with the French Infantry at Sautrecourt. Attack on a Strong Point, 7 June 1918,' 1–2

48 NAC, RG 9, v.4201, folder 11, file 15, '3rd Division, 25 February 1918'; v.4239, folder 8, file 17, '12 C.I.B. Tactical Scheme Number 3, 5 July 1918,' 1; v.4064, folder 15, file 1, 'Report on Tank Training Carried Out on August 5th 1918'

49 NAC, MG 30, E100, Arthur Currie Papers, v.37, file 167, 'Canadian Corps Exercise No. 4, 29 June 1918'

50 NAC, RG 9, v.4201, folder 11, file 15, 'Canadian Corps, 24 July 1918

51 C.E.W. Bean, *The Australian Imperial Force in France during the Allied Offensive, 1918* (Sydney 1942), VI: 329

52 Ibid., 245, 247, 267, 330; Terraine, *Smoke and Fire*, 196; P.A. Pederson, *Monash as Military Commander* (Melbourne 1985), 226

53 John Swettenham, *McNaughton* (Toronto 1968), 1: 130–1

54 NAC, MG 30, E100, Arthur Currie Papers, v.37, file 167, 'Canadian Corps Exercise No. 4, 29 June 1918'

55 Bird, *Ghosts*, 123

56 NAC, RG 9, v.4099, folder 1, file 3, 'First Army No. 1613(G), 19 December 1917'; v.4201, folder 11, file 10, 'Canadian Corps, 11 March 1918,' 1; v.4033, folder 4, file 8, 'Khaki Brigade Operation Order No. QQ,' 2
57 NAC, RG 9, v.4239, folder 8, file 17, '12th C.I.B. Tactical Scheme No. 3, 5 July 1918,' 1; RG 9, v.4099, folder 1, file 3, 'Third Army, 20 April 1918'
58 Foster and Duthie, *Letters from the Front*, 255
59 Ibid., 261
60 S.F. Wise, *Canadian Airmen and the First World War* (Toronto 1980), 517
61 NAC, RG 9, v.4099, folder 1, file 3, '2nd Division Artillery, 8 February 1918,' 1; '2nd Division, 2 December 1917'; '2nd Division, 23 April 1918'
62 NAC, RG 9, v.4099, folder 1, file 3, 'First Army, 8 January 1918'; '4th C.I.B., 8 April 1918'; v.4202, folder 14, file 2, 'Report on Experiments by a Stokes Mortar Battery Firing at Low Enemy Aeroplanes, 11 February 1918'; v.4099, folder 1, file 3, '2nd Division, 3 May 1918'

CHAPTER 8 The Final Offensives

1 Hubert Essame, *The Battle for Europe 1918* (London 1972), 87
2 G.W.L. Nicholson, *Canadian Expeditionary Force* (Ottawa 1962), 394; D.J. Goodspeed, *The Road Past Vimy: The Canadian Corps, 1914–1918* (Toronto 1969), 141
3 Charles Lyons Foster and William S. Duthie, *Letters from the Front: Being a Record of the Role Played by Officers of the Bank in the Great War, 1914–1919* (n.p. 1920), 306
4 NAC, RG 9, v.4052, folder 22, file 4, 'Canadian Corps Artillery Instructions, 4 August 1918,' 8
5 Ibid.
6 John Swettenham, *McNaughton* (Toronto 1968), 1: 139, 143
7 NAC, RG 9, v.4052, folder 22, file 4, 'Canadian Corps Artillery Instructions, 4 August 1918,' 1
8 NAC, RG 9, III, v.3855, folder 74, file 13, '4th Tank Brigade to Subordinate Units, c. 6 August 1918.'; MG 30, E100, Arthur Currie Papers, v.37, file 167, '4th Tank Battalion, Report on Operations with 1st Canadian Division, Luce Valley, August 8th 1918,' 1
9 NAC, RG 9, III, v.3855, folder 74, file 13, 'CO 4th Tank Bde to Cdn Corps G, 4 August 1918'; '4th Tank Bde Order No. 19, 5 August 1918'
10 NAC, MG 30, E100, Arthur Currie Papes, v. 37, file 167, '4th Tank Battalion, Report on Operations with 1st Canadian Division, Luce Valley, August 8th 1918,' 1

11 NAC, RG 9, v.4052, folder 22, file 4, 'Narrative of Operations Carried out by 5th Battalion on 8th and 9th August 1918,' 1; MG 30, E100, Arthur Currie Papers, v. 37, file 167, '3rd Brigade Report on Operations August 3rd to August 20th,' 2; '4th Tank Battalion, Report on Operations with 1st Canadian Division, Luce Valley, August 8th 1918,' 2–3

12 B.T. White, *Tanks and other Armoured Fighting Vehicles 1900–1918* (London 1974), 176

13 NAC, RG 9, v.4052, folder 22, file 4, '8th Battalion, Narrative of Events No. 1, Night of 6/7th August to midnight 8th August, 1918,' 1

14 Foster and Duthie, *Letters from the Front*, 296–7

15 NAC, MG 30, E100, Arthur Currie Papers, v.37, file 167, '3rd Canadian Infantry Brigade, Report on Operations August 3rd to 20th 1918'

16 NAC, RG 41, v.7, 4th Battalion. W.H. Joliffe

17 NAC, RG 9, v.4052, folder 22, file 4, 'Canadian Corps Artillery Instructions, 4 August 1918,' 8; DHist, Biog File, Catchpole, – Leslie Arthur, Memoirs, 210; *The 60th C.F.A. Battery Book, 1916–1919* (London 1919), 73

18 NAC, RG 9, v.5042, folder 22, file 4, 'Narrative of Operations Carried Out by 5th Battalion on 8th and 9th August 1918, Prepared 14 August 1918,' 1; MG 30, E100, Arthur Currie Papers, v.37, file 167, '3rd C.I.B. Report on Operations August 3rd to 20th 1918,' 2; RG 9, v.4033, folder 3, file 4, '1 Battalion Narrative,' 2

19 NAC, MG 30, E100, Arthur Currie Papers, v.37, file 167, '3rd C.I.B. Report on Operations, August 3rd to 20th 1918,' 5; DHist, 82/1070, 'The Training and Employment of Divisions – 1918,' 32; RG 9, v.4238, folder 4, file 3, '12th C.I.B. Order No. 1, 6 August 1918,' 4; RG 9, v.4052, folder 22, file 4, 'Narrative of Phase A – Operations Taken Part in by the 10th Battalion from the Night of 7th/8th–8–1918 to 9–8–1918,' 5

20 NAC, MG 30, E100, Arthur Currie Papers, v.37, file 167, '14th Battalion, Report on Operations of August 9th 1918,' 2; v.4052, folder 22, file 4, 'Headquarters 5th Battalion to Headquarters 2 C.I.B. 15 August 1918,' 1

21 NAC, MG 30, E100, Arthur Currie Papers, v.37, file 167, '14th Battalion, Report on Operations of August 9th 1918,' 1

22 NAC, RG 9, v.4163, folder 11, file 4, 'Report on Operations, Demuin-Le Quesnoy, August 8th–10th, 1918,' 1; MG 30, E100, Arthur Currie Papers, v.37, file 167, 'No. 3 Company 1st Battalion C.M.G.C. Report on Operations August 5th to August 12th, 1918,' 1–2. MG 30, E100, Arthur Currie Papers, v.37, file 167, '14th Battalion, Report on Operations of August 9th 1918'

23 NAC, MG 30, E100, Arthur Currie Papers, v.37, file 167, '14th Battalion,

Report on Operations of August 9th 1918'

24 NAC, MG 30, E100, Arthur Currie Papers, v. 37, file 167, 'No 3 Company 1st Battalion C.M.G.C. Report on Operations August 5th to August 12th, 1918'

25 NAC, RG 9, v.4052, folder 22, file 4, 'Narrative of Phase A – Operations Taken Park in by the 10th Canadian Infantry Battalion from the night of 7th/8th–8–1918 to 9–8–1918,' 3; MG 30, E100, Arthur Currie Papers, v.37, file 167, '14th Battalion report on Operations of August 9th 1918,' 2

26 NAC, MG 30, E100, Arthur Currie Papers, v.37, file 167, '14th Battalion report on Operations of August 9th 1918,' 2

27 Gordon Reid, *Poor Bloody Murder: Personal Memoirs of the First World War* (Oakville 1980), 222

28 NAC, MG 30, E100, Arthur Currie Papers, v.37, file 167, '3rd Brigade Report on Operations August 3rd to August 20th'

29 NAC, MG 30, E100, Arthur Currie Papers, v.37, file 167, '3rd C.I.B. Report on Operations August 3rd to 20th 1918'; MG 30, E100, Arthur Currie Papers, v.37, file 167, '4th Tank Battalion, Report on Operations with 1st Canadian Division, Luce Valley, August 8th 1918'

30 NAC, MG 30, E100, Arthur Currie Papers, v.37, file 167, '3rd Brigade Report on Operations August 3rd to August 20th,' 3–4

31 NAC, MG 30, E100, Arthur Currie Papers, v. 37, file 167, '4th Tank Battalion, Report on Operations with 1st Canadian Division, Luce Valley, August 8th 1918,' 1

32 NAC, RG 9, v.4052, folder 22, file 4, 'Canadian Corps Artillery Instructions, 4 August 1918,' 9

33 NAC, RG 9, v.4052, folder 22, file 4, 'Narrative of Phase A ...,' 4

34 Ibid., 1

35 Ibid.

36 Ibid.

37 Ibid.

38 Erich Ludendorff, *Ludendorff's Own Story* (Freeport 1971), 2: 210

39 NAC, MG 30, E100, Arthur Currie Papers, v.37, file 167, '3rd Brigade Report on Operations August 3rd to August 20th 1918,' 4, 6

40 NAC, RG 41, v.15, 54th Battalion, Interview with Eric Grisdale, 2

41 NAC, RG 9, v.4052, folder 22, file 4, 'Narrative of Phase A ...,'

42 Ibid.

43 NAC, RG 9, III, v.4230, folder 21, file 5, '12 CIB Report Llandovery Castle Operation 8th August–13th August 1918'; MG 30, E100, Arthur Currie Papers, v.37, file 167, '3rd Brigade Report on Operations August 3rd to 20th 1918,' 1–2; '4th Tank Battalion, Report on Operations with 1st Canadian

Division, Luce Valley, August 8th 1918,' 1; RG 9, v.4238, folder 4, file 3, '12th C.I.B. Order No. 1, 6 August 1918,' 3

44 NAC, RG 41, v.20, Machine Gun Corps, Professor A. Logan

45 NAC, MG 30, E100, Arthur Currie Papers, v. 37, file 167, '4th Tank Battalion, Report on Operations ...,'

46 John Terraine, *The Smoke and the Fire: Myths and Anti-myths of War* (London 1970), 154

47 NAC, RG 9, v.4052, folder 22, file 4, '8th Battalion Narrative No. 2 from 12.00 Midnight 8/9th August 1918 to 5.00 p.m. 10th August 1918,' 1

48 NAC, RG 9, v.4052, folder 22, file 4, 'Narrative of Operations Carried out by 5th Battalion on 8th and 9th August 1918,' 2

49 NAC, RG 9, v.4052, folder 22, file 4, '8th Battalion, Narrative ...,' 1–2

50 Ibid.

51 NAC, RG 9, v.4052, folder 22, file 4, 'Narrative of Operations Carried out by 5th Battalion ...,' 1

52 NAC, MG 30, E100, Arthur Currie Papers, v. 37, file 167, '4th Tank Battalion, Report on Operations ...'

53 Ibid.

54 NAC, RG 9, folder 2, file 4, '8th Battalion, Narrative ...'

55 Ibid.

56 NAC, RG 9, v.4052, folder 22, file 4, 'Narrative of Operations Carried out by 5th Battalion ...'

57 NAC, MG 30, E100, Arthur Currie Papers, v.37, file 167, '3rd Brigade Report on Operations ...,' 8; RG 9, v.4238, folder 4, file 3, '12 C.I.B. Order No. 1, 6 August 1918,' 4; v.4052, folder 22, file 4, '8th Battalion Narrative ...,' 3

58 NAC, RG 9, III, v.3895, folder 1, file 5, 'Canadian Corps to Divisions, 15 July 1918'

59 NAC, RG 9, v. 4052, folder 22, file 4, 'Narrative of Operations Carried out by 5th Battalion ...,' 3; '7th Battalion Narrative of Operations East of Amiens Commencing 8th August 1918,' 2; v.4238, folder 4, file 3, '12th C.I.B. Order No. 1, 6 August 1918,' 3; Brereton Greenhous, 'Close Support Aircraft in World War I: The Counter-Anti-Tank Role,' *Aerospace Historian* (Summer 1974), 89; MG 30, E100, Arthur Currie Papers, v.37, file 167, '14th Battalion Report on Operations of August 9th 1918,' 3

60 Wise, *Canadian Airmen and the First World War* (Toronto 1980), 521, 523, 525, 530–2, 535–6

61 NAC, RG 41, v.13, 42nd Battalion, Lieutenant-Colonel J.M. Morris

62 Nicholson, *Canadian Expeditionary Force*, 407, 261, 413, 419, 465; NAC, RG 24, v.2844, GAQ 11-11B, 'Casualties'

63 NAC, RG 9, v.4238, folder 4, file 3, 'G.9/2.L.C. Notes and Some Lessons

Learned from the Experience Gained during the Operations August 8th to 12th, on the Somme,' 1–2; v.4239, folder 6, file 10, 'First Army to Canadian Corps, 24 August 1918'

64 NAC, RG 9, v.4238, folder 4, file 3, 'G.9/2.L.C. Notes and Some Lessons Learned ...,' 1–2

65 NAC, RG 9, v.4239, folder 6, file 10, '78th Battalion, 22 August 1918,' 1

66 Ibid.

67 The final three months of the war were later labelled 'The Hundred Days.'

68 NAC, MG 30, E100, Arthur Currie Papers, v.37, file 168, '1st Division, Report on Arras Operations, Drocourt-Quéant Line, August 28th–September 4th, 1918'

69 NAC, MG 30, E100, Arthur Currie Papers, v.37, file 168, '1st Division, Report on Arras Operations ...,'. iv, 1; v.37, file 167, '3rd Brigade, Report on Drocourt-Quéant Operations – September 2nd 1918,' 1

70 NAC, RG 41, v.13, 46th Battalion, J.L. Hart

71 NAC, MG 30, E100, Arthur Currie Papers, v.37, file 168, '1st Division, Report on Arras Operations ..., iv, 1; v.37, file 167, '3rd Brigade, Report on Drocourt-Quéant Operations–September 2nd 1918,' 1

72 NAC, MG 30, E100, Arthur Currie Papers, v.37, file 167, 'Report on Attack of September 1st 1918 on Crow's Nest and Chateau Wood,' 1; file 168, '10th Brigade Narrative of Operations, Battle of Arras, 1–3 September 1918,' 1, Appendix G, Appendix H; file 167, '3rd Brigade Report on Drocourt-Quéant Operations – September 2nd 1918,' 1

73 NAC, MG 30, E100, Arthur Currie Papers, v.37, file 168, '1st Division, Report on Arras Operations ...,' s. iii, 3

74 NAC, MG 30, E100, Arthur Currie Papers, v.37, file 167, 'Report on Attack of September 1st 1918 on Crow's Nest and Chateau Wood,' 1; file 168, '10th C.I.B. Narrative of Operations, Battle of Arras ...,' Appendix I, 2

75 NAC, MG 30, E100, Arthur Currie Papers, v.37, file 168, '1st Division, Report on Arras Operations ...,' s. iii, 5; '10th C.I.B. Narrative of Operations, Battle of Arras ...,' Appendix H, 2; Appendix I, 2; file 167, '3rd C.I.B. Report on Drocourt-Quéant Operations – September 2nd 1918,' 3; file 168, '3rd C.I.B. Report on Operations, August 26th–September 3rd, 1918'

76 NAC, MG 30, E100, Arthur Currie Papers, v. s. 37, file 168, '1st Divison, Report on Arras Operations ...,'. iii, 8

77 NAC, MG 30, E100, Arthur Currie Papers, v.37, file 168, '10th C.I.B. Narrative of Operations, Battle of Arras ...,' Appendix H, 3, 6; Appendix I, 4; file 167, '3rd C.I.B. Report on Drocourt-Quéant Operations – September 2nd 1918,' 6

78 Nicholson, *Canadian Expeditionary Force*, 438

79 NAC, MG 30, E100, Arthur Currie Papers, v.37, file 168, '10th C.I.B. Narrative of Operations, Battle of Arras ...,' Appendix H, 3, 6; Appendix I, 4; file 167, '3rd C.I.B. Report on Drocourt-Quéant Operations – September 2nd 1918,' 6

80 Swettenham, *McNaughton*, 1:154; Nicholson, *Canadian Expeditionary Force*, 442

81 NAC, RG 9, v.4158, folder 2, file 6, '42nd Battalion Narrative of Operations 25th–30th September 1918,' 2

82 A.J.L. Kerry and W.A. McDill, *The History of the Corps of Royal Canadian Engineers: Volume I, 1749–1939* (Ottawa 1962), 189–90

83 NAC, RG 9, III, v.3873, folder 120, file 10, 'Interim Report on the Operations of the Canadian Corps during the Year 1918,' 76

84 NAC, RG 9, III, War Diary, v.4995, 3rd Battalion CE, Appendix, 'Narrative of Bourlon Wood Operations, September 27th–28th–29th, 1918'

85 NAC, MG 30, E100, Arthur Currie Papers, v.1, 'Canadian Corps Headquarters to Sir Robert Borden, 26 November 1918,' 4

86 NAC, RG 9, III, v.3873, folder 120, file 10, 'Interim Report on the Operations of the Canadian Corps during the Year 1918,' 76

87 NAC, RG 9, III, v.3912, folder 42, file 10, 'Artillery Notes on Operations of the Canadian Corps, September 27–October 1, 1918'

88 NAC, RG 9, III, War Diary, v.4938, 38th Battalion, 27 September 1918

89 NAC, RG 9, III, War Diary, v.4944, 87th Battalion, 27 September 1918

90 NAC, RG 9, III, War Diary, 102nd Battalion, September 1918, Appendix H, 'Narrative of Operations from 27th September to 2nd October 1918'

91 NAC, RG 9, v.4033, folder 3, file 6, 'Report on Battalion Operations of Oct 1st by Capt. MacLaren (1 Battalion),' 2

92 NAC, RG 9, III, v.3912, folder 42, file 9, 'Notes on Recent Fighting No. 21'

93 NAC, RG 9, v.4052, folder 22, file 7, '7th Battalion Narrative of Operations September 27th to October 2nd, 1918,' 5; 'Narrative of Events – Bourlon Wood Operations, 8th Battalion, September 27th, 28th, and 29th 1918,' 2–3; 'Narrative of Operations Taken Part in by the 10th Battalion, 27–29 September 1918,' 3. v.4163, folder 12, file 3, '1st C.M.R. Narrative of Operations 29–9–18 to 3–10–18,' 1

94 NAC, RG 9, III, War Diary, v.4945, 102nd Battalion, September 1918, Appendix H, 'Narrative of Operations from 27th September to 2nd October, 1918'

95 NAC, RG 9, v.4238, folder 5, file 6, '78th Battalion, Report "B.W." Operations'

96 NAC, RG 9, III, War Diary, v.4922, 13th Battalion, 27 September 1918

97 Ibid.

98 Nicholson, *Canadian Expeditionary Force*, 471–2

99 NAC, RG 9, III, v.3913, folder 46, file 13, 'GS Report on Mount Houy Operations, 28 December 1918'

100 NAC, MG 30, E100, Arthur Currie Papers, v.38, file 169, 'Artillery Report on Mount Houy (Valenciennes) Operation by Canadian Corps No. 1st 1918,' 4

101 Swettenham, *McNaughton*, 1: 163

102 Ibid.

103 NAC, MG 30, E100, Arthur Currie Papers, v.38, file 169, 'Artillery Report ...,' 5–7

104 Ibid., 10

105 Ibid., 5

106 Ibid., 14

107 Swettenham, *McNaughton*, 1: 165

108 NAC, MG 30, E100, Arthur Curie Papers, v.38, file 169, 'Artillery Report ...,' 5–6, 10, 15; DHist, 709.(D1), A.G.L. McNaughton, 'The Development of Artillery in the Great War' (n.d)

109 NAC, RG 41, v.15, 54th Battalion, A.W. Strudwick

110 Swettenham, *McNaughton*, 1: 166

111 NAC, RG 24, v.1883, file 27, 'Return of Killed, Wounded and Missing (by Months) for all Canadian Units in France'

CONCLUSION

1 John Terraine, *The Road to Passchendaele, The Flanders Offensive of 1917: A Study in Inevitability* (London 1977), 32

2 NAC, RG 24, v.1866, file 9

3 NAC, RG 24, v.1844, GAQ 11–11B

4 Ibid.

5 Ibid.

6 G.W.L. Nicholson, *Canadian Expeditionary Force* (Ottawa 1962), 172

7 Ibid., 183, 185, 190, 197

8 NAC, RG 24, v.1844, GAQ 11–11B, 'The Great War – Strength of Canadian Troops Engaged and Casualties in Battle'

9 Nicholson *Canadian Expeditionary Force*, 272

10 Ibid., 277

11 NAC, RG 24, v.1874, 22(5)

12 Ibid.

13 Nicholson, *Canadian Expeditionary Force*, 320

14 Ibid., 323

15 Ibid., 326
16 NAC, RG 24, v.1844, GAQ 11–11B, 'The Great War ...'
17 Nicholson, *Canadian Expeditionary Force*, 419; NAC RG 24, v.1844, GAQ 11–11B, 'The Great War ...'
18 Nicholson, *Canadian Expeditionary Force*, 440
19 NAC, RG 24, v.1874, 22(4); RG 9, III, v.3873, folder 120, file 10, 'Interim Report on the Operations of the Canadian Corps during the year 1918'; RG 24, v.1844, GAQ 11–5
20 Statistics from NAC, RG 24, v.1844, GAQ 11–11B, 'The Great War ...'
21 George Basalla points out, in *The Evolution of Technology*, that *perceived* necessity is the mother of invention, since technology is not required to gather food or find shelter. One could argue, however, that to the men in the trenches using and adapting technology was a matter of life and death.

Index

Acheville (Fresnoy), 133
aerial photography: origins, 61; at St-Eloi, 61; at Vimy Ridge, 88; and training, 98, 100; and mining, 106; and counter-battery work, 111, 190; usefulness at Vimy, 132; used in training, 138; used for orienteering, 194, 195
African troops, 188
aircraft: contribute to violence, 3; troops learn to take cover from, 20; and bombing, 26; as artillery spotters, 26; infantry unable to deal with, 29, 54; cooperation with infantry on the Somme, 75, 80–1; and lessons of the Somme, 86; and communications at Vimy Ridge, 127; and forward airfields at Hill 70, 139; German, active at Passchendaele, 163, 165; contact patrols at Passchendaele, 163; ground support at Passchendaele, 164; and infantry-artillery liaison, 171; armament, 177–8; and infantry training in 1918, 184–5; Fokker D-VII, 186; at Amiens, 191, 201–2

Aisne River (Arras), 87
Alderson, Sir E.A.H.: commands Canadian Division, 25; relieved of command after St-Eloi, 61; misgivings about Turner, 64
Allen, W.D.: comments on German aircraft at Passchendaele, 163
Allied and Associated Powers: prepare 1918 offensives, 188; press on to German border, 212; materiel, 215
American armies: experience, 6; enter the war, 87; involvement warrants optimism, 167; in Second Battle of the Marne, 188; try to maintain pressure, 207
American Civil War: as example of industrial warfare, 4, 216
Amiens, battle of, 188–206; compared with the Somme, 5; tactics at, 6; lessons of Cambrai applied, 168; planned, 188; German defences at, 188; importance of all-arms cooperation, 189; compared with Somme and Passchendaele, 202; lessons of, 205–6; advance compared with other battles, 215

against snipers, 134; German, at
Hill 70, 139, 140; German use of,
at Passchendaele, 144, 145, 152–3,
155, 158; as part of barrage at
Passchendaele, 147, 152, 161,
165; and attack of 26 Oct. 1917,
152; in assault at Passchendaele,
153, 160; and problems of weight,
154; at Decline Copse, 155; dangers machine-gunners faced, 161;
and consolidation at Passchendaele, 164; organization in 1918,
177; and battlefields of First
World War, 178; on tanks, 182,
205; use of tanks against, 182;
tactics against, 184, 189, 194–5;
as anti-aircraft, 185–6; Germans rely on, at Amiens, 188,
200; and tactics of 1918, 203,
205; German, at Drocourt-
Quéant, 207; German, at Canal
du Nord, 210; and nature of
fighting at Canal du Nord, 211;
in attack at Valenciennes, 214
Macintyre, Duncan E.: and communications at Vimy, 126
Mackenzie, John: describes creeping
barrage at Passchendaele, 158
McNaughton, A.G.L.: lectures on
role of artillery, 19; view of artillery's role in 1915, 23; seeks to
improve artillery, 93–5; and
counter-battery work, 111, 116,
123, 190; view of machine-guns
in indirect role, 115; evaluates artillery at Valenciennes, 214; orders comparison of machine-guns
with artillery, 214
McNight, G., 162; describes mud
and artillery at Passchendaele,

148; describes barrage at Passch-
endaele, 161; describes attack of 6
Nov. 1917, 164
Macpherson, S.: reports shorts, 180
Marne, Second Battle of, 188
Marquion, village of (Canal du
Nord), 212
Marquion Line (Hindenburg Line),
208
Mauser Ridge, 32; and simple tactics, 216
Maxim machine-gun: as replace-
ment for Colt, 38
Maxse, Ivor: innovations on the
Somme, 69
Menin Road (Passchendaele), 144
Mercer, M.S.: commands 3rd Division, killed at Mount Sorrel, 62;
criticizes Ross, 64
Messines: and mine warfare, 54
militia: and lessons of nineteenth
century, 8; amateurism in, 13;
pre-war training and small-unit
tactics, 91–2
Mills Number 5: appears in 1916,
57–8; operation, 58; at Vimy,
106, 124; little used at Passchendaele, 147; against pillboxes, 162;
in raids of 1918, 172
Mills Number 23: at Vimy, 124; in
raids of 1918, 172
Milne, William: wins Victoria
Cross, 124
mining: origins, 53; at St-Eloi, 61;
at Mount Sorrel, 62; at Vimy
Ridge, 88, 103, 106–7, 111, 126;
and trench raids, 104
Monash, Sir John: commands Australian Corps, and training, 183
Mons: and armistice, 215

from 1915 to 1918, 222; nature of
evolution, 223
telephones: reliability, 33, 85, 151;
at Second Ypres, 33; artillery-in-
fantry liaison, 46, 52; on trench
raids, 48; on the Somme, 70, 80;
at Vimy, 125, 126; evaluated
after Vimy, 135; compared with
power buzzer, 171; in 1918, 187;
at Amiens, 193; at Drocourt-
Quéant, 208
Thelus, 88, 111, 125
Thiepval Ridge (Somme), 71; and
artillery, 75, and machine-guns,
78; and failure of infantry-artillery cooperation, 86
thirteen-pounder: first appears, 10
Tommy Tickler's Artillery. *See*
bombs
Toronto: second contingent trains
at, 19
training: importance, 7, 90, 183; in
1906, 12; hampered at Valcartier,
16, 18; of artillery in 1914, 20; in
the trenches, 1915, 23; of artillery
in trenches of 1915, 23; while in
reserve, 24, 135, 174; importance
of, for trench raids, 50; hampered
by Sam Hughes's organization,
54–5; in British Army, 55; of replacements, 55; of bombers, 55–7,
98; between battles on the
Somme, 74–5; and lessons of the
Somme, 82; tank-infantry cooperation, 83; related to success on
the battlefield, 86; before Vimy
Ridge, 88, 97–100, 107, 111; of
Lewis gunners, 98; comments by
Arthur Currie, 131; assessed, at
Vimy, 131; in summer of 1917,

135; for Hill 70, 139; for Passchendaele, 151; between battles
at Passchendaele, 159–60; and
British input, 167; after Passchendaele, 168–9; for signallers, 171;
importance of, with rifle-grenades, 172; in summer of 1918,
175, 183, 189; of machine-gunners, 178; of artillery in 1918,
184; of tanks and infantry, 195;
in 1918, evaluated, 215
Transloy Ridges (Somme), 71; disaster at, 74
Tremblay, Thomas: commands
22nd Battalion, condemns Regina
Trench operation, 84
Trench Mortar Corps: never
formed, 179
trench warfare: routine, 24, 50, 143,
172, 174; Canadian Corps becomes experienced in, 37; casualties, 50; and rifle grenades, 50;
weapons of, 1916, 86; unchanged
to 1917, 97; weapons of, 1917,
101, 106; artillery and, 111; and
changing tactics of 1918, 169;
deadlock, 218
Tsar Nicholas II, 10
tunnelling: *See* mining
Turner, R.E.W.: commands 3rd Brigade, orders adoption of new formations, 42; commands 2nd
Division, supports the Ross, 64

Upton Wood (Drocourt-Quéant),
206

Valcartier, 37; and mobilization, 16;
machine-guns, 18; Canadian contingent leaves, 19; not used for